WALT WHITMAN

Books by the Same Author

The Heresy of Self-Love (1968)

The Adventurer (1974)

Three Journeys (1976)

WALT WHITMAN

The Making of the Poet

PAUL ZWEIG

Basic Books, Inc., Publishers

NEW YORK

The author gratefully acknowledges the Oscar Lion Walt Whitman Collection of The New York Public Library for use of the frontispiece photograph.

Library of Congress Cataloging in Publication Data

Zweig, Paul
    Walt Whitman : the making of the poet.

    Includes bibliographical references and index
    1. Whitman, Walt, 1819–1892.   2.   Poets, American—
19th century—Biography.   I.   Title.
PS3231.Z87   1984   811′.3 [B]   83–45258
ISBN   0–465–09059–1   (cloth)
ISBN   0–465–09060–5   (paper)

For Vikki, and Genevieve

CONTENTS

WALT WHITMAN

INTRODUCTION

"The Long Foreground"

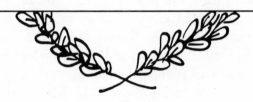

1

IN 1848, Walt Whitman was twenty-nine years old and had not yet written a single text that we now remember. During the previous two years, he had been the editor of a newspaper, the Brooklyn *Daily Eagle* and, before that, had run a series of Democratic electoral campaign sheets across the river in Manhattan. He had acquired something of a reputation as a polemical journalist with a sharp tongue, a radical Democrat, who could be uncomfortably shrill in his opinion of immigrant workers, especially the Irish. He had also published some extremely bad poems, some intriguing but negligible stories, and a potboiler temperance novel which in his lifetime sold more than anything else he ever wrote.

However carefully we examine the writing Whitman published during these years, we find no sign of immature but struggling genius, no aborted trace of any literary adventure, however misguided. We find instead a drab, excitable journalist; a man so undistinguished from the swarm of his colleagues that it is almost impossible to tell how many of the newspaper articles attributed to him he actually wrote, they are so completely expressions of the age itself at its lowest and most ordinary.

Yet, seven years after his twenty-ninth birthday, this ordinary American man with no visible talents would publish the most unusual book of poems ever to be written in the United States. He would publish it at his own expense, design its florid green cover, personally set type for it at a friend's printing shop in Brooklyn, and then persuade America's leading phrenologists to distribute it for him. Among the book's other unusual features was the omission of an author's name from the title page. Instead, on the facing page, was an engraving of a bearded man wearing a large hat, an open shirt collar showing his flannel underwear, and worker's trousers. The man stood with his hand on his hip looking from the page with an air of challenge, of invitation.

To stimulate interest in his book, Whitman wrote a series of anonymous reviews and placed them in magazines. The reviews were peculiar not only because of the dubious ethics of anonymously puffing one's own work (as a journalist, Whitman had been caustic about the dishonesty of paid journalistic puffs for plays and operas), but because the reviews made the most extravagant claims about the author:

large, proud, affectionate, eating, drinking, and breeding, his costume manly and free, his face sunburnt and bearded, his posture strong and erect, his voice bringing hope and prophecy to the generous races of young and old . . . talking like a man unaware that there was ever hitherto such a production as a book, or such a being as a writer. Every move of him has the free play of the muscle of one who never knew what it was to feel that he stood in the presence of a superior. Every word that falls from his mouth shows silent disdain and defiance of the old theories and forms. . . . If health were not his distinguishing attribute this poet would be the very harlot of persons. Right and left he flings his arms, drawing men and women with undeniable love to his close embrace.

Not only was this unnamed man a poet, he was apparently a new breed of American, unaffected by social constraints, exuberantly healthy, magnetic, inwardly balanced and spontaneous, so that poems seemed to shower from him as his native speech and not as artifacts of language on a page.

It has happened before that a mature writer, with no accomplishment to speak of, has produced a masterpiece seemingly out of nowhere. Defoe and Stendhal are examples. Yet Defoe had been a surprisingly good polemical journalist before he wrote *Robinson Crusoe,* while Stendhal had been a sensitive essayist and critic before he wrote *The Red and the Black.* Even in their early failures, we detect a strong intelligence that finally, after long searching, discovered its medium. In Whitman, however, we can detect no preliminary rumble of talent, no nervous casting about for a medium. In a famous letter to Whitman in 1855, America's most famous man of letters, Ralph Waldo Emerson, wondered about the "long foreground" that must have preceded *Leaves of Grass,* which he called, "the most extraordinary piece of wit and wisdom that America has yet contributed." But was there, truly speaking, a foreground? Surely the braiding of interests and personal traits, beliefs, commitments, talents that we identify as Whitman's history, seemed destined to produce an ordinary man—indeed, had gone far toward producing him.

Here, then, is the first puzzle Whitman presents to his reader. Strictly speaking, it is the puzzle of all genius. But Whitman offers it in a starker form. More than that, he capitalized on the puzzle, made it part of his personal paradox. He always insisted that he was not a literary man, properly trained by college and foreign travel, supported by a library of diligently read books. When he spoke, unadorned human nature spoke. The mystery of his poems, he never tired of repeating, was the lowest common denominator of all the mysteries of human achievement: the mystery of ordinariness.

This puzzle was signified by the picture facing the book's title page: here was clearly no waistcoated man of letters. It was signified less directly by the name drifting midway through the book's first monumentally long poem: "Walt Whitman," a casual sort of name, without the multisyllabled pomp of Henry David Thoreau, Ralph Waldo Emerson, or Walter Whitman, Jr. And, finally and foremost, there was the book's title, *Leaves of Grass:* "grass," the most nondescript, universal form of life; and not spears or blades of grass but leaves, as in the leaves of a tree or—in a characteristically "furtive" pun—of a book. The poems were to be seen as springing

5

out of the ground, as though no one could truly claim to have written them. And the man who did write them, this "Walt Whitman" mentioned on page 29 of his first edition seems so healthy and good-natured that he apparently did it without noticing, as Saint Paul told us charity must be done: the left hand ignoring what the right hand has accomplished, so as to avoid the traps of ambition and spiritual pride.

These are strong claims, more on a level with the mythical boasting of the American frontier—the Pecos Bills and Mike Finns—or with the titanic egotism of a James Gordon Bennett, founder of the much-despised but highly successful twopenny newspaper, the *New York Herald,* than with the usual claims of a poet and man of letters. Yet, by Whitman's day, the nineteenth century had given rise to a tradition of poetic extravagance. For Wordsworth, the poet was a "priest of nature." For Shelley, he was one of the world's "unacknowledged legislators." Carlyle called him a "hero" of humanity. For Emerson, he was the only "complete man" among "partial men." Whitman knew all this. He had grown up on the bardic archaisms of Ossian and seen the awesome fame acquired by a poet, Byron, whose well-publicized life appeared as a foundation for the wild emotions of his poems.

During Whitman's literary apprenticeship, in the early 1850s, he annotated magazine articles on the Romantic poets, and on literary theory; he read Carlyle, Emerson, and Epictetus; he read the Bible, especially the Old Testament, with its rhythmic prose-poetry and its thundering parallelisms. He also read, and gathered hints from, the dwindled race of third-rate Romantics who, now thankfully forgotten, made literary news in his day: Alexander Smith, Martin Farquar Tupper, Samuel Warren. These were grist for the mill that was churning in his mind, issuing into notebooks and scraps of paper which he carried about with him, or filed in envelopes, to assemble later into poems. Whitman did all this while remaining the unremarkable journalist he had previously been, as if his mind managed, somehow, to live two separate lives: one breathtakingly daring, almost foolhardy in its originality; the other workmanlike and harried, a perfect echo of the banal public intelligence of his time.

Let us not underestimate Whitman's enthusiasm for the national clichés of his day: his raucous patriotism; his brassy belief in "progress" and "democracy"; his broad sentimentalism about anything concerning home life and its presiding angel, "mother," who, according to the sentimental fable of the contemporary ladies' novel, incarnated Christlike virtues and suffered a sort of crucifixion at the hands of an insensitive world. As a journeyman editor in the edifying mode of Horace Greeley, who was one of the first to understand the possibilities of mass journalism in the United States, Whitman wrote what he truly believed, and he wrote it in the inflated style of his journalistic colleagues, who knew, or thought they knew, what Americans wanted to read over breakfast.

Whitman usually kept journalistic clichés out of his poetry, but not always. There are flat programmatic poems in almost every edition of *Leaves of Grass,* where Whitman seems to be trying to complete a formula, to touch on all the issues, like an editor filling out his front page. Yet in his 1855 preface ("The direct trial of him who would be the greatest poet is today. [The poet must] flood himself with the immediate age as with vast oceanic tides,") he might be describing not only the greatest poet but the journalist of the 1850s, with his newly expanded information-gathering services—the telegraph, the teams of reporters—assembling every day a miscellany of the "immediate age" for the appetite of an ever-growing public. "The newspaper is so fleeting," Whitman mused to the young friend of his later years, Horace Traubel, "is so like a thing gone as quick as come: has no life, so to speak: its birth and death almost coterminous." Such is the price of hugging the "immediate age," by cataloguing its events, moment by moment in a kaleidoscopic form that seems to be, and almost is, contemporary with the events themselves. A newspaper is a recitative on actions as they occur; it is the opposite of a formed response to events, certainly not anything that has been, as Wordsworth put it, recollected in tranquillity. And, like the "immediate age" itself, it is "gone as quick as come." All this is to say that a newspaper is not literature.

But *Leaves of Grass,* too, Whitman needed us to believe, was not literature. It, too, claimed to be contemporaneous with the experiences it rendered miscellaneously, inclusively, like one of those new independent newspapers—the *New York Times* or Greeley's

Tribune (founded in 1851 and 1841, respectively)—devoted to current events, human interest, and a dosage of strong opinion.

Much remains to be said about the influence of mass journalism on literature in the nineteenth century. Not only did newspapers help to create an unprecedented reading public, they influenced the shape of the literature itself. The novels of Balzac and Dickens, with their sprawling episodic structure, their play of coincidences, their interweaving of fiction and contemporary fact, were first written for serial publication in newspapers. They competed with the news for a reader's attention and were a version of the news in wholeheartedly embracing the "immediate age," as Whitman also enjoined the great poet to do. We call such storytelling "realism," and it owes much to the most programmatically "realistic" form of writing ever conceived: the mass-circulation newspaper.

In America, only Whitman among our great writers grasped the possibilities of the new journalistic culture and, all his life, used newspapers to publicize himself. Far from being offended, he might only have chuckled at Emerson's exasperated description of *Leaves of Grass* as a mixture of the "*Bhagavad Gita* and the *New York Tribune.*"

Whitman himself was never more than an average journalist. Yet, as a poet, he transposed the idiom of the contemporary newspaper—its broad miscellaneous esthetic, if I may so call it—into a new tone and a new form. His poet was not only bard, prophet, and priest; he was a sublime editorialist and wide-ranging commentator on the "immediate age." Whitman first tried out his larger-than-life style as a newspaper editor during the 1840s. He was a bard of daily life, his words diffused every morning into thousands of households across the city. It was an exciting accomplishment for a young man, and he remembered it years later when he created a voice for his poetry.

2

"No one will get at my verses who insists upon viewing them as a literary performance, or attempt at such performance, or as aiming mainly toward art or aestheticism." Whitman wrote this warning a few years before he died, but it had been implicit all along in everything he did. Because of it, readers have found it hard to pin him down. If not a writer, then who is he? All the subtlety and wisdom of Whitman's language—those compact gems first noticed by the poet Randall Jarrell—seem like accidents befalling a genial carpenter or fireman or popular journalist.

Here is Whitman's radicalism. It is a matter of voice, rather than of ideas. When Whitman spoke, there was no institution supporting him, not even that invisible institution that is an agreed-upon tone, a place on the spectrum of roles. Despite the radicalism of Emerson's philosophy, he was instantly recognizable—whether speaking from a podium or in his essays—as a man of refinement and education. But with Whitman, one couldn't be sure. Maybe he didn't really know what he was doing. Maybe his exquisite poems were really accidents. If so, he might very well be the new kind of man he claimed to be, more in touch with nature than the rest of us; offering in his person and in his poems (an actor and his text?) the spectacle of a man saved from the duplicity of culture, as a saint in former times offered the spectacle of a man saved from the Fall.

This is probably why Whitman's strictly literary influence has been bad. He made it hard for a reader simply to look at his poems and understand what he was doing in them. One either "adhered" to his book, as his circle of fervent friends ("the hot little prophets," as they came to be called) put it during his last years in Camden; or one did not. This intense partisanship resulted in overheated minds, like Maurice Bucke's, of *Cosmic Consciousness* fame;* in loose and baggy writing, like the poet, Vachel Lindsay's; in defensive worship, like Emory Holloway's, who nevertheless pioneered much of the important early scholarship on Whitman.

When, in the 1950s, the tools of literary criticism became refined and overrefined, *Leaves of Grass* seemed to slip between them; while anyone who felt oppressed by the detached and civil inter-

---

*Dr. Richard Maurice Bucke was an English born psychiatrist who directed a mental hospital in Ontario, Canada. Upon meeting Whitman in 1877, he seems to have had a powerful conversion experience which, he later claimed, changed his life. He wrote a biography of Whitman, parts of which have been attributed to the poet himself; and *Cosmic Consciousness,* in which he placed Whitman along with Jesus and the Buddha, among the avatars of a new evolutionary stage of human consciousness. Throughout Whitman's later years in Camden, Bucke was one of his staunchest friends and supporters.

lude provided by that decade, and longed for raw meat, became a Whitman fan, and the myth lived on: Whitman the people's poet, the hero of sexual liberation, the flag bearer of the 1960s.

In a famous aphorism, the poet William Butler Yeats wrote that a man must choose perfection of the life or of the work, thereby summing up a familiar belief in the compensatory power of art, its ability to rise above the sickness from which man suffers. In art, man "sublimates" his unfulfillable needs, creates horizons of wholeness. The Romantic poets—Keats excepted—might have resented Yeats's formula; but Whitman would not have understood it, for he believed the contrary was true: perfection of the life *was* perfection of the work. His poems were not "literature," because they annihilated the formal distance that literary works traditionally placed between themselves, as shaped entities of language, and the turbulent puzzles of experience. Wordsworth had announced the nineteenth-century's revolution in style by arguing for a poetry based on spoken language and common subject matter. Yet even he wrote as a "priest"; his revered predecessor and constant stylistic reference was Milton.

As a stylist, Whitman's genius lay in his ability to write as if literature had never existed. He did this cannily, with unerring artistic instinct. In his earlier notebooks, we find remarks like these:

Make no quotations and no reference to any other writers.
Lumber the writing with nothing—let it go as lightly as a bird flies in the air—or a fish swims in the sea.

Rules for Composition—A perfectly transparent, plate-glassy style, artless, with no ornaments, or attempts at ornaments, for their own sake— they only looking well when like the beauties of the person or character by nature and intuition, and never lugged in to show off. . . .
Take no illustrations whatever from any ancients or classics. . . . Make no mention or allusion to them whatever except as they relate to the new present things. . . .
Clearness, simplicity, no twistified or foggy sentences, at all—the most translucid clearness without variation.
Common idioms and phrases—Yankeeisms and vulgarisms—cant expressions when very pat only.

Whitman was so good at this "plate-glassy," "artless" style that we tend to forget that he, like other poets, knew exactly what he was doing. When in his poem, he tells us that we are not reading a poem but touching a man, that the distance of paper and abstract signs is unbearable to him, and that he is glad to have passed through it into our arms, we are jarred and charmed. Maybe we don't believe him, but we willingly suspend our disbelief, reading passages like the following as something more than either wit or Romantic piety:

> Push close my lovers and take the best I possess . . .
> This is unfinished business with me . . . how is it with you?
> I was chilled with the cold types and cylinder and wet paper between
>   us.
> I pass so poorly with paper and types . . . I must pass with the contact
>   of bodies and souls.

This is the special claim Whitman makes upon his readers: the claim of intimate presence, as if the poem were the outcry of a heart, were not a text but an embrace. If there is a model here, it is probably the theater, the one art Whitman had thoroughly known and loved during his pre-literary days. His poems are, in some sense, a script brought to life by the voice and physical presence of the player, who speaks beguilingly to an audience of rapt souls, each one intimately alone with the masterly presence filling his attention. Theater is, after all, the art of which it is undeniably true that perfection of the life is perfection of the work. The life in question is, to be sure, the ambiguous and mysterious one before you on the stage—the actor, who may be magnified into genius by the power of the words that have been written for him. An illusion? Yes, but of a peculiarly convincing sort: the man is there, he speaks.

Keeping in mind this figure of the theater, we understand Whitman's fascination, especially strong in the 1850s, with public speaking. His 1850s notebooks are filled with ideas for a new style of American oratory. In particular, he was fascinated by the dramatic effect of voice, gesture, and tone, the merging of the man with his text, which transfigures the speaker and makes him, momentarily, more than a man, almost a god. In Whitman's papers are such impassioned notations as these:

The place of the orator and his hearers is truly an agonistic arena.
There he wrestles and contends with them—he suffers, sweats, undergoes his great toil and ecstacy. . . .

From the opening of the oration and on through, the great thing is to be inspired as one divinely possessed, blind to all subordinate affairs and given up entirely to the surgings and utterances of the mighty tempestuous demon.

Whitman's orator was not merely a purveyor of thoughts, not a word master; his aim was not simply to convince. The spoken text was a channel for his very being. For such a man, to speak was a form of self-making, the consequences of "long previous perfect physique through food, air, exercise, etc. etc." The result was not literature or cultural statement but expanded moral being.

This was no less true of Whitman's poet. He, too, was one with his text. He, too, gained the power to speak, by means of a persistent moral discipline which fused him with his poem. "Here is what you shall do," he tells the reader in his preface to the first edition of *Leaves of Grass:*

Love the earth and sun and the animals, despise riches, give alms to everyone that asks, stand up for the stupid and crazy, devote your income and labor to others, hate tyrants, argue not concerning God, have patience and indulgence toward the people, take off your hat to nothing known or unknown or to any man or number of men, go freely with powerful uneducated persons and with the young and with the mothers of families, read these leaves in the open air every season of every year of your life, reexamine all you have been told at school or church or in any book, dismiss whatever insults your own soul, and your very flesh shall be a great poem and have the richest fluency not only in its words but in the silent lines of its lips and face and between the lashes of your eyes and in every motion and joint of your body.

Whitman's poet and his reader meet on a plane of generous impulse, of—in Whitman's terms—"nature." The place of meeting is the poem: a kind of Jacob's ladder leading upward into health, sympathy, fearlessness.

The nineteenth century transposed the religious quest for salvation into a variety of secular idioms. Emerson's poet, as the "complete man," was also the saved man, delivered from partialness and dependency, Emerson's version of original sin. This was Whitman's idea, too. It is worth noting that *Leaves of Grass* was written during one of America's periodic religious revivals. In a personal note, Whitman referred to his book as a "New Bible" and thought he might have a parallel career as a charismatic lecturer whose words, text, and gestures would transform him into a veritable "god." The religious analogy is important here. Although Whitman was a free thinker, with a streak of Tom Paine (received from his father) in his make-up, and although all his life he had a disdain, amounting to horror, of the official clergy, he was too American not to have absorbed the country's leaden devotion to religious reference. America's public rhetoric was evangelical, whether it spoke of manifest destiny, moral reform, slavery, sectional conflict, even personal health. Newspapermen were secular evangelists. There was ample ground for Whitman's turn to the Bible as a model for moral amplitude and prophetic scope as well as for prose-poetic style.

Perhaps we must look here, too, for a key to Whitman's broadcast denial of literature as a separate skill, his peculiarly convincing demonstration that his life and his work were necessarily one. Such had always been expected of saints and demanded of the clergy: their work and their lives had to be one, or they were nothing. Eighteenth-century Europe had produced a vast comic literature based on the failure of this expectation. The charismatic evangelist of Whitman's day stood in the "agonistic arena" of his church, as a living embodiment of the truth he spoke. He was himself the message, a living word, without which the other spoken word, however eloquent and impassioned, was mere art, mere performance.

Victorian America was relentlessly moralistic—a tendency that included a conventional insistence on the moral usefulness of art. An extreme, almost comic result of this moralizing pressure was the tractarian fiction of the time, promoting, for example, urgent improvements in the country's drinking habits. Whitman's novel *Franklin Evans,* published in 1842, had been such a book. Indeed, of all the writers who, in the 1850s, contributed to what the critic F. O. Matthiessen has called the American Renaissance, only Whitman was genuinely at ease with the moralizing idiom of Victorian America. Only he did not take up arms against the prevailing preachiness, as Poe, Melville, and—more subtly—Hawthorne had done. Instead, Whitman breathed a new and grandiose life into it. We think of him, rightly, as a poetic rebel who, in his day, was less famous than notorious. Yet, ironically, he believed passionately in the moral import of his poetry. He believed, as few writers ever have, that a poem's true aim is to change a man's life, to make him anew by inviting him to share, in a mode of intimate love, the poet's own remade personality:

> Have you reckoned a thousand acres much? Have you reckoned the earth much?
> Have you practiced so long to learn to read?
> Have you felt so proud to get at the meaning of poems?
>
> Stop this day and night with me and you shall possess the origin of all poems,
> You shall possess the good of the earth and sun. . . . There are millions of suns left,
> You shall no longer take things at second or third hand . . . nor look through the eyes of the dead . . . nor feed on the spectres in books,
> You shall not look through my eyes either, nor take things from me,
> You shall listen to all sides and filter them from yourself.

The historian Daniel Boorstin tells us that the self-made man was America's ideal during the nineteenth century. If so, then Emerson was his preacher and metaphysician, Thoreau his pastoral philosopher, Whitman his poet and—in a wild, almost comic, and finally tragic way—his saint.

I used the analogy of the theater earlier to describe the deliberate immediacy of Whitman's voice in *Leaves of Grass.* It is a rich analogy, serving also to characterize a whole aspect of Whitman's behavior as a public figure: his stagy workingman's costume in Samuel Hollyer's engraving for the 1855 edition of *Leaves of Grass*; the florid beard he had cultivated by 1860, to go with his high boots and tucked-in pants legs. When Whitman "spouted" Richard III from the top of a Broadway stage, he was more ham than unself-conscious child of nature. In fact, if there is one thing Whitman surely never was, it is unself-conscious. Rarely has a writer demonstrated such exquisite care for his appearance and been so aware of the effect he had on others. Here, Whitman's counterpart is not the cocky Yankee peddler striding America's "open road," but Baudelaire's esthete and dandy, Samuel Cramer, in the short story "La Fanfarlo"—or, more vividly, Oscar Wilde who, one likes to think, guessed Whitman's deepest nature when he made a pilgrimage to Camden to visit him, in 1882.

As an example of Whitman's half-humorous, but persistent, artfulness as an American-style dandy, mirroring himself gleefully in people's eyes, let this delightful passage from an 1860 letter stand for volumes of similar evidence. Whitman was writing to his friend Abby Price, while visiting Boston to supervise the printing of his new book: "I create an immense sensation in Washington Street. Everybody here is so like everybody else—and I am Walt Whitman!—Yankee curiosity and cuteness, for once, is thoroughly stumped, confounded, petrified, made desperate." Whitman could be broadly playful and "cute." Yet there is more here than some New York strutting on a proper Boston street. "I am Walt Whitman!"—this in a letter to a friend! Whitman's swagger, his peculiar self-grooming, belongs not only to the street, where it is impersonal, a kind of circus, but apparently to his private life, to his friendships. Where, we wonder, does the theater end and the undisguised player begin? How much, for example, the Boston letter and the anonymous self-portrait I quoted a few pages back resemble each other.

We are here, at the heart of the puzzle Whitman willfully created for his readers. Do we respond to his poem as we might to a poem by a more conventional poet—Wordsworth, say, or Shelley—or as followers of an impassioned saint speaking radical new words? In the 1850s, Whitman played exuberantly upon all the aspects of this puzzle. His genius, as we shall see, was to have shaped a poetic style to embody his claim, thereby preserving it vigorously and intact for those future readers—those "others"—he appeals to in his great poem, "Crossing Brooklyn Ferry": "A hundred years hence, or ever so many hundred years hence." That is why, more than a century later, we continue to question him; we are those "others." Yet, for all Whitman's literary triumph—he is probably America's greatest poet—we still ask the unliterary question he forced upon his contemporaries: not only, What is this book?—a formidable enough question—but, Who is this man?

It is the question contained in Whitman's anonymous self-reviews of 1855. It runs through his notebooks and his scattered reflections on oratory. It surfaces in the hearty, spiritual, benign, haughty, imposingly healthy personage he presented to the world, as of the early to middle 1850s. But the theatrical image has its limits. It supposes another, temporarily suspended self the player can return to and actually be when the performance is done. Whitman's performance was seemingly never done. There is something grandiose and public, even in his most fragmentary notebook entries. In 1856, Thoreau dropped in to see him in Brooklyn and, afterward, remarked, with some exasperation, that Whitman seemed to know everyone they met on their walk down Fulton Street to the ferry. Thoreau had never encountered such a thoroughgoing democrat. Yet Whitman's younger brother George remembered, years later, that Walt's "association with neighbors and strangers" was something new at the time. Before that, "he was scarcely so apt to chime in—establish an acquaintance."

Whitman was a self-made man in the most complete sense: self-constructed, made out of an idea; a personage who had written his own part. But somehow not the fraud he has often been accused of being—or not only a fraud. It is a subtle point, but one worth making. The part can become the man. The cagey, self-scrutinizing dandy, calculating, persistent in his lifelong devotion to every variety of personal publicity, was also, and profoundly, absorbed in a personal experiment as radical as his literary one, and fused with it. The "Walt Whitman" who emerges, as if produced by the poem, on page 29 of *Leaves of Grass,* in 1855, is not merely an exemplary American as portrayed in a polemically American poem; he is not only a character in a text, but the man who lived on Portland Street in Brooklyn with his mother, four brothers, and a sister-in-law, in an upstairs room he shared with his retarded, probably epileptic brother Ed.* Perfection of the work is perfection of the life.

---

*The Whitman family originated on Long Island, near Huntington, and came to live in Brooklyn in 1824, when Walt was five years old. Walt was the second oldest of six brothers and sisters. During his youth, the family moved almost every year, as his father built houses, lived in them with his family for a while, and then tried, usually unsucessfully, to sell them for a profit. In later years, the family fell on difficult times, as the youngest brother, Ed, turned out to be mentally defective; the oldest brother, Jesse, developed a pathologically violent personality and died in a mental hospital; the third brother, Andrew, died young of a

Introduction: "The Long Foreground"

At some point during 1853 or 1854, Whitman began to give an explicit form to his idea of the perfect man, by writing a poem in which he, Walter Whitman, Jr.—renamed "Walt" in honor of the casual democracy composed of his friends and lovers—would speak as that man. Not only would he speak as that man, he would become him. Refocusing the notions of "progress" and "amelioration" that were intrinsic in America's political rhetoric, Whitman, in a startling reversal, would apply them to his concept of personality. He would change himself, as America and contemporary science were visibly changing the world. In order that his poems be true, he would himself become true.

An extravagant proposition? Perhaps, but the 1850s were an extravagant period in American history. Even as forebodings of civil war were paralyzing the nation's political life; even as urban poverty and the extension of factory labor were making a mockery of Jeffersonian ideals, Americans talked piously, almost frantically, about the wholesale improvability of virtually everything. This tension-filled decade was also a heyday of utopianism, health reform, temperance, penal and educational reform. "Spiritualists" talked to the dead, thereby proving the "scientific" truth of religion. Never had human affairs seemed so easily changeable for the better. This vision of unimpeded expansion stirred Whitman deeply. The reading notes he made in the 1850s give the impression that he had set about to master all of human knowledge. His notebooks are filled with bold suggestions for improving the rules of American grammar and spelling. He wanted to rename New York "Manahatta," to change the methods of American government, to improve the armed forces.

Were Whitman's ambitions of the 1850s incredibly naïve, maybe even a little mad? Perhaps! As a thirty-six-year-old journalist, he should have known better—and in a sense he did know better, having labored for a dozen years at the nuts and bolts of the political process. But not knowing better was also very American. We

---

tubercular throat, and his wife became a prostitute. Sister Hannah married an irascible landscape painter, to whom she had been introduced by Walt, in 1852 and declined into a lifelong hypochondria. Walt was closest to his younger brother, Jeff, the only member of the family who had some inkling of Walt's artistic ambitions and shared his love of opera. Jeff was a depressive, highstrung man. Of all the Whitman children, only George and Mary led reasonably normal lives.

will see the support Whitman found in the popular thinking of his day for his extravagant habits of mind.

While writing his first important poems, Whitman experimented with being a new man. His poems were the voice of an unimaginably grandiose self; or else—more complicated, more risky—they expressed the arduous processes by which "Walt Whitman" traveled his "open road" to perfection. "Song of Myself" is probably the finest enactment in all literature of the adventure of selfmaking, akin to such great quest poems as *The Epic of Gilgamesh* and *The Divine Comedy*. It is what I would call a "therapeutic epic," based on Whitman's fundamental belief in the malleability of human personality.

During the experimental years of the 1850s, Whitman made extravagant demands upon himself, living intensely, erratically, veering from expansive highs to paralyzing lows. He also published the first edition of *Leaves of Grass,* containing several of the greatest poems in our language. Yet in the half-dozen years between its publication and the Civil War, his reputation was at best that of a marginal poet. At forty-two, he still was unable to earn a living and lived with his family in a disintegrating, increasingly strident household, held together by his mother whom it was becoming ever harder to idealize at close quarters as she squabbled with her sons and daughter-in-law.

Yet the Civil War brought a terrible renewal to Whitman. On a December afternoon in 1862, he threw some clothing into a suitcase and left for Fredericksburg, Virginia, where his brother George had been reported wounded in battle. George's wound was only a scratch, but Whitman lingered near the battlefield, "absorbing" the panoramic confusions of the war, the comradeship of the young soldiers. Soon he would be plunged into the most trying and exciting experience of his life.

By the beginning of 1863, he had gone to Washington and was visiting the war hospitals around the capital for hours every day. He sat with the young soldiers, and watched them die of cholera, wrote letters to their families, brought little treats for them: a few sheets of letter paper, some cake or candy, a sip of brandy. Most important, he brought himself—ruddy and large, white-bearded, magnetic with "health," as he put it. Holding their hands and kissing them, he felt he was feeding them his life energy. The boys called him "old man" and loved him with the helpless, grateful love of frightened adolescents.

Whitman visited the hospitals for the next four or five years, even after the war. For him, the war took place in these vast white-washed sheds, among lonely, dying young men. In the 1850s, he had imagined himself a healing spirit, in touch with all of America. It had been a profound ideal, but also a desperate one, and the "slough" he had fallen into during his last years in New York reflected his sad sense of the failure of his experiment: the life and the work were, after all, not the same. The poems might stand, but the man was only a man.

Yet now, roving the hospitals around Washington, it seemed to Whitman that he had literally become the ubiquitous spirit of his poems. All around him in the dim wards lay the America he had always spoken to in his poems: the young mechanics and the farmers, those comrades whose "adhesive" natures formed the basis for the "democracy" he loved. Once he had imagined himself uniting the country with his magnetic presence. An unfulfillable wish, it would seem—a fantasy clinging to the magnificent poems he wrote. Yet now, in the hospitals, he had become that very man. It is no wonder that, in later years, Whitman retold his life with the Civil War at its center. During the war, the dream that, for almost a decade, had shaped his life and his poems, appeared to have become a reality.

Yet how tragic that reality was! Like the brooding wanderer in his poem "The Sleepers," Whitman walked among these bodies drained by cholera, amputated in makeshift surgeries, delirious with fever. He was too honest not to know how personally exalting these hospital visits were to him. In a letter to a New York friend, he wrote:

There has not passed a day for months (or at least not more than two) that I have not been among the sick and wounded, either in hospitals or down in camp—occasionally here I spend the evenings in hospital—the experience is a profound one, beyond all else, & touches me personally, egotistically, in unprecedented ways—I mean the way often the amputated, sick, sometimes dying soldiers cling & cleave to me as if it were a man overboard to a plank, & the perfect content they have if I will remain with them, sit on the side of the cot awhile, some youngsters often, & caress them, etc. It is delicious to be the object of so much love and reliance, & to do them such good, soothe & pacify torments of wounds etc—You will doubtless see in what I have said the reason I continue so long in this kind of life—as I am entirely on my own hook too.

Whitman's excitement as he wandered through the wards bordered on the erotic. He felt fulfilled, wildly alive. It did not matter that the young men had never heard of his poems, and he never spoke of them. His kisses and caresses seemed truer to him than poems could ever be.

Yet men died in these hospitals. They had been young and healthy, their lives before them, and now they were dying. The irony must have been overpowering: Whitman had gotten his wish, but in a charnelhouse. He was alive and loved because others died. He was, in a sense, feeding on death. Never had love, death, and suffering been so urgently mingled for him:

Mother, one's heart grows sick of war, after all, when you see what it is— every once in a while I feel so horrified and disgusted—it seems to me like a great slaughterhouse and the men mutually butchering each other. . . . I see so much of butchersights, so much sickness and suffering, I must get away a while I believe for self-preservation.

The Civil War was the great event of Whitman's life. His small book *Drum-Taps* (1865) contains a handful of the finest poems to come out of the war. *Specimen Days* (1882), *Memoranda during the War* (1876), along with his letters to his mother and friends, are among the most vivid memoirs we have of those catastrophic years. Without his experience of the war, he later claimed, *Leaves of Grass* could not have been written.

Whitman was being careless here, for all but a handful of his greatest poems pre-date the war. Yet he was telling his own truth. Although his book depended less on the war than he claimed, the war rewrote his life. In the war hospitals, Whitman became the man of his book. Thoreau's "experiment" had taken him to a lakeside near Concord. Whitman's took him to the hospitals, where he learned, at the cost of mental exhaustion and finally physical collapse, that a man's life and his work could, after all, be one.

Whitman's dual experiment is my subject in this book. I begin in 1848, with Whitman's trip to New Orleans, and end with the Civil War years. These are the years of Whitman's greatest work. They are also years when he worked arduously to make himself into the new American man. He was not yet the celebrated, often controversial figure of his later years. During the 1850s, he worked alone; he lived in his notebooks and in the streets, played his grandiose role for friends and family and then for a trickle of famous visitors. During these years, the "experiment" was uncertain, and failure often seemed imminent. Although Whitman's life was uneventful during the decade before the war, in his emotions he lived recklessly and forged poem after poem in the "white heat" of his ambition.

Yet the poems are not simply effusions, too reckless to be art. Here is where Whitman reserves the deepest surprise for us. He was a self-critical artist, a stubborn craftsman who knew the effect he strove for, and developed a language to obtain it. Perhaps he drew here on that same faculty of self-distancing which drove him, as if by compulsion, often to write about himself in the third person. In the midst of the "fit" was a watcher, always cautious and prudent, who learned to construct the poems, even while the dancer danced.

3

Criticism and biography were once considered to be closely allied enterprises. The literary work and the person who wrote it were seen to provide a context for each other. How else to approach the literature of the nineteenth century, with its emphasis on personality, its theory of art as self-expression? This attitude gave rise, in the twentieth century, to a form of biographical criticism which includes such masterful works as Lionel Trilling's *Matthew Arnold* and Leon Edel's *Henry James*. To this day, one of the best studies ever written of Walt Whitman is Bliss Perry's early critical biography, published only a few years after Whitman's death.

Then, several decades ago, under the influence of what was then called the "new criticism," biography and criticism parted company. The writer's life might be interesting in itself, all well and good, declared these critics, but the work as a pattern of language existed apart. It required to be read by itself and for itself: its internal laws of rhythm and form, its chaste play of meanings, its "layers" of significance, its figures of speech. The poem was a self-enclosed creation from which the god had been forever banished. It is no wonder that Whitman's reputation suffered during the decades when this "new" critical approach prevailed. His personality was so intrusive, his poems sprawled so copiously, that the play of irony, the tensions of meaning, the controlled ambiguities, were drowned in what seemed to be, and often was, an open-ended flow of images and assertions that assaulted the very notion of form and resembled nothing so much as the limber, erratic course of actual conversation.

In recent years, however, the austerity of the "new criticism" has lost much of its appeal. Again, the impassioned echoes that resound between a writer and his text have awakened a response in some of our best critics. I think of William Pritchard's *Lives of the Modern Poets* or Joel Porte's excellent study of Emerson, *Representative Man.* These signs of a new blending of biographical and critical intelligence have encouraged me in my work on Whitman. Because Whitman's life and work were radically intertwined, they must be treated together, as parts of one enterprise, and that is my intention here. It is, after all, in his poems that Whitman spoke most completely. It was for them that he shaped his life as the exemplary American man and spontaneous wanderer of the open road.

PART I

The 1840s

PART 1

The 1840s

CHAPTER 1

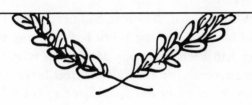

"The *Bhagavad Gita* and the *New York Tribune*"

1

WALT WHITMAN could not normally be called an impulsive man. Large-boned and fleshy, easily two hundred pounds, he appeared to be loafing even when he was busy; and his mind worked the same way. It took a while for an idea to become settled in it. "Curiously deliberate" is the way his brother George described him during the half-dozen years before *Leaves of Grass*. Yet this slow-moving man who, during his long life, contrived to act so rarely, to walk and sit so much, usually with a pencil in his hand; who was scolded for his "laziness" from childhood on, by employers, family, and friends; who remembered himself to have been as slow as glue in the thought department—this "prudent" man, to invoke a virtue he praised in his 1855 preface to *Leaves of Grass,* twice leaped impulsively into the unknown, and these two leaps delimit the most startling and productive period of his life. The second of these leaps occurred in December 1862 when, having seen his brother George's name on a list of wounded at the battle of Fredericksburg, Whitman was that evening on a train heading for the Virginia battlefield to look for him.

Whitman made the first leap in New York, on a Thursday evening in February 1848. He was standing in the lobby of the Broadway Theater, between acts of Byron's *Werner,* when friends introduced him to a southern newspaperman named Sam McClure. The two men talked, and McClure offered Whitman a job on a newspaper, the *Crescent,* he and a partner were starting up in New Orleans. Whitman accepted on the spot. The men shook hands, and McClure peeled off two hundred dollars for travel expenses and an advance of salary.

In his twenty-nine years, Whitman had never been farther from New York than Montauk, on the South Fork of Long Island. Most of his traveling had been from one Manhattan roominghouse to another or, more recently, on the Fulton Street Ferry going over to Manhattan from the office of the Brooklyn *Eagle* of which, until a few weeks before, he had been the editor in chief. For years, Whitman had gone from job to job with short-lived Manhattan newspapers; but lately, he had become an established citizen of Brooklyn, running the town's most important newspaper and living at home with his parents, his four brothers, and his sister Hannah. (His sister Mary had married in 1840, at the age of nineteen, and lived with her husband in Greenport on Long Island's North Fork.) But now, a handshake with a stranger was going to change all that. McClure's new paper was scheduled to start publishing in a few weeks. Whitman would have to leave by Saturday morning at the latest. For almost a decade, he had been writing editorials about America's heaven-given abundance and its new breed of man, native to the rude, crude West; now he was going to see for himself. In many ways, the time was ripe for it.

Only three weeks before, he had been fired at the *Eagle.* It had been a good job with a good salary, and he had kept it for almost two years, a record in his erratic career. Whitman had lost and found jobs often enough over the years, but the pressures were different now. The previous June, he had taken over the mortgage on his parents' house on Prince Street, and there were payments to be met. He also contributed heavily to the family's support now that his father's health and cranky disposition made it hard for him to earn a living. Yet Whitman had money in the bank and time before him. One imagines him enjoying the glow of the gas lamps and the well-dressed theater crowd. Ever since boyhood, he had spent his evenings at the theater. Indeed, it is fitting that Whitman's transition to a new life should be decided in one, for the theater would play an important part in his future thinking about poetry.

In one way, Whitman's decision to go to New Orleans hardly needs explaining. He was out of a job and needed the money. The war with Mexico had made New Orleans a journalist's paradise, with all the war news funneling through its booming newspapers. Only a few years before, McClure had helped to launch the famous *New Orleans Delta,* and now was recruiting staff for another paper. It was a glamorous opportunity for an out-of-work journalist with large ambitions. Yet actions often spring from emotions one has not wholly thought through; and, in fact, much had been brewing in Whitman's mind before he leaped at Sam McClure's offer.

Melville once wrote that he had not begun to live until he was twenty-five; but then a spirit of relentless change seized hold of him. In his novel *White Jacket* (1850), he describes a drowning man who slits his immaculate coat open with a knife and slips free—an act of salvation and self-hurt, sudden, precarious. Whitman was not given to images of self-assault; yet he might have used some equally dramatic image to characterize the changes of his twenty-ninth year, 1847.

2

Foremost was the loss of his job at the *Eagle.* For months he had been embarrassing the newspaper's owner, Isaac Van Anden, with editorials in favor of "Free Soil" and strident attacks on Democratic party policy. In 1846, Democratic Representative David Wilmot of Pennsylvania had tacked a "proviso" onto an appropriations bill for the Mexican War: all new territories acquired by the United States as a result of the war were to be free of slavery. The proviso had enraged Southern Democrats and was defeated in Congress; but the Free Soil debate had split the New York Democratic party—and the country—between a conservative faction called "Hunkers," who sympathized with the South, and a radical faction, derisively called "Barnburners" or "Locofocos," who rallied around Wilmot's Free Soil idea. Van Anden was a Hunker; and for two years, Whitman had walked a political tightrope between his radical sympathies and loyalty to his party and his paper. But the 1847 election had been a disaster locally for the Democrats, and Whitman lashed out at the Hunkers for betraying the party's true Jacksonian spirit. He must have known that the attack would mean his job. In personal terms, however, it meant more than that. It meant the end of his allegiance to the political party he had grown up in. It meant the collapse of the Jacksonian ideal he had lived for and defended publicly for almost ten years. Whitman was not yet through with politics; but in February of 1848, he was, at least temporarily, a man without a party. And for someone who had relished his personal stake in the "turmoil" of the democratic experiment, this was a forlorn turn of events, thrusting him into more isolation than he was prepared for.

For two years, the *Eagle's* daily deadlines had forced Whitman to think in print about a variety of subjects. In the early days of mass journalism, newspaper editors tended to be flamboyant personalities. James Gordon Bennett, Horace Greeley, William Cullen Bryant, as well as many lesser figures, were vehemently present in their newspapers. Like the great orators of a previous generation, newspaper editors had become highly visible public figures. Dickens, in 1842, had been shocked at the stridency of American journalism, as editorial giants thundered at each other in print, took each other to court, and even fought duels. Bennett, with an impudence that might have appealed to Whitman, did not hesitate to compare himself to Napoleon and his newspaper to the Bible. Whitman himself was probably closer to Greeley, a progressive, reform-minded editor, for whom journalism was a form of mass pedagogy, and a newspaper an aggrandized lyceum reaching into households at every level of society. The aim of the *Tribune*, Greeley had announced at its inception seven years before, was "to advance the interests of the people, and to promote their Moral, Political and Social well being."

This would not be a bad description of Whitman's *Eagle,* with its democratic enthusiasm, its frequent tone of fatherly advice—above all, its effort to disseminate culture to a wide audience, in the form of reprinted poems and stories, book reviews, articles on theater, the opera, exhibitions of painting and photography. Whitman thought of himself as a popular spokesman and educator. In his *Eagle* editorials he strove for grandeur, large effects. His political editorials especially have a broad, bludgeoning tone, purporting to be the voice of the people. After a while, the stream of hyperbole becomes deadening. Yet we sense Whitman trying to stretch his voice, make it large enough to speak for the workingmen and farmers whom, in his radical vision, he saw as the substance of the nation.

Although Whitman proved skillful at navigating the *Eagle* amid warring Democratic clans, it is clear that he was happiest when he was embracing large ideas about human nature and the national destiny. He was aiming not to be a politician, he announced in his first *Eagle* editorials, but a social philosopher, regarding "principles . . . in their application to the widest humanity, in their fitness to the unchanging nature of the heart . . . and not through an artificial medium, tinged by fashion, temporary possession, precedent, and the monotony of things around us."

America, he declared, was principally an "experiment of how much liberty society will bear," and a "test" of man's capacity for "self-government." America as a "test," an "experiment." These words convey a tentativeness, a note of anxiety, for America's historical adventure could fail: "O dark were the hour and dreary beyond description the horror of such a failure." Later he would call *Leaves of Grass,* too, an "experiment," and wonder at times whether it had failed. Whitman's grandiose vision had a dark side, a feeling for the precariousness of America's—and his own—venture and of "progress," which, as it propelled man toward his future, left much behind.

In Whitman's view, "liberty" and government were intrinsic enemies: "Men must be a law unto themselves," he wrote, and "the best government is that which governs least." This is pure Jeffersonian theory, a kind of Enlightenment anarchism. During Whitman's years at the *Eagle,* it had been his most consistent and passionately held belief. The true law of democracy, he continued, would never be written "by mere politicians . . . sweating and fuming with their complicated statutes," but "must spread from its own beauty and melt into the hearts of men." Arguing in particular against the morality and temperance laws that had become popular during the 1840s, Whitman had declared, "We would hunt immorality in its recesses in the individual heart and grapple with it there—*but not by law*. We would direct our blows at the substance not the shadow."

These ideas governed Whitman's opinions on specific issues of the day. All his life, he was an advocate of free trade, an enemy of the morality laws, and of the Whig program for "internal improvements"; he was against a national bank. Despite his sympathy for the workingman, he was also against trade unions. During the spring of 1846, he had written a series of angry editorials about a strike at a large south Brooklyn construction site. Workers were entitled to higher wages if they could get them, but unionism was a misguided weapon: it created counter-governments and ever more complicated statutes. In Whitman's America, the workingman, too, had to be a "law unto himself," and not a joiner of unions.

Largely speaking, these ideas formed the basis of Democratic party philosophy. Yet more was at stake here than political allegiance. Whitman was moved by a vision of liberating upheaval, a chaotic play of interests and ideas capable of shattering the constraints of mere good government and sweeping all of society into its liberating orbit. To those who were troubled by the violence of American public life, Whitman answered:

Why, all that is good and grand in any political organization in the world, is the result of this turbulence and destructiveness; and controlled by the intelligence and common sense of such a people as the Americans, it has never brought harm, and never can. A quiet contented race sooner or later becomes a race of slaves. . . . But with the noble Democratic spirit—even accompanied by its freaks and excesses—no people can ever become enslaved; and to us, all the noisy tempestuous scenes of politics witnessed in this country—all the excitement and strife, even—are *good* to behold. They evince that the *people act*; they are the discipline of the young giant, getting his maturer strength. . . . God works out his greatest result by such means; and while each popinjay priest of the mummery of the past is babbling his alarm, the youthful Genius of the people passes swiftly over era after era of change and improvement. . . . It is the fashion of a certain set to despise "politics" and the "corruption of the parties" and the unmanageableness of the masses: they look at the fierce struggle, and at the battle of principles and candidates, and their weak nerves retreat dismayed from the neighborhood of such scenes of convulsion. But to our view, the spectacle is always a grand one. . . . Is it too much to feel this joy that among *us* the *whole surface* of the body politic is expanded to the sun and air, and each man feels his rights and *acts* them? . . . We know well enough that the workings of Democracy are not always justifiable, in every trivial point. But the great winds that purify the air, and without which nature would flag into ruin—are they to be condemned because a tree is prostrated here and there, in their course?

In this vigorous editorial, we hear accents that would become familiar in Whitman's prose. Turbulence, he asserted, is the life blood of democracy; it is a counterforce to mere government, a solvent in which laws, and history itself, dissolve.

During the previous decade, American political life had become a free-for-all of torchlight rallies, street gangs, and fulsome demagogic speechmaking. Both parties were divided, quarreling among themselves. Abolitionists like William Lloyd Garrison and Wendell Phillips worked to enflame sectional conflict, in a language of apocalypse which eventually was heard. Indeed, Whitman's theory of democratic "turbulence" resembles that of Phillips ("A republic is nothing but a constant overflow of lava"), who saw himself as a mover of the democratic earthquake. The convergence is curious, for Whitman's political positions were, for the most part, moderate. He abhorred the abolitionists' disregard for national unity. Yet his emotions often swamped his opinions. On the whole, the *Eagle's* rhetoric tended to be more enflamed than its politics. We touch here on one of those "contradictions" Whitman later insisted on in his poetry. This truculent innovator, enlarging the limits of experience, was temperamentally conservative, with always a "latent sympathy for the reactionary side," as he once put it. It is remarkable, for example, how steadfastly he held onto opinions that he expressed first as a youthful newspaper editor with the *Aurora,* when he was only twenty-three, and then more amply with the *Eagle.* His famous doctrine of "prudence" corresponded to a genuine cautionary strain in his character which, many years later, he captured amusingly in his advice to his young friend Horace Traubel: "Be radical, be radical, be not too damn radical." Yet Whitman was an emotional radical. The "mighty joy" of his *Eagle* editorial has a personal ring. The broad accusatory tone, boiling into righteous rage ("each popinjay priest of the mummery of the past is babbling his alarm") almost jars Whitman out of journalistic cliché. In his view, it was precisely the violence of American life, its crudeness and rough-hewn exaggerations, that infused it with natural energy, giving rise to a new creation: the "young giant," of democracy, whose "freaks . . . and excesses" express the exuberance of youth, as the "surface" of his body expands "to the sun and air." When this truculent giant reappeared as the voice of Whitman's poetry, he would burst apart the "good government" of orderly speech. Instead of subordinating his poem to an imperious theme, he would give every line a density and a mobility that would expand the "surface" of the poem to "the sun and air."

These seeds of Whitman's later imagery and tone, scattered in his dutiful prose of the 1840s, offer a clue to the adventure he was about to embark on. It is a typical Whitmanesque movement, from the clichés of American national feeling to the interior vision of his new poetry. These passages also reveal an aspect of his character that becomes less visible as time passes. As a newspaper editor, Whitman was an angry man. He raged at the European past, at Whig conservativism, at the antiwar faction in his own party, at Brooklyn's inadequate water supply. He raged in his personal life, too. Once an overzealous usher at Grace Episcopal Church removed Whitman's hat for him. Twisting the hat into a rope, Whitman beat the usher over the head with it, before sweeping out of the posh church he had never liked much anyway. In his writing, Whitman's angry rhetoric, his contribution to the American "turbulence," could crackle with immediacy. Before Whitman became a poet, outrage occasionally made him one, as in the article I have quoted, but also in nuggets of wild language scattered throughout his *Eagle* journalism. Repeatedly, America's "uncorrupted core of primal fresher soul" is called upon to overthrow Europe's "moral rottenness," "with one unanimous prompt shrieking yell of scorn, hate and horror, so wild and high that the old fabric of royalty might come tumbling in ruins to the ground."

Whitman would use this tone, in 1850, in his first experimental poems, several of which are as much angry editorials as poems. And occasionally in the first editions of *Leaves of Grass,* there is a satirical stridency:

> Here and there with dimes on the eyes walking,
> To feed the greed of the belly the brains liberally spooning . . .
> The little plentiful manikens skipping around in collars and tail'd
>   coats. . . .
> Down-hearted doubters dull and excluded,
> Frivolous, sullen, moping, angry, affected, disheartened, atheistical.

Eventually Whitman would suppress this note, as he made himself into a robust democratic father, the "greatest lover of the universe." Yet it is worth noting that poetry, for Whitman, began in anger.

3

For almost three years, Whitman had been living with his family on Prince Street in Brooklyn; although, for a while, he may have kept a room of his own downtown near the *Eagle*'s office. He had not always lived at home. In 1833, when he was fourteen, his family had left Brooklyn and moved back to the ancestral property at West Hills, Long Island, where for some years his father had tried his hand at farming and carpentering, with his usual bad luck. Whitman stayed behind in Brooklyn as a printer's apprentice. For the next dozen years, he boarded around in the city and on Long Island, working as a printer, a schoolteacher in various country school districts on Long Island, then—going over to Manhattan— as a journalist, hopping from newspaper to newspaper and from roominghouse to roominghouse. When his family returned to Brooklyn in 1845, Whitman joined them. Despite a busy career as political journalist and writer, he does not appear to have made friends easily. Indeed, it is remarkable how few testimonies have come down to us from friends or acquaintances during these years. Not until Washington and the Civil War would Whitman begin to have a durable circle of friends. The loneliness of his Manhattan life may have influenced him to return home when he did.

Mid-nineteenth-century Americans wrote piously about the sanctity of home and mother (although police records in New York City show that almost 20 percent of all court cases during the 1830s and 1840s were for divorce). Whitman, too, though he knew better, dreamed of home, mother, and even more of father— was, indeed, obsessed by them, if we are to judge from the stories he wrote in the early 1840s. It is worth considering these much maligned stories, for they have a bearing on the most subterranean of the changes that made 1847 a decisive year for Whitman.

The stories were written mostly while Whitman was between newspaper jobs, and they resemble a lot of other stories people were writing in those days, full of ghastly deaths, tearful dreams, suffering parents, and wayward boys. But they are far better than the poems Whitman was dashing off at the time. Indeed, his reputation in the magazine world of the 1840s was for his prose, not his inept verse. And the reputation, in a way, was deserved, for these are not entirely negligible stories. What they lack in skill and distinct style, they make up for in obsessiveness, and the obsession is always the same. In story after story, a son is driven from home or driven mad by his father's cruelty or indifference. It was a theme Whitman thought about all his life. During the Civil War, walking among the shattered bodies of the soldiers in the makeshift army hospitals around Washington, Whitman would wonder how many valiant sons had been driven to enlist by the need to escape an unfeeling father.

These stories take a haunting turn, however, which might be called Whitman's signature as a fiction writer: at last, the errant boy returns, a prodigal son, to embrace his family but also to punish it. The story "Wild Frank's Return," published in 1841, in the *Democratic Review,* is an example. Frank is a rebellious boy who can't bear his father's harsh ways. ("Oh, it had been a sad mistake of the farmer that he did not teach his children to love one another.") He runs away from home, wanders the world, and at last—

feeling remorse—returns, excited at the prospect of being reunited with his dear ones. As he approaches, riding a spirited black horse, he feels sleepy and lies down under a tree with the horse's bridle tied to his arm. A storm comes up; lightning terrifies the horse; and it bolts wildly across the field, dragging Frank to his death. The horse finally stops in front of Frank's house, where his parents are standing on the doorstep. Horrified, they witness the mangled homecoming of their son. The son in the story punishes his father's failure of love by displaying its result: his own death at the hands of unleashed nature—the horse, the storm—from which only the protective love of his family might have shielded him.

In another of these stories, "Bervance: or, Father and Son," a father feels increasing dislike for his son, Luke, who bears an uncanny resemblance to him. At last the father cannot hide his feelings, and Luke becomes embittered. He begins to lead an erratic, dissipated life until, one night, after a heated argument, he knocks his father down. Overcome with loathing for his son, the father has him committed to an insane asylum. Weeks later, already disturbed by remorse, the father thinks he sees a ghost in the mirror and turns around in terror: it is the ghastly form of his son Luke, escaped from the madhouse, "unwashed, tangly-haired, rag-covered," with "the vacant, glaring, wild look of a *maniac.*" The son is never heard from again, but the father spends the rest of his life in a torment of guilt.

Although these stories are remembered only because of Whitman's later accomplishments, they are strangely effective—in particular, the turn of plot I have just described, which recurs at least half a dozen times in one form or another. In later years, Whitman understandably dismissed these stories. They were written from the surface of his mind, he said, and contained no glimpse of the depths that soon would give rise to a radically new kind of poetry. On the whole, critics have followed Whitman's judgment here, but I am not so sure they are right. Depths are not always where we think, nor are surfaces always negligible.

In these stories, for example, Whitman deals far more openly with the family obsession that dominated his youth—indeed, his entire life—than he ever did in his great poetry. After 1847, fathers disappear from Whitman's writing; but during those unstable, solitary years of the 1840s, living in the squalid, brassy atmosphere of the most violent period in New York City's history, Whitman wrote over and over again the story of a rejected son who longs to come home; an angry son who longs for revenge; a guilty son who discovers, in a terrifying economy of mental symbols, that he can take revenge and punish himself in the same act.

Relatively little is known about Walter Whitman, Sr. A photograph I have seen shows him as severe and dignified, a touch of bitterness in his mouth. The bitterness would not be hard to understand, for Walter, Sr., never possessed the valuable American talent for making money. The 1830s and 1840s had not been kind to skilled artisans like Walter Whitman. As a group they were a declining class, increasingly replaced by foreign factory labor. The building trades had seen a series of innovations, such as the balloon frame technique, which enabled workers to throw a house together with a minimum of skill, thereby devaluing the training and experience of an old artisan carpenter. To make things worse, Walter, Sr., was not an astute businessman. Throughout Walt's childhood, his father built houses for speculation; but the building boom, which had turned Brooklyn from a collection of suburban villages into a large city, had somehow passed him by. By 1847, Walt was helping to support the family, for neither his older brother, Jesse, nor Andrew, only a year younger, was inclined or able to do so.

Yet Walter, Sr., seems not to have been a bad man. His children liked him, and Walt's relations with him "were always friendly, always good," in the words of his brother George. As a young man, Walter, Sr., had known Tom Paine—a fact that impressed Walt, and Paine would always be one of his heroes. Walt's father also knew the old Quaker rebel Elias Hicks, and Walt remembered going with his parents to hear him speak at the ballroom of Morrison's Hotel on Brooklyn Heights, in 1829. It was probably in the company of his father, a sympathizer and possibly a member of the radical Workingman's party in the early 1830s, that Whitman first heard the woman he admired above all others, his mother excepted: the English socialist and reformer, Frances Wright, whose *A Few Days in Athens* Whitman read as a boy and valued all his life. The Workingman's heritage that Walt carried with him into the Democratic party in 1840 came to him from his father, and we will see the importance of this heritage to the broad American voice Whitman was to create only a few years later. Clearly, he took a great deal from his father. We must not assume that the nightmarish stories Whitman wrote in the 1840s are autobiographical in any simple sense. Yet the obsessive return to the same theme, with its unexpected conclusion, surely tells something about his submerged feelings at the time.

As a young man, he was haunted in his mind by a father who was not his actual father—a brave, "troubled-looking" artisan who, by all accounts, did his best to keep his family together—but the father a disturbingly sensitive, isolated boy might imagine for himself. This is the boy whose mother later remembered as being "very good, but very strange"; and who, in the 1870s, in a rare moment of candor about his early life, described his youth to his friend Anne Gilchrist as "restless and unhappy."*

Among Whitman's papers, there is an unfinished story that almost certainly dates from the 1840s. In it, his youthful obsession with family is expressed in a different way. A boys falls asleep and dreams that he is a busy, successful man living in a distant city. One day he receives a message that his mother is dying, and he hurries night and day to her side, only to find that he is too late. He bends his ear close to her lips, hoping to hear "two little words, *I pardon,* but the words came not."

From the moment when he first saw his mother's face, and whenever he looked at her, a wondrous faculty had awoke within him. All that was present—everything connected with his business—his schemes of ambition, his worldly gains, his friendships and his plans of life, seemed entirely melted from his thought. A doubly refined memory called up before him and around him all he had ever done in his life that seemed directly or indirectly unfilial toward his mother. Each word, each look, each action returned; not the minutest trifle connected with them but stood in brilliant light before him.

* Anne Gilchrist, the widow of William Blake's biographer, Alexander Gilchrist, was the friend of many English writers, including the Rossettis, Tennyson, Carlyle, Swinburne, and others. Upon reading *Leaves of Grass* in the 1860s, she became a passionate believer in Whitman's genius, and in the man himself, whom she felt to be the incarnation of his book. She wrote love letters to him, which he answered clumsily, and finally came to the United States, hoping to marry him. Whitman seems to have been flattered by her attentions and even shared her house in Philadelphia on occasion. But he managed to elude her, as he did every other woman who tried to get close to him.

At last the boy wakes up, sweating, from his "horrid slumber," thanking God that "the future years yet lay before him." The fate of the man in the dream has taught him a lesson: from now on, he will forsake conventional ambition and devote himself to his mother while there is still time.

This story reverses the published ones in a number of ways: It is about a loved mother, not a hated father; about a wrong done, not a wrong suffered. The guilt also is reversed: it is the boy who feels it, not the parent. Above all, it can still be expiated, for the wrong was committed in a premonitory dream. The boy can change his life, will change it.

How hard can one press a conventional tale for biographical hints? Not very hard, I agree. Yet consider this: in 1845, Whitman came back from Manhattan to live at home. Within two years, he was paying the mortgage on his parents' house. He had assumed a large responsibility for his brothers and his sister Hannah, buying clothes for them, and helping to furnish the house. In another sketch published in 1844, Whitman described his brothers and sisters as if they were his own children, and he apparently often treated them as such. It "seemed as if he had us in his charge," his brother George remembered of those early years, adding that the younger Whitmans often found Walt's "guardianship . . . excessive."

As a magazine writer, in the 1840s, Whitman used the pious conventions of the domestic tale with middling skill, to describe a personal drama more openly than he would ever describe it in later years. Literary conventions have their uses. Their stock scenarios and large impersonality can allow a writer to say more than he knows—especially when that writer is an uncannily responsive soundingboard for popular mythologies. Just as Whitman, in the 1850s, would ransack the national slogans to create a personage of his own, so, in the 1840s, he ransacked the smaller slogans of the domestic dream, and its attendant nightmare, to describe his most urgent personal feelings.

Whitman's family would never be far from the center of his story. For many years, he would be its main support and, along with his mother Louisa, its central figure. He accepted this role in 1847 and never relinquished it. Nor did he ever again try to describe the confusion of his motives and the fantasies that underlay them. There would be no more stories about cruel or insensitive fathers—indeed, no more fathers at all, as critics of *Leaves of Grass* have often remarked. When Walter, Sr., died in 1855, after an illness that had gradually disabled him, the family seems hardly to have noticed, so completely had the younger Walter taken his place. There would be no real mothers either in Whitman's writing, but only a voluminous mother-legend: beautiful, sacred, sweet-scented, surrounded by many children who are equally beautiful and sacred.

So little is known about this period in Whitman's life that I may be forgiven a speculative note. During his years at the *Eagle,* Whitman had become the mainstay of the house on Prince Street. He was already his mother's unfailing support in her struggle to keep the Whitman family together, despite the idiocy of one brother, the insane angers of another, and the father's gradual physical decline. As Whitman took his father's place, it seems that he also took on some element of his father's character. Walter, Sr., was known to have a terrible temper, which he alternated with equally terrible silent spells. In the recognizably autobiographical poem "There Was a Child Went Forth," a vignette describes the father as "strong, self-sufficient, manly, mean, anger'd, unjust,/The blow, the quick loud word." It is curious to discover, at the birth of Whitman's strong language, this liberating complicity with the father he was edging aside. Much of *Leaves of Grass* was written in a "white heat" during the months his father was gradually losing his hold on life. Although *Leaves of Grass* often refers to "the mother of many children," and its floating lines and richly varied imagery of the embrace are supremely "motherly," the muse of Whitman's new language was his absent, "troubled-looking" father.

In placing Whitman's family at the heart of his turn toward poetry, I realize that I am treading ground that is all-too familiar to biography—and to the conception of personality—in our time. In the modern life story, fathers and mothers loom ineluctably as personal legends more than actual people. This emphasis on family, taught most profoundly by Freud, has become the modern equivalent of genealogy. We consider a person to be a history of linkages in which fathers, mothers, their fathers and mothers be-

fore them, bind us to them forever by means of obscure transactions that are never quite remembered, yet never forgotten either, for they have become our character, our choices.

Here, it was Whitman himself, however, not Freud, who drew
the circle of family around him in almost every aspect of his life.
There was the obsession of the early stories, the move home in
1845, the emerging role as family provider and resolver of tensions; surrogate, at times heavy-handed, father to his brothers and
sisters. Throughout most of the 1850s, he shared a room with his
retarded brother Ed, to whom he left most of his possessions when
he died. Whitman was embedded in his family and, in some ways,
never left it. During much of his life, it is the only place we see
him; there or, alternatively, in America, as the partner of "ma
femme," Democracy, in a grandiose, happy marriage of which
Leaves of Grass is the epithalamium.

Alexis de Tocqueville wrote, in a well-known passage of *Democracy in America:* "In democratic societies, each citizen is habitually
preoccupied with a very small object, himself. If he looks further
off, all he can see is the immense image of society, or the even
larger image of the human race. All his ideas are very singular and
clear, or very general and vague; the space between is empty." This
remark, written in the late 1830s, announces the revolution that
was soon to take place in American literature, when writers like
Emerson, Whitman, and Thoreau would display a sublime "democratic" agility as they passed from the privacy of personal experience to the most dizzying expansions of the imagination, while
lingering as briefly as possible in the "space between." For Whitman, as we have seen, the "space between" was stormy and unpredictable, an arena of angry politics, construction sites, milling
crowds, rich audiences at the opera. In his Civil War poem "Give
Me the Silent Splendid Sun," Whitman would compare America's
"splendid" social turbulence to its immense natural setting: both
were examples of nature unleashed; in both, a salutary violence
shattered the "indoor" proprieties of Old World manners. In the
midst of this milling scene, the "very small object" Whitman had
always before his eyes, in Tocqueville's phrase, as a secure and solid
anchorage, included "home" and "mother" raised to the level of
myth.

Here again, Whitman fills an American piety with his own peculiar intensity. Nineteenth-century Americans worshiped the family with an ardor that was probably unique. Ladies' magazines were filled with stories of innocent women suffering under the scourge of angry drunken husbands. The American woman was described as a saint whose presence defined a small heaven on earth, the family. Unfortunately she was likely to be too trusting and innocent to deal with the dangerous realities of Tocqueville's "space between." She represented everything good; yet, like Christ Himself—become a softened, half-hidden paradigm of feminine virtues—she was nailed to the cross of the world.

Mid-nineteenth-century America was a "great heyday of feminine authorship." Hundreds of novels poured forth every year, describing the sacrament of family, its presiding saint, her sweet decline and fall. Melville raged at the appalling sentimentality of the women's novels and, in *Pierre* (1852) even wrote one, twisting it with ferocious glee into a tale of Job-like torment. Melville's rage was shared by Hawthorne and, to a degree, by all the writers of that extraordinary flowering of literary genius we now call the American Renaissance. Whitman was the exception. He felt peculiarly at home with the idealized sentiments of the domestic novel. In an *Eagle* article, he had called the popular Swedish novelist Frederika Bremer "that sweet authoress" and set her novels beside the New Testament to be read by his own children, should he ever have any:

The mild virtues—how charity and forebearance and love are potent in the domestic circle—how each person can be a kingdom of happiness to himself—how indulgence in stormy passions leads invariably to sorrow—and depicting in especial the character of *a good, gentle mother*—these are the points upon which Miss Bremer labors like some divine painter, who revels in his art, and whose work is in a double sense, a work of love.

Echoing the diluted Christian sentiments of the popular novels, Whitman praised "woman" as the "savior" of a harsh world:

If goodness, charity, faith and love, reside not in the breasts of females, they reside not on earth. . . . In their souls is preserved the ark of the covenant of purity. To them is given the mission of infusing some portion of those good things in the minds of all young children; and thus it is that amid the continuous surging of the waves of vice, each generation is yet leavened with the good withal.

Whitman applied this ethereal ideal to his own family and his own mother, in what must surely be one of the most stubborn acts of faith on record. When he designed the first edition of *Leaves of Grass,* he used on the cover a motif of embossed leaf patterns he had almost surely seen on the enormously popular *Leaves from Fanny's Fern,** which his very title seems to echo. There are passages in the early stanzas of "Song of Myself" which evoke a curiously interior domestic encounter, a happy marriage of self and soul: one partner busy with the coming and going of worldly occupations; the other, like the woman standing demurely apart from the pulling and hauling, in the editorial I just quoted. A few stanzas later the two meet on the grass, in a justly famous celebration of conjugal delight. The entire poem "Song of Myself" echoes the pieties of the Victorian marriage myth while soaring boisterously beyond them—a fine illustration of Whitman's fundamental "twoness."

4

Although Whitman at the *Eagle* had been an able spokesman for Brooklyn's Democratic party, politics accounted for only a part of his interests during these years. Upon taking over the paper in 1846, he had inaugurated a literary department which occupied several columns on the first page. Here he reprinted an occasional poem by Longfellow or a story by Hawthorne, but mostly he filled the literary columns with the sort of high-minded sentimental tales he himself had been writing.

Like many Americans of his day, Whitman was sternly moralistic where literature was concerned. A book had to "do good"; it had to be "democratic," like the French Feuilleton novelist, Eugene Sue's *Martin the Foundling* which Whitman thought was the most morally potent novel he had ever read. At the time, he de-

*Fanny Fern, the pen name of Sara Payson Willis Parton, was a highly popular writer of the 1850s, with weekly newspaper columns, children's books, and poems.

plored the novels of Walter Scott which he had loved a dozen years before and would read again with pleasure almost half a century later. Scott's greatness, like Shakespeare's, was marred for Whitman by his "feudal" mentality and his condescension to the common man. He was "dangerous" to democrats. Whitman was particularly offended by Scott's insulting portrayal of Oliver Cromwell whom Whitman admired as a heroic enemy of priests and kings.

While these schematic views did not make for a distinguished literary page, and the *Eagle* was no rival to Greeley's *Tribune,* they do tell us that Whitman in 1846 was thinking about literature as much as he was about politics. The list of books he reviewed in the *Eagle* includes most of those that were later at his fingertips when he began to think about a new democratic poetry. Carlyle, Emerson, Goethe, Coleridge, Margaret Fuller, Schiller, Georges Sand, Schlegel, Ruskin, Martin Farquhar Tupper; dozens of popular novels, histories, treatises on health and phrenology. Many of the books Whitman kept with him all his life were review copies from his *Eagle* days.

In one of his first newspaper articles for the Long Island *Democrat,* at the age of twenty-one, Whitman had announced that he would one day write "a wonderful and ponderous book." During his *Eagle* years, he did not yet know what kind of book this would be, but he fully understood the power of the written word in his literate century. "Where is, at this moment, the great medium or exponent of power, through which the civilized world is governed?" he asked in an early *Eagle* editorial:

Neither in the tactics or at the desk of statesmen, or in those engines of physical terror and force wherewith the game of war is now played. The *pen* is that medium of power—a little crispy goose quill, which, though its point can hardly pierce your sleeve of broadcloth, is able to make gaping wounds in mighty empires—to put the power of kings in jeopardy, or even chop off their heads—to sway the energy and will of congregated masses of men, as the huge winds roll the waves of the sea, lashing them to fury, and hurling destruction on every side!

When Whitman described democracy as a young giant exposed all over to the life-giving air, he meant that in a democracy every citizen was free to think and feel for himself. The air bathing the giant was composed of ideas, opinions, information, and their vehicle was the written word. That was why kings trembled when the "pen" stirred. That was why, too, in this age of literacy, the wielder of the pen could look forward to fame beyond all imagining:

At this hour in some part of the earth, it may be, that the delicate scraping of a pen over paper, like the nibbling of little mice, is at work which will show its results sooner or later in the convulsion of the social or political world. Amid penury, and destitution, unknown and unnoticed, a man may be toiling on to the completion of a book destined to gain aclamations, reiterated again and again, from admiring America and astonished Europe! Such is the way, and such the magic of the pen.

During Whitman's newspaper years, in the 1840s, he apparently thought, now and then, of a larger ambition, beyond the desultory poems and stories he had been publishing. He would write something that would shake the world. As a newspaper editor, he had already been stirred by feelings of "love" for the thousands of unknown readers who took his words into their homes every morning. Writing newspaper editorials was a kind of communion, and one in which Whitman reveled.

Perhaps it is this underlying, and almost secret, ambition which convinced Whitman that his lack of education was a drawback for a man of the "pen." Except for a few years in Brooklyn public schools before he was twelve, Whitman had never been to school at all, except, ironically, as a schoolmaster in several Long Island communities between 1838 and 1841. This lack, as much as anything, separated him from the group of literary nationalists calling themselves "Young America" who had taken over the *Democratic Review* in 1844. The group was led by the critic Evert Duyckinck and the novelist and playwright Cornelius Matthews. Duyckinck was a wealthy man who possessed a library of seventeen thousand books. He and Matthews were college graduates; both of them had been to Europe. Although Whitman published stories in the *Democratic Review* and echoed the literary nationalism of Young America, he must have felt cowed by the extensive culture of men like Duyckinck and Matthews.

When in an *Eagle* editorial dated 17 December 1846 Whitman

remarked, "Some of the wisest and most celebrated men, whose names adorn the pages of history, educated themselves after they had lost the season of youth," he was probably thinking about himself, for that is what he had started to do only the year before. Around 1845, Whitman began to clip out of magazines articles that interested him on a variety of subjects: literature, of course; but also history, geography, geology, even law. It was a self-directed, often scattered enterprise, which ranged from purely personal items, such as an article on "Egotism" from *Graham's Magazine* he clipped and annotated in 1845, to the almost comically encyclopedic notations he made, in the mid-1850s, on all of world literature, culled from popular manuals of self-culture like Charles Knight's six-volume compilation, *Half-Hours with the Best Authors.* Maurice Bucke described Whitman in 1882 sitting at a table with half a dozen books open before him, sampling passages from each one. We can take this as an example of Whitman's method: idiosyncratic, no doubt superficial, but peculiarly intense and wide-ranging.

The *Eagle* became Whitman's college and his library. By 1849, he was reading with a growing sense of purpose, although his effort was still unfocused. If he had an ambition during his years at the *Eagle*, he did not know yet what it was. He had stopped writing poems and stories, as if he had begun to feel his limitations but had not learned how to outwit them. Although he reviewed quantities of books, most of the reviews were perfunctory; we hear in them no voice of intellectual authority, as in Poe's literary criticism, one of the forgotten intellectual monuments of the Jacksonian era. Whitman's *Eagle* reviews of such works as Goethe's *Autobiography* foreshadowed his later interests, and his all-around moralizing laid the groundwork for his radical moral vision of later years, but the Whitman of the *Eagle* was not really a man of letters.

5

The most unlikely development of 1847 was Whitman's enthusiasm for the Italian opera, which was to play a curious part in his artistic education. By the late 1840s, opera had become extremely popular in New York. The art form was still in its youth. Each year, such masters as Verdi, Bellini, and Donizetti, were writing their finest works, and some of the greatest singers ever to perform grand opera were in full career. Sooner or later, most of them came to New York, and the opera seasons were perhaps the most brilliant the city has ever known. Europe's best-known performers—Alessandro Bettini, Marietta Alboni, Henriette Sontag—sang to audiences drawn largely from New York's recent aristocracy of money, which had become a glittering feature of the city's life. During these years, some of the best opera companies in the world performed in the Park Theater, Niblo's Gardens, and Palmer's Opera House.

What opera meant to sophisticated New York audiences may be guessed from a critic's description of the new Astor Place Opera House in 1847: "Never perhaps was any theater built that afforded a better opportunity for the display of dress." New York's "upper ten thousand" gathered there in all their splendor: the "daintily-arrayed men, who spend half their income on their persons, and shrink from the touch of a woollen glove, . . . delicate and lovely women, who wear the finest furs and roll in the most stylish equipages." Surely, this is not expected company for a querulous Locofoco Democrat. But all his life, Whitman had a complicated reaction to the sumptuousness of upper-class living. In 1843, as editor of the *Aurora,* a small fashionable Manhattan daily, he had passed through a somewhat dandyish phase himself. The Brooklyn boy from a poor carpenter's family had crossed more than the East River when he established himself in Manhattan. Like countless young men and women after him, he had crossed into the great world where, on a snowy winter morning, he remembered seeing John Jacob Astor bundled into a sleigh hitched to a magnificent team of horses. Here was the cruel oligarch of his party's egalitarian rhetoric. But Whitman also noticed the well-groomed horses, the expensive woolen blankets, the severe black suit, and the terrible old man himself, a dazzling focus of power. As ideologue and shy outsider, Whitman saw one thing. Yet he was fascinated by rich colors and fine appearances; he was transfixed by a smell or a voice and loved the quiet luxury of the gas-lamp clusters outside the theaters and opera houses of the city. This is the Whitman who, several years later, described the recently built Academy of Music on a night of gala performance:

We see the rows of globe lamps outside on the balconies as we approach. The light falls softly, but plentifully, on the chocolate-colored walls, and on the iron railings, and on the dark painted sashes of the windows, and down over the four or five broad steps of the front, where the entrance lets in to the parquet and boxes.

And, once inside the theater:

It is a full house—it is splendid! What costly and fashionable dresses! What jewelry! What a novel sight to you—those white-gloved hands, lifting or holding the large opera glasses! What an odor of the different perfumes—the whole combined and floating in one faint, not unpleasant stream, into one's nostrils. What an air of polished, high-bred, deliberate, heartless, bland, superb, chilling, smiling, repelling fashion! How the co-pious yet softened gas-light streams down from hundreds and hundreds of burners! What a rim of fire up overhead encircling the base of the dome! What a rich and gay aspect from the profusion of gilt ornaments on the iron pillars, and on the white ground! What a magnificent spectacle to see so many human beings—such elegant and beautiful women—such evi-dences of wealth and refinement in costume and behavior!

In such a place, Whitman could only be a charmed onlooker who, in the midst of his delight, had to remind himself: "What an air of polished, high-bred, deliberate, heartless, bland, superb, chilling, smiling, repelling fashion." Evening after evening, he saw not only "death under the breast-bone" of these high-styled man-nikins, but also their extravagance, which moved him, as the fash-ionable shops on Broadway also did, to delight, even awe at the wonderful wastefulness of the human animal.

Whitman's "conversion" to opera seems to have taken place early in 1847. A few months before, he was still comparing the "heart-music" of American family singing groups like the Hutch-insons (a popular group of the time), to "the stale, second hand foreign method . . . with its trills, the agonized squalls, the lacka-daisical drawlings, the sharp ear-piercing shrieks, the gurgling death-rattles, the painful leaps from the fearfullest eminences to a depth so profound that we for a while hardly expect the tongue to scramble up again." But early in 1847, a new tone crept into

Whitman's opera reviews. On 16 January, the tenor in *Lucia di Lammermoor* reminded him of "an exquisitely played flute, at once dazzling and soothing." A few months later, he exulted over the lead soprano's performance in *Linda of Chamounix:*

Her voice is the purest soprano—and of as silvery clearness as ever came from the human throat—rich, but not massive—and of such flexibility that one is almost appalled at the way the most difficult passages are not only gone over with ease, but actually dallied with, and their difficulty redoubled. They put one in mind of the gyrations of a bird in the air.

Here, for the first time, is the man who would write: "O what is it in me that makes me tremble so at voices? Surely, whoever speaks to me in the right voice, him or her I shall follow, as the water follows the moon, silently, with fluid steps, anywhere around the globe"; and whose 1850s notebooks would contain the following paragraph, later refined into a key passage of "Song of Myself":

I want that tenor, large and fresh as the creation, the orbed parting of whose mouth shall lift over my head the sluices of all the delight yet discovered for our race.—I want the soprano that lithely overleaps the stars, and convulses me like the love-grips of her in whose arms I lay last night.—I want an infinite chorus and orchestrium, wide as the orbit of Uranus, true as the hours of the day, and filling my capacities to receive, as thoroughly as the sea fills its scooped out sands.—I want the chanted Hymn whose tremendous sentiment shall uncage in my breast a thousand wide-winged strengths and unknown ardors and terrible ecstasies—putting me through the flights of all the passions—dilating me beyond time and air—startling me with the overture of some unnameable horror—calmly sailing me all day on a bright river with lazy slapping waves—stabbing my heart with myriads of forked distractions more furious than hail or lightning—lulling me drowsily with honeyed morphine—tightening the fakes of death about my throat, and awakening me again to know by that comparison, the most positive wonder in the world, and that's what we call life.

Opera was no ordinary theatrical event for Whitman. When the curtain went up, the sarcastic observer was overwhelmed by sensual excitement, moved to ecstasy by *bel canto* virtuosity. God was a "vast pure tenor ... rising through the universe"; and Whitman later heard Him in the person of the great Bettini, a "beautiful, large, robust, friendly young man" who in the early 1850s dazzled New Yorkers in Verdi's *Ernani,* among other famous roles.

On first hearing grand opera, Whitman wrote, "A new world— a liquid world—rushes like a torrent through you. If you have the true musical feeling in you, from this night you date a new era in your development." One of his greatest poems, "Out of the Cradle Endlessly Rocking," describes a boy listening to the mournful "aria" of a mockingbird on a Long Island beach. From that moment, a "new era" opens in his "development": he is so deeply stirred that he, too, becomes a "singer," a poet. The operatic form of "Out of the Cradle . . . ," a sequence of arias and recitatives, is suggestive. Whitman is apparently telling us that he learned to sing at the opera; that his awareness of how language and the inspired voice could overleap the distance between selves in their isolation, had come to him as a member of the audience, in one of New York's overdecorated opera houses. Whitman's "barbaric yawp" was apparently modeled on "the agonized squalls . . . the sharp ear-piercing shrieks" of the *bel canto* soloist. The "reader," whom Whitman implores to hug him lovingly, is the audience he felt himself to be when the tide of singing voices washed over him.

6

Although Whitman's book reviews at the *Eagle* tended to be perfunctory, what a difference we find when we read his articles on the theater. Here he needed no prompting from hastily read clippings. The great performers and performances of a dozen years and more were at his fingertips, and he spoke of them with a noticeable swagger: "We consider ourselves no 'chicken' about stage matters." It is the voice of a man who has seen plenty and remembered it all. The great actors of the time—Charles Kean, Fanny Kemble, Ellen Tree, Charlotte Cushman—had left indelible impressions. To have seen as a boy the English actor Charles Macready walking down the stage in the part of Richard III had moved Whitman beyond words. Now, in the *Eagle,* he wrote ringingly of the actor's genius:

Though we never acted on the stage, we know well enough, from the analogy of things, that the best way in the world to represent grief, remorse, love, or any given passion, is to feel them at the time, and throw the feeling as far as possible into word and act. This is a rare art, we admit; but no man or woman can be really great on the stage who has it not. The strange and subtle sympathy which runs like an electrical charge through human hearts collected together, responds only to the touch of the true fire.

. . . Sock, and Buskin! let us whisper in your ear . . . the whole secret of penetrating your hearers' hearts: Throw into your identity . . . the character you are to represent.

Whitman was arguing here for Macready's "mental style" as opposed to the physical posturing and loud tirades that, under the influence of the great Edwin Forrest, had become the "American" style of acting. To be an actor, Whitman noted, it was not enough to "enact passion . . . by all kinds of unnatural and violent jerks, swings, screwing of the nerves of the face, rolling of the eyes." An actor had to become the part he played; in his performance, art and nature had to become one. Whitman was no indiscriminate nationalist. He admired Forrest and probably included his memory of Forrest's histrionic "magnetism" in his own later personage as "one of the roughs"—"nude, eating, drinking," and so on. But Macready's "mental style" of indirect effects, of art melting seamlessly into feelings, skill into spontaneity, seemed truer to Whitman. This was the effect he would later strive for as a poet: to translate personal presence into language so completely that the art would seem not to be art at all, but an act of electrifying intimacy.

Whitman had been going to the theater since he was a boy. Theaters had schooled him more deeply than books. Starting in 1834 or 1835, he had ferried over regularly from Brooklyn to see performances at the stylish Park Theater, but especially at the old Bowery, where Forrest and the elder Booth* drew enthusiastic audiences from the whole spectrum of New York society. It was here that Forrest's "robustious" performance in the popular playwright John Howard Payne's *Brutus, or the Fall of Tarquin* had "permanently filtered into [Whitman's] whole nature." Here, too,

---

*-This was Junius Brutus Booth, the great Shakespearean actor and father of Edwin and John Wilkes Booth.

he saw "what has been reckoned by experts one of the most marvelous pieces of histrionism ever known"—a benefit performance of *Richard III* by the elder Booth which Whitman recalled in his article "The Old Bowery," written in the 1880s:

> I can, from my good seat in the pit, pretty well front, see again Booth's quiet entrance from the side, as, with head bent, he slowly and in silence (amid the tempest of boistrous hand-clapping) walks down the stage to the foot-lights with that peculiar abstracted gesture, musingly kicking his sword, which he holds off from him by its sash. Though fifty years have passed since then, I can hear the clank and feel the perfect following hush of perhaps 3,000 people waiting.

Nothing Whitman read during those early years—not Scott's novels or *The Arabian Nights* or Count Volney's *Ruins*—"filtered" as thoroughly into his "whole nature" as did experiences like this. He certainly never recalled his early reading in as passionate detail.

The experience of the stage, in particular the intimate collaboration of actor and audience, was preternaturally intense for the young Whitman. "Seems to me I ought to acknowledge my debt," he later wrote, "to actors, singers, public speakers, conventions, and the Stage in New York, and to plays and operas generally." He even did some acting of his own, probably in the early 1850s, in "a small but well-appointed amateur-theater up Broadway . . . I was myself a member for some time, and acted parts in it several times. . . . Perhaps it too was a lesson, or help'd that way." What the lesson was is not entirely clear. Whitman's earliest ambition, as I have said, was to write a book, not a play, and was certainly not to be an actor. While teaching school in Smithtown on Long Island in 1837 and 1838, he joined the town debating society; and a few years later, he is known to have given at least one electoral speech at a rally in Battery Park. But that is about the only real performing he is known to have done, aside from that in the 1850s and a few unimpressive lectures given at long intervals during the rest of his life.

Yet Whitman was stirred by the actor's power. As a man on the verge of discovering a new poetry, his truest experience of artistic pleasure had come to him as a member of the audience in the theaters and opera houses of New York. When he was an old man,

Whitman remembered those audiences as intensely as the plays themselves—and in particular the audience at "the old Bowery":

alert well dress'd full-blooded young and middle-aged men, the best average of American-born mechanics—the emotional nature of the whole mass arous'd by the power and magnetism of as mighty mimes as ever trod the stage—the whole crowded auditorium, and what seethed in it, and flushed from its faces and eyes, to me as much a part of the show as any—bursting forth in one of those long-kept-up tempests of hand-clapping peculiar to the Bowery—no dainty kid-glove business, but the electric force and muscle from perhaps 2,000 full-sinewed men.

It was such "power and magnetism" that Whitman himself would soon aspire to, such a communion of robust men he would describe as the ground level of true democracy, his republic of comrades. Whitman's idea of democracy, and of the poet's role in it, would draw strongly on his experience of the theater. The relationship between the actor merging himself bodily into a part, and the audience, freed from their social and personal differences by a communion of love and admiration, would be a model for the relationship he would eventually seek with his readers. His great poems—I think in particular of "Song of Myself"—are best read as performances, dramatic monologues. Whitman himself would always be exquisitely conscious of the impression he made personally on others. He "staged" himself with gusto as a "rough," as a benign peace-giving savior, as a brave garrulous old man, pitching his personal life so that his poems would appear not as artifacts but as natural extensions of his conversation. The idea is profoundly theatrical, and Whitman knew that. "These actor people always make themselves at home with me," he once told Horace Traubel, "I feel close to them—very close—almost like one of their kind."

7

Whitman took the warning of his literary dream about the man who returned home too late. In 1845, he came home to stay; and the return, with its charged domestic implications, apparently was liberating, for, some time during 1847, he began to carry around a small notebook with improvised leather loops and a pencil stuck through them. The notebook contains the date 1847 and two addresses: the Whitman home at 71 Prince Street, and the *Eagle* office at 30 Fulton Street. These addresses, however, are crossed out, and in their place is "106 Myrtle Avenue," the address of a house Walt built for himself and his family during the winter of 1848–49. (They moved there in April 1849, although Walt may already have been using the storefront office on the ground floor of the house for a short-lived Free Soil newspaper, the *Freeman.*) Whitman seems to have used the notebook at first for keeping accounts. But some time between 1847 and the spring of 1849, he started making entries of another sort:

Be simple and clear.—Be not occult.
True noble expanded American character is raised on a far more lasting and universal basis than that of any of the characters of the "gentlemen" of aristocratic life, or of novels, or under the European or Asian forms of society or government.—It is to be illimitably proud, independent, self-possessed generous and gentle. It is to accept nothing except what is equally free and eligible to any body else. It is to be poor, rather than rich—but to prefer death sooner than any mean dependence.—Prudence is part of it, because prudence is the right arm of independence.

It is hard to know what Whitman intended by these notations. They read like notes for an essay or a lecture. As a newspaper editor in the manner of Horace Greeley, he had long been used to speaking with a tone of grand assertion; yet there is something new here: the feeling of a more complex intelligence than one detects in his editorials; a more interesting expression of moral qualities; the surprising insistence on "prudence" as an American virtue.

Nothing in the notes enables us to date them with any certainty. There is a trace of Emerson, whom Whitman had read while at the *Eagle,* and possibly before; some Epictetus, whom he is known to have read as late as 1851, although he also claimed to have read him as a boy of eighteen. There may be one small clue: by the fall of 1849, Whitman was introducing into his journalism ideas and images that would later serve in *Leaves of Grass,* although none of them appears in this earliest notebook. Could at least part of the notebook date from an earlier period, and the first essaylike entries have been written as early as 1847? In any case, the tone of these notes has nothing to do with the conventional piety of a newspaper editor. The rhetoric is not Jacksonian "spread-eagle," but lofty, even-tempered. A new ambition is fermenting here.

On the other hand, these first notebook entries remind us how long it took for an idea to work itself through in Whitman's mind. The reference to a distinct "American character," and the need to disregard the old European models, echoes a debate that had reached its peak in 1845 and then died down, after stirring up some excitement and more derision: the campaign waged by the "Young Americans," Cornelius Matthews and Evert Duyckinck, for a genuine American literature, emancipated from the cultural tyranny of England.

The campaign had first been waged in Duyckinck's short-lived magazine, *Arcturus,* and then in the columns of the *Democratic Review.* The Young Americans' most fervent wish, expressed in numerous articles and manifestos, was for a literary genius who would shuck off the debilitating influence of England and Europe, a writer who would be as purely American as the continent itself.

Despite the grandiose tone, the debate was really a quarrel of Manhattan intellectuals. Evert Duyckinck, amid his seventeen thousand books at his townhouse at 20 Clinton Place, wrote genial manifestos; and his adversary, Gaylord Clark, cultivated and supercilious, as only a highbrow American could be, made venomous fun of them in his magazine, the *Knickerbocker.* The debate churned on, but it was a war of generals with no army, of critics but no writers. As Duyckinck wryly noted, if all the writings on "this prolific text of a possible native authorship, could be brought together in one mass, they would constitute a very respectable library, and go a long way toward settling the question by making a national literature themselves."

Young America is remembered today only because two writers listened to the shrill debate and then produced works of eccentric genius claiming to be American epics. These writers stood deliberately on the ground the Young Americans had staked out for them. They were, of course, Herman Melville and Walt Whitman; their books, *Moby Dick* (1851) and *Leaves of Grass* (1855). Each writer set out to occupy the place defined by Duyckinck and Matthews, and each was greeted with appalling silence by the remnants of Young America, who had long since lost their war of the magazines and were apparently no longer listening. It is shocking that Duyckinck and his friends should have been so blind to Melville's achievement, for Melville, already famous as the author of *Typee* (1846), had been one of them, spending evenings with Duyckinck in his impressive library and playing host to the Young Americans in Massachusetts, the summer before *Moby Dick* was published. But there was never much chance that Walter Whitman, Jr., a half-educated carpenter's son and political journalist, would ever cross the threshold on Clinton Place. When Matthews had expounded his ideas on "home literature," Whitman echoed them in the *Eagle.* More than once he had publically defended Matthews, but the Young Americans, who could have used a friend, never noticed; and Whitman paid them back by never mentioning them in later years.

Yet the first items in Whitman's notebook carry on Duyckinck's war of generals by sketching, in the Matthews manner, yet another critical assertion—on the need for an American literature. Thus, Whitman began his literary adventure as a critic, not a poet, for critics were his models—unless he was stirred by Cornelius Matthews's lumbering prose romances, *Behemoth* and *Big Abel and the Little Manhattan,* as Melville surely had been.

8

Thus, the man who shook Sam McClure's hand in the lobby of the Broadway Theater that February night in 1848, was already feeling his way toward a new idea of himself. His political commitments were crumbling, and with them, his settled vocation as a journalist. The most intense, artistic pleasure he had ever experienced was heightening an element in his character which he had previously kept hidden, even from himself. Under and amidst these changes was a dimly understood feeling of internal expansion, of self-confidence and release, because of his new, oh so complex position in his family as protector and provider.

In 1844, Nathaniel Hawthorne had published a story called "The Select Party" in the *Democratic Review*. A personage called the "Man of Fancy" entertains a number of allegorical guests, including a shadowy figure with a high white forehead and intensely burning eyes: he is "the Master Genius for whom our country is looking anxiously into the mist of Time, as destined to fulfill the great mission of creating an American literature, hewing it, as it were, out of the unwrought granite of our intellectual quarries." The figure is ghostly, for "he dwells as yet unhonored among men, unrecognized by those who have known him from his cradle."

The evening of Whitman's first leap—when, accepting Mc-Clure's offer, he hurried home to pack his trunk—he may already have been playing with the extravagant dream that would soon possess him: to become the Master Genius of American literature. True, he hadn't written anything that could justify such a dream, but neither had anyone else; the Young Americans had made that clear. And there were times when he felt so elated, as if the traffic along Broadway, the crowds at the opera, the quick sparkling tides of the East River, belonged to his very being. And so they did, as the world had once been Adam's, and as it now belonged to the democratic man of the new continent. Wasn't that what democracy meant: that everything belonged to everyone? If not in legal title, then in the unlegislated realm of experience?

At the age of twenty-nine, Whitman's ambitions had suddenly become complex. He had succeeded in raising himself part way out of the working class. He was a man of the pen, a journalist, able to salt his articles with showy quotations from Byron and Shakespeare. Politics were his business; his emotions were stirred by words like "freedom," "democracy," "feudalism." He held strong opinions and angrily defended them in the *Eagle*. The opinions, for the most part, were those of his party, its radical branch. Although Whitman had no love for black people, he was increasingly passionate about Free Soil, and this issue finally shoved him out of practical politics and made a place for his other, gradually emerging interests.

As we have seen, Whitman did not simply shrug himself out of politics. His phrenological "caution" rating was too high for that. He let the changes ferment; let his long-standing love of the theater, his growing passion for opera, shape a still vague literary ambition. He listened to the arguments of cultural nationalists like Duyckinck and Matthews, mulled over the popular Romantic idea of the "genius," of the poet as voice of a nation. He absorbed a potpourri of ideas about poetry, largely from British magazines. And he privately tried out a style in a small leather-bound notebook: some evocative prose; some scattered lines of poetry; some dictums that seem to be the seeds of essays and may or may not echo Emerson or Carlyle, or the Germans, none of whom was much appreciated in the overworldly circles of New York intellectuals.

This, as near as one can tell, is Walt Whitman at the threshold of the most important decade of his life. He is neither intellectual nor poet, although he has begun to think critically and write lines of experimental verse. He is not, and perhaps never has been, a man of the popular culture; yet, more than any important American writer of his day, he vibrates at times like the Romantic Aeolian harp to the popular passions of mid-century America: the jingoistic fervor of war, the sentimental cult of home and mother, the hagiographic love for the old heroes of the Republic, amounting, in Whitman, to a cult of old age itself.

CHAPTER 2

"I Saw in Louisiana"

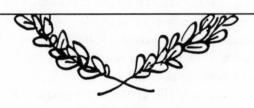

1

LATER, Whitman told about months, years, of wandering through the South and West. His journey to New Orleans became a legend. It was his baptism, his initiation into the vastness of the American land. In fact, he got there as quickly as he could: by railroad to Baltimore and Cumberland in Maryland; an overnight stagecoach ride to Wheeling, West Virginia; and then a long descent by steamboat along the Ohio and Mississippi rivers. He brought his fourteen-year-old brother Jeff with him and took notes along the way for a series of articles that he published in the *Crescent*.

The brothers reached Cumberland by sunset of the second day and had a few hours to see the town, before going on by stagecoach. They admired Cumberland's public buildings and its two newspapers. Cumberland was the eastern gathering point for the famous Conestoga wagons, with their arched canvas hoods, resembling the Chinese junks Whitman had recently seen exhibited in

New York. Hundreds of wagons were camped in "Tartar-looking groups" near the town, waiting to load on goods brought this far by the railroad, and fan out with them across the western country. Whitman's evening in Cumberland inspired his first printed attempt at the sort of nonliterary imagery that, in a few years, would become his trademark:

Night now falling down around us like a very large cloak of black broadcloth, (I fancy *that* figure, at least, hasn't been used up by the poets) and the Alleghenies rearing themselves up "some pumpkins" (as they say here) right before our nasal members, we got into one of the several four-horse stage coaches of the "National Road and Good Intent Stage Company," whereby we were to be transported over those big hills.

There is still plenty of New York superciliousness here, but Whitman had started thinking about a new, homely imagery, something Wordsworth or William Cullen Bryant could never have used. He had also begun his collection of colloquialisms (in the 1850s, he would make lists of them). Whitman had an ear for American street talk and would soon be using it in his writing, without the ironist's quotation marks.

At the coach station, the brothers' baggage was thrown onto a weighing machine, and their names were ticked off the passenger list. Soon they were packed into a low compartment, along with seven other passengers, and were racing up the mountains on a head-thumping ride: "Up we toiled and down we clattered . . . over these might warts on the great breast of nature." It was a cold night. The moon flashed between clouds and cast a milky light on the snow-covered ground. The coach stopped to change horses every ten miles, and the passengers stretched their legs or warmed themselves in the one-story way houses, where "stupendous fires" of locally mined soft coal gave off a flickering heat. Whitman described the impression of that night:

the mountains on all sides, the precipitous and turning road, the large bare-armed trees looming up around us, the room half filled with men curiously enwrapped in garments of a fashion till then never seen—and the flickering light from the mighty fire putting a red glow upon most objects, and casting others into a strong shadow.

This is finer descriptive writing than Whitman usually managed. The "large bare-armed trees" and "men curiously enwrapped" might almost be images in the 1855 *Leaves of Grass*. These articles for the *Crescent* are still far from the prose Whitman would write in a few years, but they are remarkably visual. He had begun to see as a painter and almost wished he were one.

Inside the coach, the nine "boxed" riders tried to talk the cold away, although, recalled Whitman, an old Ohio farmer did most of the talking. During the War of 1812, he had captured a becalmed British merchant brig off the coast of Maine and was still trying to collect his five-thousand-dollar bounty. "Poor old man!" Whitman noted, "if he lives till he gets Congress to pay him, he will be immortal."

Walt and Jeff jolted over the frozen Alleghenies, stopped in weirdly lit taverns which came alive during the night hours when wagoners and stage passengers staggered in for a few minutes to melt their frozen bones. Whitman was awed by the land-ocean stretching from the porch of one of these late-night way stations:

Just off on one side of us was a precipice of apparently hundreds of feet. The silence of the grave spread over this solemn scene; the mountains were covered in their white shrouds of snow—and the towering trees looked black and threatening; only the largest stars were visible, and they glittered with a tenfold brightness. . . . Faith! if I had an infidel to convert, I would take him on the mountains, of a clear and beautiful night, when the stars are shining.

At last, after a bone-breaking twenty-eight hours, the brothers reached the Ohio River at Wheeling and boarded a side-paddling river steamer, the *Saint Cloud*, for the trip to New Orleans.

These western riverboats were a uniquely American creation. "Except that they are in the water," Charles Dickens had written, "and display a couple of paddle-boxes, they might be intended, for anything that appears to the contrary, to perform some unknown service, high and dry, upon a mountain top." A riverboat consisted of:

a long, black, ugly roof, covered with burnt-out feathery sparks; above which tower two iron chimneys, and a hoarse escape valve, and a glass steerage house. Then, in order as the eye descends toward the water, are the sides, and doors, and windows of the state-rooms, jumbled as oddly together as though they formed a small street, built by the varying tastes of a dozen men: the whole is supported on beams and pillars resting on a dirty barge, but a few inches above the water's edge: and in the narrow space between this upper structure and the barge's deck, are the furnace fires and machinery, open at the sides to every wind that blows, and every storm of rain that drives along its path.

Dickens did not like to think about those glaring fires tended by "reckless men whose acquaintance with [their] mysteries may have been of six months' standing," while the traveler overhead went nervously about his business, in a "frail pile of painted wood."

To Jeff at least, the "frail pile of painted wood" was a floating palace: a splendid passenger deck, fine staterooms with real beds, enormous meals—"everything you would find in the Astor House in New York," he wrote to his mother—even if the river outside was a gruel of mud, with miles of uncultivated riverbank, toppled-over trees, occasional cabins sending a thread of blue smoke into the sky, near a forlorn wheatfield full of stumps. The *Saint Cloud* halted at gray towns or on empty stretches of river, where passengers rowed out to it while others were put ashore with their trunks, their bundles of linen, and their rocking chairs at the foot of a high bank with a faint trail zigzagging up to the crest. Dickens described such a scene:

The men get out of the boat first; help out the women; take out the bag, the chest, the chair; bid the rowers "goodby"; and shove the boat off for them. At the first plash of the oars in the water, the oldest woman of the party sits down in the old chair, close to the water's edge, without speaking a word. None of the others sit down, though the chest is large enough for many seats. They all stand where they landed as if stricken into stone; and look after the boat. . . . There they stand yet, without the motion of a hand. I can see them through my glass, when, in the distance and increasing darkness, they are mere specks to the eye.

Even Whitman had to admit that the shores of the Ohio were "barren of interest," although he was certain that "the period must arrrive when cultivation will bend [them] nearly all to man's use." Cairo, Illinois, at the junction of the Ohio and Mississippi was a dreadful muddy town, good for "the ague," and little else.

On the way to Cairo, Whitman was amazed at the quantity of freight that shuffled on and off at every stop, enough to make "a very fair cargo to a New York liner." There were hundreds of barrels of pork and lard, "bags of coffee, rolls of leather, groceries, dry goods, hardware, all sorts of agricultural products, innumerable coops filled with live geese, turkeys, and fowls . . . divers living hogs, to say nothing of a horse and a resident dog." The boat zigzagged between the Ohio and Kentucky shores, following its cargo manifest. It stopped at Cincinnati and Louisville, rich, active cities, bursting with trade and new buildings. Below Louisville, there was a nerve-wracking stretch when the captain of the *Saint Cloud* decided to run the rapids, which drop twenty feet in less than three miles, instead of looping around them by means of a canal on the Kentucky side. The boat lurched into the "boiling place" and slid along the main channel at frightening speed, grating on the bottom and steering precariously around half-submerged rocks. Walt shrugged the danger off, but Jeff's letter home was full of the bumps and sudden turns, a wheel that jammed, the fright everyone had, although he "not so much as some of the men."

At night, Whitman strolled along the side deck, peering into the muffled darkness. For the first time in years, he wrote a poem— about the onrushing river and its starless nights:

> How solemn! sweeping this dense black tide!
> > No friendly lights i' the heaven o'er us;
> A murky darkness on either side,
> > And kindred darkness all before us!
>
> Now, drawn near the shelving rim,
> > Weird-like shadows suddenly rise;
> Shapes of mist and phantoms dim
> > Baffle the gazer's straining eyes.
>
> River fiends, with malignant faces!
> > Wild and wide their arms are thrown,
> As if to clutch in fatal embraces
> > Him who sails their realms upon.
>
> Then, by the trick of our own swift motion,
> > Straight, tall giants, an army vast,

Rank by rank, like the waves of ocean,
　　On the shore march stilly past.

How solemn! the river a trailing pall,
　　Which takes, but never again gives back;
And moonless and starless the heaven's arch'd wall,
　　Responding an equal black!

Oh, tireless waters! like Life's quick dream,
　　Onward and onward ever hurrying—
Like Death in this midnight hour you seem,
　　Life in your chill drops greedily burying!

This is not quite Poe, although it tries. But neither is it the pallid Walter Whitman of his earlier verse. There is an experience here looking for a language, and not yet finding it. The Mississippi murk strains to express Whitman's deeper "doubts" about "appearances," his puzzled glimpses of the "flashes and specks" that the solidest reality may, after all, be. The shorelessness of the river at night suggested to him an interior shorelessness that, in only a few years, would flow into his great poems of night and death.

Days before reaching New Orleans, the Mississippi became a southern river, flowing lazily past groves of cypress trees, luxuriant mats of hanging moss, orange trees, rows of slave huts, and the large white plantation houses. Here was an America Whitman had only read about, with its slow, musical speech, its exaggerated gentility. Northerners tended to have complicated feelings about the South. Just as they thought of Europe as a "past" to improve upon, they dreamed—confusedly, maybe a little guiltily—of the South as an escape from the arduousness of too much change, too much busy self-reliance. Wealthy New Yorkers looked to the aristocratic South for legitimacy of manner, a kind of native Englishness. But the city's working classes, too, felt a curious sympathy for southern ideas and the southern tone. (Indeed, during the Civil War, New York was a "Copperhead city,"* sympathetic to the southern enemy.) Whitman, too, had been fascinated by the South. In *Franklin Evans,* in 1842, he had written about corrupt plantation owners and their overseers and the sexual wickedness of mulatto

* Southern sympathizers in the North, during the Civil War, were called Copperheads.

slave women: it was a South culled from magazines, a stereotype of tropical idleness, drink, honor, and sexuality; yet it was a sympathetic, at least a fascinated portrait.

Whitman, as I have said, would always have an appreciative eye for the idle rich. His democratic outrage would be tempered by a lingering curiosity for the accouterments of expensive living. As a Locofoco Democrat, too, he had expressed a respect bordering on awe for the South's greatest intellect, John C. Calhoun who, during the 1830s and 1840s, had scathingly criticized the relationship between capital and labor, arguing that the "free" northern worker was himself little more than a slave to capitalist manipulation. Calhoun's defense of slavery was oddly popular with northern workingmen and it accounts, in part, for the New York workingman's sympathy with the South—a sympathy that Whitman talked about in later years, attributing to it both his slow response, as a young man, to the question of slavery, and his relative indifference to the actual plight of the blacks, whom he never liked much, according to the evidence of friends like John Burroughs (later, one of America's greatest naturalists), and of his own Civil War letters to his mother, which contain mocking accounts of the behavior of black people.

Toward afternoon on Thursday, 24 February, the *Saint Cloud*'s passengers sighted the packed-earth embankments called "levees," which start about 120 miles north of New Orleans to keep the river from flooding the low-lying country to the east. Hours before the city itself came into view, the famous dome of the Saint Charles Hotel seemed to float on the horizon: a dazzling promise of the legendary city, built on mud, slave wealth, and tropical temperament.

For hours, the *Saint Cloud* maneuvered past a confusion of keelboats, ferries, and gaudily painted river steamers, with square-rigged ocean craft lying thickly at anchor in their midst. The wharves curved along the broad loop of the river for three miles, like a vast amphitheater, backed by massive warehouses and office buildings. To the steamboat traveler, inching through this cluttered river scene toward the dock, New Orleans was surely one of the most extraordinary commercial spectacles in the world. Then came the wharves: a broad curving thoroughfare heaped with cotton bales; with hogsheads of sugar, flour, fruit; with sacks of ice, barrels of pork; and over everything, the pungent aroma of coffee. After weeks of the empty river, and the exasperatingly silent, unvarying landscape of the western countries, New Orleans, for all its southern strangeness, must have seemed like a city out of the Arabian Nights.

2

After trying several roominghouses, the brothers settled at the Trement House across the street from the Crescent's offices, where almost immediately Walt began putting in long days. In addition to Whitman, the *Crescent* employed a full-time editorial writer who went by the name of "Larue"; a "city news" man named Reeder who, in Whitman's opinion, drank too much; and "a young fellow named Da Poute" [Da Ponte] who translated "Mexican and foreign items" and served as "factotum in general." It is one of history's smaller curiosities that young Da Ponte was the grandson of Lorenzo Da Ponte, one of Mozart's librettists. As the *Crescent's* "exchange editor," Whitman went through the dozens of out-of-town newspapers which arrived by mail every morning, and "made up the news," as he called it, with "pen and scissors." It was common for newspapers at the time to cannibalize each other by mutual agreement, exchanging free copies in a countrywide network of news swapping, which amounted to an informal news service. Occasionally Whitman contributed feature articles to the *Crescent.* He also sent several chatty "letters" to the *Sunday Times,* a New York weekly edited by a journalistic friend of his. Along with Jeff's letters home, and some short memoranda Whitman jotted in his notebook, these journalistic pieces are virtually the only source of information on Whitman's life in New Orleans.

Here, as so often, we see Whitman only in outline. Of his friendships, his daily routine, his opinion about personal matters, he left no word, either in letters or in his notebook; and the people he knew—his fellow journalists; his friend, the New York poet, Theodore Gould, who lived in New Orleans during these years—

never bothered to record their impressions. Not only was Whitman secretive about his private life, but it is as if he had none, as if the hunger for a human presence that he wrote passionately about in *Leaves of Grass* were a hunger not for individuals but for crowds passing in a street—one of his favorite images for life in its unshadowed overflow and abundance. A poem written almost ten years later, has caused biographers to speculate about a love affair in New Orleans:

> Once I pass'd through a populous city imprinting my brain
>   for future use with its shows, architecture, customs, traditions,
> Yet now of all that city I remember only a woman I casually met
>   there who detain'd me for love of me,
> Day by day and night by night we were together—all else has long
>   been forgotten by me,
> I remember I say only that woman who passionately clung to me,
> Again we wander, we love, we separate again,
> Again she holds me by the hand, I must not go,
> I see her close beside me with silent lips sad and tremulous.

The "populous city," with its "architecture, customs, traditions," is almost surely New Orleans, the only city Whitman had visited by the time he wrote this poem, in 1858. Yet a poem is not evidence that a biographer can use without infinite precautions. A poem is a sort of fiction. The truth it tells is "indirect." It lies and conceals in order better to reveal. In this poem, for example, Whitman was "lying" about a matter of importance: the "she" in the version he published was "he" in his original manuscript. Because his group of poems celebrating the love of woman—"Children of Adam"—seemed skimpy, he transferred "Once I Pass'd . . ." into it from the abundant "Calamus" section, celebrating male love. Thus, this poem tells us about Whitman's willingness to manipulate the tone and imagery of his poems for literary effect, but not much about the life he led in New Orleans; it tells about the power of his love fantasies for men, but not much about his sexual habits.

The *Crescent* seems to have been an immediate success, collecting two thousand subscribers within a few weeks. Whitman's former employer, the Brooklyn *Eagle,* complimented the paper on its tasteful printing and wished its publishers and editors luck, as did the *Crescent*'s New Orleans rivals, the *Delta* and the *Picayune*. Within days, Whitman was in the thick of New Orleans life, meeting his fellow journalists and haunting the large noisy cafés near Lafayette Square. "I frequently thought . . . that I felt better than ever before in my life," he wrote in his notebook.

New Orleans was tropical and curiously foreign, a blend of frontier brutality and the most refined romantic gentility. Yet Whitman felt at home there. Like New York, it was an immigrant city and a busy port; its active streets opened onto a spindly crowd of masts and overhanging prows along the river. Like New York, too, New Orleans was a city of moral contrasts. A few years later, after a visit there, the landscape architect Frederick Law Olmsted wrote:

I doubt if there is a city in the world, where the resident population has been so divided in its origin, or where there is such a variety in the tastes, habits, manners, and moral codes of the citizen . . . so that nowhere are the higher qualities of man—as displayed in generosity, hospitality, benevolence, and courage—better developed, or the lower qualities, likening him to a beast, less interfered with, by law or the action of public opinion.

Whitman loved the New Orleans custom of lounging in dimly lit barrooms, where he sipped "cobblers" or brandy and made notes about the city's idle rich. Here, undoubtedly, he met some of the characters he sketched in his articles for the *Crescent:* "John J. Jinglebrain" with his up-to-the-minute dress and his greased locks; "Daggerdraw Bowieknife, Esq." a deadly southern character, in whom elegance and good breeding combined with a murderous expertise in every conceivable killing tool.

Occasionally Whitman's barroom sketches manage a more personal note. Among the habitués of the hotel lounges, Whitman noticed an "old grey haired farmer," whose "firm and honest" soul he compares, with Jacksonian echo, to a "hickory stick." This old farmer is the father of a senator. He has spent his life cultivating potatoes and turnips, threshing wheat, occasionally selling off a stand of corn. Now, grasping his cane in an "iron clutch," he reads in the newspaper, with tears of pride, that his son has been discussing the important issues of the world, that he has spoken out plainly to monarchs.

Whitman's writings are filled with portraits of fierce, benevolent old men. Many of his articles in the *Eagle* had shown a respect verging on awe for America's legendary elders: Jackson, the Mexican War generals, and, of course, the Founding Fathers themselves. Here, as so often, Whitman's personal vision was rooted in the popular culture. Nineteenth-century America was a country of hero worshipers. One aspect of the headlong experiment that gripped American public life during these years of expansion was a passion for great individuals, who were shouldered into myth by the popular imagination. Within years after they died, Washington, Jefferson, Jackson had become saints. As legendary fathers, they anchored the "democratic turbulence" Whitman praised in the *Eagle,* by giving it a human face. They were intercessors, models of wisdom and forgiveness, exemplifying the properly spiritual ambition that nineteenth-century democracy came to stand for, in the midst of its violence and its miseries. This may help to explain the flamboyance of American political lingo in the second quarter of the century. Statesmen Henry Clay, John Calhoun, and Daniel Webster struggled to satisfy the popular craving for immense men, by inflating their speech, grafting it onto the Bible. Emerson, too, was not merely listened to, but, as the poet-philosopher George Santayana once remarked, was worshiped as prophet and saint.

Whitman's hickory-souled father belongs to a gallery of beloved old men in Whitman's writings: the manly patriarch in "I Sing the Body Electric"; Abraham Lincoln, whom Whitman mythologized in "O Captain, My Captain" and "When Lilacs Last in the Dooryard Bloomed." Within a few years, Whitman's most striking patriarch would be himself: crinkled ruddy face, peaceful eyes, cheerful halo of beard.

As always, Whitman lived in the streets. He spent hours strolling on Lafayette Square or along the levees. One morning in late April, he got up with the sun and strolled out along the river. In the early haze, the city seemed "lazy and idle," except for a dozen bare-legged German sailors scouring the deck of their ship, and a negro who threw a large stone at the head of his mule. Whitman wished he owned the negro; he swore he wouldn't treat him the way he treated that mule, but would give him a cowhide and get him to whip himself. Farther along, he saw a longshoreman in a red shirt and blue cottonade pants, snoring on a bench. His socks were missing, and he was drunk. Poor man, he had probably spent his last "picayune" in a grog shop and then gotten kicked out by his landlord.

Soon the sun was comfortably perched just above the horizon. Shopkeepers were opening for the day. Stevedores hurried toward their ships. Whitman wandered into Saint Mary's market, where he noticed a famous lawyer chewing on a long stick of sugar cane and a woman stirring up a bucket of live crabs with iron tongs. In their stalls hung "rounds of beef haunches of venison and legs of mutton . . . that would have made a disciple of Graham forswear his hermit-like appetite."* By the middle of the morning, Whitman was passing the gaudy display windows on the downtown shopping streets. The newsboys, he remarked, were "cute as foxes." The "savory smell of fried ham, broiled beef-steak, with onions," stealing out of "the half unshut doors" of restaurants, made him hungry. So he headed over to the Tremont House for breakfast: "tea, a radish, a piece of dry toast, and an egg," accompanied by "one of the morning papers."

Let this walk stand for many others, along the levee or in the French Quarter, near the old Spanish cathedral. As a newspaper man, Whitman probably visited the former Hotel de Ville, now a city courthouse, located on the Place d'Armes, thickly planted with orange and lemon trees and beds of roses. Olmsted describes this part of town with its "narrow dirty streets . . . grimy old stuccoed walls; high arched windows and doors, balconies and entresols, and French noises and French smells." Whitman peered into the famous New Orleans grog shops; listened to street vendors like "Timothy Goujon," trilling his operatic sales pitch: "Ah-h-h-h-h-h a bonne marché—so cheep as navair was—toutes frais—var fresh. Ah-h-h-h un veritable collection—jentlemens and black folks. Ah-h-h come and buy de veritable poisson de la mer—de bonne huitres—Ah-h-h-h-h!"

Whitman had been using half-understood French phrases in his

---

* On Graham, see page 96.

articles since his days as editor of the *Aurora*. It was the sort of thing American journalists did—a provincial mannerism—much as they salted their gangly prose with quotes from Milton and Shakespeare. In fact, Whitman did not have much of a gift for languages. He never learned more than a journalist's smattering of French, Spanish, or any of the other languages with which he strewed his mature poetry as part of the stylistic expansion—the "language experiment"—he claimed *Leaves of Grass* to be.

But New Orleans was itself a sort of language experiment, a babble of phrases transplanted from half of Europe. Olmsted was amused by the street signs in the French Quarter, with their "funny polyglomatic arrangements":

APARTMENTS TO LET

A la Fée aux Roses

WEIN BIER EN DETAIL

Chambres à Louer

Upholsterers in all its Branches

Kossuth Coffee House

Depot des Graines Pour Les Oiseaux

To Loyauge Intelligence Office, only for the girls and women answering ho! On demande, 50 hommes pour le chemin-de-fer. Wanted to work on the railroad some men now.

Défense d'afficher!

Linguistic pastiche was part of the urban genius of New Orleans; and Whitman, on the verge of his own radical experiments with language, was surely struck by the city's polyglot style.

Although the Mexican War had been over for several months, New Orleans was still dominated by the presence of the military. For two years, the war effort had funneled through here. Soldiers bivouacked in open fields and even set up tents in Lafayette Square. The neighborhood around the Tremont House had been a combined armed camp, staging area, and hospital depot. Steamers shipped regularly for Vera Cruz in Mexico, loaded with recruits, and returned with the sick and wounded; while all the public places in town clanked and shone with the parading victors. Whitman wrote of those weeks: "No one who has never seen the society of a city under similar circumstances can understand what a strange vivacity and *rattle* was given throughout . . . [by] the crowds of soldiers, the gay young officers . . . the receipt of important news, the many discussions, the returning wounded." This might be Washington fourteen years later during the Civil War. In New Orleans, as in Washington, Whitman felt himself to be at the heart of a great American event.

Yet the Mexican War was complicated for Whitman, as the Civil War would be later. At first he had been in favor of the war. Under Whitman's tutelage, the *Eagle* had clamored about illustrious generals and invincible troops and had featured pious exhortations to spread the light of democracy southward into Central America. This point of view was Democratic party policy, but it also reflected Whitman's personal, strident nationalism which, half a dozen years before, had won him more allies than he wanted among the bigoted Native American groups.* Unlike Thoreau and the New England intellectuals, Whitman had no qualms about the country's expansionist aims, advertised under the slogan of "manifest destiny": Mexico, Oregon, Cuba, Canada—nothing was too much for America's continental appetite.

But the Wilmot Proviso had exacerbated national feelings about the war. People had been forced to recognize an awkward complicity between expansionist Democrats, shrill with Jacksonian ideals, and the partisans of slavery. To many patriotic Americans, democracy was the summit of human history. A democratic America blessed the world by overflowing the national boundaries. But slavery was democracy's nightmare; it was dark and terrible, reality smashing the dream. Slavery stood for the inexpugnable weight of the past, a kind of original sin that democratic optimism could not will away. Yet the southern states saw the Mexican War as a chance to expand their "peculiar institution" into the conquered territories of the Southwest. This was a darker "manifest destiny." I evoke it here because the splintering of the democratic dream wrought changes in Whitman's outlook that were definitive and,

*See note, p. 222.

ultimately, made a poet of him. In New Orleans, Whitman was assailed by all sides of every issue and not professionally committed to any of them.

This is the Whitman of *Leaves of Grass*. From now on, he would be on both sides of most arguments, with a mixture of passion and caution that he, after Emerson, would call "prudence," meaning an attitude of sympathetic detachment, a "cosmic" long view conducive to feelings of impartial love, but also to a curiously comic vision of human events.

Whitman's exit from politics occurred only gradually. Within a few months of returning to New York from New Orleans, he would be a delegate to a Free Soil convention in Buffalo. The following autumn, he would create a Free Soil newspaper in Brooklyn and edit it for almost a year. The first experimental poems he published in the *Tribune* and the *Post* in 1850 were political. Thus, he did not give in without a struggle to his contradictory temperament. An enemy of quick transitions, prudent, stubbornly conservative, he eased half against his will into the broad principles of his new poetry:

> Do I contradict myself?
> Very well then I contradict myself,
> I am large, I contain multitudes.

On some days Whitman strolled from his office on St. Charles Street to the Bank's Arcade, a rendezvous for local journalists. Standing at the bar that stretched along one side of the Arcade, he listened to planters and businessmen talk about city affairs, the peace treaty. Across the floor of the Arcade, he saw slave auctioneers sipping brandy and water, while they sold off, sometimes for thousands of dollars, human beings who were obliged to open their mouths so that buyers could inspect their gums and teeth. Yet Whitman knew the terms of his employment and kept his peace about controversial matters: he never mentioned the slave trade during his stay in New Orleans. Turning to a less controversial subject, he wrote a daring appreciation of a show of nude models performing at a local theater. They stood, he wrote, in "graceful and beautiful groupings—most of them—after models in sculpture." Angered by the fuss made in some out-of-town newspapers, he added: "It is a sickly prudishness that bars all appreciation of the divine beauty evidenced in Nature's cunningest work—the human frame, form and face." Here was a safe controversy, and Whitman threw himself into it. Yet within half a dozen years, the slave auction and the "divine beauty" of the nude models would be conflated in a memorable passage of "I Sing the Body Electric," in which the poet, standing beside a slave auctioneer, helps him to praise the mysteries of the human body:

> A slave at auction!
> I help the auctioneer . . . . the sloven does not half
>   know his business.
>
> Gentlemen look at this curious creature,
> Whatever the bids of the bidders they cannot be high
>   enough for him,
> For him the globe lay preparing quintillions of years without
>   one animal or plant,
> For him the revolving cycles truly and steadily rolled.
>
> In that head the allbaffling brain,
> In it and below it the making of the attributes of heroes.
>
> Examine these limbs, red black or white . . . . they are very
>   cunning in tendon and nerve;
> They shall be stript that you may see them.
>
> Exquisite senses, lifelit eyes, pluck, volition,
> Flakes of breastmuscle, pliant backbone and neck, flesh not
>   flabby, goodsized arms and legs,
> And wonders within there yet.

The early spring weather matched Whitman's expansive mood. The air smelled of magnolia blossoms, and the sky was so clear it looked as if it had been "newly shingled." At night the brothers strolled in Lafayette Park. By day they walked out toward Lake Pontchartrain. On Sunday mornings, Whitman visited the old French market and "got a large cup of delicious coffee, with a biscuit . . . from the immense shining copper kettle of a great Creole mulatto woman." Thousands of shoppers crowded the marketplace, speaking a dozen languages: it was a tropical version of some great Paris *marché*.

Springtime in New Orleans resembled a long holiday, beginning with Mardi Gras, followed by a raucous volunteer fireman's parade, and then a highly touted horserace at the Jockey Club across the river. For a few weekends in March and April, a woman made elaborate preparations for going up in a hot-air balloon. At first, people were curious; but when, after four or five tries, the balloon kept blowing up, they decided they'd been taken. "They all laid hold of it," wrote Jeff, "and dragging it over the fence tore it all to pieces, they did not leave a piece a foot square."

There were the courtrooms and theaters and the opera; the large barrooms and hotel saloons; the Saturday-night balls; the miles-long arc of the levee rumbling with commerce; the candle-lit cathedral on holy days; the marketplaces; above all, the parades which, to Whitman, were the quintessence of city life, and which he would always love, as living poems, the city's own "catalogues."

That spring, news came from Europe of revolution. The people of Paris had taken to the streets; the French king was in exile; a poet, Lamartine, had been made foreign minister of a new republic which had decreed universal male suffrage and abolished the death penalty. Newspapers all over the country ran fat headlines across their front pages. In New York, Horace Greeley and William Cullen Bryant led a mass rally in favor of the revolution. In New Orleans, there were banquets, toasts to world freedom. The army fired a one-hundred-gun salute, and the *Crescent* printed the text of the *Marseillaise*. Whitman wrote: "One's blood rushes and grows hot within him the more he learns or thinks of this news from the continent of Europe!"

It was one of the few times in Whitman's life when he was in the right place to share the excitement of a great event. New Orleans swarmed with European refugees who were delirious with joy at the news from across the ocean. "The whole civilized world is in commotion," Whitman wrote. "Everywhere the people have risen against the tyrannies which oppress them."

The memories of that spring stayed with Whitman. Two years later, in Greeley's *Tribune*, he would publish a lurid historical poem entitled "Resurgemus," evoking the upheavals of 1848:

Suddenly out of its stale and drowsy lair, the lair of slaves,
Like lightning Europe le'pt forth . . . . half startled at itself,
Its feet upon the ashes and the rags . . . Its hands tight to the
   throats of kings. . . .

Yet behind all, lo, a Shape,
Vague as the night, draped interminably, head front and form in
   scarlet folds,
Whose face and eyes none may see,
Out of its robes only this . . . the red robes, lifted by the arm,
One finger pointed high over the top, like the head of a snake appears.

The poem's personified abstractions hark back to the Poe-like stories Whitman had been writing in the early 1840s, and all but
disappear from his later poems. The images are bloated, filled with
Gothic alarm. Yet this is one of the first poems Whitman would
publish in his new style, and it is among the twelve to comprise the
first edition of *Leaves of Grass,* in 1855. The "lair of slaves" in the
poem's first line represents a curious transfer of the imagination.
For New Orleans, too, was a "lair of slaves." There Whitman had
tasted exhilarating personal freedom. There, too, in a slave city, he
had shared in the effervescence of revolutionary hope. "Slavery"
and "liberation" were uneasy partners in Whitman's memory. In
"Resurgemus," he bends them into a political rhapsody, where
they supply the articulating drive of his first published verse
experiment.

Whitman probably never planned to stay long in New Orleans.
He knew about the city's stifling summers, when the levee was
deserted, and the barrooms and hotel lobbies stood empty. Summer
also brought the yellow fever epidemics which gripped the city
every few years. Although he was earning a good living, prices
were high in New Orleans. An apple that cost a penny, or maybe
two, in New York, cost ten cents here. Still, Walt saved what he
could: "already he has quite a sum," Jeff wrote, "as soon as he gets
a thousand dollars, he is coming north." It's not likely that Whitman saved a thousand dollars during his few months in New Orleans; and as weeks passed, his prospects for doing so dimmed. For
after a cordial beginning at the *Crescent,* his relationship with the
owners began to sour. Here is how Whitman describes the change
in a memorandum written a few weeks later:

both H. and M'C, after a while, exhibited a sort of coldness, toward me, and the latter an irritability toward Jef., who had, at times, much harder work than I was willing he should do. . . . I had been accustomed to having frequent conferences, in my former situations with the proprietors of newspapers, on the subject of management, etc.—But when the coldness above alluded to broke out, H. seemed to be studiously silent upon all these matters.—My own pride was touched—and I met their conduct with equal haughtiness on my part.—On Wednesday May 24th I sent down a note requesting a small sum of money.—M'C returned me a bill of what money I had already drawn, and stated that they could not make "advances." I answered by reminding them of certain points which appeared to have been forgotten, making me *not* their debtor, and told them in my reply I thought it would be better to dissolve the connection. They agreed to my plan (after some objections on the part of me); and I determined to leave on the succeeding Saturday.

Although Whitman and McClure quarreled about money, the source of the tension was probably elsewhere. It is hard to imagine that "Free Soiler" Whitman managed to hold his peace at all times about the *Crescent*'s racial policies, and his attitude would have been good reason to exclude him from editorial conferences. Also, Whitman had never worked on a newspaper with a large staff, and he never would again. The *Aurora,* and the political campaign sheets he had run in the mid-1840s, even the *Eagle,* had been one-man shows, as the Brooklyn *Daily Times* would be in 1857. As Whitman did not like to share responsibility or act on another person's ideas, I imagine that he may well have been an inconvenient employee. Whatever the reason, he was too proud not to take McClure's hint. Besides, Jeff had never gotten over his homesickness and now, with the May heat, had fallen ill, probably with dysentery. All told, it was time to leave. Next Saturday, 27 May, the Whitman brothers boarded the *Pride of the West* and steamed upriver toward St. Louis.

They reached Brooklyn late in the afternoon, on 15 June, having been away exactly four months. Everything was fine at the Whitman home on Prince Street. Whitman had seen a lot, had written his quota of slapdash editorials, had as usual quarreled with his employer, and been fired. And he had come back, "large as life, but quite as vain . . . his brown face smiling like a wicker basket

filled with wooden particles cleft from timber," as his friend Henry
Lees announced in the Brooklyn *Advertiser.*

In later years, as Whitman repeatedly daubed at his personal
legend, New Orleans would be the gateway: before it, a dim pre-
history; after it, the "simmering" that in 1853 or 1854 came to a
"boil." The poet-tree "uttering joyous leaves of dark green," in a
beautiful short poem of the late 1850s, was a Louisiana live oak
that Whitman might have seen in the swampy lowlands toward
Lake Pontchartrain. Poetry, for Whitman, would luxuriate in
moss-hung branches and glossy tropical leaves; it would never be
far from the Southern theme. During the 1850s, while the country
frenetically drove itself apart, Whitman worked at a poetic labor of
union, a sort of national pastoral, in which he attempted to overcome the ugliness of sectional conflict, reaching back to an earlier,
happier vision of America. The memory of New Orleans would
give concreteness to his healing vision. It would enable him to
gravitate to his temperamentally right place on both sides of the
conflict: a Free Soil man, yes; on occasion, a hysterical populist
critic of those "few hundred rich plantation owners" whom he saw
as bending not only blacks but all Americans to their feudal wills;
an appallingly warlike Yankee when the fighting actually started.
And yet never entirely at ease with sectional hatred; always eager
to meet and personally know his enemies; above all, always happy
with the southern way of slow living, stiff personal pride, and
stylish individualism. In a Civil War letter to his mother, he wrote
coyly that, with his broad ruddy face, flowing beard, and domed
gray hat, he had recently been taken for a Southern plantation
owner, and he liked that.

It was inevitable that Whitman—and his biographers—would
make a great deal out of these months in the South. The change
that was taking place in Whitman's literary ambition was so unprecedented, and apparently so abrupt, that we want to hang it on
some event. So we imagine the mystical shock of a new country
expanding before a novice traveler's eyes; or a love affair with a
well-born Creole lady that had to be kept secret because of the
threat of scandal.

In later years, Whitman dismissed the idea that his poetic faculties had been awakened by any profound personal change; and I think, here, we can accept his view. The truth, we know, was at once more ordinary and more mysterious. Only the year before, Whitman had begun to write prose notes in his leather book. It was, as yet, merely an orgy of bold rhythms awaiting a form and a framing vision. The journey to New Orleans did not supply either the form or the vision, which took several more years to emerge; although when they did, they would enable Whitman to sweep all these scraps and trials into a broad form-without-form. When the time came, he remembered, he did not leave much out. Nor did the trip mark as clear a break with the past as it might seem. Whitman went to New Orleans as a journalist. Newspapers were an expanding field in the 1840s. Whitman knew that and wanted to cash in on his decade of professional experience. Things didn't work out for him down South; but he kept at it when he got home, and would keep at it for three more years, with a self-made man's fantasy of making it big as the editor of a widely read newspaper, like his friend William Cullen Bryant or like Horace Greeley, both of whom he admired and would have liked to emulate.

3

Earlier that year, in January, when Whitman lost his job at the *Eagle,* his friends talked of finding him another paper, and they hadn't forgotten while he was away. All that spring, factions in both political parties had collided so angrily over Wilmot's question of slavery in the new territories that, looking toward the presidential election in the fall, the parties could manage only an embarrassed silence on the overwhelming problem of the day. The party conventions in May and June had made the embarrassment official. Neither the Democrats nor the Whigs had been able to unite behind any of their eminent leaders. Clay and Webster were little more than bystanders. Calhoun's powers were concentrated in an old man's last effort to forestall the catastrophe that he already knew would destroy his precarious and beloved South. When he spoke, it was not as a political leader but as a prophet

preferring war to compromise, a cleansing struggle to the accom-
modations of politics. In January, Free Soil had been a matter of
party politics; and Whitman, taking his stand, had lost his job. By
summer, it was becoming a national nightmare. The Democrats
met in Baltimore, on 22 May, and nominated a conservative, Lewis
Cass, as their candidate for president. Outraged Barnburners from
New York made Baltimore "lurid with their wrath," according to
a contemporary newspaper account. Already plans were afoot to
hold a Free Soil convention in Buffalo that August, in the hope of
creating a new party. Later Whitman spoke of a short period in his
life when he flirted with abolitionism, and this was surely the
time.

A Free Soil newspaper was planned in Brooklyn to oppose the
Eagle, now firmly in conservative hands. Judge Samuel Johnson, a
strong advocate of the rights of black people and an old friend of
Whitman's, was the force behind the paper. A list of subscribers,
dated 11 July, exists to the *Banner of Freedom,* "which shall oppose
the extension of slavery and support for elective offices persons
who will advocate the same." Later in the summer, Johnson signed
the list over to Whitman, who became the editor. By the time the
paper appeared on 9 September, Whitman had changed its name to
the Brooklyn *Freeman.*

It had been an exciting summer for Whitman. On 5 August, the
local Barnburners had met in Washington Hall, to appoint fourteen Brooklyn delegates to the Free Soil Convention in Buffalo. As
a "martyr" to the cause, and a well-known polemicist, Whitman
had been chosen. On Monday, 7 August, Bryant's *Evening Post*
reported on the Brooklyn meeting:

Mr. W. Whitman made some remarks introducing a resolution instruct-
ing the delegates from King's County to go unconditionally for the
nomination of Martin Van Buren. At the particular desire, however, of
some of the members of the meeting, he accepted an amendment preserving the spirit of the resolution, but leaving out the positive instructions,
which was adopted—though many preferred it in its first form.

The convention met on 9 and 10 August, in a huge tent on the
shores of Lake Erie. As many as 30,000 delegates gathered from all
over the country in an atmosphere that was part country fair, part

revolutionary assembly, and part campmeeting, with many delegates getting up at five in the morning to sing hymns in the cool of the dawn. By afternoon, the heat was fierce, as the crowd milled through the enormous tent and listened to some of the greatest speakers of the day. Somehow, 465 official delegates were winnowed from the thousands of fervent participants, and the business of the convention was attended to, with torchlit sessions lasting until after midnight. Now and then, the Hutchinsons, the family singing group Whitman had praised before opera captivated him, sang uplifting songs. As with any political convention that brings together not altogether trusting allies, there was plenty of wheeling and dealing in the back rooms. But the participants would long remember the Buffalo convention, and the third-party movement that sprang from it, "as a magnificent expression of crusading righteousness."

It was the sort of moment Whitman loved: the sweating crowd squeezed into the mammoth tent; torchlight; good oratory; group singing; the expansive feeling of unanimity as at the political meetings he had always relished, but with an added evangelical tone. Whitman would call this feeling, "ensemble-individuality," in a later neologism, and it expressed his lifelong experience of aliveness and exhilaration whenever he "bathed" himself in a crowd. The days in Buffalo were an essential crowd-bath. Delegates streamed in from all over the country. Free blacks like abolitionist Frederick Douglass spoke, and men of all parties merged their differences in a solid reform platform, centered on the Wilmot plank of Free Soil but including virtually all the progressive ideas of the day. The Buffalo convention was democracy made visible and physical. It is no surprise that Whitman felt himself to be a bit of an abolitionist during the summer of 1848.

Upon returning from Buffalo, Whitman equipped the *Freeman* with as good a press as he could afford, and wrote his first edition. The plan was to bring the paper out every Saturday at two cents a copy. In October, when the electoral campaign was heating up, he planned to turn it into a penny daily. The 9 September deadline was upon him almost before he knew it, but Whitman was ready to fulfill the *Advertiser*'s friendly prediction of two months before:

"No grimalkin ever worried horror-stricken mice . . . more than our amiable locofoco friend will be likely to clutch and worry old Hunkerism in King's County."

In his first issue, Whitman made it clear that the *Freeman* was going to be an instrument of combat:

Hardly any one who takes the trouble to look two minutes at our paper will need being told, at any length, what objects we have in view . . . our doctrine is the doctrine laid down in the Buffalo Convention, and expounded in the letters of Van Buren and Adams. . . . We shall oppose, under all circumstances, the addition to the Union, in the future, of a single inch of *slave land*, whether in the form of state or territory.

The Brooklyn *Eagle,* he claimed, had poisoned the moral atmosphere of the county, and now the *Freeman* was going to cleanse it. Whitman was gearing up for a fight, but luck was against him. That very night a fire broke out in a crockery store on Fulton Street. It was a windy night, and Brooklyn, with its rows of pinewood houses, was a tinderbox. Before long, the fire had roared across twenty downtown acres, destroying hundreds of buildings, including the *Freeman*'s office on Orange Street. Several dozen fire companies, mostly from Manhattan, raced to the rescue, but they spent most of their time brawling with each other. Looters took over the streets, until the City Guard moved in to restore order.

Although the fire frustrated any role Whitman might have had in the election, he did not give up. By 1 November, he was ready with a new weekly *Freeman,* a "remarkably handsome" paper with a hopeful future according to the *Long Island Democrat.* Unfortunately, no copies of the paper have survived, but apparently it did not do well. Perhaps Whitman's heart was not in it. A fair number of the articles on poetry he clipped and saved from British magazines date from this winter. When he wasn't reading, or printing the *Freeman,* he was supervising the construction of a house on Myrtle Avenue for his family: a corner frame building with two squat stories over a wide-windowed shop. By April 1849, the house was finished, and the Whitmans moved in. For several years, Walt used the ground-floor space for a bookstore and printing shop, but it does not seem to have been a very active business, and he never mentioned it in later years, although some time in 1849 he started taking books on consignment from Fowler and Wells, the phrenological publishing house and reform emporium that would play an important part in his future.

A theme runs through many of the glimpses we get of Whitman in these early years. He appears to have been easy-going, perhaps even lazy. According to his political adversaries at the *Eagle,* he was "too indolent to kick a musketo." But even Whitman's friends saw this side of him. An old acquaintance remembered him in his printing office and bookstore in 1849:

The superficial opinion about him was that he was somewhat of an idler, "a loafer," but not in a bad sense. He always earned his own living. I thought him a very natural person. He wore plain cheap clothes, which were always particularly clean. . . . He was quite grey at thirty. . . . His singular coolness was an especial feature. He had a look of age in his youth, as he has now a look of youth in his age.

Whitman worked to his own rhythm. Large and slow-moving, he was slow-thinking too, he admitted, which may be why he failed to make his mark as a journalist. And the "singular coolness": that, too, crops up elsewhere. Whitman had a way of suddenly withdrawing that could jar people. It made him seem impregnable. What a tantalizing mixture: easy-going, vain, remote without warning, angry, lazy. Yet through it all, a practical busy man when he had to be. He had written a newspaper virtually single-handed for two years and was now writing another.

Whitman had a last flurry as a journalist. By April, he persuaded his backers to fund the *Freeman* as a morning daily. He managed to get some of the town government's official printing work. He advertised for a few reporters, claimed a large circulation—mostly giveaways, scoffed the *Star*—and, in a characteristically defiant act, sent his newsboys to hawk their papers at a cut rate in front of his rivals' offices. Whitman was flying now. He crowed about the electoral victory that was coming, and boasted of his own prospects: the *Freeman* would keep on expanding; it would become a powerful newspaper; as the editor, he would earn four thousand dollars a year, maybe more, until he decided to retire to a "good farm . . . when we get too much vex'd with our official duties."

Boasting was something of an art in nineteenth-century America and it came easily to Whitman, as easily as his daydream of leisure and early retirement.

Whitman's high did not last long. Feuding Democrats had begun to talk in private. On 12 September, Free Soil Democrats met in Utica and voted to accept a joint ticket with their former Hunker enemies. Whitman got wind of the upcoming deal, which put a personal enemy of his on the ticket. This was too much for Whitman. Stubborn to the last, he wrote his final editorial for the *Freeman* on 11 September:

After the present date, I withdraw entirely from the Brooklyn Daily Freeman. To those who have been my friends I take occasion to proffer the warmest thanks of a grateful heart. My enemies—and old hunkers generally—I disdain and defy just the same as ever.

By joining the crusade against slavery, Whitman had, in a sense, reaffirmed the politics of his earliest years, when he frequented Workingman party meetings with his father and heard the English reformer Frances Wright, whom he once called the greatest woman he ever knew. Once again, he stood with a vocal minority against the powers of government. Once again, his militant minority spoke in tones of moral self-confidence, persuaded that it was the conscience of the nation. During the preceding decades, American political life had received much of its radical terminology—its orotund flag waving of democracy, freedom, and progress—from these vocal minorities which it neutralized and absorbed, while stealing their slogans. This was to happen again. The third-party effort of 1848 failed; yet within a few years, it would express the passion of the decade and prepare the nation for civil war. As a battling Free Soil editor, Whitman, had he stayed with the movement, could have hoped to serve his personal ambitions as well. Yet he, as much by character as by principle, was an absolute protestant; like Milton, the only party he could belong to happily was his own. When, in 1856, he wrote his never-published pamphlet, "The Eighteenth Presidency"—his last volley in the Free Soil wars—it was as a lone sharpshooter, a political Natty Bumppo.

In 1848 and 1849, Whitman was still very much the man his political friends knew. But now there was also a leather notebook with a pencil stuck through its loops, small enough to be carried in a pocket. The notebook spoke of other matters, in a bold, hard-edged language. Here was no trace of politics, nor was there much that could be called personal. It is as if, in these notebooks, Whitman was experimenting with tone, addressing an audience of immortals, instead of an audience of citizens.

The notebook tells us that, appearances to the contrary, Whitman in 1848 and 1849 had entered a new phase. Not only was he the man his political friends knew; he was also a man of whom they had no idea. We must now begin to think of him as a paradox: on the one hand, a writer of limited originality, practiced in laying end to end expected phrases that reassure; on the other hand, a writer obsessed with originality who had decided to reinvent the idiom of literature. There is an entry in one of his notebooks: "I cannot understand the mystery: but I am always conscious of myself as two (as my soul and I)." If there was ever a time of "twoness" in Whitman's life, it was now: both parts of himself were passionate and articulate; yet, as often with Whitman, they seemed not to know each other.

4

In June of the previous year, Whitman's first story in several years appeared in the *Union Magazine of Literature and Art*. "The Shadow and Light of a Young Man's Soul" is an awkward story, showing little improvement over the bleak family romances he had been writing in the early 1840s, but it shows that, despite his later disclaimers, Whitman was fascinated by the idea of a radical personal change. The obsessive themes of his previous fiction are all present in the story: a father who selfishly dissipates his wealth, a widowed mother, and a son who devotes his life to her. But the story draws more directly on autobiographical material than anything Whitman had yet written, or would write until *Specimen Days,* more than thirty years later.

The boy, Archie Dean, is forced to leave New York City, after the great fire of 1835, and go to live on Long Island, where he teaches school. He has an invalid younger brother whom he loves dearly. An outcome of the story is that he manages at last to provide a secure and happy home for his mother; and "never did his tongue utter words other than kindness, or his lips, whatever annoyances or disappointments came, cease to offer their cheerfulest smile in her presence." All of this is so close to Whitman's own life that we wonder whether the character of Archie Dean represents Whitman's view of himself as a boy and young man. His description of Archie's character seems revealing and recalls both a photograph of Whitman taken in the early 1840s showing a young man's sleepy-eyed face, his chin resting on a foppish cane, his elegant suit and hat; and Louisa Whitman's remark about Walter's "strangeness" as a boy:

"Unstable as water," even in his youth, was not a sufficient excuse for his want of energy and resolution; and [his mother] experienced many sad moments, in her maternal reflections, ending with the fear that he would "not excel." The young man had too much of that inferior sort of pride which fears to go forth in public with anything short of fashionable garments, and hat and boots fit for fashionable criticism. His cheeks would tingle with shame at being seen in any sort of working capacity; his heart sank within him if his young friends met him when he showed signs of the necessity of labor, or of the absence of funds. Moreover, Archie looked on the dark side of his life entirely too often; he pined over his deficiencies, as he called them, by which he meant mental as well as pecuniary wants.

But Archie Dean has an important lesson to learn. At first he is upset by the country crudeness of his Long Island neighbors, "to whom grace and refinement are unknown." But soon his spirits are revived

by his long walks over the hills, by his rides on horseback every Saturday, his morning rambles and his evening saunters; by his coarse living, even, and the untainted air and water, which seemed to make better blood in his veins. Gradually, too, he found something to admire in the character and customs of the unpolished country folk; their sterling sense on most practical subjects, their hospitality, and their industry.

He makes friends with a "yellow-faced" old spinster, whose life has been devoted to reacquiring the ancestral property that her father's youthful dissipation had lost, and her story encourages Archie Dean to a new resolve:

The change was not a sudden one; few great changes are. But his heart was awakened to his weakness; the seed was sown. Archie Dean felt he *could* expand his nature by means of that very nature itself. Many times he flagged; but at each fretful falling back, he thought of the yellow-faced dame, and roused himself again . . . he felt that on him rested the responsibility of making [his mother's] last years comfortable. "I shall give up my teacher's place . . . and come to live with you; we will have the same home, for it is best so." And so he did. And the weakness of the good youth's heart never entirely got the better of him afterward, but in the course of a season was put to flight utterly. . . . With an iron will he substituted action and cheerfulness for despondency and fretful tongue. He met his fortunes as they came, face to face, and shirked no conflict. Indeed, he felt it glorious to vanquish obstacles.

He had been a disconsolate boy; now Archie Dean makes himself into a man, through a program of outdoor living and filial loyalty that resembles Whitman's own program during these years. The story is prophetic, for the most radically willed of Whitman's changes lay several years in the future when, almost overnight, he created himself as a new man.

Under cover of fiction, Whitman described himself movingly in "The Shadow and Light of a Young Man's Soul": his angry masculine personality was shored up by an "iron will," but a "dark side" was ever straining to express itself, as in this very story or in a notebook entry written a few years later and never fully worked into a poem:

I am not glad tonight. Gloom has gathered round me like a mantle tightly folded.
The oppression of my heart is not fitful and has no pangs; but a torpor like that of some stagnant pool.

Archie struggles out of his self-enclosed adolescence, but the change is ambivalent. How secure is his new manly character when it depends on an ever-renewed act of will that could falter at any moment? His maturity seems deliberate, theatrical. As a fiction writer, Whitman was not capable of probing such questions. When the story ends, Archie Dean has been tucked into his role in the family romance as the stalwart happy son. But Whitman has stumbled upon a rich insight: any change that depends so completely on the will expresses not only a persistent longing, but also a half-suppressed feeling of helplessness, an inability freely to be that which one admires most. We think of Whitman's vacillating temperament, his spurts of constructive effort, followed by periods of passiveness and depression.

There is, moreover, a further change that is not foreshadowed by the character of Archie Dean. To become a poet in full possession of his powers, the two sides of Whitman's character—the rough-mannered man and the passive, vacillating boy—would have to become, in some manner, friends, even lovers. This liberating self-marriage is accomplished, symbolically, in the opening stanzas of "Song of Myself," which is at once the ceremony of marriage and its consummation; out of it is born the poet, as Whitman came to understand him. Only then would Whitman's touchy, angry self give way to the celebrator of "sympathy," the "greatest lover."

In Jacksonian America, change, unlimited, frantic with possibility, had become a national romance. Myriads of reform movements evangelized tirelessly across the country, in an effort to improve everything from drinking habits to the tight lacing of corsets. Government, modes of dress, even the character of individuals seemed caught up in the flow of "progress," which, for many Americans, was not simply a philosophical doctrine but a name for the nature of things. The Puritan, shadowed by his obsession with original sin, had been replaced by the American Adam for whom nothing was irredeemable—who, indeed, had no "past" in the grim Puritan sense: his past was but a husk bursting and falling away under the pressure of his ripening. Emerson was the stylist of this expansive American innocence. An essay of Emerson's is a moment immobilized and richly repetitive. Not an argument that moves forward inexorably to a culminating point, but a bursting free, a daguerreotype of the mind at play.

Whitman had been educated in the rousing years of Jacksonian optimism. As a partisan journalist, he had learned to speak with his party's Biblical fervor. America as he knew it was careening into the future. But the American he knew best, the victimized boy of his early stories, was somehow not aboard. Out of such a dilemma

Poe, Melville, and Hawthorne made great fiction. It finds curious expression in the paintings of the mid-nineteenth-century American Luminists: their immense empty landscapes dwarf the human figures tucked in a corner, and seem to crush them. Even the light flooding the gigantic scenes tends toward a savage mournfulness, as if to say that mere individuals must be defeated by such grandeur.

This moral tension, however, did not feed Whitman's imagination. He stood instinctively with the Young Americans or with Hawthorne in "The Select Party," and dreamed instead of a personality large enough to inhabit the American landscape. Someone strapping and robust, like the actor Edwin Forrest, or like the oversized half-humorous folk figures of frontier legend. As Whitman turned toward poetry, he turned toward a dream of personal expansion that was no less American than the patriotic fervor of his earlier newspaper articles. Already we have caught the flavor of this dream in "The Shadow and Light of a Young Man's Soul." It would grow more passionate and more complex during the early 1850s, becoming at last the key, not only to Whitman's radical esthetics but to the personality he forged as the living product and the expressive source of his poetry.

5

On 16 July 1849, Whitman visited the busy phrenological emporium of Fowler & Wells, on Nassau Street, in the newspaper district of lower Manhattan. There, for the sum of three dollars, Lorenzo Fowler examined the exterior of Whitman's head, to determine the strength and proportion of his mental faculties, as they had influenced the shape and the size of his brain. Analyzing cranial bulges, forehead, and overall volume, Lorenzo translated his measurements into numerical values on a scale of 1 minimum to 7 maximum. The result was as follows:

Size of brain	6	Benevolence	6 to 7
Strength of system	6	Constructivenss	5
Degree of activity	5	Ideality	5 to 6

Propelling or executive		Sublimity	5 to 6
faculties	6	Imitation	5
Vital temperament	5	Mirthfulness	5
Motive apparatus	6	Intellectual faculties	5 to 6
Mental apparatus	5	Observing and knowing	
Amativeness	6	faculties	6
Philoprogenitiveness	6 to 7	Individuality	6
Adhesiveness	6	Form	6
Inhabitiveness	6	Size	6
Concentrativeness	4	Weight	5
Combativeness	6	Color	3
Destructiveness	5 to 6	Order	5+
Alimentiveness	6	Calculation	5
Acquisitiveness	4	Locality	6
Secretiveness	3	Eventuality	6
Cautiousness	6	Time	3
Approbativeness	4	Tune	4
Self Esteem	6 to 7	Language	5
Firmness	6	Causality	5
Conscientiousness	6	Comparison	6
Hope	4	Suavitiveness	4
Marvellousness	3	Intuition of human nature	6
Veneration	4		

Fowler's categories are bizarre, but this is clearly a flattering estimate to which Lorenzo added several pages of even more flattering character analysis, and a paragraph-long summary which so uncannily resembled the idea of himself Whitman would soon broadcast to the world that he reprinted it in several editions of *Leaves of Grass:*

This man has a grand physical construction, and power to live to a good old age. He is undoubtedly descended from the soundest and hardiest stock. Size of head large. Leading traits of character appear to be Friendship, Sympathy, Sublimity and Self-Esteem, and markedly among his combinations the dangerous faults of Indolence, a tendency to the pleasure of Voluptuousness and Alimentiveness, and a certain reckless swing of animal will, too unmindful, probably, of the conviction of others.

This was probably not Whitman's first visit. For years the Fowler & Wells Phrenological Cabinet had been a New York curiosity, rivaling Barnum's famous museum. Thousands of visitors every year came to consult with Orson and Lorenzo Fowler and their associate, Samuel Wells, or simply to gawk at the world's largest collection of skulls, including the skulls of "murderers, thieves . . . lions, tigers, hyenas," savages, famous individuals, noted madmen, and, in fact, "all the valuable phrenological specimens . . . in the civilized world." During his newspaper years, in the early 1840s, Whitman had worked around the corner from the Fowler & Wells establishment and may have had his head examined even then. Within months of taking over the *Eagle* in 1846, he reviewed favorably several phrenological handbooks, including Johann Kaspar Spurzheim's *Phrenology,* the fundamental text in America, about which he wrote:

Breasting the waves of detraction, as a ship dashes sea-waves, Phrenology, it must now be confessed by all men who have open eyes, has at last gained a position, and a firm one, among the sciences . . . perhaps no philosophic revolutionizers were ever attacked with more virulence— struck by more sinewy arms, or greater perseverence—than Gall, Spurzheim, and the other early Phrenologists . . . but the Phrenologists withstood the storm, and have gained the victory.

Among the "persevering workers" whose "inquiry after truth" secured victory for the new science, Whitman singled out "the two Fowlers and Mr. Wells." Years later, in "Good-Bye My Fancy," he remembered:

One of the choice places of New York to me then was the "Phrenological Cabinet" of Fowler and Wells, Nassau Street near Beekman. Here were all the busts, examples, curios and books of that study obtainable. I went there often, and once for myself had a very elaborate and leisurely examination and "chart of bumps," written out (I have it yet).

We know that Whitman eventually saw a connection between his "chart of bumps" and his expansive poetical character. In reprinting the Fowlers' "chart," he improved his score by small amounts, feeling perhaps that, after all, he knew himself better than even the famous Lorenzo Fowler: his score for Self-Esteem, had been almost a perfect 7.

Whitman's July visit intensified his interest in phrenology; and for the next half-dozen years, Fowler & Wells played an important part in his affairs. His journalism at this time is sprinkled with awkward phrenological terms, such as "philoprogenitiveness" and "alimentive." He sold Fowler & Wells pamphlets in the abortive bookstore he set up on the ground floor of his house on Myrtle Avenue. In 1855, he wrote for their general interest magazine, *Life Illustrated.* Fowler & Wells distributed the first edition of *Leaves of Grass* and published the second, in 1856. After that, Whitman's collaboration with them cooled; yet he continued to use their peculiar word "Adhesiveness" to designate one of his most important themes: the impassioned love of man for man. All his life, he preserved his "chart of bumps"—maybe to remind himself that, before it all really began, someone without prompting had seen him as he wanted to be seen.

Phrenology is remembered today as one of the "sports" of nineteenth-century science; yet its claims were not altogether unreasonable and had, at least initially, a sort of elegance. The mind and its physical organ, the brain, cannot be separated, argued the Austrian physician Franz Gall, the founder of phrenology; therefore, a quantifiable relationship must exist between them. To this extent, Gall was right, and almost two-hundred years ahead of his time. Neurologists are only now beginning to develop a convincing topography of the brain. The problem comes with Gall's next axiom: each of the mind's faculties is directly linked to a specific area, or "organ," of the brain. The bulkier and more prominent that area, the more generously endowed the corresponding mental faculty.

In order to prove Gall's theory, phrenological doctors became the best brain surgeons of the nineteenth century; but phrenologists also developed a less intrusive method of research. By examining the exterior of an individual's head, they claimed to determine the size and placement of the "organs" composing his brain. Using this method, a skilled phrenologist believed he could read a person's character from the shape of his head, decipher his true self, so to speak. Here, phrenology touched the century's most sensitive nerve, as psychoanalysis (related to phrenology on more than one count) has in our own. To know oneself scientifically; to touch the physical substratum of all philosophy and all morality; to read, in the creases and folds of the brain, an interior physiognomy, a text that the phrenologist, with his invaluable map, could decode for all to understand: this was revolutionary. Yet it was so probable, so exactly the practical result one expected of the scientific method, that proof was hardly needed.

In America especially, phrenology presented itself as the essential science of man. By analyzing the morphology of the brain, the phrenologist claimed to be studying the measurable translation of matter into spirit, of flesh into mind, nothing less. If anyone could be said to know how, and with what results, body and spirit were one, it was the phrenologist. It is not surprising that many of the best minds of the nineteenth century accepted Gall's thesis, even if they were repelled by some of its more extravagant applications. In Europe, Hegel; in America, Horace Greeley, William Cullen Bryant, Horace Mann, among many other prominent figures, were convinced of its worth. By Whitman's day, many businesses required a "chart of bumps" from prospective employees, as today they might require a battery of psychological tests.

By the time Whitman wrote the great poems of his 1855 edition, the fundamental outlook of phrenology had become thoroughly familiar to him. In his preface, he listed "phrenology" among the sciences that are the "lawgivers of poets," and mentioned phrenology in the poems themselves. He used the phrenological jargon tactfully along with his own neologisms, foreign words, and Quakerisms, as part of a conscious effort to enlarge American literary usage: "O adhesiveness! O pulse of my life." He described a rollicking Manhattan-bred man: "Voluptuous, inhabitive, combative, conscientious, alimentive, intuitive, of copious friendship, sublimity, firmness, self-esteem, comparison, individuality, form, locality, eventuality." The form here is the phrenological "chart of bumps," one of Whitman's "found" catalogues.

Other references are less visible, but probably more important, because they indicate how intuitively Whitman drew on phrenological ideas in the 1850s. When he wrote, in his preface: "All beauty comes from beautiful blood and a beautiful brain," and declared of the greatest poet, "His brain is the ultimate brain," he was thinking as a phrenologist, for whom the brain was the reigning organ—what the "soul" had been to traditional thinkers and in other contexts to Whitman himself. Elsewhere in the preface, the "chart of bumps" becomes a model for the description of personality:

Extreme caution or prudence, the soundest organic health, large hope and comparison, and fondness for women and children, large alimentiveness and destructiveness and causality, with a perfect sense of the oneness of nature and the propriety of the same spirit applied to human affairs . . . these are called up of the float of the brain of the world to be parts of the greatest poet.

During these years, Whitman was something of an intellectual magpie, taking from every source and using what he read as raw material for a broad attack on the conventional boundaries of poetic subject matter. In a notebook, we read, "Everything yet is made the subject of poetry—narratives, descriptions, jokes, sermons, recipes, etc., etc." To bring the unpoetic into poetry became one of the axioms of modern poetry: what Ezra Pound called making it new. It is a quality we admire in poets as diverse as Rilke, Eliot, and William Carlos Williams. But in this area, Whitman is the master. Apparently there was nothing he could not use: his personal knowledge of house building, Italian opera, Olmsted's lessons on astronomy, the world atlas. In this welter of influences, phrenology holds a place of importance, not only as a source of provoking new words but as a source of ideas that would eventually shape Whitman's poetry.

Take the phrenological emphasis on the body as a source of mental vitality. "The qualities of mind correspond with the build of the body," wrote Orson Squires Fowler. "If the latter is beautifully formed, well-proportioned, handsome, etc., not only will its motions be easy and graceful, but the feelings will be exquisite, the mind well balanced, and a beauty, perfection, taste, refinement, elegance, and good taste will characterize everything he says and does." Orson Fowler tended to be quick on the draw—he called himself "the great gun of phrenology in America"; and his descriptions of healthy manhood have a tone of religious exaltation: "Beauty inimitable characterises every joint; every muscle; every physical organ; every propensity; every element of Man." As Orson saw it, a great man had to have "great physical strength and vital stamina." Even a poet drew more "on the physiology than on the phrenology," he wrote; more on the bouyancy of his body than on his faculties of brain and mind! This might be Whitman, who had been thinking similar thoughts for years. He hated the Victorian prudery that had wanted to clothe nude models in New Orleans or had shrunk from Lorenzo Fowler's frank discussions of "matrimony" in its physiological aspects. In 1846, reviewing *The Use of the Body in Relation to the Mind,* by the health reformer George Moore, Whitman remarked: "Few persons realize how intimate [is] the relation of mental causes and processes toward the body and its well or ill being." The Fowlers carried this reasoning a step further. Not only did "mental causes and processes" influence the body, they did so legibly and predictably, for the body was the mind's open secret, its visible text. We hear Orson Fowler's evangelism of the body in Whitman's early notebook:

The effusion or corporation of the soul is always under the beautiful laws of physiology—I guess the soul itself can never be anything but great and pure and immortal; but it makes itself visible only through matter—a perfect head, and bowels and bones to match is the easy gate through which it comes from its embowered garden, and pleasantly appears to the sight of the world.

By the time Whitman wrote his great poems, the oneness of body and spirit had become more than a conviction to him: it was a principle of his imagination, a spontaneous source of countless images. Above all, it gave solidity to his most intimate theme: the merging of the poet with his poem:

Writing and talk do not prove me,
I carry the plenum of proof and everything else in my face,
With the hush of my lips I confound the topmost sceptic.

Whitman develops this phrenological theme in the fifth stanza of "Song of Myself," where body and soul meet as equals on the grass and make love. Their meeting is sexual and of the body. Yet the most ecstatic caresses are given by the "voice" and "tongue" and are of the soul.

Whitman did not hear of William Blake until many years later; yet there is a remarkable convergence between the two poets. Whitman's dramatic sense of the relationship between body and spirit, and their sexual marriage; of the "soul" as an "effusion . . . of physiology," has the ring of Blake's aphorisms in *The Marriage of Heaven and Hell.* The reason is that Whitman's teachers, the phrenological Fowlers, were Blakeans without knowing it. They evangelized and popularized a form of spiritual materialism that would have startled the revolutionary poet, and their preaching bore fruit in Whitman's own fluid, flighty materialism.

The Fowlers never encouraged Whitman to write poetry and supported him only reluctantly when it came to publishing his book in 1855. Lorenzo Fowler thought that, "with practice," Whitman might make a good accountant. So much for character reading as a science! But they supported Whitman far more substantially by encouraging him to rethink his life at a time when he longed with his whole being for a new outlet. They supplied a philosophy to go with Archie Dean's iron-willed determination to make himself into a new man. For the heart and soul of the Fowlers' enterprise was their conviction that man can and must change. This conviction was Orson Fowler's specific contribution to the development of phrenology.

Early in his career, he had toured the South and West, demonstrating the phrenological method on numbers of willing heads. During the tour, he later wrote, his own organs—"of size, individuality, form, locality, eventuality, comparison and language"— were necessarily in constant use. Afterward, it seemed to Orson that these organs "had very much increased." Could it be that exercise strengthened the organs of the brain, as it did the muscles of the body? The implications were enormous, and Orson was quick to formulate them as a doctrine: "The exercise of particular mental faculties, causes the exercise, and consequent enlargement, of corresponding portions of the brain."

How simply stated! Yet here is where phrenology moves beyond Gall and Spurzheim to become an extravagantly Romantic science. For if exercise could alter the organs of the brain, then the phrenological "chart of bumps" became a personally tailored blueprint for personal change. In the words of a nineteenth-century admirer:

One of the real benefits of [phrenology] was that it inspired courage and hope in those who were depressed by the consciousness of some inability. . . . Phrenology also showed us how, as Goethe says, our virtues and vices grow out of the same roots; how every good tendency has its danger, and every dangerous power may be so restrained and guided as to be a source of good.

The Fowlers endowed American phrenology with a moral amplitude that went beyond its crude theory of the brain. During the 1840s, they allied phrenology with the temperance movement; with Sylvester Graham's vegetarian crusade; with one of the early forms of feminism, the "anti-lacing" movement, which argued against tight corsets and stays; with the anti-medicine movement, and the "water-cure" movement, which preached that water, taken internally or applied to the body in the form of wet sheets, was nature's supreme medicine. The Fowlers favored new methods of agriculture, new materials for house building, and new architectural designs, culminating in Orson Fowler's famous octagonal house, built near Peekskill in upstate New York.

The Fowler & Wells Phrenological Cabinet, and its associated publishing firm, became an eclectic bazaar of reforms; yet there was a logic to it all. If man was morally and organically improvable, as Orson Fowler had demonstrated, then it was necessary to improve man by every possible means. For improved behavior was not merely good, it was a form of therapy. Orson Fowler's calls to battle were so hectic and urgent that grammar failed him. Phrenology, he trumpeted, "has laid the foundation on which those glorious superstructures of reform now so rife—now sweeping into oblivion the evils that enthrall society, and placing man upon the true basis of nature—are based."

The Fowler & Wells motto, "Self-made or never made," is a huckster's version of Emerson's chaste virtue of self-reliance. If the American was on a footing with Adam, it was because he had the power to be his own Pygmalion, his own self-perfecting shaper and maker.

There is undoubtedly a comic side to the Fowlers' phrenological optimism, which managed to combine high principles with a keen American eye for business. For all their moral seriousness, the Fowlers are not entirely unrelated to phrenological gypsies such as "His Royal Highness Prince Luximon Ray, M.D.," with his "Grand Hindoo Poetical Chart," or Huck Finn's friend, "the celebrated Dr. Armand de Montelban of Paris" lecturing "on the Science of Phrenology at ten cents admission." Yet under their influence, phrenology became a genuine promoter of social experiment. Horace Mann's educational reforms; the new therapeutic idea that the insane should be treated with warmth and loving care; Samuel Gridley Howe's revolutionary pedagogical method for teaching the deaf-mute girl, Laura Bridgman: these were all directly grounded in the encouraging phrenological theory of man's improvability. Today's therapeutic ideal—although it is more puzzled, more diffident of results—was first promoted by the publicists of this dead-end science who, in Whitman's New York, believed the human condition to be curable.

What did Whitman think about all this? We know the importance he attached to his "chart of bumps," and we know that he kept in touch with Fowler & Wells for half a dozen years, first as a bookseller and a journalist, finally as the author of a book they distributed. Yet Whitman had never been much of a reformer, despite his interest in the temperance movement in the early 1840s. Generally speaking, reformers struck him as a hectic lot, and he made fun of them in the *Eagle* as impractical dreamers who talked too much. Personally, he liked a friendly drink and a good steak. Nor could the Fowlers' ideas about poetry have interested him much. The poet, they felt, belonged to the "nervous" type: physically thin, emotionally highstrung, best exemplified in modern times by Edgar Allan Poe. Whitman's sparing use of phrenological terminology in his early poems, even his deft phrenological portraits in the poem "Faces," and his possible use of Orson Fowler's ideas on heredity in "Unfolded Out of the Folds," while worth noting, are no more than anecdotal. They show the range of Whitman's eclecticism and his unparalleled ability to use "scientific" material in his poems.

Yet Whitman shared some fundamental attitudes with the Fowlers. He was an anti-medicine man; he believed in the health-giving virtues of water, at least in the form of daily plunges at Grey's Baths and of the vigorous cold water brushings he gave himself every morning. In the *Eagle*, he had written rhapsodic editorials about the delicious waters of the new Croton system, as compared with the stale, evil-smelling liquid that came from Brooklyn's pumps.

As a family, the Whitmans tended to be nervous about health, as well they might be, with a chronically ill father and a defective, probably epileptic son, Ed; with another son, Jesse, who may already have been showing signs of mental breakdown; and still another son, Andrew, who within a few years would die of a tubercular throat. Their letters to each other are obsessive and troubled when asking about each other's health. Later, Whitman's favorite sister, Hannah, carried the family obsession to a repulsive extreme, becoming a reclusive hypochondriac. Whitman took another path and made "health" a metaphor for all the expansive values he dramatized in his poems. He made himself visibly "healthy." What he brought with him to the hospitals when visiting his sick stage-driver friends in New York, and later during his years of hospital visiting in Washington, was the "magnetism" of his unexampled physical well-being which, he was convinced, had a therapeutic effect on the weakened systems of the wounded and the ill.

During the late 1840s, Whitman compiled a folder of newspaper and magazine articles on health and "physiology"; and in 1849, the year Lorenzo Fowler drew up his "chart of bumps," Whitman apparently planned to give a series of lectures on "diet, exercise and health." In a sense, the subject governed the themes of Whitman's life: his idea of the poet as the supremely healthy man; his fascination with hospitals and with the sick, leading to his service as a male nurse during the Civil War; his bouyancy and courage during the last twenty years of his life when he was an invalid, following the stroke he suffered in 1873.

Health was Whitman's passion. Pride in his body and in his poems, went hand in hand. When he became chronically ill, in the 1860s, his poems too shrank. In his old age, Whitman published a poignant meditation entitled "Health (Old Style)" which conveys the exalted well-being that he connected all his life with a healthy body:

In that condition the whole body is elevated to a state by others unknown—inwardly and outwardly illuminated, purified, made solid, strong, yet bouyant. A singular charm, more than beauty, flickers out of, and over, the face—a curious transparency beams in the eyes, both in the iris and the white—the temper partakes also. Nothing that happens—no event, rencontre, weather, etc.—but it is confronted—nothing but is subdued into sustenance—such is the marvellous transformation from the old timorousness and the old process of causes and effects. Sorrows and disappointments cease—there is no more borrowing trouble in advance. A man realizes the venerable myth—he is a god walking the earth, he sees new eligibilities, powers and beauties everywhere; he himself has a new eyesight and hearing. The play of the body in motion takes a previously unknown grace. Merely *to move* is then a happiness, a pleasure—to breathe, to see, is also. All the beforehand gratifications, drink, spirits, coffee, grease, stimulants, mixtures, late hours, luxuries, deeds of the night, seem as vexatious dreams, and now the awakening;—many fall into their natural places, wholesome, conveying diviner joys.

Whitman's emphasis on robust outdoor healthiness, his magnificent praise of the body in "Song of Myself," where bodily well-being becomes a form of religious worship, are phrenological themes. Here he describes himself in one of his anonymous reviews of *Leaves of Grass,* in 1855:

Of pure American breed, of reckless health, his body perfect, free from taint from top to toe, free forever from headache and dyspepsia, full-blooded, six feet high, a good feeder, never once using medicine, drinking water only—a swimmer in the river or bay or by the sea-shore—of straight attitude and slow movement on foot—an indescribable style evincing indifference and disdain—ample-limbed, weight a hundred and eighty pounds, age thirty six years—never dressed in black, always dressed freely and clean in strong clothes, neck open, shirt collar flat and broad, countenance of swarthy transparent red, beard short and well mottled with white, hair like hay after it has been mowed in the field and lies tossed and streaked—face not refined or intellectual, but calm and wholesome—a face of an unaffected animal—a face that absorbed the sunshine and meets savage or gentleman on equal terms—a face of undying friendship toward men and women, and of one who finds the same returned many fold—a face with two grey eyes where passion and hauteur sleep, and melancholy stands behind them—his physiology corroborating a rugged phrenology.

This is not the highstrung, thin-bodied poet of the Fowler and Wells ideal, but it is a Fowler & Wells man in every other respect: a water drinker, a temperance man, an anti-medicine man, an anti-lacing man; above all, a glowingly healthy man, whose poems directly translate the free-flowing life that everyone sees in him and loves.

If Whitman, in the early 1850s, was rethinking his belief in the democratic "experiment" and in "progress"; and if, like Melville, at the same time, he was looking for an idea that would give a private dimension to the exalted claims of American political life, an idea that would provide the largest conceptual scope to his own longing for personal change, he surely found it in the Fowlers' therapeutic vision, with their emphatic belief that all of man's good, and the best hopes of history, had as their goal the inception of a completely healthy human being.

6

In the fall of 1849, shortly after resigning as editor of the *Freeman,* Whitman went to spend a few weeks with his sister Mary at Greenport, the last stop on the recently completed Long Island Railroad. In 1840, when Mary was only nineteen, she had married a hard-working shipbuilder, Ansel Van Nostrand; and now the Van Nostrands owned a small white house in the old whaling town on the north fork of Long Island. Mary rarely came to Brooklyn, and kept her distance from the family's painful decline over the next decades; yet she was very much part of the Whitman dream. Already in New Orleans, Walt had written to his mother of "the day when we can have our own quiet little farm and be together again—and have Mary and her children come to pay us long visits." If Whitman had anywhere a family that corresponded to his sentimental fable of home and mother, it was Mary's, and there he retired to pass his disappointed autumn.

He did not leave quietly. On 4 October, the *Advertiser,* his bitter-sweet Whig adversary, published an anonymous swan song for "Editor Whitman, that transcendentally fast politician . . . at whose coat tails time and events must keep pulling." It is an affectionately mocking portrait and, despite its clumsy irony, a revealing one. Whitman is described as Brooklyn's best-known editor, as "full of egotism" as the first block of Fulton Street was of politicians. Apparently Whitman had not been entirely silent about his literary ambitions, for the *Advertiser,* with tongue in cheek, hails him as a future "literary genius—one of the shining lights of the age." The article goes on:

In person as well as in feeling, our biped is a pretty fair specimen of the "native raw material," what you call a civilized but not a polished *Aborigine*. And, by the way, it has been asserted by one of his brother Editors that he is a lineal decendant from some Indian tribe, with what truth we will not venture to say. In dress and gait he apes in some degree the gravity of the student, with inverted shirt collar, of course, after the manner of "Childe Harold." His face, good looking but remarkably indolent in expression, is sometimes "bearded like the pard," and at other times, probably to suit the season, as free from hair as the fair cheek of "Justice". . . . From the South he brings the French motto "Liberty, equality, fraternity," and he stands before us as a "Freeman." But, like all hot-headed ultras, he awards no "liberty" unless they belong to the "spirit of progress"; as for "equality," . . . 'twould be ridiculous for foreigners to claim such a privilege; as for "fraternity" the old hunkers would not, by any manner of means, take him into their brotherly embraces, and so our motto and our little sheet are gone, or, which is the same thing, our distinguished biped is gone from it, and is again "on the town."

Here is virtually our only glimpse of Whitman before he began to remake himself into a bardic poet and representative American man. The traits are familiar: the "indolent expression" curiously allied with a reputation for hot-headedness; the Byronic shirtcollar, with its hint of bohemian pleasures and of a self-consciousness about dress which had marked him as early as his dandyish days on the *Aurora,* in 1842. The appearing and disappearing beard show a man still experimenting with his appearance; a man who, at thirty, has not yet settled who he is, although he is certainly not "one of the roughs" and not a bluff, straightforward workingman. This specimen of "native raw material" may lack "polish" but he is "civilized," a social amphibian.

During his autumn retreat at Greenport, Whitman wrote, for the New York *Sunday Dispatch,* a series of articles called "Letters from a Travelling Batchelor." They are rambling and gossipy, full of country talk, local characters, a visit to a cemetery, an exuberant sail to Montauk, some reflections on city versus country living. The "Letters" represent Whitman at his journalistic best—in places, crisp and authoritative, as if the notebooks, with their experimental style, were aching for an audience.

Whitman knew the Long Island countryside well. He had been born at West Hills, near Huntington, and his family had never lost touch with the area. During his childhood, Whitman remembered riding back to Brooklyn in his uncle Cornelius Van Velsor's dray cart, and feeling nauseated by the relentless jolting of the hard-wheeled wagon and the tar smell of the tarpaulin drawn over the load of goods. When the depression of 1837 caused Whitman, then eighteen, to lose his job as a printer's apprentice in Brooklyn, he spent several years drifting about the Island, working mostly as a schoolteacher. In Smithtown in 1838, he started a local newspaper, the *Long Islander,* wrote it, set it up in type, and trotted around the countryside in a carriage he bought for the purpose, to deliver his paper to local subscribers.

The "old friend" mentioned in "Letter VI," who "for the last fifteen years has made it his annual custom to go down on Long Island for purposes of recreation, sporting, and to get sniffs of the sea air that sweeps over every part of that amphibious sort of territory," was most likely Whitman himself. Later, in *Specimen Days* (1883), Whitman would write about his Long Island youth with a rustic realism that recalls William Sidney Mount's lovely genre paintings:

Here, and all along the island and its shores, I spent intervals many years, all seasons, sometimes riding, sometimes boating, but generally afoot (I was always then a good walker) absorbing fields, shores, marine incidents, characters, the bay-men, farmers, pilots . . . always liked the bare sea-beach south side . . . the soothing rustle of the waves, and the saline smell—boyhood's times, the clam-digging, barefoot, and with trousers rolled up—hauling down the creek—the perfume of the sedge meadows—the hay-boat, and the chowder and fishing excursions . . .

Whitman's childhood was so enmeshed in these scenes of the Long Island countryside that he sometimes felt as if he had "incorporated" them. Even the rolling line of his new poetry, he claimed, had been inspired by the "soothing rustle" of the surf on the beaches of Long Island.

While he roamed the countryside around Greenport, Whitman may have been consoling himself for yet another journalistic failure, further evidence that, like his father, he was not very good at the important American endeavor of making a living: here he was, thirty years old and a "famous editor," with nothing to edit and no prospects either. Yet Whitman's "defeat" was curiously liberating, to judge from the alert prose of his "letters" to the *Dispatch*.

In his first article, he describes a fisherman and his dog on a wave-rimmed beach near Montauk. The dog was "magnificent . . . black as tar":

All of a sudden, while his master was talking to me, and his brilliant (I really cannot find the right word) vitreous eyes were vibrating from mine to the surface of the sea, he broke off from the talk . . . pointing to something like a small black chip, slowly moving edgeways on the surface of the water.

Those "vitreous" vibrating eyes had been beyond Whitman's powers not long before. The cruising "black chip"—a shark—would supply an excellent detail in the long untitled poem that is the centerpiece of *Leaves of Grass* in 1855, as would the bluefishermen observed earlier that day:

Two hundred men, in a hundred skiffs, catching bluefish by trailing! Imagine the skiffs, real beauties too, darting like swallows, and managed by five-score bold and expert water-dogs, each ambitious of doing some daredevil maneouver that would eclipse his fellows—the sails bulging like the puffed cheeks of an alderman, and anon dipping in the water, or making the boat turn sharper corners than I ever saw a boat turn before—a hundred men ceaselessly employed in hauling in the lines, taking off the fish, and casting out again—and then such a casting out! Such a length as they made the bones fly! such a twirl of the rope! no twisting, although the coils be many! such superb attitudes, equal to anything in Greek statues! such ready expedients to avoid any obstacle to the incessant hauling in, and throwing out of those lines, and the rapid depositing of fish in the boats, which seemed, to my eyes, to rival the celerity with which the "fast compositor" deposits type in his stick! the flashing of the white bones in the sunlight, and the ornamental flourishes which the "fancy ones" among the young fishermen would cut with their lines in the air—and all this done under the swiftest motion of their vessel in a stiff breeze over the dark sparkling waters! All silent, too, was the spectacle, except the slapping of the waves on the shore of the promontory, and the occasional screetch of a sea-bird. Here they intertwined among each other, to and fro, in and out and around—much like the sparkles of moonlight that you can see sometimes of a summer night dancing in the East River—or any other river, I suppose, when the water is smooth, and the moon bright.

Not only is this better journalism than any Whitman had yet written, but it shows him at the threshold of a new ambition: to excel at doing what no important American writer had truly attempted, although Emerson expressed the idea when he wrote: "I embrace the common, I explore and sit at the feet of the familiar, the low." Emerson could never follow his own dictum, but Whitman did. He expanded downward; he cast his remarkable eye upon the ordinary doings of ordinary men, endowing them with a vividness and a pungency that the "feudal" poets of the Old World and the "artificial" poets of the new still reserved for the memorable deeds of heroes. Having removed himself from the wearisome quarrels of Jacksonian politics, Whitman was developing a Jacksonian esthetics. The robust American man Whitman loved to write about was first of all a Long Islander: part farmer, part fisherman, and tough as a Homeric pirate:

Imagine a community of straggle-limbed, yellow-faced, hard-fleshed sea-dogs—or a goodly infusion of such communities in the nation; do you suppose such a nation could ever degenerate and decay, as old Rome did with her Sybarites? No, indeed. And though my compound adjectives above do not describe the ideal of masculine good looks, there is something surpassingly welcome in the sight of these sinewy and huge-pawed fellows.

I went down to Montauk Point a day ago . . . and we came among a band of such amphibious men—great, unshaved, gigantic-chested beings, with eyes as clear as coals, and flesh whose freedom from the gross humors of artificial life told its tale in the dark and unpimpled brown of their faces and necks. . . . These men . . . make their beds and sleep soundly on the salt hay, or in the sails of a boat, or on the ground—go half-stripped for days and days up to their waists in water—eat raw salt pork, seasoned with a little vinegar, (or perhaps bad rum)—and, thus continuing for many seasons, live to a good old age, and die of Time more than of Sickness.

Here we see the first visible stirring of the colloquial realism that Whitman would soon forge into an artless-seeming anti-poetry. His "Letters from a Travelling Batchelor" contain many such stylistic trials: a bell that "winds off" with a "sort of twirl or gulp, (if you can imagine a bell gulping)"; a stream running smooth as "plate glass"; the "firm fine-grained meat white as snow and of indescribable sweetness" of freshly caught Long Island fish. A miserly farmer's wife he ran across on an excursion to Gardiner's Island provoked him to a wicked portrait:

The old woman was fat, but her face, the color of copper, had none of the jolly or motherly expression of most fat old women. Her restless black eyes shifted constantly to and fro, and she seemed to be under the influence of an unsatisfied demon of motion, for she waddled and trotted without a single moment's cessation.

The most spirited of these letters tells about a sail to Montauk for an overnight party, with a group of chance acquaintances. Here Whitman is, unexpectedly, a gay New Yorker, witty, Rabelaisian, like the clever sketch writers who entertained the readers of Gaylord Clark's *Knickerbocker Magazine:*

To a minerologist, I fancy Montauk Point must be a perpetual feast. Even to my unscientific eyes there were innumerable wonders and beauties all along the shore, and the edge of the cliffs. There were earths of all colors, and stones of every conceivable shape, hue, and density, with shells, large boulders of pure white substance, and layers of those smooth round pebbles called "milk-stones" by the country children. There were some of them tinged with pale green, blue or yellow—some streaked with various colors—and so on.

We rambled up the hills to the top of the highest—we ran races down—we scampered along the shore, jumping from rock to rock—we declaimed all the violent appeals and defiances we could remember, commencing with "Celestial states, immortal powers, give ear!" . . . I doubt whether those astonished echoes ever before vibrated with such terrible ado. Then we pranced forth again, like mad kine—we threw our hats in the air—aimed stones at the shrieking seagulls, mocked the wind, and imitated the cries of various animals in a style that beat nature all out! We challenged each other to the most deadly combats—we tore various passions into tatters—made love to the girls, in the divine words of Shakespeare and other poets, whereat the said girls had the rudeness to laugh till the tears ran down their cheeks in great torrents. . . . We hopped like crows; we pivoted like Indian dervishes; we went through the trial dance of *La Bayadere* with wonderful vigor . . . there was not a sensible behaved creature among us, to rebuke our mad antics by comparison.

Far from moping and licking his wounds, Whitman wrote with a boyish glee that expands gently into one of those melodious silences that would soon be among his most attractive modes:

I made my bed in the furled sail, watching the stars as they twinkled, and falling asleep so. A stately and solomn night, that, to me—for I was awake much and saw the countless armies of heaven marching stilly in the space up there—marching stilly and slowly on, and others coming up out of the east to take their places. Not a sound, not an insect, interrupted the exquisite silence,—nothing but the ripple of the water against the sides of the vessel. An indescribable serenity pervaded my mind—a delicious abnegation of the ties of the body. I fancied myself leaping forward into the extent of the space, springing as it were from star to star. Thoughts of the boundless Creation must have expanded my mind, for it certainly played the most unconscionable pranks from its tabernacle lying there in those fields of hempen duck.

This is no journalistic hack but a genuine writer, drawing on a side of his imaginative life he had never expressed before. Striding greedily from star to star, prancing like some cosmic Yankee peddler across geological ages and astronomical distances would be a form of robust child's play to the "orbic" self that was apparently already stirring in Whitman's mind.

Perhaps the most startling evidence that Whitman had begun to think as a poet comes in two "letters" written from New York in late November and December. Among Manhattan's most imposing structures in 1849, was the recently built lower Croton Reservoir, at Fortieth Street and Fifth Avenue, where the New York Public Library now stands. The four-acre reservoir was surrounded by thick forty-five-foot battlements and topped by a promenade offering a splendid view of the rivers and the crowded skyline of the city farther downtown. Here, one day in November, Whitman started out on one of his journalistic rambles about town:

Of the latter part of an afternoon, it makes a delightful little jaunt to go out . . . and see the sunset, from the broad walk on the top of this reservoir. A hundred years hence, I often imagine, what an appearance that walk will present, on a fine summer afternoon! You and I, reader, and quite all the people who are now alive, won't be much thought of then; but the world will be just as jolly, and the sun will shine just as bright, and the rivers off there—the Hudson on one side and the East on the other—will slap along their green waves, precisely as now; and other eyes will look upon them about the same as we do.

The walks on the battlements of the Croton Reservoir, a hundred years hence! *Then* these immense stretches of vacant ground below, will be covered with houses; the paved streets will clatter with innumerable carts and resound to deafening cries; and the promenaders here will look down upon them, perhaps, and away "up town" toward the quiet and more fashionable quarters, and see great changes. . . .

Ages after ages these Croton works will last, for they are more substantial than the old Roman aqueducts, which were mostly built on the surface of the ground. And crowds of busy feet will patter over this flagging, years hence, and here will be melancholy musings, and popping the question, and perhaps bargains and sales, long long after we of the present time are under the sod.

In itself Whitman's journalistic meditation is not remarkable, yet the reader will recognize the theme of one of his greatest poems, "Crossing Brooklyn Ferry":

> Others will enter the gates of the ferry and cross from shore to shore,
> Others will watch the run of the flood-tide,
> Others will see the shipping of Manhattan north and west, and the heights of Brooklyn to the south and east,
> Others will see the islands large and small;
> Fifty years hence, others will see them as they cross, the sun half an hour high,
> A hundred years hence, or ever so many hundreds years hence, others will see them,
> Will enjoy the sunset, the pouring-in of the flood-tide, the falling back to the sea of the ebb-tide.

The difference between Whitman's newspaper stroll of 1849 and the poem published seven years later (in the second edition of *Leaves of Grass*) measures the distance he would travel in a few years. Here, at the center of his meditation, he placed the reservoir with its solid walls, its view over the distant rivers and the city. In 1856, the scene would be the river itself; its flow, the flow of time. No dour monument can withstand it; no reservoir can safely distribute its waters. For this, something more spacious and permanent than a reservoir is required, able to flow with the river, to merge with its sights and pleasures—the poet's expansive mind:

> It avails not, time nor place—distance avails not,
> I am with you, you men and women of a generation, or ever so many generations hence.

Whitman's homily on the impermanence of life would, by 1856, be internalized: the time-defeating monument would be the poet; the work that attests to its bouyancy upon the waters, would be his poem. Even the poem's masterful parallelism is present in the 1849 article as a clumsy journalistic device. The theme would ripen for half a dozen years before taking its final shape, when it would draw upon yet another idea Whitman broached in the "Letters." On 23 December, he described a second ramble about town:

Many books have been written, to describe journeys between the Old and New World, and what was done or seen therein, and afterward. But we know of no work . . . describing a voyage across the Fulton Ferry.

There can be no mistake. In the fall of 1849, Whitman's real work had begun.

PART II

The Making of a Poet:
The 1850s

CHAPTER 3

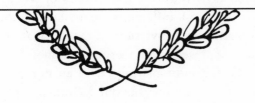

"A Blessing on the Young Artist Race"

1

THESE NEXT YEARS—the early 1850s—are surely the most intriguing of Whitman's life. He was writing in his notebook and thinking, a man awakening from a lifelong sleep. But how? Why? These years were filled with elusive activity—the kind that leaves a man changed, yet no one has seen it happen, and nothing has happened: an ordinary man has become extraordinary, a conventional writer has become a genius.

Occasionally we catch glimpses of Whitman in the newspaper articles he continued to write, but his journalistic activity thinned out drastically after 1852. There were, of course, the notebooks and, as we will see, they were crucial. But they are undated, largely impersonal. We recognize in passing the germs of poems, the development of a style, a handful of ideas he would hold onto all his life. There are also quantities of receipts and bills which survived all the expurgating bonfires Whitman lit in his later years. They are staccato, telegraphic signs, tapping out what the daily demands on him were during this period of silent upheaval. But Whitman seems to have worked hard to erase these years—not, I think, out of personal delicacy or fear of later scandal (his was always apparently a fairly blameless life), but because he wanted to keep intact the mystery of his poetic origins. This desire fueled several unsettling controversies in later years. Had he read Emerson before 1855? Had he read anything at all, aside from Walter Scott and the Bible? Had he really been a carpenter, as in William O'Connor's fable about a saintly uneducated workingman who was transparently Whitman, as O'Connor, with Whitman's help, imagined the poet in the mid-1860s?* I will do my best to answer these and other questions concerning the years of experiment, both literary and personal, that now begin. The contours of Whitman's new poetry; the patchwork of influences he mobilized to shape his thinking; above all, the conviction of a personal stake in his poetic vision, an unprecedented merging of moral and esthetic aims, such as even the most radical Victorian never dreamed: all this will emerge from behind the veil Whitman drew over the early 1850s.

Later Whitman scoffed at the idea that becoming a poet had changed him in any way. On the contrary, he insisted, his poetry and his personal "magnetism" had developed inexorably from the flow of his life. He liked, and may even have written the following passage in Maurice Bucke's 1883 biography of him:

Walt Whitman's early years provided the most comprehensive equipment ever attained by a human being, though many things that the schools prescribe were left out. It consisted in absorbing into himself the whole city and country about him, New York and Brooklyn, and their adjacencies; not only their outside shows, but far more their interior heart and meaning. In the first place he learned life—men, women and children; he went on equal terms with everyone, he liked them and they him, and he knew them far better than they knew themselves. Then he became thoroughly conversant with the shops, houses, sidewalks, ferries, factories, taverns, gatherings, political meetings, carousings, etc. He was first the absorber of the sunlight, the free air and the open streets, and then of interiors. He knew the hospitals, poorhouses, prisons and their inmates. He passed freely in and about those parts of the city which are inhabited by the worst characters; he knew all their people, and many of them knew him; he learned to tolerate their squalor, vice and ignorance; he saw the good . . . and the bad that was in them, and what there was to excuse

* For William O'Connor, see p. 344.

and justify their lives. It is said that these people, even the worst of them, while entire strangers to Walt Whitman, quite favorably received him without discourtesy and treated him well. Perhaps only those who have known the man personally, and have felt the peculiar magnetism of his presence, can fully understand this. Many of the worst of these characters became singularly attached to him. He knew and was sociable with the man that sold peanuts at the corner, and the old woman that dispensed coffee in the market.

This is legend, although a legend that is close enough, in many respects, to Whitman's actual life: as a youth, and later as a journalist, he had explored the city from end to end. His habit of talking with strangers came later, according to brother George; not until the early 1850s when he began to think of himself as a working-man-poet and exemplary democrat. In Bucke's description, Whitman was not really a poet at all but a man of the people with his eyes open and his senses hungry for experience. Like his Louisiana "live-oak," he had grown from his roots. This was an important part of Whitman's self-made myth. If *Leaves of Grass* was a song of the common man, Whitman had to be the common man incarnate: a pure product of his American upbringing and blood. The myth required that he not particularize himself sexually or temperamentally; that his very past be exemplary, not individual and personal. Eventually Whitman's self-editing harmed his poetry by diverting it toward abstract feelings and self-imitation.

It is difficult to establish a chronology for these years of self-discovery. A merest skeleton of events underlies the inner advances and retreats, the doubts and the flashes of certainty by means of which Whitman established for himself a new area of feeling, and a new skill. His notebooks are the invaluable text, but they are largely undatable. We know what happened, and we have an idea of the contributing elements that ranged from Whitman's reading to the temperamental shifts brought about by his family life, his father's gradual decline, his failure as journalist and politician. But there is no secure order which can be translated into a story. From here on, therefore, I have changed my approach, separating out themes and trains of thought and treating them in separate chapters in order, I hope, to give the reader a sense of the elusive unfolding that culminated, in 1855, with the publication of *Leaves of Grass.*

2

In the spring of 1849, the Whitman family had moved into their boxy frame house on Myrtle Avenue; and for the next few years, the bookstore and printing shop on the ground floor was at the center of Walt's activities. He took on small printing jobs, distributed a variety of books and pamphlets for the firm of Fowler & Wells, sold stationery, children's books, phrenological paraphernalia, knives, forks, and toothbrushes. During the winter of 1850, an opportunity came his way. He was asked to be the principal editor of a new penny newspaper, the *Daily News,* which was being started in Manhattan. The owner had invested in modern steam presses and type. He had joined the Telegraphic News Agency; had hired an ample staff of reporters, compositors, and carriers. This was to be a serious journal, with no vulgar advertisements or eye-catching love stories. It was a good idea—too good apparently, for the paper failed within a month, and Whitman's last brief return to Nassau Street and Printing House Square was over. The next year, he started a modest commercial weekly, the *Salesman and Traveller's Directory for Long Island*, but that, too, failed almost immediately.

By now, Whitman was imbedded in his family. Receipts show him buying household equipment and clothing. His store seems to have been a sleepy sort of an affair, but he was getting money from somewhere; maybe the free-lance writing he did for the Brooklyn *Advertiser* and the *Star,* for Bryant's *Evening Post,* and the abolitionist weekly, the *National Era.* He bought chinaware, a carpet, a watch fob, an old painting of a "colossal human figure," along with a teapot and a round clock. A few years later, he bought a piano for his brother Jeff and a plot in Brooklyn's Cypress Hills Cemetery for his father.

Around this time, Whitman condensed a four-hundred-page (in double columns) prose epic by the Swedish writer Bernhard Ingemann—*The Childhood of King Erik Menved*—and tried to persuade the *Sun* to serialize it under a new name, "The Sleeptalker" (a foretaste of Whitman's best word making). Here, too, he failed. He seems also to have thought about writing stories again but the ideas he came up with are utterly lacking in moral subtlety and depth. Thieves steal money from a dying smallpox victim, but the bills spread contagion to the thieves, who also die. A pickpocket runs away to California to escape punishment, but later it turns out that he has been hung there for some other reason; Whitman added: "make the pickpocket the husband of a worthy woman who has been inveigled into marriage with him." Another sketch conveys Whitman's anticlerical feelings: "make a character of a ranting religious exhorter—sincere but a great fool." He apparently thought he could make some money with these ideas; but—in contrast to Melville, say, who was an irrepressibly original writer trying, with relative success, to bend himself to the popular market—Whitman was simply a hack who wrote magazine filler as he had a decade before in his comically awful temperance novel, *Franklin Evans.*

Here is the baffling, often irritating fact of Whitman's temperament: that he was a hack and yet was also America's most original poet. Time and again, in his journalism, in his attempts at fiction, even in *Leaves of Grass* (especially the plodding programmatic poems he filled out his books with), he sank to the lowest level of popular taste with a homey directness that is not without charm. While he was toying with low moral melodrama, Whitman was also experimenting in his notebooks with new conceptions of poetic style and form, unleashing a verbal mania that burst forth occasionally in his journalism and in a few published poems. His "twoness" was apparently integral and fertile. It fed his comradeship with stage drivers and ferry boatmen, who knew him, not as a literatus who liked to lower himself, but as a vivid, eccentric man who was completely comfortable with them on their terms. It accounts for the ease Whitman would feel with illiterate farm boys in the Civil War hospitals, writing firm spare letters for them to their families. The letters stand as small masterpieces of American vernacular, showing no glimmer of "poetry" or sensitivity, more than might be expected from a good-hearted man of the people. Never, he recalled later, did he bring a copy of *Leaves of Grass* to the hospitals. Thus, we come to see Whitman's anti-literary style, his supple grasp of the uses of the vernacular tone, as not simply a form of impersonation, a masterful lie which, in a merry flash, a sort of practical joke, stripped away the overcultivated tone of American literature. Although Whitman's family never knew what to make of his literary ambitions, he was more one with them than they knew. He remained all his life the son of a poor carpenter and a semi-literate mother. He thought as they thought, never rose above them, any more than he rose above the dozens of workingmen whose names fill his notebooks.

Here, again, Whitman blurs when we think we possess him. Other writers come to us as one. Emerson with his spare body and his remote, sweet face, his cultured tone, is visibly and reliably a man of literature. Even Melville exists as a single, intensely wrought voice, unfailingly intelligent, unfailingly at a distance from the popular imagination. To see Whitman, however, we need bifocals. He was a verbal adventurer, listening to his own rhythms and setting them down in a deliberate style. He was also a semi-cultivated newspaperman. The popular Whitman—half cultivated, surprisingly crude—supplied a rich raw matter, vividly lived and vividly remembered, to the verbal adventurer. Here the "twoness" that has made Whitman seem uncomfortably alien, and almost questionable, to literary minds, becomes one indeed: in his poetry, which rings the changes on the popular tone with beguiling directness, while weaving a net of syntax and form that one can, without being facetious, compare to Mallarmé, for example. In return, the poems became Whitman's model. The man whose poems developed a myth of "merging," who wrote voyages that were ecstatic in-pourings of the miscellaneous wonders of the world, enabling the "self" to become fleshed and bold with the meat of experience; this man found in his poems a template for a personality beyond "twoness," bold with the spontaneous confidence of his animal spirits, like that "strange, natural, quick-eyed and wondrous race" of stage drivers he loved and probably studied with the eye of a divided man longing to be whole.

Much nineteenth-century literature exists in a passionate often awkward dialogue with the popular culture. Balzac and Dickens wrote baggy monsters of novels shaped to the needs of newspaper serialization, and modeled on the lurching melodramas of such as Eugène Sue. Poe's severe and elegant fantasies were grounded in the well-forgotten crudities of the Gothic novel. Romantics everywhere drew on folk tales. Like Wordsworth, they sought to apply their deepest imagination to rendering simple people who, as Rousseau had taught a whole civilization, lived close to nature and possessed an unchanging truth of human experience. What I have called Whitman's "twoness"—his simultaneous personalities of adventurous wordmaster and unsophisticated man of the people— internalized this dialogue and made it the most visible signature of his literary achievement.

In 1850, Whitman had yet to forge a new poetry from the débris of his political enthusiasms, from the years of journalism, the ferry riding, the theater and opera going, and from his autodidact's fascination with Romantic literary theory. The pieces were not yet in place. As far as the world was concerned, Walter Whitman was still an excitable journalist, whose sickly prose piece "Tomb Blossoms," written in the early 1840s, had just been anthologized in a book called *Voices from the Press*.

That spring, however, Whitman burst into print with a series of "queer little poems," as the Brooklyn *Advertiser* called them. Appearing in the *Tribune* and Bryant's *Evening Post*, they joined a chorus of outrage, from Free Soil Democrats and other opponents of slavery, at an elaborate compromise bill that Daniel Webster was shepherding through Congress, in the hope of settling the slavery question once and for all. The most controversial provision of Webster's omnibus bill was for a fugitive slave law that would require escaped slaves captured anywhere in the United States to be arrested and returned to their owners. On 11 March, Senator William Seward (later Lincoln's secretary of state) made an inflammatory speech attacking the Webster compromise and predicting that slavery was ineluctably doomed. Although the Constitution does not expressly forbid the enslavement of human beings, "there is a higher law than the Constitution. . . . The territory [of the United States] is a part . . . of the common heritage of mankind, bestowed upon them by the Creator of the universe. We are his stewards and must so discharge our trust . . ." Seward's "higher law" speech brought public feelings to a boil, and Whitman echoed it in his notebook: "I tell you Americans the earth holds on her huge bosom not a creature more base and abject than that man who takes all that is dictated to him by a superior power, whatever it may be,

117

and having no other text for his obedience than political laws, then obeys."

Although Whitman's notebooks rarely reflect the political events of the moment, in 1850, he was still an activist, making himself heard at political meetings. The *Eagle* taunted him as that grim "shirt collar man" whose "eye like a furnace glows." One night he and eight others were thrown out of a Democratic party meeting to cries of "Down with the traitors." Political outrage fueled his "queer little poems" of 1850, as if conventional form and meter has been exploded by the heat of invective. One of the poems takes its text from the Old Testament: "And one shall say unto him, What are these wounds in thine hands? Then he shall answer, Those with which I was wounded in the house of my friends."

> If thou art balked, O Freedom,
> The victory is not to thy manlier foes;
> From the house of thy friends comes the death stab. . . .

> Virginia, mother of greatness,
> Blush not for being also mother of slaves.
> You might have borne deeper slaves—
> Doughfaces, Lice of Humanity—
> Terrific screamers of Freedom,
> Who rear and bawl, and get hot i' the face,
> But, were they not incapable of august crime,
> Would quench the hopes of ages for a drink—
> Muck-worms, creeping flat to the ground,
> A dollar dearer to them than Christ's blessing;
> All loves, all hopes, less than the thought of gain;
> In life walking in that as in a shroud:
> Men whom the throes of heroes,
> Great deeds at which the gods might stand appalled
> The shriek of a drowned world, the appeal of women,
> The exulting laugh of united empires,
> Would touch them never in the heart,
> But only in the pocket.

Whitman's long angry rhythm suggests the kind of line he would soon be writing: the "creeping" and the "muck-worms" would find a place in "Song of Myself." This poem's form of public address is still closer to an inflated editorial than to the scale of

Whitman's later poetry, but we see the direction: here, maybe, is the very dividing line between the two styles.

"Blood Money," the loveliest of these early poems, was published a few weeks after Seward's "higher law" speech and shows how, even then, Whitman could lift his theme beyond merely partisan outrage:

I

Of olden time, when it came to pass
That the beautiful god, Jesus, should finish his work on earth,
Then went Judas, and sold the divine youth,
And took pay for his body.

Curs'd was the deed, even before the sweat of the clutching hand grew dry;
And darkness frown'd upon the seller of the like of God,
Where, as though earth lifted her breast to throw him from her, and heaven refused him,
He hung in the air, self-slaughter'd.

The cycles, with their long shadows, have stalk'd silently forward,
Since those ancient days—many a pouch enwrapping meanwhile
Its fee, like that paid for the son of Mary.
And still goes one, saying,
"What will ye give me, and I will deliver this man unto you?"
And they make the covenant, and pay the pieces of silver.

II

Look forth, deliverer,
Look forth, first-born of the dead,
Over the tree-tops of Paradise;
See thyself in yet-continued bonds,
Toilsome and poor, thou bear'st man's form again,
Thou art reviled, scourged, put into prison,
Hunted from the arrogant equality of the rest;
With staves and swords throng the willing servants of authority,
Again they surround thee, mad with devilish spite;
Toward thee stretch the hands of a multitude, like vulture's talons,
The meanest spit in thy face, they smite thee with their palms;
Bruised, bloody, and pinion'd is thy body,
More sorrowful than death is thy soul.

Witness of anguish, brother of slaves,
Not with thy price closed the price of thine image:
And still Iscariot plies his trade.

The movement here is stately and measured and surprisingly controlled. The image of Christ heaved from the earth and refused by heaven is memorable. The "beautiful god" and the stalking "cycles" of time would contribute to later poems. Whitman might have included "Blood Money" in *Leaves of Grass* without embarrassment. Perhaps he did not include it because the poem's Biblical theme was too conventional for the ebullient, unlettered "rough" of 1855. "Blood Money" is closer to the objective tone of many poems in Whitman's Civil War book, *Drum-Taps* (1865).

In these poems of 1850, Whitman is still a voice from the press. But the voice has begun to mutate. There are a new tone and a new precision of diction. "Blood Money" is a poet's poem, not a journalist's, just as the prose in "Letters from a Travelling Batchelor" had risen, however unevenly, beyond mere journalism.

On 21 June, the *Tribune* published that other "queer little poem," "Resurgemus," which I have already mentioned: a lurid allegory of the struggle for liberty, the arrogant triumph of despots, and the mysterious rebirth, like the unkillable resilience of grass, of "the seed of freedom":

God, 'twas delicious!
That brief, tight, glorious grip
Upon the throats of kings.
You liars paid to defile the People,
Mark you now:
Not for numberless agonies, murders, lusts,
For court thieving in its manifold mean forms,
Worming from his simplicity the poor man's wages;
For many a promise sworn by royal lips
And broken, and laughed at in the breaking;
Then, in their power, not for all these,
Did a blow fall in personal revenge,
Or did a hair draggle in blood:
The People scorned the ferocity of kings.

But the sweetness of mercy brewed bitter destruction,
And frightened rulers come back:
Each comes in state, with his train,
Hangman, priest, and tax-gatherer,
Soldier, lawyer, and sycophant;
An appalling procession of locusts,
And the king struts grandly again.

Like the other 1850 poems, "Resurgemus" resembles an angry editorial more than a poem. Yet Whitman liked it enough to include it in *Leaves of Grass,* and we see why. Whitman's rhythmical instinct—his finest trait as a poet—is present in "Resurgemus," which he would simply reset into the longer lines of his book, leaving the phrasing of the poem largely intact.

3

Around 1850, it is possible to recognize attitudes, opinions, even particular words that will come to characterize Whitman as we know him. In a paragraph sketch for the *Advertiser,* he praised the "bold masculine discourses," without "prettiness and correctness of style," of the popular Brooklyn pastor, Henry Ward Beecher; and we hear in embryo the future rough-shod poet with his distrust of ornamental language. He admired Beecher's angry retort to a heckler, but "if we might take such a liberty [we would] advise more coolness, even contempt or indifference toward those who violently assault him." Whitman would soon be giving himself the same advice, gleaned from Epictetus. His notebook would contain such personal slogans as "Boldness. Nonchalant ease and indifference."

> Backward I see in my own days where I sweated through fog with linguists and contenders,
> I have no mockings or arguments. . . . I witness and wait.

In another article, he objected to the delirious acclaim that greeted the Swedish singer Jenny Lind on her visit to New York in 1850. Miss Lind's vocal technique was dazzling, he admitted, "performing the same feats with sound, that leapers and 'India rubber men' perform with their limbs." Such vocal gymnastics are "curious to hear"; yet a more ordinary voice will often possess far more "sweetness and music." Five years earlier, in an article entitled "Art Singing and Heart Singing" for Edgar Allan Poe's *Broadway Journal,* Whitman had made a similar distinction. There he had preferred the "heart-songs" of American family singers like the

Hutchinsons to the agonized squalling of foreign art singers. After the revelation of grand opera, however, Whitman wrote more subtly:

Music, in the legitimate sense of that term, exists independently of technical music, as much as language exists independently of grammar—or perhaps I might say, just as poetry exists independently of rhyme. The science of music, with all its rules and conventionalisms, may at times be almost disgusting to the purest and highest appreciation of the surpassingly beautiful reality which those rules are the mere shadow of.

Art's highest aim, Whitman had come to know, is not simply to be artless and direct, a language of the heart: its "surpassingly beautiful reality" is beyond technique, yet is somehow suggested by it and bodied forth by it, as the voice, apart from any words, envelops the hearer and lifts him to an oceanlike heaven of pure sounds. "Ah, welcome that I know not the mere language of the earthly words in which the melody is embodied," he wrote about the librettos of Italian opera, "as all words are mean before the language of true music." "The words of my book nothing, the drift of it everything," he would write in only a few years.

Whitman's occasional journalism changed at this time. Even when he was writing for the abolitionist *National Era,* it was about music and painting. He rambled up Broadway, describing the exotic appeal of the world's busiest street. He remembered the first time he ever went to the theater and "had a dim idea of the walls of some adjoining houses silently and suddenly sinking away, to let folks see what was going on within." He was thinking less about politics, more about the arts and his own experience. And the art he was writing most about is not poetry, or even literature, but music. A decade or so later, the French Symbolist Paul Verlaine's poem-manifesto, *Art Poétique,* would begin, *"De la musique avant toute chose,"** inaugurating the Symbolist preoccupation with verbal music. For Whitman too, but more profoundly and more subtly, poetry would aspire to the condition of music—not in a Poe-like chiming of exotic rhymes and assonances, but in a pattern of suggestive imagery, interweavings of theme, shifts in tone, suggested by the alternations of recitative and aria.

*"Music before everything."

122

Whitman wrote about painting, describing his visits to the American Art Union and the competing International Union, two popular galleries in Manhattan. He liked William Sidney Mount's painting of a black fiddler calling out steps at a square dance, and another of Mount's Long Island scenes: a Negro winning a goose at a raffle. Whitman wrote about the Brooklyn landscape artist, Jesse Talbot, a friend of his, and about another young Brooklyn painter, Walter Libbey, who would soon paint Whitman's portrait. He especially admired Libbey's painting of a boy playing a flute:

I don't know where to look for a picture more *naive,* or with more spirit or grace. The young musician has stopped, by the wayside, and, putting down his basket, seats himself on a bank. He has a brown wool hat, ornamented with a feather; rolled-up shirt sleeves, a flowing red cravat on his neck, and a narrow leather belt buckled round his waist—a handsome healthy country boy. The face, the position of the hands holding the flute, the expression of the features, are exquisitely fine. I have looked several long looks at this picture, at different times, and each one with added pleasure and admiration. The scene in the background, clear and sunny, is yet subdued as a subordinate part—a servant to the main purpose; and it is a beautiful scene too. The basket, half of which you see, the light resting here and there on the wide withes; the folds of the trousers, and their shadowed creases made by the open legs; on all these, the work shows the true artist. There is a richness of coloring, tamed to that hue of purplish gray, which we see in the summer in the open air. There is no hardness, and the eye is not pained by the sharpness of outline which mars many otherwise fine pictures. In the scene of the background, and in all the accessories, there is a delicious melting in, so to speak, of object with object; an effect that is frequently enough in nature, though painters seem to disdain following it, even where it is demanded.

Just as Whitman enjoyed the play of visual detail in Libbey's painting, his poetic "catalogues," too, would be distinctly pictorial. He was a passionate observer, "absorbing" visual impressions, "devouring" colors. The drama of eyesight—the world flowing variously and smoothly into the "space of a peachpit"—would be a cornerstone of "Song of Myself."

Whitman's delight in the visual drew him to both painting and photography. In the *Eagle,* he had written about the uncanny immediacy of daguerreotyped faces; and the first ambitious poem he wrote in the 1850s was a miscellaneous cataloguing of "pictures" hung in the "gallery" of his mind. Eventually he would become the most photographed and painted poet of modern times, with a carefully pondered sense of the visual effect he created. In later years, he would speak with a delicacy of preference that could seem fatuous about the numerous portraits he dredged from the morass of papers on his bedroom floor.

Strolling up Broadway in 1850, he remarked the skylighted studios where dozens of daguerreotypists pursued their newly fashionable trade: "Whatever artistical objections may be brought against this sort of picture, it is not the less true, that some of the Broadway operators do produce the form and spirit of the face to a degree that defies criticism. Some pictures taken, at Lawrence's rooms, by Gabriel Harrison, are perfect works of truth and art." On a sweaty summer day in 1854, this same Gabriel Harrison would take Whitman's best-known photograph: hand on hip, broad hat, flannel shirt showing under his open collar, high boots, wide lips. So we see him in Samuel Hollyer's etching based on Harrison's photograph—an etching that Whitman placed as his signature and visual identity at the beginning of the anonymous book of poems he published in 1855.

In his description of Walter Libbey's painting, Whitman was taking sides in a debate that divided the New York art world and contributed importantly to his thinking about poetry. Libbey's "richness of coloring," Whitman wrote, was "tamed" to the "purplish grey" of open summer air. There is "a delicious melting in . . . of object with object," without any hardness or painfully sharp outline. Whitman was comparing Libbey's natural play of light and color to the virtuoso realism of painters schooled in the famous Dusseldorf academies which were popular in the 1850s. Dusseldorf realism aimed at literal reproduction, vivid, cleanly drawn outlines; a faithfulness to the object so labored that a student painter was rumored to have posed a horse beside his easel, and shot it, in order to paint its death agony. According to Whitman, such realism violated the natural movement of the eye which sees ensembles, not a uniform filigree of details, however superbly rendered. Of a painting called "The Death of Bayard," which he saw exhibited in a Manhattan gallery, Whitman remarked:

There is too little soul in the picture, whose subject demands that is should be specially full of that element. The plumes, the armor, the velvet tunic, and all the small fixings, are carefully and elaborately rendered. An upholsterer's or dry-goods man's wife might be in rapture with it. . . . [The picture] seems to thrust itself from its frame, and "stand out" as they call it. This effect is openly sought after. It is fatal to the truth and life of art. Not protruding but retiring . . . must be that picture which deserves a place among the things of genius. Nature never thrusts anything forward in this way—it will do for a melo-drama on the stage but is no part of true greatness in life or in art.

Although Whitman admired the technical brilliance of the Dusseldorf painters, as he did Jenny Lind's virtuosity, he believed there was a more profound realism which was truer to nature:

Too many of our young fellows, among those who ought to know better, are carried away with the false principle of working up the details of a picture to the minutest specification. This is the business of the modelist, not the artist. . . . Aim to produce that beautiful resemblance which will excite the motion that the real object might produce—the rest is the mere drippings, the shavings and sawdust. Keep them out of sight, unless you would mar the perfect work.

When Whitman wrote, a few years later, that his poems were to be "indirect" and "subjective" instead of linear and narrative; when he wrote that he was letting "nature speak" in his wayward stanzas which refused to gel into objective scenes and stories but spilled forward like waves of the ocean—a favorite image of Whitman's—he was translating into literary terms values he had defended in the articles he wrote about his young Brooklyn friends, Walter Libbey and Jesse Talbot. Consider Whitman's own impressionistic landscapes, their "delicious melting in" of object with object, their experiments with light:

Smile O voluptuous coolbreathed earth!
Earth of the slumbering and liquid trees!
Earth of departed sunset! Earth of the mountains misty-topt!
Earth of the vitreous pour of the full moon just tinged with blue!
Earth of shine and dark mottling the tide of the river!
Earth of the limpid gray of clouds brighter and clearer for my sake!
Far-swooping elbowed earth! Rich apple-blossomed earth!
Smile, for your lover comes!

And this "luminist" celebration of a sunrise:

> To behold the daybreak!
> The little light fades the immense and diaphanous shadows,
> The air tastes good to my palate.
>
> Hefts of the innocent world at innocent gambols, silently rising,
>   freshly exuding,
> Scooting obliquely high and low.
>
> Something I cannot see puts upward libidinous prongs,
> Seas of bright juice suffuse heaven.

As a cultural journalist, Whitman was certainly not the masterful magazine writer that Poe was; yet he knew what he liked, and he knew why. Perhaps we see here the first unmistakable sign of Whitman's originality. These ideas did not come to him from any pronunciamento by Cornelius Matthews or Evert Duyckinck; they were not jarred awake by the obscure mid-century poets who influenced him in lesser ways: Alexander Smith or Martin Farquhar Tupper. Although Whitman would soon formulate his idea of the poet's role in ways that are indebted to Emerson and Carlyle, neither of these influences are present here. In his articles on painting, Whitman was thinking for himself about artistic pleasures that mattered to him. Although he would soon see America as a "truculent giant" and create a giant's voice to speak for it, Whitman here affirms his belief in a curiously modest artistic aim: to become a channel for nature's subtlest sensations; to awaken in himself a kind of "negative capability," to use Keats's term. In Whitman's great poems, the "rough" swaggering in the American foreground will be complemented by an exquisitely passive personality who observes a spear of summer grass or waits, full of the night's echoes, for his lover. This "negative" personality will provide the texture of Whitman's poems, their impressionistic concreteness. It will save him from Ossianic bombast and divert him from the self-display of a Byron to the allusive style he called "indirect." We see it here, shaping his esthetic choices, providing a ground for the new poetry he would soon be writing.

Jesse Talbot and the Brooklyn sculptor Henry Kirke Brown (whose bronze statue of George Washington stands in Union

Square, in lower Manhattan) were at the center of a group of Brooklyn artists who usually met at the latter's studio. Whitman liked their company. When he was among them, he was not only a voice from the press but a partner in their experiment to create a new American esthetic. He sympathized with their marginal lives and deplored the American "locomotive" as a symbol of the brash profit making that never slowed down long enough to consider the solitary labor of artists. In the *Evening Post,* he called for his painter friends to join together in a counterdemocracy of the arts, "a close phalanx, ardent, radical, progressive":

These thousands of young men . . . are in the main composed of the nobler specimens of our race. With warm, impulsive souls, instinctively generous and genial, boon companions, wild and thoughtless often, but mean and sneaking never. . . . Unlike the orthodox sons and daughters of the world in many things, yet it is a picturesque unlikeness. For it need not argue an absolute miracle, if a man differ from the present dead uniformity of "society" in appearance and opinion, and still retain his grace and morals. A sunny blessing, then, say I, on the young artist race!"

Samuel Longfellow, brother of America's best-known poet, Henry Wadsworth Longfellow, was the pastor of a small church in Brooklyn during these years; and Whitman knew him but felt uncomfortable among his cultivated friends: "they were literary, polite: I was not their kind—was not *au fait*—so preferred not to push myself in, or, if in, to stay in." He preferred Brown's sculpture studio which was more like a carpenter's shop, with Brown

always modelling someone—always at work. . . . There I would meet all sorts—young fellows from abroad stopped here in their swoopings: they would tell us of students, studios, the teachers, they had just left in Paris, Rome, Florence: one sparkling fellow in particular I fancied: he spoke of Béranger—I was greatly interested; he either knew Béranger or knew a heap about him. In this crowd I was myself called Béranger: my hair had already commenced to turn grey.* My mother and sister would say to me: You're an odd one Walt: whereas everybody else seems to try all they can to keep young you seem to glory in the fact that you are already beginning to look venerable.

---

*Pierre Jean de Béranger was a liberal French poet of the time, with a wide following among the masses of the French people. One sees why Whitman would have been flattered by the resemblance.

THE MAKING OF A POET: THE 1850s

As a Brooklynite, Whitman encouraged his friends to form a local art union; and when they did, he wrote about it for Bryant's *Evening Post*. Without making exaggerated claims for their work (none of it, he wrote, approached "the highest order of merit," yet it was a "very agreeable collection," containing "some works of taste and talent"), Whitman became their spokesman. He wrote about the importance of encouraging young artists, about the enfeebling effect of neglect; and here, faintly, we may hear an expression of Whitman's own intellectual solitude. If "literary" and "polite," went together, as they largely did in 1850s New York, where did that leave Whitman? Where was that small, maybe half-talented group of contemporaries which T. S. Eliot supposed to be important for the nurturing of a poet's talent? Whitman's revolt against literary standards was more wholesale than Melville's, because Whitman stood completely outside the institution of literature, as Melville did not. Melville's upheaval had the anguished feeling of a family quarrel, Whitman's was a revolution; it was, in its way, not only literary but class warfare.

In the spring of 1851, Whitman's friends invited him to lecture at the newly formed Brooklyn Art Union, on Fulton Street. The speech is an inventory of the reading Whitman was doing at the time: Emerson's *Nature* and "Divinity School Address," Carlyle's *Sartor Resartus,* Epictetus, Frances Wright's *A Few Days in Athens.* Whitman would soon remind himself to leave all the "stock touches" out of his writing, including references to other books— this would be his revolutionary plan; but in 1851, he still aspired to be a man of letters, with history and the classics at his fingertips. He spoke of "beauty" and left the "stock touches" in. He spoke of Greece and Socrates and the great heroes. The twin supports of his speech were Emerson and Carlyle: one standing for the ecstatic dialogue between nature and art; the other, for the fulminating wit of the prophet attacking the "profit-motive," and the "uniforms" worn by the foppish classes who neglected true artists and were laughable models for artists to waste their gift upon.

When God called his creation "good," Whitman began, he was referring to nature's ability to be always new and fresh, always a beginning. Among men, the artist perceives God's fresh beginning and makes it visible to others. Emerson had asked: "Why should not we also enjoy an original relation to the universe?" We can, said Whitman, or rather the artist in us can. For all men are artists, although few are aware of it; few know, therefore, that we live in the first minutes of the creation, instead of at its dwindling end:

Who would not mourn that an ample palace of surpassingly graceful architecture, filled with luxuries and gorgeously embellished with fair pictures and sculpture, should stand cold and still and vacant, and never be known and enjoyed by its owner? Would such a fact as this cause your sadness? Then be sad. For there is a palace, to which the courts of the most sumptuous kings are but a frivolous patch, and, though it is always waiting for them, not one in thousands of its owners ever enters there with any genuine sense of its grandeur and glory.

Whitman's palace is nature and art, and it is man's perceiving mind: a place in which to stroll, aimless and delighted. Nature as a palace, an indoors? Whitman would not long put up with such "feudal" tropes. He would make a religion of unhousing himself and his poetry. The next time he would write of art as nature's utterance, the trope would be humbler: leaves of grass.

Whitman's next remark must have surprised his Art Union audience. Great art, he told them, had the power to humanize death and make it almost appealing:

In the temple of the Greeks, Death and his brother Sleep, were depicted as beautiful youths reposing in the arms of Night. At other times Death was represented as a graceful form, with calm but drooping eyes, his feet crossed and his arms leaning on an inverted torch. Such were the soothing and solemnly placed influences which true art, identical with the perception of the beauty that there is in all the ordinations as well as all the works of Nature, cast over the last fearful thrill of those olden days. Was it not better so? Or is it better to have before us the idea of our dissolution typified by the spectral horror upon the pale horse, by a grinning skeleton or a mouldering skull?

At the heart of Whitman's poetry would be a soothing myth of death: as a husky-voiced old mother; as an ocean; as a night filled with amorphous shapes; as a perpetual expansion, a metempsychosis based on the natural cycles of death, decay, and rebirth. Whitman's fascination with death would save his poetry from the one-dimensional optimism—William James called it "healthy-mindedness"—he has often been accused of. Whitman was haunted by death. His youthful stories are driven by a genuinely personal nightmare, clinging to Poe-like conventions. He collected articles about examples of longevity and dreamed of an ageless old age, full of "joy joy joy." *Leaves of Grass* was wedded to death, written under "great pressure," while his father lay dying in another room of the house, and published days before his death.

In his speech at the Art Union, Whitman described Death as a beautiful boy enfolded with his brother, Sleep, in the comforting arms of night. The image is classical, perhaps inspired by Frances Wright's *A Few Days in Athens*. It conveys an erotic wistfulness. The figure with "calm but drooping eyes" might almost be a self-portrait. Elsewhere Whitman described his own "singular eyes of an indistinct light blue, and with that sleepy look that comes when the lid rests half-way down over the pupil." Lounging on an inverted torch, the figure also resembles the "singer" in "Song of Myself," who "bends an arm on an impalpable certain rest,/Looks with its sidecurved head curious what will come next." Death exists in the speech as a curious self-mirroring, wedded to "art" and to the Greek vision of boys reclining in each other's arms.

A friend of Whitman's, Abby Price, remembered a conversation Whitman had about death a few years later: "For a few minutes," she said, "his face wore an expression she had never seen before—he seemed rapt, absorbed." In describing it afterward, she said he appeared like a man in a trance. This "rapt" fascination may be the source of Whitman's sweetly haunted lines in "Out of the Cradle Endlessly Rocking," and "When Lilacs Last in the Dooryard Bloomed," and provides the compelling lyricism of one of Whitman's most puzzling poems, "Scented Herbage of My Breast," in which the longing for "comrades," the leaflike growth of poetry, and the vision of death, (the very themes Whitman invoked in his Art Union speech) are woven together with peculiar intensity:

> Scented herbage of my breast,
> Leaves from you I glean, I write, to be perused best afterwards,
> Tomb-Leaves, body-leaves growing up above me above death,
> . . . .
> O slender leaves! O blossoms of my blood! I permit you to tell in your
>   own way of the heart that is under you,

O I do not know what you mean there underneath yourselves, you are
not happiness,
You are often more bitter than I can bear, you burn and sting me,
Yet you are beautiful to me you faint tinged roots, you make me think
of death,
Death is beautiful from you (what indeed is finally beautiful except
death and love)
O I think it is not for life I am chanting here my chant of lovers. . . .

The concluding theme of Whitman's speech became the ground
note of his poetry and his life: "The perfect man is the perfect
artist"; in Emerson's phrase, the poet is the "complete man,"
among "partial men." Whitman did not yet know where this Em-
ersonian idea would lead him. In 1851, his "perfect man" was a
Greek of the age of Pericles: naturally artistic, possessing a harmony of moral qualities, a fervent citizen and a strong individual:

It refreshes the soul to bring up again one of that glorious and manly and
beautiful nation, with his sandals, his flowing drapery, his noble and
natural attitudes and the serene composure of his features. Imagination
loves to dwell there, revels there, and will not turn away. There the artist
appetite is gratified; and there all ages have loved to turn as to one of the
most perfect ideals of man.

From the first, Whitman's "artist appetite," hungered less for
great works than for great men, whom he compares sarcastically to
the "orthodox specimens" of the "present times, products not of
any artistic impulse, but of "fashionable tailordom":

the tight boot with the high heel; the trousers, big at the ankle, on some
rule inverting the ordinary ones of grace; the long large cuffs, and thick
stiff collar of his coat—the swallow-tailed coat, on which dancing masters are inexorable; the neck swathed in many bands, giving support to
the modern high and pointed shirt collar, that fearful sight to an approaching enemy—the modern shirt collar, bold as Columbus, stretching
off into the unknown distance—and then to crown all, the fashionable
hat, before which language has nothing to say.

Great art is rooted in moral grandeur and physical beauty.
Therefore, Whitman counsels the artist to learn not from other
artists, not even the "great old masters," but from the world of

magnificent behavior: Mary Stuart, Kossuth, Mazzini, as well as Socrates, and "a greater than Socrates."

All great rebels and innovators especially if their intellectual majesty bears itself out with calmness amid popular odium or circumstances of cruelty and an infliction of suffering, exhibit the highest phases of the artistic spirit. A sublime moral beauty is present to them, and . . . may almost be said to emanate from them.

Eventually *Leaves of Grass* would reverse this heroic ideal, choosing to celebrate the anonymous acts of the ordinary life. The reference to Greece would be reduced to a mere colorful detail in a world-circling catalogue and replaced by another scourge of "fashionable tailordom": the "rough," the hero of the American streets. In 1851, Whitman still had only half an idea, but it is a clear and significant idea: the artist must work to be "perfect"; making his art, he must also make himself.

There is another conceptual step Whitman had yet to take in 1851. He had still to work out the tricky esthetic that would proclaim the very making of poems to be a form of "self making," an inherently moral labor performed completely and wittily in the laboratory of language. Meanwhile, he declared himself as a poet and slyly "improved" a stanza from his friend William Cullen Bryant's "Forest Hymn" by reworking it into the sort of irregular line he himself was then experimenting with:

> There is not lost, one of Earth's charms
> Upon her bosom yet
> After the flight of untold centuries,
> The freshness of her far beginning lies
> And still shall lie.

One wonders how Bryant took this playful arrogance.

4

After three years in the house on Myrtle Avenue, the Whitmans took up their old house-hopping habit again. In May 1852, Walt bought a lot on Cumberland Street and put up two houses. A month later, the Myrtle Avenue house was sold; and in September, the family moved into one of those on Cumberland, selling the other. A few months later they sold their own house, too. In January 1853, Walt bought another lot on Cumberland and gave the contractors, Lucky and Vankeuren, a month to build him a house to live in. A year later, in May 1854, the Whitmans moved into yet another house Walt had built on Skillman Street. The following year, the family bought a house in a working-class neighborhood on Ryerson Street far out along Myrtle. This was Walt's address when, in May 1855, he walked into the clerk's office of the Southern District Court of New York, in Williamsburg, to find out the proper wording for a copyright on a book he was going to publish.

Whitman's collection of receipts from these years reflects a more important change. His bookstore was gone; the journalism thinned out too. In 1852, Walt and his brothers rented a storefront on the corner of Cumberland Street and Atlantic Avenue and set themselves up as carpenter-contractors. Whitman was no misty-minded businessman. The receipts were carefully itemized, payments noted to the penny and dated. His father had not been good at business, and Walt was trying to do better. He supervised the work and kept his accounts in order. He made a profit, too. In May 1855, Louisa Whitman paid $1,840 for the house on Ryerson Street, clear of mortgage; most of the money probably came from Walt. At last, the Whitmans had a home of their own. For a few brief years, the family achieved a measure of stability before the difficult times that were coming.

Whitman's career as a house builder and contractor lasted only a few years, yet it may be a key to deeper changes occurring within him. His new work took him away from the world of letters, from the journalism and the shrill sentiments of a political outsider. In a way, it brought him home: to the world of "mechanics" and laborers he had fled as a younger man and was now rediscovering on his summer rambles around Long Island, but especially in his role as family provider, helping to fill his father's shoes. Whitman's life had come full circle; and as Antaeus drew his strength from the earth, he celebrated by reveling in the concreteness of the working world. We find him noting down the specific vocabulary of the trades—"pork packing . . . they wear oil-skin overalls. . . . The killer hammer—the hog hook—the gutting"—for use in his poems; or enjoying the "superb music" of workingmen's voices:

I often wander all day on Manhattan Island, through streets toward the East River, on purpose to have the pleasure of hearing the voices of the native-born and bred workmen and apprentices in the spar-yards, on piers, caulkers on the ship-scaffolds, workmen in iron, mechanics to or from their shops, drivers calling to their horses, and the like.

Although as a newspaperman and Locofoco Democrat, Whitman had often written about the working classes, his sympathy had been abstract, a matter of democratic principles. His ear for street talk had been there, but in quotation marks, defining a distance Whitman had preferred: the distance of ambition, of a higher social horizon. That has gone now. Whitman was not only listening to the "superb music" of the streets, he was chiming in, striking up acquaintance with strangers. This was a recent development, brother George remembered. When Thoreau walked down Fulton Street with Whitman in 1856, he was impressed, and a little piqued, by Whitman's casual friendships with the tradesmen and workers. The man was the greatest democrat he had ever met, Thoreau wrote to a friend.

The poems in Whitman's first book bristle with the terminology of the shop. Here, for Whitman, was a new heroism; here were the unnamed acts by which men lived. Melville celebrated the "epic tools" of whale-fishing; not spears and shields, but try-pots, blubber spades, harpoons, and coiled ropes. This became Whitman's subject, too, as he "catalogued" the clanking, hammering, and smelting; the work shops and the skills:

The anvil and tongs and hammer . . . the axe and wedge . . . the square
    and mitre and jointer and smoothing plane;
The plumbob and trowel and level . . . the wall-scaffold, and the work
    of walls and ceilings . . . or any masonry-work;
The ship's compass . . . the sailor's tarpaulin . . . the stays and lanyards,
    and the ground-tackle for anchoring and mooring,
The sloops tiller . . . the pilot's wheel and bell . . . the yacht or fish-
    smack . . . the great gay pennanted three-hundred-foot steamboat
    under full headway, with her proud fat breasts and her delicate
    swift-flashing paddles; . . . .

The etui of surgical instruments, and the etui of oculist's or aurist's
   instruments, or dentist's instruments;
Glassblowing, grinding of wheat and corn . . . casting, and what is cast
   . . . tinroofing, shingledressing,
Shipcarpentering, flagging of sidewalks by flaggers . . . dock-building,
   fishcuring, ferrying;
The pump, the piledriver, the great derrick . . . the coalkiln and
   brickkiln,
Ironworks or whiteleadworks . . . the sugarhouse . . . steam-saws, and
   the great mills and factories; . . .

The cylinder press . . . the handpress . . . the frisket and tympan . . . the
   compositor's stick and rule,
The implements for daguerrotyping . . . the tools of the rigger or grap-
   pler or sailmaker or blockmaker.

The first epic of the working life was probably *Robinson Crusoe*,
in 1719, which can be read as a variant of utopian fiction: an
account of how the drudgery of housebuilding, weaving, farming,
sewing, cooking can become a satisfying and morally luminous
activity. The nineteenth century, too, was devoted to a dream of
happy work, most spectacularly in the odd theories of the French
utopian writer Charles Fourier, whose American disciple, Albert
Brisbane, Whitman met and may have echoed in his poems. Happy work was a kind of beatitude, even for a grim prophet like Karl
Marx, who imagined his future communists fishing, working, and
playing in millennial contentment. Thomas Jefferson dreamed of a
country of small farmers, inhabiting a heaven of private property
and farm work: America's version of the shepherds who, since
Theocritus and Virgil, had piped delightful melodies under trees,
far from the imperfect world.

Whitman's first great poem, "Song of Myself," is a siren song of
"union," of "merging"; it is, profoundly, a pastoral poem, but it
differs from the familiar Romantic pastoral of Wordsworth or
Shelley, because its happy place is not a green meadow beside a
brook but the onrushing world of ordinary experience: the world
of carpenters building houses, of tram drivers, of paving stones
echoing the sounds of living men and women. For Whitman, democracy itself was a new sort of pastoral; its music was not that of a
lone piper but something like a chorus of voices, a free-form opera

raveling half out of control, "a barbaric yawp." What can we say of a poem that extends its pastoral embrace to every creature, trade, and place, leaving nothing out, resorting to the inclusive form of the random list to express its capacity for sympathy? Such a work can hardly be called a poem. It reflects an indiscriminate appetite, a mind that sees all the dreamed-of fulfillments of religion and literature in the unvarnished, shaggy particulars of the everyday world.

In retrospect, we see this as an expression of Whitman's Americanness. Jacksonian rhetoric had turned America into a Romantic idea: a secular heaven in which social justice, the healing powers of nature, and the fellowship of men appeared to be changing the conditions of history. Yet only two writers—Whitman and Melville—at the fading end of this romantic American dream, managed to give it full original expression. Before these two, Evert Duyckinck's wistful complaint seemed all too justified: so many manifestos, so much excited theorizing. But where was the literary genius to make the dream live? Surely not those respectable half-giants, Washington Irving, William Cullen Bryant, or James Fenimore Cooper. Hawthorne and Emerson were closer, but even they were too decorous; their very strength had an Old World sobriety, a constrained style that made them seem half-English. Only Melville and Whitman managed the feat of creating—beyond the rich Biblical rhetoric of American politics, beyond the down-home coziness of American "heart-singing" and black-face Jim Crow performing—a spacious American art that D.H. Lawrence would compare to the Greeks.

Whitman did not find his Americanness; he created it all on his own in his rooms on Skillman and Ryerson Streets, while toting up invoices for building materials, paying bills, buying and selling quickly built frame houses. He later imagined himself as an orator traveling from the halls of Congress to the western cities, to the streets of New York. His "voice" would raise the conflicts of American life to a new level, at once resolving and intensifying them. For he believed that the "turbulence" of democracy and the evolutionary brutality of nature were the same: a benign law guided both nature and democracy toward ever greater "development." Harmony was not a formal dance under trees but an urging of all conflicts, a sexual prodding from within life to produce more and better life. It is no wonder that, a decade later, Whitman was fascinated by Hegel and saw everywhere around him a dialectic of tooth, claw, and sexual feeling which was, to him, the music of unity:

Urge and urge and urge,
Always the procreant urge of the world.

Out of the dimness opposite equals advance. . . . always substance and increase,
Always a knit of identity . . . always distinction . . . always a breed of life.

Because of this sexual dance, he could envision a society of clashing but free atoms gravitating toward ever better combinations. In his unpublished political pamphlet, "The Eighteenth Presidency" (1856), he loosed a verbal onslaught of political invective in the service of this hope. Shatter the rigid layers of class privilege and political self-seeking, Whitman thundered, and then maybe you will see some ordinary "mechanic," rough-mannered, naïve, instinctively honest, who will stride from his workshop to the nation's capital, to run his country's affairs for a time, and then return in all simplicity to his shop like one of Pericles' Athenians.

Whitman would always be a newspaperman. Even now, he freelanced when he could, and would shortly begin a life-long campaign via the newspapers to keep himself before the public eye, as no serious poet has ever done. Yet in 1852, he liked to see himself as one of Brooklyn's regular young men, a builder and businessman. It was part of his double vision of the heroism of the ordinary, and it took shape amid his practical activities as a contractor. When he wrote to Senator John Parker Hale before the 1852 elections, encouraging him to accept the Free Soil Party's nomination for the presidency, it was not as the experienced politician and local literary figure but as one of the city's talkative young workingmen who, better than politicians, as he said, could be counted on to know the hearts of the people.

To be sure, Whitman did not invent this romance of democracy. A decade before, the Whigs had promoted their candidate, William Henry Harrison, as a leathery old farmer wise with log cabin lore and apple brandy. Within a few years, Abe Lincoln would become an American legend, with his school lessons charcoaled on a wooden shovel and his fence-rail splitting. Here was the American pastoral, feeding public rhetoric, enabling Americans to see the glimmerings of a unique destiny in the brutal, often nasty affairs of their growing country.

5

The vision was Jefferson's. But America had changed in half a century. There were large cities now, foreign-speaking immigrants, and sectional conflict. Whitman's pastoral hope is grounded in the city. Its ordinary man is not a farmer, but a "mechanic." Even so, it is more a swan song than a celebration. Whitman saw Shakespeare as an elegist of the "feudal scene," its last wondrous voice. He might have described his own sprawling, entrepreneurial poems of the 1850s in similar terms. For the world he celebrated was fading. His own father's waning career as an artisan carpenter might have been a symbol of that decline. Increasingly, the artisan—never comfortably established in America anyway—was being replaced by the factory worker; and skill, by the sort of repetitive labor that Carlyle and other English social critics had been deploring for decades. Whitman's New York in the 1850s was built on large-scale commerce and factory labor. Its opera houses, luxurious stores, and thousand-room hotels depended to a large extent on the desperately low wages paid to immigrant workers. Alongside the glitter was another New York Whitman knew equally well: the New York of disease-ridden tenements, of Five Points*; and the Bowery; the brutalized existences that Melville gave glimpses of in *Pierre* (1852), and that Americans probably first learned to see, ironically enough, by reading Dickens. New York was both the showcase and the rubbish heap of America's industrial revolution; a city devoted to stock manipulations, rail-

*The downtown neighborhood east of Broadway, toward the present Bowery and beyond was known as Five Points. It was a poverty-stricken neighborhood, full of cheap bars, beer halls, and seedy roominghouses. The "Bowery Boys" and "roughs" made Five Points a notoriously violent and suspect neighborhood which more fortunate frequenters of Broadway, a few blocks to the west, did their best to ignore.

road interests, and wage-depressing unemployment. The simpler America of farmers and mechanics may never have existed outside of booster legend and the hagiography of the Founding Fathers. It was certainly not the America Whitman had known during a dozen years of political infighting and newspaper reporting. Yet in 1852, he began to imagine it on the model of an earlier time, when solid, solitary individuals seemed able to control their destinies.

The burly workingman Whitman would later describe in 1856, leaping lithely onto the siderail of a Broadway stagecoach, is an anachronism: "Tall, large, rough-looking man, in a journeyman carpenter's uniform. Coarse sanguine complexion; strong, bristly, grizzled beard, singular eyes, of a semi-transparent, indistinct light blue . . ."

For none other than Walt it is who . . . turns up with springing and elastic motion, and lights on the off side top of the stage with his hips held against the rod as quietly as a hawk swoops to its nest. . . . As onward speeds the stage, mark his nonchalant air, seated aslant, and quite at home.—Our million-hued and ever changing panorama of Broadway moves steadily down; he, going up, sees it all, as a kind of half dream.— Mark the salute of four out of five of the drivers, downward salutes which he silently returns in the same manner—the raised arm, and the upright hand.

Whitman liked to stage himself, and he did so here as someone he had never been. No one who knew him during those years could imagine him with carpenters' tools in his soft, clumsy hands.

Whitman's poet would embrace the "immediate age" like a lover; yet the "age" of his poems was, in fact, not quite contemporary. In this displacement he resembled the great social novelists of the century—Dickens and Balzac—who described a world of rapidly changing cities and denatured social relationships, in which the passing of even a decade had begun, just barely, to reveal a new destiny. Whitman's pastoral America was contemporary, and it was not. His society of free selves attuned to their best by a journeyman singer who bestrides the country, was a dream that drew broadly on themes of decades-old fantasy. It reflected the American legend of democratic giants, such as Ben Franklin, Daniel Boone, and Andrew Jackson: ordinary extraordinary men who stood so tall, that, as in Emerson's famous dictum, the country might seem to be the shadow cast by their strong presences. Whitman's fantasy embroidered and clarified a vision that remembered a past several decades earlier, when Brooklyn was a collection of scattered villages, and Broadway still had the leafy busyness of city and country intertwined.

Whitman's unifying vision resembled the city he observed with tireless curiosity, as it expanded up Manhattan Island and across the villages of Brooklyn onto the landfill of South Brooklyn. He saw as no other writer of his century. Superimposing his fantasy of a younger America on a reality that was visibly pulling apart, socially and politically, Whitman would combine his poetic realism (remember his admiration for the daguerreotype) with an expansive form that was a version of American pastoral.

The "realism" of the nineteenth-century novel was not simply a form of reportage. It was an attempt to expose the "lies" of Romantic fantasy and the appalling consequences of contemporary social change. The realist was not a celebrant of the "immediate age." He rendered, with cruel exactness, the disintegration of values, personalities, hopes. His essential landscape was the city—for Europeans, a frantic, frightening place, full of building and destruction: the epic gloom of Dickens's London, of Baudelaire's Paris, of Zola. This would be the burden of the American realists, too: Frank Norris, Dreiser. The city became an analogue of Darwinian nature: a place so random and brutal that the specifically human values of morality and religion, compassion, communal feelings, were replaced by the pressures of natural selection.

When Americans of Whitman's time saw the city at all, they saw it as a place where the democratic dream had gone smash; where Europe had gained a fatal toehold. A decade earlier, from Concord village, Emerson had launched his cultural challenge to an America of small-town lyceums frequented by literate farmers and merchants. Emerson's admiring letter to Whitman in 1855, upon reading *Leaves of Grass,* is one of the brave surprises of America's literary history. Yet Emerson was never comfortable with Whitman, or with his city, and Whitman played to the hilt his part of a bad city boy. We wonder at the bravado that led the unknown poet to bring his famous patron—a man he had just publicly called "Master"—to a fireman's club on Mercer Street, in

1856. Was he simply showing off as the greatest democrat in the world, as he had to Thoreau a few months earlier? Or was he underscoring the specific power of his idea of America: that the city was its home and its form. For Whitman, the city was "democratic turbulence" incarnate.

There is an uncanny parallel between his miscellaneous form-less-seeming poems and the oceanlike miscellany of the city, as seen, for example, from lower Broadway, "up over the porpoise-backs of the omnibuses, as they lift and toss in that unquiet sea, and over the tossing spray of ribbons and plumes that give back rain-bows to the eyes of him that gazes on the living waves."

In the eighteenth century, another self-educated journalist, Daniel Defoe, had glorified London as a great arena of self making and saw in it a human frontier ready to be colonized by the initiative of such as Moll Flanders or Robinson Crusoe. To master the city, one had to be somewhat criminal, like Moll; one had to be self-willed and sharkish. Transgression became a normal enterprise, in a world that shoved social levels and moral norms into a heap. Whitman, too, grasped the moral revolution contained in his idea of the city. He made it a signature of his poetic "self," who included the criminal and the prostitute, the Bowery "bhoy" and the poor, among his multitude of lovers. *Leaves of Grass* is the voice of a wayward, slightly dangerous man, who calls for "comrades," while also warning them against himself; who flirts boldly with the polite taboos of his age, in particular the sexual taboos. His poems celebrating male love are so unequivocal, so limpid, that they challenged with virtual impunity, the even deeper taboo surrounding homosexuality. Nothing, not even the poems of "Calamus," could make Americans confront that sealed subject openly enough even to be outraged. It is as if the "Calamus" poems were not read, as if they slipped through blanks in the minds of readers who were so disgusted by Whitman's more conventionally erotic poems that James Russell Lowell threw his book into the fire, and Thoreau complained, "it is as if the beasts spoke."

When Whitman called himself "one of the roughs," he was not simply referring to his shaggy beard and casual workingman's out-fit. "A more despicable, dangerous, and detestable character than the New York rough does not exist," begins a contemporary article on the subject. "His chief affinities are with bar-keepers, prize-fighters, harlots and ward politicians." He stuffs ballot boxes, mugs passers-by. He is urban danger personified, the complete city dweller. The "rough" is human nature reeling out of control, as the city was human environment reeling out of control. But where Europeans and most Americans saw only the danger, Whitman, like Defoe, saw the power of personality unleashed.

Needless to say, Whitman was not a "rough," any more than he was a journeyman carpenter. He was a political journalist, a book-shop owner, a building contractor; finally, a poet. Yet the tone of his poems, the limber truthfulness of his personage make it hard even now to be sure where the poems end and the man begins. Whitman wanted very much for his reader to have this difficulty. He wanted one not to know—in contrast to one's experience with, say, Emerson, Thoreau, Dickens—that what one is faced with is a text, a voice transposed by recognizable mannerisms of style from a living throat to a book; from the loose threads of immediate experience to the woven patterns of a timeless utterance. Thoreau set out to "live deliberately" in his shack on Walden Pond and to write equally deliberately in his book. Emerson's essays raised his speaking voice to a level of compression, paradox, and wit that no conversationalist could hope for: he speaks for eternity and from eternity. The casual immediacy of Whitman's style goes further than any major writer of his century toward blurring the boundary between the life and the work.

Whitman's originality was also a deliberate provocation. Readers in Victorian America were all too ready to apply moral criteria to the books they read. Above all, a good book had to "do good" and express goodness of heart. The sentimental novels that crowded out Hawthorne and Melville obeyed this cloying formula. Whitman obeyed it, too, but in reverse. His poems were not "good," but tantalizingly "bad" and their author too, it was hinted, was "bad," as any full-bodied American was bound to be. Strong feeling could not be tailored to esthetic or moral limits. To be flooded by the "immediate age," especially an age of noisy streets and miscellaneous crowds, was to dissolve the close boundaries of the moral self, along with the equally close boundaries of rhyme and iambic rhythm.

CHAPTER 4

"A Copious Book Man"

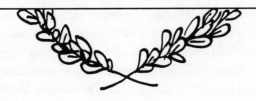

1

WHITMAN'S LIFE was surprisingly "uneventful," his younger brother George once wrote; and the early 1850s appear to have been as lacking in event as any. Family responsibilities; the house building Whitman undertook with his brothers and ailing father; some journalism; plenty of opera, city streets, and ferry rides; visits with his painter friends; summers at his sister Mary's in Greenport. None of the literary friendships we associate with a writer's shaping years. Only Emily Dickinson was as formidably alone. Yet during these years, Whitman developed a voice capable of rendering his experience as a working-class man and a city man. By stepping outside the institution of literature—not a simple step, but an intuitive and crafty one, for which he had little precedent— Whitman stepped into the formless tangle of the present age, armed with a tone of voice that could "digest hard iron," as Marianne Moore wrote of the ostrich, that unwieldy, powerful symbol of the poet's miscellaneous temperament.

These choices arrived at stubbornly and silently, while living amid his semi-literate family, must be borne in mind when we ask what properly literary influences Whitman experienced during these elusive years. What congenial books did he come across in the Astor Library, where he spent many of his days; in the articles he annotated; in the few books he owned and kept by him? Whitman's intellectual solitude was not as complete as he wanted his readers to believe. He had the company of books. After Gay Wilson Allen's and Floyd Stovall's patient work of detection, Whitman's reliance on books is no longer a secret or even an issue. Americans in the nineteenth century were probably the most bookish people on earth, and Whitman would react against this in a few years by creating a belligerently unliterary style such as might come from a man who had never read anything more than a newspaper. Yet, for all the brilliant deception of his poetic style, Whitman was no less a reader of books than Thoreau or Melville, as his voluminous notes and his conversations in old age with Horace Traubel testify. He read, as we have seen, to garner materials for his poems: Charles Lyell, on the new science of geology; Denison Olmsted and O. M. Mitchel, on astronomy; George Robins Glidden, on ancient Egypt; articles on Hindu epic; books of travel; census reports; newspaper articles. He read also to strengthen his idea of a representative voice; a hero-poet who was, paradoxically, an ordinary man anchored in the toil of daily life. How could the last truly become the first, as it was claimed in the New Testament? How could the laborer, enmeshed in the "immediate age," attain bardic heights?

Ever since Wordsworth, this question had become a Romantic commonplace. The literary "genius" for whom Emerson and the Young Americans scanned the horizon in the 1840s, was to speak from and for the "people." Like the Bible or like Shakespeare, his poems would be the products not of a cultivated class but of the nation itself.

Carlyle showered extravagant praise on the worker-poet of his "Corn-Law Rhymes" essay. In *Sartor Resartus* (1833–34), a book that fascinated Whitman, Carlyle wrote dramatically of the divine inner speech that had been revealed to the Quaker, George Fox, while he sat "in his stall; working on tanned hides, amid pincers,

paste-horns, rosin, swine-bristles, and a nameless flood of rubbish."
Carlyle's "weird," "rapt," style affected Whitman deeply. Carlyle
wrote that he honored first among all men the "toil-worn Craftsman that with earth-made Implement laboriously conquers the
Earth"; after him the artist,

who is seen toiling for the spiritually indispensable; not daily bread, but
the bread of Life. . . . Unspeakably touching is it, however, when I find
both dignities united; and he that must toil outwardly for the lowest of
man's wants, is also toiling inwardly for the highest. . . . Such a one will
take thee back to Nazareth itself; thou wilt see the splendour of Heaven
spring forth from the humblest depths of Earth, like a light shining in
great darkness.

Whitman was particularly stirred by a book belonging to his
mother which he claimed to have read so often that "the sheets
[were] often loose, ready to drop out." This was George Sand's
Consuelo, the story of a simple country girl who becomes a singer
of surpassing fame. When, in 1858 Whitman conceived of a "new
school" of oratory, "far more direct, close, animated, and fuller of
live tissue and muscle than any hitherto," he compared the effect
he sought to "Consuelo's free and strong Italian style" when she
sings in the "respectable village church." In the scene Whitman
was referring to, Consuelo has come back to perform in her native
village after a dazzling career in the capitals of Europe:

A sort of dizziness seized upon her, and as it happened to the pythonesses
in the paroxism of their divine crises . . . she was led to manifest the
emotion with which she overflowed, by the expression that was natural
to her. She began to sing in a brilliant voice.

George Sand's overheated style suggested to Whitman a connection
between the feats of the operatic voice which gave him such intense
pleasure, and the bardic expansion—the "song"—he sought for his
poetry.

Sand's sequel to *Consuelo, The Countess of Rudolstadt* contains several scenes that appear to have influenced Whitman even more
directly. In the novel, two young men visit a ruined country
church, where they hear a journeyman laborer playing beautiful
melodies on a violin. The local countrypeople hold the man in

awe, with his craggy face and his quiet muscular body: "thick grey hair waving around his face increased the brilliancy of his large black eyes. His mouth had an indefinable expression of strength and simplicity." The journeyman violinist is, in reality, an esoteric master whose very music expresses a form of divine philosophy. When the young men implore him to reveal what he knows,

he composed the most magnificent poem that can be conceived. He interpreted all the religions of the past, all the mysteries of the temples, of the poems and of the legislations; all the efforts, all the tendencies, all the labors of anterior humanity. In those things which had always seemed to us dead or condemned, he discovered the elements of life, and, from the darkness of the very fables, he made to shine the lightnings of truth. He explained the ancient myths; he established in his lucid and ingenious demonstration, all the bonds, all the points of contact of the religions among themselves. He showed us the true requirements of humanity, more or less understood by the legislators, more or less realized by the people. He reconstituted before our eyes the unity of life in humanity, the unity of doctrine in religion; and from all the materials scattered in the old and new world, he formed the bases of his future world. . . . He filled up the abysses of history which had so terrified us. He unrolled in a single infinite spiral the myriads of consecrated bandages which enveloped the mummy of science. And when we had received with the quickness of the flash what he showed to us with the rapidity of the lightning, when we had seized the aggregate of his vision, and the past, father of the present, stood before us like the luminous man of the Apocalypse, he stopped.

There was plenty here to fascinate Whitman: a rhapsodic poem embracing all the human prospect; an orator-poet whose words approximate the condition of music; a humble journeyman who is also a bard and a sage; a benign old man such as Whitman had always loved, and would himself become, even while relatively young.

Whitman casually pillaged the books he read, rephrasing and "translating," until the original has become all but invisible. Paraphrase was a profound gift of Whitman's. By means of it, he "digested hard iron," while preserving the unliterary diction of his poems. We catch him at it in one of his early notebooks, where he enlarged a passage from *The Countess of Rudolstadt,* into a paragraph rich with suggestions for his poetry. Here is Sand:

The unknown refused to explain himself. "What could I say to you that I have not said in another (my own) language? Is it my fault that you have not understood me? You think I wished to speak to your senses, and it was my soul spoke to you. What do I say! It was the soul of the whole of humanity that spoke to you through mine."

And here, elaborately playful, is Whitman:

Every soul has its own individual language, often unspoken or lamely (feebly) spoken; but a true fit for that man and perfectly (haltingly) adapted for his use.—The truths I tell to you or to any other may not be plain to you, because I do not translate them fully from my idiom into yours.— If I could do so, and do it well, they would be as apparent to you as they are to me; for they are truths.—No two have exactly the same language, and the great translator and joiner of the whole is the poet. He has the divine grammar of all tongues, and says indifferently and alike, How are you friend?, to the President in the midst of his cabinet, and Good day my brother, to Sambo, among the hoes of the sugar field, and both understand him and know that his speech is right.

Whitman has more than paraphrased here. Where Sand's language is vague, he particularizes; he gives a sampling of the idioms his "joiner" can speak, and they are American. He does not only echo Sand, he improves her. The result provides material for Whitman's 1855 preface and for a short poem he included in that edition and, a year later, expanded, calling it "Song of the Answerer":

Every existence has its idiom . . . every thing has an idiom and tongue;
He resolves all tongues into his own, and bestows it upon men . . . and
    any man translates . . . and any man translates himself also:
One part does not counteract another part . . . He is the joiner. . . . He
    sees how they join.

Throughout *The Countess of Rudolstadt* are sentences that might have been written by Whitman:

There is but one sure road to truth; it is that which corresponds to complete human nature, to human nature developed under all its aspects.

no one lives in vain; nothing is lost.

And we also, we are on the road, we walk forward! Life is a journey.

As Whitman cast about for a conception of art that was large enough for his bardic ambition, yet humble enough to include his actual life and experience, he apparently came upon George Sand's journeyman-poet. Whitman's contradictory nature overrode ideology and trampled on principles. Italian opera? French novels? Foreign models alien to the natural springs an American genius ought to drink from? Clearly Whitman knew when to set aside his ideological preferences. There seems little doubt that he used *The Countess of Rudolstadt.* But questions of influence are never simple, especially where Whitman is concerned. Many of Sand's ideas, even her phrasing, can be found elsewhere. Her exalted humanitarian prose and her sentimental pantheism belonged to the age. We cannot be sure that Whitman read Jules Michelet's *The People,* for example; although years later, a poem of Whitman, "To the Man-of-War Bird," would paraphrase another text by the French historian. Yet we hear in *The People* a voice that might be Whitman's:

This book is more than a book, it is myself. . . . Receive this book of *The People,* because it is you, because it is I. . . .
Son of the people . . . I have lived with them, I know them, they are myself . . . I unite them all in my own person.
The people in the highest sense of the word, is seldom to be found in the people . . . it exists in its truth, and at its highest power in the man of genius; in him resides the great soul . . . the whole world (vibrates) at the least word he utters. . . . That voice is the voice of the people; mute of itself, it speaks in this man. . . .
The rise of the people, the progress, is often nowadays compared to the invasion of the *Barbarians* . . . straining to give everything at once—leaves fruit and flowers—till it breaks or distorts the branches. But those who start up thus with the sap of the people in them, do not the less introduce into art a new burst of life and principle of youth; or at least leave on it the impress of a great result.

There are echoes of other voices. In 1852 appeared a new edition of *Festus,* a copious third-rate epic by the English poet Philip Bailey. *Festus,* first published in 1839, was based on the Faust story and contains twenty thousand lines in which divine love triumphs over evil, and such useful Whitmanesque words and images as "deific," "Uranus," an "electric" touch, a poet who "wakes and walks by night." A year later, the Scottish poet Alexander Smith published a long dramatic poem, *A Life Drama,* in which he announced,

a mighty poet whom this age shall choose
To be its spokesman to all coming times.

These lines impressed Whitman so much that he quoted them in an anonymous review of his own book, two years later. And no wonder! Smith's young yearning bard was, prophetically, named Walter.

Whitman was comfortably able to digest the flabby romanticism of English poets who inflated their careers by flooding the American market with their books. And not only their books. In 1851— his arrival trumpeted beforehand in the New York papers—came Martin Farquhar Tupper, whom Whitman had praised in the *Eagle* for the loosely written dithyrambs of his best-selling *Proverbial Philosophy* first published in 1838. Tupper was lionized, and over the years *Proverbial Philosophy* sold a million copies in America, especially to women who loved his "abundant imagery" and "the pure morality everywhere inculcated." The book was rough, loose, easy to digest. Its Biblical phraseology provided a tone of sublimity. Owing to its diffuse, rambling line, the polite reader could take in large amounts of poetry without needing to furrow his or her brow. Tupper was something of a comic figure to the educated American audience. Hawthorne found him good-hearted but a little ludicrous. To Whitman, however, Tupper was no joke. He demonstrated that a poet could reach an audience vaster even than Longfellow's; that poetry could make use of the printing industry's new capacity to produce large numbers of books inexpensively, and get them into the hands of uncounted readers. Whitman was the first important poet to shape his conception to the possibilities of what we would now call the mass media. When he wrote, in 1855, "The proof of a poet is that his country absorbs him as affectionately as he absorbs it," he was not simply making a pious wish, thanks to the steam-driven rotary presses that, only a decade before, had given Americans the penny newspaper and now gave them, along with Martin Farquhar Tupper, the much-deplored deluge of feminine novelists. An English reviewer, in 1857, called Whitman "a wild Tupper of the west"; and Henry James, a few years later, in an article he wrote for the *Nation,* had the "melancholy task," of agreeing in print. Whitman did not share their scruples. He liked Tupper's *Proverbial Philosophy* and was not ashamed to find in it added license to cast aside traditional forms and rhythms.

Whitman's rhythmic experiment was not completely foreign to his contemporaries. Ruskin and Carlyle had both written a form of rhythmic prose that slid easily into poetry. As Bliss Perry points out, the journals of Thoreau and Emerson are full of rhapsodic passages and sketches for poems, reflecting "a metrical and rhythmical lawlessness that was in the very air, although the classical training of Thoreau and Emerson doubtless made them hesitate to print these fresh formless transcripts of emotional experience." Whitman's flight from culture into nature had been enacted for more than a generation by other poets, who promoted a new freedom from the chained cadences of the iamb or the ballad—and, in fact, a new prosody. We see how deliberate this movement was in William Blake's preface to his *Prophetic Books,* which can stand as a (largely unread) manifesto for the prosodic freedom writers came to insist on in succeeding decades:

When this verse was first dictated to me I considered a Monotonous Cadence like that used by Milton and Shakespeare, and writers of English Blank Verse, derived from the modern bondage of Rhyming to be a necessary and indispensable part of the verse. But I soon found that in the mouth of a true Orator, such monotony was not only awkward, but as much a bondage as rhyme itself. I therefore have produced a variety in every line, both of cadences and number of syllables. Every word and every letter is studied and put into its fit place: the terrific numbers are reserved for the terrific parts, the mild and gentle for the mild and gentle parts, and the prosaic for inferior parts: all are necessary to each other. Poetry Fetter'd Fetters the Human Race.

Here was a doctrine Whitman could accept, if not from Blake, whom at the time he had not read, then from Macpherson's *Ossian* which he remembered declaiming by the seashore in his youth; from Carlyle and Emerson; but most powerfully from the English

Bible, which offered the full range of rhythmic effects Whitman found congenial. The Bible was still America's inescapable book, even to a family like the Whitmans, with their tradition of radical politics and their anticlericalism. From sources as different as Carlyle and the Young Americans, Whitman heard the call for a poetry capable of creating a new "Mythus" and a new Bible. It is no wonder that he schooled himself in the prose poetry of the "old" Bible at this time of tumultuous inner change. In Bliss Perry's words:

Here was precisely that natural stylistic variation between the "terrific," the "gentle," and the "inferior," parts so desired by William Blake. Here were lyric fragments, of consummate beauty, imbedded in narrative or argumentative passages. The parallelism which constituted the peculiar structural device of Hebrew poetry gave the English of the King James version a heightened rhythm without destroying the flexibility and freedom natural to prose. In this strong rolling music, this intense feeling, these concrete words expressing primal emotions and daring terms of bodily sensation, Whitman found the charter for the book he wished to write.

If Whitman was looking for a link between the prosodic freedom of the Bible, and a voice that could range through the "immediate age," with the flexibility of a contemporary newspaper, he may have found it in a striking long poem commemorating the 1851 Crystal Palace Exhibition in London. Written by the popular poet, Samuel Warren, the poem is entitled *The Lily and the Bee, A Lyrical Soliloquy*. It was first published in America in 1851 and republished two years later for the opening of New York's Crystal Palace Exhibition, where Whitman spent afternoons and evenings for more than a year. *The Lily and the Bee* celebrates "Man—a unity" amid his creations, during a day, a night, and an early morning at the Crystal Palace. As the poem ranges from exhibit to exhibit, it uses almost every stylistic device we now associate with Whitman. In some cases we seem to hear his very cadences: "Prussia, proud, learned, thoughtful, martial." The sweep and irregularity of the poem, its world-embracing stanzas, sliding from prose into poetry and back again, are everywhere reminiscent of Whitman's broad manner:

THE MAKING OF A POET: THE 1850s

In dusky, rainless EGYPT now!
Mysterious memories come crowding round—
From misty Mizraim to Ibrahim—
Abrama! Joseph! Pharaoh's Plagues!
Shepherd Kings! Sesostris! . . .
Behold Napoleon, deeply intent on the great project!
See him, while the tide of the Red Sea is out, on the self-same sites
　　traversed three thousand years before by the children of Israel!
He drinks at the Wells of Moses, at the foot of Mount Sinae:
He returns and so the tide: The shades of night approach . . .

A unit unperceived,
I sink into the living stream again!

Like Whitman, Warren expands and narrows his kaleidoscopic vision centering on the hovering personage of the poet who explores
the glass and cast-iron "hive" of his fellows:

Poor Bee! Dost thou see ME?
And note my speculations,
Thinking so curiously, all so confident!
Of thee, thy Being, Doings!
—Myself! the While!
Unconsciously contemplated by Intelligence, unseen!
Transcending mortal man. . . .
This moment loftily scanning ME,
Suspending for awhile his cares sublime,
And gazing down on ME,
On all MY Fellows clustering round
In this our Hive,
Of fancied splendour! vastness!

We cannot know for certain that Whitman read *The Lily and the
Bee,* as we know he read *A Life Drama* and Bailey's *Festus,* but the
echoes of diction make it hard to believe that he did not. The
Crystal Palace was one of Whitman's passions in 1853 and 1854: a
heightened analogue to the wealth of the city's store windows, the
cargoes heaped in healthy disorder along the quays, the "oceanlike" thronging of the crowds on Broadway.

While writing *Leaves of Grass,* Whitman enjoined himself to
"make no quotations and no reference to any other writers." He

wrote and rewrote his book, to get out all the "stock touches," all the literary echoes. It was a hard job, he remembered. Yet in the end he covered his tracks so well that we have come to know him as a purely intuitive poet who had only an approximate idea of his best gifts—a man who had, indeed, begun afresh, with all the mixed blessings of unliterate newness. Yet not only did Whitman read, he scavenged, paraphrased, and pastiched. He looked alertly for hints to advance his poetic experiment. And he found them, everywhere. In George Sand and Michelet; in inflated English bards who impressed the popular audience; in the Bible which, despite his respect for Tom Paine's free thinking, he read, if not religiously, at least pragmatically, as a quarry for tonal and rhythmic effects.

We are unlikely to know everything Whitman read, although the list we have is long enough. Years later, in 1880, he visited the mental hospital that Maurice Bucke directed in Ontario, Canada; and Bucke described him sitting in the library with a dozen books open before him, not so much reading as savoring ideas, turns of style. I like this scene of Whitman at his reading table. He was not so much a reader, as a gleaner. He read widely, if not always profoundly. He was like the "young giant" of his *Eagle* editorial, some years before, nourished by a life-giving air of words, of print, which fed his independence. Whitman wrote the following comment in the margin of an article entitled "Thoughts on Reading," which he had clipped from the *Whig Review* and annotated repeatedly over a period of years: "all kinds of light reading, novels, newspapers, gossip, etc., serve as manure for the few *great productions,* are indispensable or perhaps are premises to something better." Whitman might be describing his own reading habits here. He was not a self-sufficient bard, "letting nature speak without check," or ignorant of voices that expressed similar ideas and strove toward similar effects. Whitman lived in a cultural air full of hints and suggestions. More than most writers, he mulled them over until they became part of his own nature, and he drew on them deeply when it came to articulating his art—not only deeply, but variously, mingling the diction of bad poets with the excited arguments of literary nationalists like Margaret Fuller, whose famous taunt he remembered forty years later: "It does not follow, because the United States print and read more books, magazines and newspapers than all the rest of the world, that they really have, therefore, a literature." Whitman tore Fuller's chapter on American literature from her book *Papers on Literature and Art* and kept it by him as a reminder, no doubt, that a morning's work was yet to be done in his self-consciously new country:

What suits Great Britain, with her insular position and consequent need to concentrate and intensify her life, her limited monarchy, and spirit of trade, does not suit a mixed race, continually enriched with new blood from other stocks and most unlike that of our first descent, with ample field and verge enough to range in and leave every impulse free, and abundant opportunity to develop a genius, wide and full as our rivers, flowery, luxuriant and impassioned as our vast prairies, rooted in strength as the rocks on which the Puritan fathers landed.

That such a genius is to rise and work in this hemisphere we are confident; equally so that scarce the first faint streaks of that day's dawn are yet visible.

Whitman loved to hear this kind of call, and he heard it everywhere, as a rumble in the press, the trumpet call of American particularity: because American nature was grandiose, Americans had to speak with a new voice; because American rivers were wide, her books, too, had to be abundant and natural. It was easy for conservatives like Richard Henry Dana (author of *Two Years Before the Mast*) and his Boston friends to make fun of this preposterous equation which they took as proof, if any were needed, that the day was far off when well-read men, in comfortable circumstances, would be able to make an adequate literature for their country. Within only a few decades, American writers had forgotten the high-flown claims of our first literary chauvinism; and the poet Sidney Lanier, making affectionate fun of a poet he admired, could write: "As nearly as I can make out, Whitman's argument seems to be, that, because a prairie is wide, therefore debauchery is admirable, and because the Mississippi is long, therefore every American is God."

Yet in the 1840s, literary nationalists like Margaret Fuller and her friends at the *Democratic Review* believed that Americans lived under a unique dispensation; that here, in this gargantuan land, furrowed by a restless population, nature and culture interpenetrated with unparalleled urgency.

Whitman listened to this excitable chorus. He read its claims in that volatile American institution, the daily and weekly press which, by the 1840s, had become an expression of the country itself: voluble, contradictory, articulate; a seedbed of public emotions, often outrageous and violent, but comprehensive too. Fuller was right: simply because Americans had so many newspapers and magazines to read did not mean they had a literature. But Fuller also saw what Whitman would see more profoundly: a national consciousness was being forged in that stew of ephemeral journalistic language. As a journalist with literary ambitions, Whitman must have enjoyed the poem by Cornelius Matthews which Margaret Fuller quoted in her essay—a poem celebrating the press for its epic sowing of the seeds of American life:

As shakes the canvass of a thousand ships,
    Struck by a heavy land-breeze, far at sea,
Ruffle the thousand broad sheets of the land,
    Filled with the people's breath of potency.
. . . .
How beautiful who scatters, wide and free,
    The gold-bright seeds of loved and loving truth!
By whose perpetual hand, each day supplied,
    Leaps to new life the empire's heart of youth.
. . . .
There is an inwrought life in every hour,
    Fit to be chronicled at large and told.
'Tis thine to pluck to light its secret power,
    And on the air its many-colored heart unfold.

No wonder Whitman had to work hard to eliminate the literary echoes from his poetry. The "nature" he let speak "without check," as if he had never read "such a thing as a book," was surprisingly compounded of books and more books; was fed liberally by the press; was left fallow in a mind saturated by the voices of American public life and American public speech. Whitman was right in his canny way to underplay specific questions of influence and source. He was lying, but he knew what he was saying. In those early years, he had not merely been susceptible to influences; he had soaked them up. His very lack of formal education had left him free to read without regard for standards, taking from Aeschylus as well as from Frederika Bremer, from Emerson as well as from Fanny Fern. There is something glorious and bewildering in Whitman's esthetic sympathies. Yet they are his signature and helped create his remarkable style.

From early on, Whitman had turned his excitable nature outward. As a Democrat and a journalist, he had thrown himself into the public life of the country, made its flightiness and its obsessions his own. His editorials had cultivated a crude "bardic" tone, impersonal, larger than life; they were a daily epic crowded into columns and transported with awesome directness into the hands of readers. His passions had been public before they were private; he had lived the nation's life before he had lived his own. As a young man, growing up in the 1840s, it had been easy, even exalting, to do this. For America, in the Jacksonian lingo, was not merely a nation but the hope of all humanity. Whitman had fled himself to find himself on the largest of all stages, and he liked the roominess, the expanded emotions. He liked himself better as an American than as the secretive gloomy son of a decaying family that roped him in with its tensions, its incomprehension.

As a poet, he would use his early training. His poems would become an argument with others, not with himself. The larger life he had thrown himself into as a young man and a journalist had been discredited by the mediocrity of 1850s politics. Now Whitman would create it again. No longer a journalist, but a poet, he would make it his legend: hopeful, poignant, arrogant. That he could have this aim indicates how accurate his youthful instincts had been. He had known early on that he had to live large or not at all. He had to be filled with the passions of the nation—its slogans, its daily ephemera (the "immediate age"), its newspapers, its literary fashions, its public voices—or be silent. Whitman was profoundly a man of his times, played upon by every stray breeze, every gust and storm of the national life. Practically speaking, this means that he read, talked, gossiped; that he lived in the streets, the newspapers, the lecture halls, and the libraries.

2

Reading was so much a part of Whitman's life that he could use it as a figure for the mind's natural activity. Broadway contained "many lessons"—he wrote in an article for *Life Illustrated*—some of them "so plain that they who walk may read," while others required exegetical forays up flights of stairs, to where an alert "reader" found other "lessons" that were invisible from the sidewalk. In 1853 and 1854, Whitman frequently climbed such stairs, at "the gayest and most crowded part of Broadway" "into a suite of three large halls" that were "dim, dreamy, silent, eloquent." In these second-story rooms at 659 Broadway, an Englishman, Dr. Henry Abbot, exhibited his personal collection of Egyptian artifacts, while trying to persuade the city to buy them from him, to form a municipal museum.

Henry Abbot was plump and weary-looking, and sported a Turkish mustache. The New York Historical Society has a portrait of him wearing full Turkish regalia: a plumed fez, dark robes over a high-collared white shirt, a sash, with the curved handle of a sword showing; in his hand, the ivory mouthpiece of a hookah. One day, by appointment, he decked himself out for Whitman in his full costume.

Abbot had practiced medicine in Cairo for thirty years, while amassing his collection of antiquities at a personal cost, it is said, of one hundred thousand dollars. When the expense became too great, friends persuaded him to bring his collection to New York and sell it there. But New Yorkers were unpredictable. They went to the opera decked out in all their jewels and stood in line to get into P. T. Barnum's museum of freaks; they flocked down to Nassau Street to visit the Fowler & Wells exhibit of skulls. But Dr. Abbot's Egyptian Museum never became a favorite, and often Whitman was Abbot's only visitor, "a solitary gazer amid these wonderful relics." By the time the New York Historical Society got money together to buy the collection in 1860, Abbot had gone back to Egypt and was dead. Whitman published an article entitled "The Egyptian Museum," in *Life Illustrated,* shortly after Abbot left in 1855, having had enough of those gloomy second-story rooms containing his life's passion, which no one else seemed to care about.

Whitman remembered paying many visits to the Egyptian Museum and having "long talks with [Dr.Abbot] in connection with my reading of many books and reports on Egypt—its antiquities, history, and how things and the scenes really look, and what the old relics stand for, as near as we can now get." On friendly evenings, Abbot took Whitman around the exhibit personally and explained to him the statuettes of hawk-headed men and "the sandals, boots, knives, spoons, needles, lamps, combs . . . hollow reeds containing powder and ointments, toilet-boxes, ornaments shaped like lotus flowers, headrests, bronze mirrors"; the gold figures of "insects, bugs and beetles"; the "strips of papyrus containing whole narratives, often representing pictorially the lives of persons and their funeral ceremonies, and their judgment before the gods after death." Whitman remembered in particular a "colossal head," carved in limestone, with almond-shaped eyes and a calm expression, probably the face "of some great ruling person."

Unlike the Greeks, whose statues stood out chastely against the barbarity of nature, the Egyptians combined the animal and human worlds into a network of symbols: men with the heads of dogs or birds; a lion with a woman's face; beetles made of gold, and worshiped. The high and low were wrought into a mysterious pattern which became, as if by inner development, a language: that visual enigma of signs and stylized pictures known as hieroglyphics. These fascinated Whitman: "They are wonderful . . . as distinct as anything cut last week in New York or Boston." Having read George Sand's exalted idea of the "hermetic" mysteries rooted in a romanticized Egypt; having read Carlyle and Emerson, for whom physical facts were symbols of spiritual facts, and the world a text to be deciphered with all the senses, Whitman loved the uncanny concreteness of hieroglyphics. It was as if, for the Egyptian, facts had voices; as if things, in their inmost nature, were already parts of speech. Whitman would shortly describe the "rolling earth" as a mute assemblage of languages. The grass would be "so many uttering tongues . . . a uniform hieroglyphic." The hair on his chest would become "scented herbage," resurrecting into speech the buried parts of his psyche, as Osiris, the Egyptian Christ, was buried and then resurrected by the youth and growth of spring. A few years later, an acquaintance maliciously described Whitman walking down Broadway, "with a red shirt on, open in front to show the 'scented herbage of his breast' and [comparing] himself with Christ and Osiris." Apparently Whitman was not shy about his Egyptian interest, and we glean here the cute echo of a conversation, maybe around one of the long tables at Pfaff's, the bohemian bar Whitman frequented in the late 1850s.

As he walked among Dr. Abbot's "wonderful relics" and read the books Abbot suggested to him—John G. Wilkinson's *The Manners and Customs of the Ancient Egyptians,* Glidden's *Ancient Egypt,* and others—Whitman was awed by the immensity of human time. Men had lived and died, built cities, written books, obeyed laws, "three thousand years ago—five thousand—ten thousand years ago—and probably far back beyond that." Before Abraham, Homer, and the Greeks, there had been man in all his ordinariness. Egypt, at the dawn of time, had been a kind of America.

In the country parts were agriculture, roads, canals, conveyances, barns, implements, cattle, machines. . . . In their cities were officers, streets, aqueducts, manufactures, public institutions, quays, markets, amusements. . . . They not only had books, but these books were plentiful. Epics were common. They had novels, poems, histories, essays, and all those varieties of narratives forever dear to the people.

In time's vanishing perspective, Egypt stood for the bouyancy of man; the survival of his works, in particular his art, through eras beyond imagining. All his life, Whitman would muse about lost masterpieces and forgotten genius, civilizations risen to a pinnacle and then erased without a trace. Nineveh and Babylon had survived as mere names. How many, in the earth's backward infinity, had not survived at all? "Song of Myself" contains a romance of immense numbers: "Sextillions of infidels," "quintillions of stars," "trillions of winters and summers," "a few quadrillions of eras," "a few octillions of cubic leagues." Only in the Hindu epics do we find such a scale. But Whitman need not have reached that far to conceive his romance of numbers. Measurable immensity was one of the passions of the nineteenth century. Only seventy years before, a Scottish gentleman farmer and scientist, James Hutton, had exploded the Biblical chronology which had counted six thousand years since God's seven days of creation. On his farm near Glasgow, Hutton had guessed that the earth's mountains and valleys, its cliffs, riverbeds, and beaches, had not appeared, fully formed, on the third of God's busy days but had arisen with unimaginable slowness from the actions of wind, water, and earthquake. According to the new science of geology, not six thousand years, but many millions, maybe even a few "quadrillions of eras," had matured the gargantuan nature that Thomas Cole and his Hudson River School painted in their primeval landscapes. Nature was old in its youth; its powers of renewal were charged with the measureless miracle Whitman describes in his poem "This Compost." In this ferment of renewal and change, it would not be surprising if the few known eyeblinks of human history had been preceded by other civilizations now lost. Death and forgetting were a sea upon which floated the fragile arcs of known time. Seen from this shoreless prospect, art was the human equivalent of nature's infinite powers for self-renewal and change. Whitman saw Egypt as mankind's first collective poem, its first complete embracing of nature's high and low, of man and animal, of life and its extended aftertime, death.

Napoleon's conquest of Egypt and Jean François Champollion's subsequent deciphering of the Rosetta Stone, had given rise to a new discipline, archeology. Within Whitman's own lifetime, time's backward scroll had begun to be legible. Antiquity had taken on a vastness, within which Greece and Rome were almost recent. Geology, too, had won the day. The earth could be seen as a text written in mountains and rocks; its story was the oldest ever told. The nineteenth century was a heyday of scientific popularizing. Charles Lyell's lectures on geology drew crowds all over England and America, and Whitman probably heard him when he visited New York in 1842. Whitman almost surely read such works as S. G. Goodrich's *A Glance at the Physical Sciences* of 1844 and Richard Owens's *Key to the Geology of the Globe* of 1857, as he paraphrased passages from these books in several poems. Geological time offered a scale Whitman plays upon in "Song of Myself":

I am an acme of things accomplished, and an encloser of things to be.

My feet strike an apex of the apices of the stairs,
On every step bunches of ages, and larger bunches between the steps,
All duly traveled—and still I mount and mount.

Rise after rise bow the phantoms behind me,
Afar down I see the huge first Nothing, the vapor from the nostrils of
   death,
I know I was even there. . . . I waited unseen and always,
And slept while God carried me through the lethargic mist,
And took my time . . . and took no hurt from the foetid carbon. . . .

Cycles ferried my cradle, rowing and rowing like cheerful boatmen;
For room to me stars kept aside in their own rings,
They sent influences to look after what was to hold me.

Before I was born out of my mother generations guided me,
My embryo had never been torpid . . . nothing could overlay it;
For it the nebula cohered to an orb . . . the long slow strata piled to rest
   it on . . . vast vegetables gave it sustenance,
Monstrous sauroids transported it in their mouths and deposited it with
   care.

Here is part of Whitman's cosmic comedy: a form of boasting, of
frontier arm flapping with a broad wink and a shuffle. This Daniel
Boone cohered out of a nebula; his development required "trillions
of summers and winters." Pierre Simon de Laplace's nebula theory
of the earth's origins was still popular in Whitman's day, and its
idea of solid nature developing out of a cosmic fog appealed to his
temperament: he, too, had "sweated through fog," had cohered
bizarrely and slowly after a prolonged adolescence.

Whitman's poetry is filled with references to the sciences, often
in the form of enigmatic allusions, some of which Joseph Beaver
has cannily detected in his study *Walt Whitman and Science.* For the
most part, Whitman got his science from the popularizers and the
newspapers; although as a light sleeper, he seems to have observed
the night skies often enough to fill his writing with descriptions
that Beaver was able to verify with an almanack. Whitman's "starry
heavens," it turns out, were no more "imagined" than were his
city streets.

The crucial discoveries of science must invariably be made twice:

first by the scientist and then, in quite a different way, by ordinary people who discover, one day, that their world has been unalterably changed. Pascal in the seventeenth century had been "terrified by the silence of infinite spaces." Alone in his time, he had grasped the lesson of a recent optical tool invented by a Dutchman, and trained on the cozy arch of the night sky. A glance through the telescope had dissolved the heavenly spheres, with their music, their crystal geometry, and replaced them by an undefined space in which earth and sun were mere specks on the outskirts of infinity. Yet only in the nineteenth century was astronomy's "second" discovery truly made, not simply in the observatory (or in the mind of an isolated moralist) but in the lecture halls and in popular handbooks.

The idiom of a culture hangs together in unexpected ways. As the Romantic poets hungered for the "infinite," meaning a limitless upward aspiring of the psyche, the geologist and the astronomer supplied palpable and measurable "infinities," enlarging all space and all time. As a journalist and lover of progress, Whitman had no trouble accepting the prodigious advancements of technology that were reshaping his world: the steam engine and the steamship, the telegraph, the motorized rotor press, the transatlantic cable. Wordsworth retired to the Wey Valley, to tuck himself into changelessness. But Whitman was not shy about change. How could he be, when the very streets of his city underwent a dance of change from year to year, even month to month.

Let me not claim too much for Whitman's knowledge of science or for his Egyptology. What he knew, he knew in bits and pieces, as he knew most things. But no poet of his century grasped, as Whitman did, the uses of the immensity that science had suddenly made available to the imagination. Reading the exuberant lessons of Lyell on geology, and especially of O. M. Mitchel on astronomy, Whitman saw the confines of the universe fall away and was dazzled.

In the adventurous state of mind which produced the ecstatic prose of his notebooks, Whitman saw connections everywhere. I called him a magpie, a digester of "hard iron," compared with the New England scholars, with their prodigious libraries and their Germanic thoroughness. But Whitman had what these scholars never had, what not even Emerson or Thoreau had: a naturally omnivorous mind. Call it journalistic. Suppose it was formed by the professional habit of composing newspaper pages for all the jarring and ill-fitting tidbits of a day's news. Imagine this rangy reportorial eye casting about for images to express the eruptive moments Whitman was beginning to place at the center of his psychic life, images that might be used in poems. The books he had been reading on astronomy and geology already met him halfway; they were filled with a sense of wonder at the "deep time" of the earth's unimaginable past, at the fertile vastness of the cosmos, and tried to communicate that wonder with touches of speculative poetry. Such books were a rich trove for Whitman's gift of paraphrase.

CHAPTER 5

"A Strange Miscellany"

WHEN the transcendentalist Bronson Alcott rode the ferry over to Brooklyn to visit Whitman in the fall of 1856, he noticed an unmade bed with a full chamberpot under it, and three pictures—"a Hercules, a Bacchus, and a satyr"—pasted on the "rude walls" of Whitman's bedroom. Alcott half jokingly asked which of these pictures stood for the new poet; and Whitman, with an evasive shrug, seemed to say all three. Years later, this sort of memory irked him; for in time, he came to think of himself no longer as a natural man, one of the "roughs," but as a reassuring, prematurely old father, the good gray poet he thought America needed. Something Alcott did not mention is a large nondescript trunk, maybe the one Whitman took with him on his trip to New Orleans, seven years before. But it was somewhere around, probably serving already as a repository for Whitman's past, a kind of substitute memory. In it, he deposited his odds and ends of manuscript, bundles of receipts, the articles he tore out of magazines, a file of his old editorials, pocket-sized notebooks made of folded paper, in which names and addresses mingled with book titles, scraps of poems, and anything else that drifted into his Sargasso of written bits.

This was the trunk Whitman had his mother send on to him in Washington, when he set up there in 1863. It was his one solid belonging in his drift from one roominghouse to another, during the Washington years. It migrated with him to Camden, New Jersey, where, during the last decades of his life, it spilled over onto tables and chairs, so that to the visitors to his room on Mickle Street, Whitman seemed to be drowning in paper.

Not only did he hold on tenaciously to these fugitive scraps; he seems, from early on, to have lived with his pen in his hand. For years, this was his secret: the one thing he did not want to be, or look like, was a man of letters. He wanted his poems to sound as if they had come on their own, in the spare time left to him from merely living. An air of slowly moving flesh; a kind of garrulous ease in public, sitting next to the drivers on streetcars or in Pfaff's: this was how he wanted to be known. Writing was his secret because the poems were not supposed to be literature. Yet Whitman wrote all the time. Not only poems; but notes for lectures he never gave; stray opinions on various subjects; the names of young men, usually workingmen or soldiers, with, rarely, a personal note: "slept with me" raising the obvious question but not really answering it, the phrase not having yet become the euphemism for sex that it is today. By the early 1850s, Whitman began to accumulate literary notes scrawled on scraps of paper, or in homemade notebooks of a few pinned-together pages, or in thicker bound notebooks, usually pocket-sized and therefore probably carried around with him on his frequent excursions around the city. With the doggedness of a self-taught man, he accumulated notes on the great writers of world tradition, collected articles on the history of the English language, and compiled a personal handbook of vernacular expressions, often with a note reminding him where he'd heard them spoken.

Very rarely are these reams of notes, made on odds and ends of used paper, personally revealing; they are never intimate. Their connection to Whitman's published work is spotty. Yet he wrote them tirelessly, as if he needed this daily buckshot of words, this flotsam of language, however trivial.

For a while during the Civil War, the role of the notebooks changed, as Whitman poured into them his impressions of the hospitals, often while he sat in the long whitewashed rooms beside dying or suffering boys whom he thought of as his sons. During these years, when he served as a volunteer nurse in the Army hospitals around Washington, Whitman felt that his private life and the life of the nation had become one. The hospitals were the secret of the war; they were its inner life, so to speak; and Whitman moved through them, soothing, helping, writing. Later, in 1875, he published his jottings in *Memoranda during the War* and then, in 1883, in his compilation of autobiographical notes, *Specimen Days*. Having tried for years to form the notes into a real book, at last he gave up, deciding that their spontaneous, disorganized aspect was a good thing: a way of rendering into language the elusive shape of events, without any overlay of artifice or any cultural lie:

If I do it at all I must delay no longer. Incongruous and full of skips and jumps as is that huddle of diary-jottings . . . all bundled up and tied by a big string, the resolution and indeed mandate comes to me this day, this hour . . . to go home, untie the bundle, reel out diary-scraps and memoranda, just as they are, large or small, one after another, into print-pages, and let the melange's lacking and wants of connection take care of themselves. It will illustrate one phase of humanity anyhow; how few of life's days and hours (and they not by relative value or proportion, but by chance) are ever noted. Probably another point too, how we give long preparations for some object, planning and delving and fashioning, and then, when the actual hour for doing arrives, find ourselves still quite unprepared, and tumble the thing together, letting hurry and crudeness tell the story better than fine work.

With these words prefacing *Specimen Days,* Whitman turned into literature his wayward jottings: a miscellaneous stew of notes, fresh from the hurried pressure of events; and we think of Melville exulting midway through *Moby Dick:* "God keep me from ever completing anything. This whole book is but a draught—nay but a draught of a draught."

Since Whitman's and Melville's day, modern readers have developed a love for the fragment, the sketch, the spontaneous jotting, as being, in some way, truer than the crafted final work. This love has expressed a distrust of culture, a sense that an artist is closer to the muse when—as Kierkegaard said of his own notebook jottings—the "umbilical cord of [the] first mood" still clings to his inspiration. With Picasso, the sketch became a major form. With Eliot, Pound, and Joyce, the fragment—in a wayward pastiche of other fragments, a quilt of moments accidentally yet somehow harmoniously thrown together—became an element of style—the basic molecule, so to speak, in a new idea of form. The Surrealists believed that a man carried around in his mind and blood something like a living notebook—called the unconscious—that threw off telegraphic jottings, to be snatched as they flew past. Renaissance philosophers considered nature to be God's other book. In our day, the unconscious, taken as nature's most concentrated essence, has become God's other book; its language a form of anti-art, dissonant, elliptical, reveling in non-sense, grounded often in ugliness.

When Whitman revised "Song of Myself" for his 1882 edition, he added a sort of gloss to the first lines of the poem:

> I harbor for good or bad, I permit to speak at every hazard,
> Nature without check with original energy.

The added lines tell the reader how to approach this puzzling text which spills erratically down the page in long flaglike lines, shifting elliptically from theme to theme, image to image, over fifty undivided, apparently indigestible pages. Whitman is saying: In this poem, you will hear nature speaking; that is why it is unliterary, uncrafted. For nature's language is spontaneous utterance. Nature knows only the present, never the past or the future. My poem therefore is like the crest of a wave, billowing into the present with no echo of its beginning, no foreshadowing of its conclusion: that is to say, no form, as life itself has no form. My poem is, in fact, not a poem, but a shoreless utterance, the most satisfying analogies for which are the "open road" or the mind-stretching expanses of geological time and astronomical distance.

By the time Whitman added these lines to "Song of Myself," he had backed away from the extreme provocation of his first edition. The punctuation has been conventionalized. A scattering of thematic hints, such as the one I have quoted, has been added. Above all, the fifty pages of packed language have been skillfully divided into fifty-two stanzas. By 1882, "Song of Myself" has found its way part way back into literature. But Whitman might have described the original 1855 version as "Incongruous and full of skips and jumps"; its passages reeled out of his notebooks, "just as they are, large or small, one after another, into print-pages . . . letting hurry and crudeness tell the story better than fine work," which made it maybe "the most wayward, spontaneous, fragmentary [poem] ever printed."

While this description is literally true of *Specimen Days,* which was strung together out of notebook entries, it tells another sort of truth about "Song of Myself." Later we will see how thematically controlled and artful Whitman's greatest poem is, its apparent lack of form becoming a new kind of form. Yet the poem, and most of Whitman's writing, has effectively resisted the sort of critical intelligence lavished on other poets of Whitman's stature. It does not comfortably divide into a sequence of related parts; its themes, even its rhythms, seem too casual to support interpretation. As the poem slips through the hands of readers who have no such trouble with Wordsworth's *Prelude,* or Blake's prophetic books, or Eliot's *Wasteland,* it seems to insist that nothing can or should be said about it; that it is simply itself: nature's unparaphrasable outpouring—God's other book—and therefore fundamentally different from a "mere" poem.

To its first readers, on the other hand, and to many of its later critics, "Song of Myself" seemed truly to have tumbled pell-mell out of Whitman's trunk. To a conventional literary eye, clutter and nature can resemble each other. Yet it is this fragmentary, elliptical aspect of Whitman's poetry that has made it seem modern: its unprepared shifts in tone; its maw of a long uniambic line that digests the unpoetic without a missed breath: all those qualities Whitman meant when he called his method "indirect" and contrasted it with the narrative method of the poets he saw himself replacing—Shakespeare, Milton, Scott. Only by "indirection" could the entire man, and not merely his tellable actions, be expressed in language. "Indirection"—"elliptical and idiomatic"—was the democratic, truly American method, for it addressed itself to an obscure well of sentiments and impulses which everyman, no matter how ordinary, carried within him: his own complete "nature."

Is it too much to say that all of modernism sprang out of Whitman's trunk, as it did perhaps out of those other pell-mell masses of privacy—those trunks—that the nineteenth century turned into famous anti-books: Emerson's *Journals* and their decanted essences, his essays; the *journaux intimes* of Maine de Biron, Delacroix, or Amiel, those monuments to a lifetime's probing of the intimate rhythms of thought and feeling. Out of these grossly shaped boxes of words came the idea of a form that would be no form: words that would perform the ultimate mimetic act by pretending to be, and trying to be, life itself in all its unravelings. Proust's, Joyce's epic trunks of language, devoted to the miraculous ordinariness of a man's inner being.

The idea that his life could be represented as a miscellaneous bag of bits may have come to Whitman from one of the century's underestimated books, Thomas Carlyle's *Sartor Resartus,* which Whitman read avidly during these years. Carlyle's philosopher-hero, Diogenes Teufelsdrökh, turns out to have left, in guise of an autobiography:

Six considerable Paper-Bags [containing] miscellaneous masses of Sheets, and oftener Shreds and Snips . . . Anecdotes, oftenest without date or place or time, fly loosely on separate strips, like Sibylline leaves. Interspersed also are long purely Autobiographical delineations; yet without connection, without recognisable coherence. . . . . Selection, order, appears to be unknown to the Professor. . . . Close by a rather eloquent Oration . . . lie washbills marked *bezahlt* (settled). His Travels are indicated by the Street-Advertisements of the various cities he has visited.

By the early 1850s, the sheets, shreds, and snips had begun to accumulate in Whitman's trunk. There were copies of his early stories, newspaper articles he had written as early as the "Sundown Papers" in 1841, and his editorials for the *Aurora* in 1843, some of which he updated for use in the *Eagle* and, later, the Brooklyn *Daily Times.* He even took images from them for "Song of Myself." There were articles he tore out of magazines and annotated repeatedly over the 1850s. There were also masses of clippings from newspapers on apparently anything that caught his eye: the description of a "California belle," dated 1848: natural and wild, athletic, dark-skinned; or an account of pigeons somewhere in Indiana billowing in thick clouds, so that all a hunter had to do was shoot straight up into the air, to bring down birds by the hundred. There were clippings on swimming and Turkish baths, personal longevity, diet, anything having to do with health. He annotated a book page on "catarrh," the bronchial system, and emphysema. There were clippings on the proper training for boxers, on the ages of forty to sixty as the true prime of life, on the compatibility of "hard study" and a healthy body. On the back of a Fowler & Wells book, *The Science of Swimming* (1849), he pasted the advertisement for Henry Gibhard's Gymnasium, on Broadway. When, in the late 1880s, he came across a scrapbook of these clippings, among the odds and ends scattered across his floor on Mickle Street, he mused to Horace Traubel:

It is a strange miscellany—a hodge-podge, some of it only pulp, some of it very vital: curious, rejected reviews, critiques, odds and ends of newspaper gossip—all of it in the past, the far past—gathered together fifty years ago and on from that time for many years. I have always had it about me as a book for personal reference...." "What has that particular book to do with *Leaves of Grass*?" "Oh! everything! is full of its beginnings—is the a b c of the book—contains the first lisps of the song.... Here was my first tally of life—here were my first tries with the lute—in that book I am just like a man tuning up his instrument before the play begins."

I have remarked that America, in the nineteenth century, was a country of readers. Of all the aspects of the old cultures of Europe and England, the written word was the most easily acclimatable to the new land. Frontier cabins were a world away from the architecture and the great paintings and sculpture of Europe. Music was only sporadically available outside of New York. But every shack could have its bookshelf and receive its weekly *Tribune*. It is possibly this bookishness that D. H. Lawrence mocked when he described America as having been born old and only later becoming young. Few European books of the nineteenth century are as thickly inlaid with the echoes of other books as are *Moby Dick* or even

Walden—not to speak of the willfully cultivated styles of Longfellow, Irving, and Bryant. Whitman assaulted this bookish culture with all his might. He rose up and smote it with his workingman's posture, his loosely affectionate "Walt." In his notebooks he interspersed little reminders for himself:

> Make no quotations and no reference to any other writer.
> It seems to me to avoid all poetical similes—to be faithful to the perfect likelihoods of nature.
> Do not go into criticism or arguments at all.
> Rules for Composition—A perfectly transparent, plate-glassy style, artless, with no ornaments.

As I have said, Whitman was thoroughly devoted to books, and they were essential to the miscellaneous style of his great early poems. He reported that Emerson once said to him: "You surprise me in one way, Mr. Whitman: surprise me greatly; yet do not surprise me either: for I might have assumed as much: that is, I find you a copious book man—a readier knower of conventional things in literature than I had thought you to be."

For more than a century, readers have continued to express Emerson's surprise; yet surely the bookishness, or at least Whitman's peculiar variety of it, should have been obvious. Did Emerson really think Whitman had personally experienced all the places his poetic self visits in the poems, practiced all the professions, witnessed all the events? The poems are so concrete, so wisely selective in their material details, that they sound at every step as if they were written by a superhumanly traveled jack-of-all-trades who had meddled in all the professions. And, indeed, Whitman had! He had meddled, and traveled, by means of books, magazines, and newspapers. He had read, clipped, and rephrased so well that we still cannot tell apart the genuinely autobiographical passages from the paraphrased and impersonated ones.

Whitman liked to describe himself as an out-of-doors poet, a man of the streets and the open air, his senses tuned to the variegated spectacle of the city. He rode the Fulton Street Ferry so often that he got to know the crews and their captains, and sometimes recited poetry to them late in the evening or talked to them about the theater. He particularly loved to ride the Broadway stages and became friends with many of the drivers. Some of their names appear in his notebooks. Years later, in *Specimen Days,* he remembered them:

Broadway Jack, Dressmaker, Balky Billy, George Storms, Old Elephant, his brother Young Elephant (which came afterward), Tippy, Pop Rice, Big Frank, Yellow Joe, Pete Callahan, Patsy Dee. . . . They had immense qualities, largely animal—eating, drinking, women—great personal pride, in their way. . . . I suppose the critics will laugh heartily, but the influence of those Broadway omnibus jaunts and drivers and declamations and escapades undoubtedly enter'd into the gestation of *Leaves of Grass.*

On at least one occasion he took the place of a sick driver and gave the money to the man's family. Whitman formed the habit of visiting hospitals—so important to any understanding of his life— to comfort sick stage-driver friends in New York Hospital on lower Broadway. In the first edition of his book, he included a description of a driver's funeral:

Rapid the trot to the cemetery,
Duly rattles the deathbell . . . . the gate is passed . . . . the grave is halt-
    ed at . . . . the living alight . . . . the hearse uncloses,
The coffin is lowered and settled . . . . the whip is laid on the coffin,
The earth is swiftly shovelled in . . . . a minute . . . no one moves or
    speaks . . . . it is done,
He is decently put away . . . . is there anything more?

He was a goodfellow,
Freemouthed, quicktempered, not badlooking, able to take his own
    part,
Witty, sensitive to a slight, ready with life or death for a friend,
Fond of women . . . played some . . . ate hearty and drank hearty,
Had known what it was to be flush . . . grew lowspirited toward the
    last . . . sickened, was helped by a contribution,
Died aged forty-one years . . . and that was his funeral.

Thumb extended or finger uplifted,
Apron, cape, gloves, strap . . . wetweather clothes . . . whip carefully
    chosen . . . . boss, spotter, starter and hostler,
Somebody loafing on you, or you loafing on somebody . . . headway
    . . . man before and man behind,
Good day's work or bad day's work . . . pet stock or mean stock . . .
    first out or last out . . . turning in at night,

To think that these are so much and so nigh to other drivers . . . and he there takes no interest in them.

As a journalist, Whitman had written many rambles about town, filled with street scenes and local characters. They were his first tries at "loafing" in print, allowing the sensations of the day to accumulate in his mind. In this passage we find the same "loafing" sensibility, anchored in particulars, the drama only slightly heightened.

The scrappy, fragmentary appearance of many of Whitman's notes and the convenient pocket-size of the notebooks bear out his description of himself as an out-of-doors poet. Like Wordsworth pacing iambically in his garden, Whitman ambled, albeit with a longer, irregular step, in the streets, with his notebook in his hand. Walking was one of the nineteenth century's principal literary activities.

The walking man is partly outside of time. To his Washington friend, Ellen O'Connor, Whitman spoke of his ability to "stop thinking at will, and to make his brain 'negative.'" He never explained himself, but we remember Keats's mysterious phrase "negative capability": "when a man is capable of being in uncertainties, mysteries, doubts without any irritable reaching after fact and reason." I think of Keats's "negative capability" and of Whitman's ability to "stop thinking" as an ambulatory state of mind. Strolling without any destination, Whitman saw everything with an aimless vividness which his poems would express through long series of parallel descriptive lines, without any verb to jell them into an overall action. I am speaking of Whitman's catalogues, which don't really list at all but present a succession of "stills"—daguerreotypes, he might have said—received by a mind out on the open road or, as the case might be, on the streets of the city, with their "heavy uninterrupted street-bass" and their "never-ending human currents."

There is an idea that shows up frequently in Whitman's notes and eventually becomes the governing theme of "Song of Myself," its equivalent of a narrative thread:

What is it to own anything?—It is to incorporate it into yourself as the primal god swallowed the five immortal offspring of Rhea and accumulated to his life and knowledge and strength all that would have grown in them.

Every hour of the day and night, and every acre of the earth and shore, and every point or patch of the sea and sky, is full of pictures. No two of this immortal brood are alike, except that they are all of unspeakable beauty and perfection, and large and small alike descend into that greedy Something in Man whose appetite is more undying than hope, and more insatiate than the sand with water.

The perceiving self of Whitman's poems will also be an acquisitive self, a hungry self traveling through an edible world which it learns to know, not Biblically but carnally none the less, by digesting it. In "Song of Myself," he calls himself a "fluid and swallowing soul" and smacks his lips, after careening over the earth and into space: "All this I swallow, it tastes good, I like it well, it becomes mine." This idea is expressed somewhat differently in another passage:

The soul or spirit transmits itself into all matter—into rocks, and can live the life of a rock—into the sea, and can feel itself the sea—into the oak, or other tree—into an animal, and feel itself a horse, a fish, or bird—into the earth—into the motions of the suns and stars—

A man is only interested in anything when he identifies himself with it—he must himself be whirling and speeding through space like the planet Mercury—he must be driving like a cloud—he must shine like the sun—he must be orbic and balanced in the air, like this earth—he must crawl like the pismire—he must—he would be growing fragrantly in the air, like the locust blossoms—he would rumble and crash like the thunder in the sky—he would spring like a cat on his prey—he would splash like a whale.

To see and love, even simply to be "interested," requires a kind of ecstasy, a "merging," to use Whitman's characteristic word. Self and other flash together. The figure here is not strictly speaking of "digestion"; yet the action is similar: an emptiness is filled; a negative space—the self's inwardness—becomes whatever enters it. It is the figure of a hungry passiveness, a profound inward availability, which underlies the idiom of our language. We speak of "digesting," "taking in," "absorbing," even "swallowing" new knowledge. Whitman expands this root metaphor into a passion-poem of learning and perception—ultimately, of self making.

These passages in the notebooks probably reflect the influence of Emerson who, in his first essay, "Nature," had written that the poet:

unfixes the land and sea, and makes them revolve around the axis of his primary thought, and disposes them anew. . . . The sensual man . . . esteems nature as rooted and fast; the [poet] as fluid and impresses his being thereon. . . . The remotest spaces of nature are visited and the farthest sundered things are brought together.

Emerson dissolved the interval between man and the environing world by declaring that the world served man spiritually, mirrored his moral energies. Emerson's poet forges the world "in the apocalypse of [his] mind" and then goes forth exuberantly into his own creation. Whitman, with his genius for carnal imagery, would express this idea in his description of a touch: "My flesh and blood playing out lightning, to strike what is hardly different from myself."

The "self" of Whitman's early poems is so rarely seen doing anything that he has been described as a cosmic voyeur, passive and "feminine," a fleshed version of Emerson's "transparent eyeball." Emerson's figure for the awakened seer is curiously abstract, an eye without a body. But Whitman's view is closer; it is a walker's view. His world is alive with the paradox of its substantial separateness migrating smoothly, miraculously, into the miniature of the mind:

What is marvelous? what is unlikely? what is impossible or baseless, or vague? after you have once just opened the space of a peachpit and given audience to far and near and to the sunset and had all things enter with electric swiftness softly and duly without confusion or jostling or jam.

The mind filling with sights; the closely woven forms coming to rest in the poet's brain, made "negative" by his ability to "stop thinking": these are the essential moments in Whitman's epic of self making. They are what he sought by "loafing" on the grass. They are the underlying profit of his "lazy" disposition, his unhurried day-long walking, which gave him an ironist's view of commuters leaping onto the Fulton Street Ferry as it pulled out, or scrambling dangerously onto a moving train. He walked or rode the ferry or drove up and down Broadway because he enjoyed the raw impact and variety of the city. Like Rousseau and Wordsworth, those great literary walkers, he enjoyed aimless movement and made it the central figure of those miscellaneous epics of perception and experience, the great traveling poems of his first editions: "Song of Myself," "The Sleepers," "To Think of Time," "Crossing Brooklyn Ferry," "Song of the Open Road."

Whitman's 1850s notebooks are tantalizing documents. We find in them an accumulation of attitudes, stylistic trials, bold assertions, experiments with tone, experiments with forbidden subject matter, all of which, in 1853 or 1854—"under pressure—great pressure from within"—coalesced into the first edition of *Leaves of Grass*. To leaf through them, deciphering the large curves of Whitman's handwriting, is to examine the fossil remains of an unexampled upheaval, one of the puzzles of American literature: the emerging, with no apparent preliminaries, of a poet. In the notebooks we see it happening. We see the sweeping, hard-edged language, so different from the pudgy journalistic prose he was still capable of. We see the moments of surprising delicacy, as when he writes, near the beginning of his first notebook: "I will not be the cart, nor the load on the cart, nor the horses that draw the cart; but I will be the little hands that guide the cart." The cart, let us suppose, is America; the horses are the powers that draw it forward: its politics, natural resources, armies, history itself. But Whitman will be the "little hands," with their imperceptible pressure, their delicate control. Only the hands, so easily overlooked amid the rumbling of wheels and the pounding of hoofs—amid the masculine hard work—can express an awareness of destinations. As a story writer in the 1840s, Whitman often toyed with facile allegories; and a residue of this tendency clings, here and there, to his first experimental poems of 1850. Allegory was his first attempt at the grand mode; but here we see that his liveliest instinct led him away from allegory, toward a richer play of meanings. The cart may be America, but it is first a cart. The "small hands" are driver's hands, expressing the gentle, almost feminine skill of the burly driver, as well as the coaxing pressure of poetry. It is a power of weakness, a "feminine" power perhaps; yet without it, the horses are blind elemental beasts.

It is fascinating to peer into a writer's notebook and see the stirrings he drew on to create his finished work. In his notebooks, the writer is still only human: a patchwork of failures and successes. In his completed work, he has soared beyond us. There is another interest, too. In our day we have an inordinate curiosity about a man or a woman's private life, their accidental thoughts and discarded jottings. We suspect that this secret side of a man is truer than his more available side, which is partly theatrical, composed of attitudes that are attuned to us as audience and are therefore untrustworthy. Tell me what a man says when no one is listening, and I will tell you who he is: this has become a key to psychotherapeutic technique as well as the source of a whole literature, climaxing in Joyce's masterful stream-of-consciousness passages in *Ulysses.*

Here the reader of Whitman's notebooks will be disappointed, for he was not a diarist. He kept nothing resembling a *journal intime* composed of notes intended for no one's eyes, confined speculations about self and its private darknesses. Yeats, in a famous definition, wrote: "Out of the argument with ourselves we make poetry, out of the argument with others rhetoric." Even in the privacy of his experiment, Whitman saw himself framed by his audience, no less than Rousseau in the opening of his *Confessions,* where he invites the human race to gather round as witnesses, while he reveals himself. Whitman carried his audience with him, addressed it, spoke with the public tones—grounded in oratory and theater—that Yeats called "rhetoric." The notebooks reveal how throughgoing Whitman's publicness was. Even when speaking to himself, as in the first sentence of his first surviving notebook—"Be simple and clear.—Be not occult"—he was editorializing. Whitman's "I" required a "you," to be implored and preached to: "Never speak of the soul as anything but intrinsically great. . . . The truths I tell to you or to any other may not be plain to you. . . . We hear of miracles—But what is there that is not a miracle? What may you conceive of or name to me in the future that shall be beyond the least thing around us?" Even with the "umbillical cord of the first mood" still clinging to his words, Whitman thought publicly. Inverting the modern wisdom, we conclude that he is most himself when he keeps us in mind. His writing was a vast enterprise of keeping in touch: an argument with others, not with himself.

Occasionally we seem to glimpse the elusive moment when the raw emotion, like one of Ovid's changelings, has emerged part-way into a posture:

> I am not glad to-night. Gloom has gathered round me like a mantle tightly folded.
> The oppression of my heart is not fitfull and has no pangs; but a torpor like that of some stagnant pool.

These lines are a cry from the heart: a man groping to name his deepest feeling and thereby hold it at arm's length, master it. But no. Already the lines are half-versified. Following it are stanzas, not quite rhythmically strong but still shaped toward a meaning. At least one of the stanzas has the makings of a characteristically Whitmanesque meditation:

> O, Nature! impartial, and perfect in imperfection!
> Every precious gift to man is linked with a curse—and each pollution has some sparkle from heaven.
> The mind, raised upward, then holds communion with angels and its reach overtops heaven; yet then it stays in the meshes of the world too and is stung by a hundred serpents every day.

And the poem, which started with a cry half-hewn into a posture, ends with the posture: "O Mystery of Death, I pant for the time when I shall solve you!"

Another notebook, probably from the mid-1850s, contains a prose entry entitled "Depression":

Everything I have done seems to me blank and suspicious.—I doubt whether my greatest thoughts, as I had supposed them, are not shallow.—and people will most likely laugh at—me—My pride is important; my love gets no response—The complacency of nature is hateful—I am filled with restlessness—I am incomplete.

This passage, and the preceding one, hint at something we might not have known: during these intense, uncertain years Whitman's mood swung jaggedly at times. Still, the passage is not a confession. It is, for example, carefully reworked, its tone is dramatic, not private. The first sentence becomes a line in "Crossing Brooklyn Ferry," and the whole passage may simply be a working sheet for that poem.

The sparseness of Whitman's private notes matches the sparseness of other personal sources from these years. Whitman's "magnetic" presence, exuding confidence and a broad outreach of friendliness, left surprisingly few traces in people's minds. He was curiously invisible, as could well be true of someone whose personality is thoroughly public: people slide off him, becoming not friends but an audience. We see Whitman in the streets and the opera houses, but rarely in anyone's home. We hear him in editorials, but hardly ever in conversation. From his brother George's rambling reminiscence of this period, we glean the portrait of a stubbornly remote man:

Walt was very reticent in many particulars. For example I never knew him to explain his business projects or schemes of any kind—to communicate particulars of any plan he may have had in hand. . . . Do you ask if he was shiftless? No: he was not shiftless—yet he was very curiously deliberate . . . he would refuse to do anything except at his own notion—most likely when advised would say: "we won't talk about that. . . ." He would lie abed late, and after getting up would write a few hours if he took the notion—perhaps would go off the rest of the day. . . . I do not think he took a word of advice from anyone. This was so, first and last. It was in him not to do it—in his head, in his heart. . . . If we had dinner at one, like as not he would come at three: always late. Just as we were fixing things on the table, he would get up and go around the block. . . . Walt's hearing was very acute, especially at night. Noises in the street he would growl about. He seemed to hear sounds others did not hear or take notice of. His sense of smell, too, was remarkable.

George is describing a man who has unlatched himself from shared routines, without seeming to notice or care; although the remark about Walt's jumpiness hints that his friendly detachment may have overlaid raw nerves, a sign of the "pressure from within" that was driving him toward poetry. The walking may have helped to soothe him.

Another note from these years gives us a curious side glimpse of

Whitman's private uncertainties: "Of Insanity.—Some are affected with melancholia, in these the organ of cautiousness will be found large; some fancy themselves the Deity, in these self-esteem predominates; some are furious, in these destructiveness, or more likely, combativeness." We remember that Whitman's own "chart of bumps" had given him large organs of "cautiousness" and "self-esteem" and a somewhat smaller "destructiveness." Is this note a veiled confession of inner turmoil? Is it a slip of the pen of the sort Freud has taught us to respect? We possess only such vanishing glimpses of Whitman's inner man. Unless a handful of verbal experiments, some of which find their way more or less intact into the poems, can be considered similar glimpses.

During the summer of 1851, Whitman wrote several letters signed "Paumanok" for Bryant's *Evening Post.* In one, published on 11 August, he describes himself wandering toward sundown along "old Clover Hill (modernized Brooklyn Heights)" enjoying the sunset over the darkening harbor:

Sails of sloops bellied gracefully upon the river, with mellower light and deepened shadows. And the dark and glistening water formed an undertone to the play of vehement color above.

Rapidly, an insatiable greediness grew within me for brighter and stronger hues; oh, brighter and stronger still. It seemed as if all that the eye could bear, were unequal to the fierce voracity of my soul for intense, glowing color.

And yet there were the most choice and fervid fires of the sunset, in their brilliancy and richness almost terrible.

Have not you, too, at such a time, known this thirst of the eye? Have not you, in like manner, while listening to the well-played music of some band like Maretzek's, felt an overwhelming desire for measureless sound—a sublime orchestra of a myriad orchestras—a colossal volume of harmony, in which the thunder might roll in its proper place; and above it, the vast, pure Tenor, —identity of the Creative Power itself—rising through the universe, until the boundless and unspeakable capacities of that mystery, the human soul, should be filled to the uttermost, and the problem of human cravingness be satisfied and destroyed.

Whitman would remember this passage in "Song of Myself": "Dazzling and tremendous how quick the sunrise would kill me,/ If I could not now and always send sunrise out of me." "Song of Myself" would contain a crescendo of passages evoking the ecstatic danger of the senses, the precariousness of a "self" that has soared beyond conventional limitations of feeling; and the notebooks are full of similar passages. One of them, in carefully reworked prose, gives an excellent example of Whitman's method of composition:

I want that tenor, large and fresh as the creation, the orbed parting of whose mouth shall lift over my head the sluices of all the delight yet discovered for our race.—I want the soprano that lithely overleaps the stars, and convulses me like the love-grips of her in whose arms I lay last night.—I want an infinite chorus and orchestrium, wide as the orbit of Uranus, true as the hours of the day, and filling my capacities to receive, as thoroughly as the sea fills its scooped out sands. —I want the chanted Hymn whose tremendous sentiment shall uncage in my breast a thousand wide-winged strengths and unknown ardors and terrible ecstacies—putting me through the flights of all the passions—dilating me beyond time and air—startling me with the overture of some unnameable horror—calmly sailing me all day on a bright river with lazy slapping waves—stabbing my heart with myriads of forked distractions more furious than hail or lightning—lulling me drowsily with honeyed morphine—tightening the fakes of death about my throat, and awakening me again to know by that comparison, the most positive wonder in the world, and that's what we call life.

Only Nietzsche, in *The Birth of Tragedy,* has written this well about the ecstatic terror of musical experience, associating it with the Dionysian principle: the equivalent of the Maenads who tore Orpheus to pieces as he floated singing down the river. Whitman, too, tells of being disrupted, dislocated by the music. The images skid into each other, accumulate, spill together in unresolved clauses. The sentences waver out of control. Yet there is a guiding intelligence throughout; witness the successive "I wants," already rephrasing the passage as poetry. Even more clearly than in the lines of "Song of Myself" that are based on this paragraph, we see wave after wave of imagery, peak after peak of intense feeling, until the resolving final clause. The paragraph resembles a feat of *bel canto* virtuosity. It also indicates one of Whitman's tasks as a writer: to capture in language moments of physical delight, to devise a flexible, almost spatial style, free of directive verbs: the language of ecstasy.

Here is another more extreme example from Whitman's notebooks:

I have seen corpses shrunken and shrivelled—I have seen dismal manni-kens of abortions, still-births so small that the doctors preserved them in bottles—But no corpse have I seen—no minnied abortion—that appears to me more shrunken, from comparison to the fullest muscular health of some fine giant—more inert and blue and fit for the swiftest burial—more awfully a corpse because a perfect shaped and affectionate youth, in living strength and suppleness, stands ready to take his room, when the hearse carries the defunct away—than the whole and the best of what over this great earth has been called, and is still called, Religion, seems to me in comparison with the devotion? loving in a sort worthy that immea-surable love, stronger than the propulsion of this globe, ecstatic as the closest embraces of the god that made this globe—fiercer than the fires of the sun around which it eternally swings—more faithful than the faith that keeps it in its company and place—divergent and vast as the space that lies beyond—which belongs to any well developed man which is the great law whence spring the lesser laws we call Nature's.

There is a "too muchness" here, a sort of syntactical high jinks, pushing language to the edge of its possibilities. William Blake saw the world in a grain of sand; Whitman saw that every strong feeling could become a cosmos. In his notebooks, he elaborated a style to express this: a language that spilled forward in raging accu-mulation, disrupting its own grammar; a language that was, in some sense, not language.

This is a familiar ambition in the poetry of the late nineteenth century. The French poets Rimbaud and Mallarmé sought in their work to create a hieratic language, rescued from the "tribal lan-guage" of ordinary usage. Poetry became "difficult," purposely evasive and suggestive. It became, in some sense, the "other" lan-guage that Church Latin had become, or Hebrew, or Homeric Greek: meant not for the transactions of daily life, but only for the highest, most sacred feelings.

But wait! Can we really apply such ideas to Walt Whitman, the first genuine master of the American vernacular? A poet whose whole aim was to express the grandeur of the common man to the common man himself, in his own language? Who insisted hope-fully, at the end of his preface to Leaves of Grass: "The proof of a poet is that his country absorbs him as affectionately as he absorbs it."

Yet unless we approach Whitman in this larger perspective we risk misunderstanding him. We risk yielding, without sufficient resistance, to the open-toned style of his poetry, as if Whitman were indeed the popular poet he hoped to be and actually sounded like. The risk is that we will pass too quickly over his adventurous, surprisingly elusive imagery, his controlled balancing of long units of meaning, as if his poems were simply windy folksongs filled with obscure patches, or the effusions of an excitable adolescent.

It was Whitman's dilemma and his genius to have been brilliantly at cross-purposes with himself. He liked to see himself as an American Homer, a Milton without the dour theology, a Biblical prophet alternately thundering at his people and showering them with loving sweetness. He loved the epic pageantry of Scott and Shakespere and, in later years, compared himself to Victor Hugo. Yet Whitman also wrote about the "delicate hands" guiding the cart: the poet's intuitive mind which reached its goal by means of "indirection," never saying outright what could be suggested, so that the jolt of understanding would take place not on the page but in the reader's heart:

> Have you practiced so long to learn to read?
> Have you felt so proud to get at the meaning of poems?
>
> Stop this day and night with me and you shall possess the origin of all poems,
> You shall possess the good of the earth and sun . . . there are millions of suns left,
> You shall no longer take things at second or third hand . . . nor look through the eyes of the dead . . . nor feed on the spectres in books,
> You shall not look through my eyes either, nor take things from me,
> You shall listen to all sides and filter them from yourself.

To possess the poem's origin—in his own mind and in nature—the reader had to give up his desire for clearly marked themes and graduated arguments. He had to abandon himself to a text that was not overly concerned with "meaning" something, or whose meanings were swept aloft in the allusive play of language:

> —Hasting, urging, resistless,—no flagging not even in the "thoughts" or meditations—florid—spiritual—good, not from the direct but indirect meanings—to be perceived with the same perception that enjoys music, flowers and the beauty of men and women—free and luxuriant.

Such a poem eschewed the bold edges of literary theme; offered impressions, direct sensations, a constellation of images.

We remember Whitman's criticisms of the Dusseldorf style of painting which filled New York galleries in the early 1850s. The Dusseldorf paintings specializing in definite outlines were not true to nature which provides only flashes of form and color, washes of movement, shades of texture. The American Luminists had moved their easels out of doors several decades before the Impressionists; and in this way, Whitman too was a "luminist," an "impressionist." He, too, moved his art out of doors, not only into the streets during his long walks or in the analogue of those walks, the "catalogues" of his early poems; he moved his art out of culture into nature. He wrote poems that purported not to be poems ("Camarado, this is no book,/Who touches this touches a man") in a language that was not language, not a syntactical ordering of thoughts and themes, but something "to be perceived with the same perception that enjoys music, flowers and the beauty of men and women."

Whitman's poetry exists in this play upon the limits of language and culture. Where Rousseau had cried out *je ne sais quoi* ("how can I say it?") at moments of strong feeling, Whitman—(and Rimbaud, Mallarmé, Gerard Manley Hopkins)—worked to create a new dimension of language, amounting to a new language, that could articulate the unsayable, speak its silence. When, in "Song of Myself," Whitman recoils from the trap of language, he writes his reticence, and his silence becomes a condition of his poem:

My final merit I refuse you. . . . I refuse putting from me the best I am.

Encompass worlds but never try to encompass me,
I crowd your noisiest talk by looking toward you.

Writing and talk do not prove me,
I carry the plenum of proof and every thing else in my face,
With the hush of my lips I confound the topmost skeptic.

Whitman's desire to create a sensory music, a language of smells and eyesight, resembles that of the French Symbolist poets who, except for Jules Laforgue, never took any interest in him, although they worshiped Poe. The reasons for their neglect are easy to see.

The Symbolists were mock aristocrats, who appealed to a tradition of vanished elegance and imaginary refinements. In Poe, they found a mood brother, a biliously polemical "decadent." Yet Whitman would have been more to their purpose had they seen past his bardic stance to the practice of his poems. Like the Symbolists, Whitman's "indirect" style foreshadows the experimental poetry of the early twentieth century and surfaces strangely in such unlikely writers as Ezra Pound and T. S. Eliot.

Joseph Frank introduced the term "spatial form" to describe this elusive, fragmentary aspect of modernist literature. According to Frank, the modernist writer worked against the sequentialness of language, by creating poems that were not narratives or arguments but glimpsed wholes, their beginnings and endings somehow simultaneous. He accomplished this by means of ellipses which broke the narrative sequence; by orchestrations of imagery and symbol; by repetitions of theme. The result was a poetry that was meant not simply to be read but to be reread, so that, understood in its network of themes and imagery, it would be experienced as a space of meaning, a foray outside of time.

The "spatial" poem, it is clear, must be "interpreted," completed in the reader's mind by an act of extreme attention. It could be said that the modern institution of the university English department, with its staff of professional readers, inspecting poems as the soothsayers of ancient Greece inspected patterns of spilled intestines, originated in the arduous demands of "spatial form."

It is ironic that the best minds of modern criticism—I. A. Richards, Richard Blackmur, Lionel Trilling, Edmund Wilson, and Kenneth Burke—have had little to say about Whitman, whose "indirect" method breaks the very stylistic ground they have defined. Yet Whitman's attempt to forge a language for his moments of physical ecstasy are peculiarly "modern."

I have said that Whitman wrote at cross-purposes with himself, and these crossed purposes may help to explain the oversight of the critics. On the whole, modern critics have believed that a poem must rise to an impersonal diction, a voice speaking as a mask or a "persona," austerely separate from the feelings of the poet wielding the pen. Twentieth-century poems embodying this stringent ideal—*The Waste Land, The Cantos*—repudiated the emotion-filled voice of the Romantics, with their excited reaching after strong feeling, their belief that poems must give satisfactions that are not only literary but also moral, even religious. The Romantic poet as priest or legislator, the Romantic poem as an expression of exalted experience: to the interpreters of modern poetry, these conceptions were flawed by a disorder of merely living and merely feeling. The Romantics spoke naïvely that very "tribal language" a poet had to repudiate in order to achieve the severe timelessness of the poem.

Yet Whitman's "language experiment" revels in the play of strong feelings. It represents the far edge of the Romantic quest, the very moment when the narrative impulse bursts under the pressure of unfathomable feelings, and the splintered parts settle into a new form, offered by Whitman as an auspice of the inner man, his "authentic" self.

Neither romantic or modern, Whitman slips between critical idioms, an eccentric hybrid who further confused matters by arguing convincingly that his poems were not literature at all but unimpeded experience, accidentally spilled into language; that to read them was to embrace a bearded passionate man, who was often deliriously happy. We can see why, over the years, more searching questions have been directed at Whitman's life than at his poetry. Having located at the core of his "experiment" a language of sensory delight, we can see, too, why the idea of an explosive personal origin for the poems has intrigued many readers. While Whitman may not have been jarred into poetry by a Creole lover in New Orleans, we are inclined to look curiously at a passage like the following, from a notebook of the 1850s:

> Bridalnight
> one quivering jelly of love
> limpid transparent
> Limitless jets of love hot and enormous . . .
> Drunken and crazy with love swimming
> in its . . . in the plummetless sea
> Loveflesh swelling and deliciously aching whiteblood of love.

Some of these lines find their way into "I Sing the Body Electric"; and we recognize the "limitless jets" and "quivering jelly," the "plummetless sea," "loveflesh," "deliciously aching," sperm as the "white blood of love," from a number of poems. Here is the shore-less sexuality, an eroticism without object or subject, approximating a fantasy of masturbation, which occurs frequently in Whitman's poetry.

Shall we consider Whitman's verbal venturesomeness in purely literary terms, as a question of tone and subject matter? Or shall we suppose that he was driven by intense experience—his passion for sounds, color, and touch—to write poems that dissolved the narrative straightjacket of the conventional Romantic poem and made radical forays into pure feeling, pure sensation. Shall we suppose that Whitman's senses were overly sexualized, like an infant living a polymorphously perverse love affair with the world, its other mother? With these questions in mind, let us read two related notebook passages from the same period:

Faith. Becalmed at sea, a man refreshes himself by swimming round the ship—a deaf and dumb boy, his younger brother, is looking over . . . and the swimmer floating easily on his back smiles and beckons with his head. Without waiting a moment, the young child laughing and clucking springs into the sea and as he rises to the surface feels no fear but laughs and though he sink and drown he feels it not for the man is with him there.

This passage became the basis for a never completed poem, called "Death Song":

Joy Joy! O full of Joy
Away becalmed at sea one day
I saw a babe, laughing, kicking etc. etc.
And as a swimmer floated in the waves he
Called the child. Laughing it sprung and . . .

Whitman was rarely so successful at balancing his effects. The sensation of "Joy Joy!" swims on a "plummetless" depth of terror; tragedy wears a sunlit sensual face. It is too bad he never completed this poem, with its Melvillean paradox, its play of love, erotic confidence, and death. But we come now to one of those troubling personal questions Whitman inspires. Could he have left the poem unfinished because it came too close to genuinely forbidden ground? The splashing, laughing sea is the "plummetless sea" of

187

the erotic. The man beckons to his younger brother, inviting him to come and play. The brother, disabled, helpless, comes and plays and is sucked irremediably into the sexual element, still laughing, still confident, never fully understanding what has happened to him.

Whitman was devoted to his youngest brother, Ed, all his life, supporting him and leaving him most of his money when he died. Ed was mentally defective, probably epileptic. During much of the 1850s, he and Whitman shared a room, even a bed. How deeply do these juxtaposed texts allow us to peer into an obscure, possibly shameful zone of Whitman's sexual life? We are unlikely ever to know. Yet Whitman's poems invite us (his deaf and dumb younger brothers?) into intimacy, while they, in fact, reveal remarkably little of the actual man who hugs us through the "cold types and cylinder and wet paper." Whitman is there, and he is not. He is all direct emotions, unconcealed attitudes; yet he has no inwardness, no privacy buckling his words. His voice is swaggeringly self-assured. It tells us we can count on the man, whose words are a mere spray of his being. Yet the man eludes us, and we peer after him asking who he is. "Who touches this, touches a man." But who is the man?

The idea that Whitman had a "secret" would tantalize his young Camden friend, Horace Traubel, as it has tantalized critics ever since. The secret "might test you," Whitman told Traubel, becoming solemn; even "disgust" you. He never told Traubel any "secret"; or if he did, Traubel kept it to himself, and we can only wonder whether Whitman's "secret" was as Victorian—as sexual—as it sounds. Was it related to the other "secret" that the English critic John Addington Symonds had tried to ferret out when, over the years, he badgered Whitman about the "Calamus" poems and their suggestion of homosexual love? A century later, Whitman's sexual life is still a mystery. Was he homosexual? Did he become openly homosexual in the 1850s, his new poetry a celebration of erotic freedom? Who were the men that he listed in his 1850s notebooks: young, physically attractive, usually workingmen or stage drivers, even policemen, with some personal trait he noted—liquid eyes; handsome, round red face. One night he walked up Gold Street, after a fireman's parade, with a tall young man named Billie; on another, he bumped into "Ike" on Fifth Avenue: a fat drinking man, around twenty-eight, who rode a horse named "Fashion" in "the great race." There was also Charles Brown ("Bdway Brownie") and his friend Jakey (James, "tall, genteel,") and Johnny ("round-faced, full, eyes liquid, in Dunbar's and Engine house") and "James Dalton (20) round faced, lymphatic, lost front teeth." Also "Nick (Black eyes 40th st small)." In an 1860 notebook, a page is filled with obsessive play upon the letters of the name "Arthur Henry," with no description; and there is this note: "Dec. 28 Saturday night. Mike Ellis—wandering at the cor. of Lexington Ave. and 32 St.—took him home to 150 37th st.—4th story back room—bitter cold night—works in Stevenson's carriage factory."

There are dozens of these names in the 1850s notebooks and dozens more in the daybooks he kept in the 1870s and 1880s. Were these men Whitman's lovers? Possibly, but so many? The lists seem to be made at a sitting, as if Whitman periodically toted up his chance meetings with young men, catalogued them, made list-poems, such as he envisaged as "A New Way and the True Way of Treating in Books History Geography Ethnology Astronomy etc. etc. By long lists. . . ." These were, I suspect, part of Whitman's enterprise of keeping in touch. All his life, he was a collector of names, and one almost sees him leafing through his lists, reassured by the size of his collection. It is, after all, similar, in its way, to the editorials he had sent out, day after day, as a newspaper editor, like the "filament, filament" of the "patient spider" in his poem. In *Leaves of Grass,* too, he invited an eternity of friends to gather close to him. Whitman's lists of young men read like a sad residue of his lifelong passion to be surrounded by throngs of comrades or, at least, by names standing for comrades.

Whitman never told Traubel his "secret," and we must not dismiss the possibility that he was teasing his young friend. Anyway, it is clear by now that no simple answers are likely to be found to any of our questions. Whitman's gift of poetry was rooted deeply and variously in his life. No "secret" will disclose it, for it is all secret, and no secret as well.

Whitman's lists of young men do not tell us that he was homosexual or, if he was, that he performed athletic feats of intercourse and kept a score sheet. They do tell us, yet again, of his collector's mentality which found a perfect form in the "catalogues" of the early poems and later in *Specimen Days*.

Few poets have written as erotically as Whitman, while having so little to say about sex. For the most part, his erotic poetry is intransitive, self-delighting. It veers toward the larger self-delight of the mystical. Its analogies are with the ecstatic Sufi poet Rumi, or the Tantric hymns of India, or the erotic swoons of Saint Theresa. In practice, I suspect, Whitman was fairly chaste, the remote, edgy side of his character flaring up in intimacy, interposing an obstacle to love relationships of any sort. All observers seem to agree that there were no women in his life. Acquaintances from his Long Island days remembered that he "seemed to hate women." A former student of his at Bayside on Long Island recalled: "The girls did not seem to attract him. He did not specially go anywhere with them or show any extra fondness for their society. . . . He did not care for women's society—seemed indeed to shun it. Young as I was, I was aware of that fact." His brother George made the same point, and it is borne out by everything else we know about Whitman, including his clumsy flight from his English admirer, Anne Gilchrist, in the 1870s.

Any love he experienced was for men, that's clear enough. The lists attest to it, as do the extraordinary love poems of "Calamus," written in the late 1850s. As a young schoolteacher at Smithtown in the early 1840s, he had boarded with the family of one of his students, but "the father quite reproved him for making such a pet of the boy," he told his friend Ellen O'Connor years later. We glimpse here the ambiguity of Whitman's fondness for boys and see it again in the ties he formed with printer's devils and apprentices at his various newspaper jobs. We see it at its most passionate in his confused, exalted state of mind while visiting the war hospitals around Washington, during the Civil War, and again in his troubled friendship with a young Washington streetcar conductor, Peter Doyle, in the late 1860s. At times Whitman's attraction to men seemed to rule his character and his thinking. The "Calamus" poems are lucid rhapsodies of love and loss. They are among the finest love poems in our language, and they are addressed to a man. With "Song of Myself," "Calamus" became a cornerstone for all the future editions of *Leaves of Grass*. It is a culminating moment, when Whitman's ineradicable feelings were reinforced and clarified by a political theme. In "Calamus," Whitman saw "Democracy" as a fluid, lawless, yet orderly exchange of feelings among "comrades," a network of intimacies on a vast scale. "Democracy" could succeed only as an unimpeded flow of love, of which he, Walt Whitman, would give the first example, with the open-toned utterance of his truest feelings. The poems of "Calamus" grounded Whitman's vision and gave it a wholeness. Intense love between men became, for Whitman, the fundamental bond. Half a century later, Freud, too, would ground his idea of the communal feelings in the "homosexual" aspect of the erotic drives of men and women.

We glimpse the opposing forces of Whitman's character in a pair of incidents that occurred a dozen years apart. During the late 1850s, Whitman spent many evenings at the home of his mother's friend, Abby Price. Mrs. Price's daughter, Helen, recalled these evenings years later in a long letter which Maurice Bucke reprinted in his biography of Whitman. This affectionate letter gives us virtually the only intimate portrait of Whitman we have from these years. Helen described him discussing Swedenborgian spiritualism with a family friend, Mr. Arnold; reading aloud a draft of "Out of the Cradle Endlessly Rocking"; playing with the children; basking demurely, almost reluctantly, in his budding celebrity. One evening the discussion turned toward "friendship":

He said there was a wonderful depth of meaning ("at second or third removes," as he called it) in the old tales of mythology. In that of Cupid and Psyche, for instance; it meant to him that the ardent expression in words of affection often tended to destroy affection. It was like the golden fruit which turned to ashes upon being grasped, or even touched. As an illustration, he mentioned the case of a young man he was in the habit of meeting every morning where he went to work. He said there had grown up between them a delightful silent friendship and sympathy. But one morning when he went as usual to the office, the young man came forward, shook him violently by the hand, and expressed in heated language the affection he felt for him. Mr. Whitman said that all the subtle charm of their unspoken friendship was from that time gone.

The man was probably Frederick Huene, a young German poet who had worked with Whitman at the Brooklyn *Daily Times* in

1857. Whitman gave Huene a copy of *Leaves of Grass,* and Huene began translating it into German but gave up, perhaps because Whitman had suddenly cooled toward him. The scene completes our sense of Whitman's stubborn reserve about his intimate life. More than a concealment, the silence seems to have been a condition of Whitman's feelings. He felt, and didn't say; he took refuge in undeclared, maybe unshared feelings. "I hate to have people— throw themselves into my arms—insist upon themselves, upon their affection," he once told Traubel. "It is a feeling I can never rid myself of."

Whitman had mythology at his fingertips, and the reference to Cupid and Psyche is revealing. According to legend, after nights of anonymous love in darkness, Psyche schemes to light a lamp beside her bed in order to see her lover. The lamp falls over and spills scalding oil on Cupid, who flees forever. Knowing him, she loses him. Like the stories of Oedipus and of Narcissus, that of Cupid and Psyche portrays the temerity and the precarious adventure of the lowliest, simplest human act: to know another, and to know oneself. It was an adventure Whitman shied away from. The golden apples could be savored only at a distance.

Ellen O'Connor remembered a bit of doggerel Whitman liked to recite during his Washington years:

A mighty *pain* to love it is,
And yet a pain that love to miss,
But of all pain, the greatest pain
It is to love but love in vain.

We can imagine Whitman clowning as he recited this little poem; yet it is touchingly appropriate. It expresses in the form of a jingle what Whitman had expressed in many of his "Calamus" poems: the pain of his self-inflicted zone of silence; the lonely pride, edged with humiliation; the anxious flight from what he wanted deeply and was reluctant to possess. As the critic Stephen A. Black has remarked, the kisses in Whitman's poems are always kisses of parting:

Sit a while, wayfarer,
Here are biscuits to eat, and here is milk to drink,

> But as soon as you sleep, and renew yourself in sweet clothes, I will certainly kiss you with my good-bye kiss, and open the gate for your egress hence.

> . . . . I record of two simple men I saw to-day, on the pier, in the midst of the crowd, parting the parting of dear friends,
> The one to remain hung on the other's neck, and passionately kissed him,
> While the one to depart, tightly prest the one to remain in his arms.

The other incident dates from the late 1860s. Late one night, on an empty streetcar in Washington, Whitman sat down next to the conductor, a young man named Peter Doyle; and the two felt instantly as if they had known each other for a long time. Despite an age difference of almost thirty years, they became close friends, and more. There is an impassioned delicacy in Whitman's letter to Doyle, a mingling of fatherly care and almost girlish love. Whitman's feelings were violently stirred, as we know from a desperate confession he made, in thinly disguised code, in his journal:

cheating, childish abandonment of myself, fancying what does not really exist in another, but is all the time in myself alone—utterly deluded & cheated by *myself,* & my own weakness—REMEMBER WHERE I AM MOST WEAK, & most lacking. Yet always preserve a kind spirit & demeanor to 16. But PURSUE HER NO MORE.

It is IMPERATIVE, that I obviate & remove myself (& my orbit) *at all hazards* [away from] from this *in-*

cessant enormous & [enormous] PERTURBATION

TO GIVE UP ABSOLUTELY & *for good, from this present hour,* [all] this FEVERISH, FLUCTUATING, *useless undignified pursuit of 164—too long,* (*much too long*) persevered in,—so humiliating—*It must come at last* & had better come now—(*It cannot possibly be a success*)

LET THERE FROM THIS HOUR BE NO FALTERING, [or] NO GETTING——*at all henceforth,* (NOT ONCE, *under any circumstances*)— *avoid seeing her, or meeting her, or any talk or explanations*—or ANY MEETING WHATEVER, FROM THIS HOUR FORTH, FOR LIFE.

Here, for virtually the only time in all his notebooks, Whitman cries out to himself, for himself; writes within a privacy made even more private by the nervous substitution of a number code for the initials of Peter Doyle (P is the 16th letter of the alphabet, D is the 4th), and by the reversal of genders. This is no staged utterance or half-shaped poem but, in the most modern, most tormented sense, a rank argument with oneself. The very sort of argument that Whitman never allowed to issue into poetry. Indeed, he had to strangle and overmaster it, before it smashed his speaking voice. Whitman knew what he was feeling here, and could not bear it. In another entry, he wrote: "Depress the adhesive nature. . . . It is in excess, making life a torment. . . . All this diseased, feverish dispro-portionate *adhesiveness*." Psyche has lit her lamp; she knows whom she loves and her lover flees, or she herself flees. Her erotic drive and the knowledge of its object leave Psyche in a state of desperate perplexity. The most private core of her being is suddenly un-shielded. Yes, that is what she had longed for, but longing is not the same: it is a way of being with oneself, substituting oneself for the distant and unknown lover. But now the lover is here, a puz-zled young man, flattered by Whitman's devotion, drawn to him in complicated ways, grateful to him—but irrevocably remote and mysterious, as another human being must be. If we compound this elemental drama of self-risk with the stifling taboo on homosexual love in Victorian America, we glimpse the desperate conflict in Whitman's inmost character. He could accept his sexuality only as a form of intransitive ecstasy, its object concealed by darkness, the lamp unlit, or indirectly and coyly lit. "Indirection" was not mere-ly an esthetic principle for Whitman, but an erotic strategy. "Fur-tive as an old hen," he said half-mockingly of himself, with a sly switching of gender.

This is unlikely to be the formula for a robust sexual life. In-stead, we imagine a shy circling of the flame, a flirtation with saying the unsayable, a moral passion for the forbidden zones of behavior, for the reproved and excluded ones whom Whitman would defend as surrogates for his own self-darkened self. Whit-man would not spill burning oil on his Cupid, but he would shed a half-light on him, would hint at "secrets" and reveal them in coded ways; would change the name of love to "adhesiveness," so outlandish as to be safely unrevealing; would conceptualize the sexual bond, by raising it into the realm of the American sublime and calling it "democratic." His lists of young men, his passionate devotion to the wounded soldiers in the war hospitals, were other circlings of the flame.

Were at least some of Whitman's young men also bed partners? Such encounters—trysts in the dark, the lamp unlit—leave no trace, although I would guess that they were, and that they were not happy experiences; that the "pain" of loving in "vain" was somehow better and more sustaining for him. Whitman's genius was not, finally, for love but for poetry, and for the obscure moral courage that keeps the deep source of emotions fully alive, even when the familiar sentimental satisfactions are lacking. For a dozen years and more, Whitman lived on this precarious edge. From the body of the "truculent giant"—Whitman's figure for democratic America—he turned to his own large-boned body. And the two bodies, in a conceptual leap that remade American literature, became one.

We understand now the undertone of hysteria, and the poignancy, of some of Whitman's notes: "Poem incarnating the mind of an old man, whose life has been magnificently developed—the wildest and most exuberant joy—the utterance of hope and floods of anticipation—faith in whatever happens—but all enfolded in Joy Joy Joy, which underlies and overtops the whole effusion." Whitman would not make poetry out of the argument with himself. Instead, he would pour ecstasies of hope and anticipation into a dream of self-making, of self-transcendance, of which the fundamental discipline would be the making of poems. These poems would not be monologues of inward conflict and resolution. They would leap cleanly, with a tone of casual conviction, into a vision of expanded being. The "Joy Joy Joy" of the notebook would become the stalwart, magnificent old man of "I Sing the Body Electric":

> This man was of wonderful vigor and calmness and beauty of person;
> The shape of his head, the richness and breadth of his manners, the
>   pale yellow and white of his hair and beard, the immeasurable mean-
>   ing of his black eyes,
> These I used to go and visit him to see .... He was wise also,

He was six feet tall . . . he was over eighty years old . . . . his sons were
massive clean bearded tanfaced and handsome,
They and his daughters loved him . . . all who saw him loved him . . .
they did not love him by allowance . . . they loved him with personal love;
He drank water only . . . . the blood showed like scarlet through the
clear brown skin of his face;
He was a frequent gunner and fisher . . . he sailed his boat himself . . . .
he had a fine one presented to him by a shipjoiner . . . he had fowl-
ing-pieces, presented to him by men that loved him;
When he went with his five sons and many grandsons to hunt or fish
you would pick him out as the most beautiful and vigorous of the
gang,
You would wish long and long to be with him . . . you would wish to
sit by him in the boat that you and he might touch each other.

Whitman's old man lounges beyond sexual incompleteness, beyond the edgy inward drama of Cupid and Psyche. He stands for
the self Whitman was even then making in his poems and in his
person. Within half a dozen years, he would stride compassion-
ately between rows of hospital beds, his reddish face, large frame,
and flowing beard the embodiment of "magnetic" health and pa-
triarchal confidence.

How poignant, then, this note Whitman appended to the anguished confession of his love for Peter Doyle: the "wise man . . .
reproves nobody Blames nobody/*Nor ever speaks of himself.* . . . All
his desires depend on things within his power. . . . His appetites
are always moderate. . . . He observes himself with the nicety of an
enemy or spy, and looks on his own wishes as betrayers." Whitman's dream of an unwounded life is wistful and intense when set
beside his capitalized and underscored cry of pain. He had not only
acted his part of a "rough" or his later part of a commanding good
gray poet. He had recoiled from an inward hunger he rarely expressed. When, for once, he spilled his pain across a page he had
meant for wiser notations, he fled reflexively to the glorious fantasy that, for almost twenty years, had nourished his poetry:

> Outline sketch of a superb calm character
> his emotions &c are complete in himself irrespective
> (indifferent) of whether his love, friendship, &c are returned
> or not

He grows, blooms, like some perfect tree or flower, in Nature,
    whether viewed by admiring eyes, or in some wild or wood
    entirely unknown
His analogy the earth complete in itself enfolding in itself all processes
    of growth effusing life and power for hidden purposes.

Faced with a painful reality, Whitman called forth the image of
a magnetic large-spirited old father, drawn from the vocabulary of
the benign stoic, Epictetus, from America's hagiographical worship
of the fathers of the Revolution and from his own lifelong fascination with old age as a triumph and a release. This image became a
talisman, a companion of his mind. It became, finally, a template
for his desire to be "self-made or never-made," as his phrenological
mentor, Orson Fowler had put it.

Eventually Whitman became the sage of Mickle Street in Camden, portrayed in Thomas Eakins's marvelous portrait and in the
finest array of photographs ever taken of a poet: garrulous and
playful, superbly gifted for old age, having practiced the part all his
life, even an old age of half-paralysis, with long spells of debilitating exhaustion and dizziness and never-relenting gastric pains. He
would talk stagily and wonderfully to his little band of disciples
and dangle his "secret" before young Horace Traubel, who tran-
scribed his master's every word into a serene, opinionated, fatuous,
often wise record of an old man's musing. This was Whitman's
gift: to shape his life to his deepest musings; to become the man of
his words.

For a dozen years, during the 1850s and 1860s, the words were
superb, the self-making an open-ended, uncertain experiment.
Whitman leaped repeatedly to his pastoral vision, leaped and recoiled; and in the poems, he recorded the pendulum movement,
the exaltation and the lapse into pain.

What is important here is Whitman's instinct for his subject
matter—sensory expansion, physical ecstasy—and his ability to
mold the resources of his poetry in order to express it. From the
crucible of the erotic, he made a new form and a new tone, spacious, miscellaneous; sometimes refined to the heated intensity of a
love poem; sometimes expanded to embrace a phantasmic, yet vividly various lover: the world.

PART III

"A Man of His Words"

CHAPTER 6

"Self-Made or Never Made"

1

IN SPITE of Whitman's elusiveness about these important years, we have managed to identify the scattered signs of change in his newspaper articles and his notebooks, in the puzzled remarks of his uncomprehending brother George, in the periodic side glance of an acquaintance remembering not so much the poet or the man as the costume, the personage. It is an astonishing progress: without a career, his livelihood precarious, no accomplishments to speak of, a marginal journalist lucky to place noncontroversial "letters" in a few newspapers. It is the portrait of a floundering, almost middle-aged man, understandably possessed at times, by feelings of "torpor" and "gloom." How had he gotten himself into this situation? For one thing, as a journalist he had backed an unpopular cause, in those nervous years of the early 1850s, when politicians and newspaper editors were making a last attempt to pretend that the unspeakable would not happen: that the romance of democracy could survive the persistence of slavery and the cultural blindness that made North and South envious and frightened of each other, as in one of Strindberg's nightmarish marriages.

There were personal reasons, too. Whitman had never worked for anyone without trouble. He was stubborn and touchy, apt to stiffen unreasonably on questions of principle. There was, in him, also a streak of wild anger. For years he had been forcing himself into a corner. In a way, he had grown backward, from the edgy self-reliance of his youth, working for one newspaper after another, and living on his own in Manhattan boardinghouses, to his present role as a doting son, a lovable, yet somehow stubborn failure, in the crowded wooden house dominated by his dying father.

Yet growing backward can still be growth—not progress maybe but a peculiar sort of blundering and broadening, a probing for unused strengths. As Whitman settled into his family, as he fell away from the ambitions of his early years, he found himself stranded but also freed. He was seized by a feeling of buoyancy. His buoyancy became a voice, an ambition.

Later he spoke of simmering, simmering, and then boiling over. He had been working toward this for years; an exploratory, hesitant labor, beginning, he remembered, as early as 1848 and 1849. But now he caught fire, and he identified the igniting flame differently at different times: it was Emerson; it was Marietta Alboni's supreme vocal power; it was the sounding surf on the beaches of Long Island:

Speech is the twin of my vision. . . . it is unequal to measure itself.
It provokes me forever,
It says sarcastically, Walt, you understand enough. . . . why don't you let it out then!

and

I am a dance. . . . Play up there! the fit is whirling me fast.

The "fit" whirled him very fast. He was at work on his book by 1853 or 1854, and the first edition of *Leaves of Grass* came out in 1855, containing twelve poems, including a magnificent long poem, later called "Song of Myself": a total of ninety-five large pages. A year after that, another edition of the book appeared, with thirty-two poems and 384 pages. In June 1857, Whitman wrote his friend Sarah Tyndale that he had "a *hundred* poems ready" and was counting on yet another edition. The work multiplied and ramified. "Backward I see in my own days where I sweated through fog with linguists and contenders": Whitman was out of the "fog" now. Maybe he did not yet know where he was, had not begun to map out the place and write methodical tours of the territory. But he was creating it, writing and rewriting, "boiling." On his bedroom wall, this "curiously deliberate" man hung a reminder: "Make the works," meaning, I suppose, start quarrying poems out of the deepening pile of notes and fragments he had been bringing back with him from his street forays.

He would call one of his poems "Spontaneous Me." As a writer, however, Whitman's unit of spontaneity was probably short: a sentence, a paragraph. The fit whirled him fast, but not long, and often, as we have seen, in prose. "Make the works" has a sound of construction, as in waterworks; and it is true, Whitman was grappling with a problem of craft: How to move from the acquisitive random impulse to pile up perceptions, intuitive flows of language, small units of rhythm, to the making of actual poems? How to be faithful to his fundamental insight: that randomness, an open-ended acceptance of the mind's playfulness and of the world's variousness, could be the principle of a work of art? As Whitman cast about for an appropriate voice, he thought essentially as a Platonist: the world was real; art was merely a "picture":

> The rich coverlet of the grass, animals and birds, the private untrimm'd
>   bank, the primitive apples, the pebble-stones,
> Beautiful dripping fragments, the negligent list of one after another as
>   I happen to call them to me or think of them.
> The real poems, (what we call poems being merely pictures).

The idea, therefore, was to make poems that were as little like "pictures" as possible, or, if they were "pictures," to let them not be framed and separate but kaleidoscopic, running into one another, unframed and limitless, as the actual poems did.

Whitman's first attempt at such a poem was not successful, but the result was fascinating anyway. The trial poem, "Pictures," begins with a figure that reverberates with suggestions for Whitman's poetry:

> In a little house pictures I keep, many pictures hanging suspended—It
>   is not a fixed house,
> It is round—it is but a few inches from one side of it to the other side,
> But Behold! it has room enough—in it, hundreds and thousands,—all
>   the varieties.

On the walls of the little house hang family portraits, the busts of poets, historic scenes from ancient Greece and the French Revolution, "pictures" of American life, the wilderness, a "string" of Iroquois Indians, Ralph Waldo Emerson standing "tall and slender" at the lecturer's desk, Asian scenes, Arctic scenes, city street scenes. Mixed in with them is a charming self-portrait: "with rapid feet, curious, gay—going up and down Manhattan, through the streets, along the shores, working his way through the crowds, observant and singing": it is "the young man of Manhattan, the celebrated rough."

Celebrated by whom, we want to ask? But Whitman is simply trying out his legend; he is giving vent to the fantasy of his soaring moods: he would be celebrated for his maleness, his air of danger; yet he would also be light-footed, a kind of Ariel, singing and watching; a large, muscular, surprisingly delicate man. This may be Whitman's first recorded self-portrait, the first result of his obsessive need to stand outside himself and see himself with an appraising, celebratory eye. No writer I know has written so many third-person portraits of himself. The "fit" whirled him fast, but the watcher kept on watching and watching himself. The windows of the "little house" never stopped reaping their harvest of "pictures" to hang in thickening bunches on the inner walls. This is the poem's fable: a crude, somewhat mechanical version of the odyssey of perception that the fast-footed "singer" would undertake a year or so later in "Song of Myself."

Whitman's "pictures" hang in the gallery of the mind, but the artist is light. In overcoming his Platonic distrust of mere art, Whitman has hit on an original image. His gallery is modeled on one of the fashionable daguerreotype galleries where Manhattanites came to view the uncannily exact reproductions of famous faces. The "little house," with its apertures, is a camera, not so much observing the objects of the world as peeling their pictures from them and storing them in the inner gallery of memory.

For more than a century, photography has been arguing with art. On the one hand, it has become a stunningly democratic art (anyone can have his gallery of pictorial memories recorded in photograph albums); on the other hand, it has been accused of being an anti-art, enslaved to visual surfaces. In Whitman's day, however, this argument had not yet begun. The photographer belonged to an admired new breed. He was an artist producing miraculous replicas of the real, but also a scientist, a chemist, and a technician, mysterious in his expertise. We have seen Whitman's ability to transform the new into material for poetry. Here he seizes on the new technique of photography as a metaphor for the perceiving mind and for the act of poetry, thereby bridging the Platonic chasm between nature and art and paving the way for the anti-art of his great poems.

For the rest, "Pictures," is little more than a catalogue, and not a particularly interesting one at that. Its rhythms are slack and carelessly accented, more like prose than poetry. Yet the first hints of Whitman's poetic method are here, in the form of parenthetical asides: ("I name everything as it comes"), to explain the randomness of the "pictures" that pour forth in no order, yet in order nonetheless—that of the impulsive, unfettered mind; ("for I have all kinds"), naming the variety of these "pictures," which range superhumanly from the great events of history long past to scenes of the wild West and the busy work-life of the cities; ("abruptly changing"), indicating the sudden shifts that characterize the mind's stream of consciousness. For that is what is represented here: the flux of a mind reveling in its memories. And what memories they are! These eyes have ranged through all of time and space, they have seen Socrates and Dante and Lucifer, and the southern slave gangs, and the seven wonders of the world.

And yet the poem is surprisingly static—more like one of Teufelsdröckh's great bags full of scraps in Carlyle's *Sartor Resartus* than a poem. Whitman's camera self is as yet little more than a machine storing up images. It has no inwardness and therefore, truly speaking, no experiences. When, part-way through the poem, Whitman begins his characteristically acquisitive stance ("my woods . . . my slave-gangs . . . my congress"), the possessive carries no force, because the poem's "self" has remained empty, a mere figure of speech. Although Whitman eventually rejected "Pictures" as a failed experiment, the poem's failure foreshadows a problem in many poems Whitman would later publish. Often the self of these poems is not a developing character but a didactic voice with nothing to learn, only a deadening, repetitive wisdom.

"Pictures" was probably written quickly, and it has many of the weaknesses of Whitman's journalism: a skimming style, lines that are flatly descriptive, as if the writer had not taken the time to probe for exact words and rhythms. Whitman once told Horace Traubel that he never could think fast enough to be a successful journalist. That remark may be a key to the difference between Whitman's achievement as a serious writer and his commonplace journalism. His best poetry was written and rewritten, formed gradually to its final rhythms. The germinal idea for "Crossing Brooklyn Ferry" lay fallow for six years, before Whitman shaped it into a poem. As we have seen, he kept a series of notebooks spanning these years, and they are filled with prose paragraphs, isolated sentences, paraphrases of other writers, trial lines for poems, whole sections of verse. What is startling is the degree of transformation these raw materials underwent before taking their place in the finished poems. The prose has been worked into long rhythmic lines of verse. The notebook verse has been rewritten many times. Often it has been pulled apart, with separate lines ending up in widely separate parts of the poem. The inspired "boiling" of these years did not exclude a deliberate effort of construction, many times reworked. There is an architectonic genius here which combines, in the great poems, with Whitman's other genius for the single line, the verbal snapshot. It indicates something of Whitman's best method that "Song of Myself," the most subtle and verbally dense of these early poems, should have been worked up from such a diverse and longly crafted base. The lesser poems of the 1855 edition have left behind little such "foreground"; they were probably written more hastily, as their looser, flatter lines reflect.

2

In the spring of 1853, Whitman took time off from his contracting work to accompany his ill father on a visit to the family homestead in West Hills on Long Island. It is the only time we hear of the older Whitman during these years. Like Whitman himself in his old age, his father had gradually lost his strength and his health. During the next years, the latter's impending death would dominate the Whitman household; a suspended breath, waiting to be expelled. Whitman expressed this in an unconsciously impatient image written hastily some months before his father's death. "America," begins the prose introduction to his new book of poems, "perceives that the corpse is slowly borne from the eating and drinking rooms of the house . . . that it was fittest for its days . . . that its action has descended to the stalwart and well-shaped heir who approaches . . . and that he shall be the fittest for his days."

The "heir" had arrived, bearded and prematurely grey. The "work" he was making was not a house, but a book. Like his father, he would be good at his work: a solid constructor of poems. Yet, like his father, he would have a hard time selling his work for profit. His eventual success would be wrenched from a history of failures, as if he had to struggle—an awful wrestling with the angel—to break with his father's pattern of failure. The "heir's" triumph is the result of a long inner argument which he won only gradually and doggedly. Perhaps this is a key to Whitman's late blossoming. Yet by 1855 the signs of triumph were accumulating. Whitman had already become a kind of father. Not only did he provide money for the household and supervise domestic matters; his brother George remembers him to have been thoughtful, strong, a puzzle to his family, but looked up to, a source of moral strength. In these years, which had a quality of belated, excitable adolescence, Whitman was becoming not only his mother's but also his father's keeper. Perhaps we see here a source of that irrepressible will to become father and mother to all mankind which shapes the elusive tone of his poetry and fashions his very personality as a delicate "rough," a mother-man, swaggering yet gentle, assertive yet coy and sentimental.

Soon another failure pushed Whitman toward the life he was already choosing. By the winter of 1854, economic conditions had worsened throughout the country. New houses were selling at a loss of twenty to thirty percent. Brooklyn's building boom was over for a time, and the Whitman brothers were out of business. Walt had never given himself completely to house building anyway. He had gone on writing for the *Star* and even for his old employer, the *Eagle*—proof that whatever hard feelings there had been, had long since faded. His stubbornly personal schedule had always given him time to walk the streets and fill envelopes with scraps of notepaper; to read the newspapers assiduously and clip out articles containing raw material for a poetry of the "immediate age": in Brooklyn, a burning house collapses on a fireman; the ship *San Francisco* is disabled in a storm while another ship circles it for four days, with a sign chalked on a board: "Be of good cheer, we will not desert you." These will be fragments for Whitman's "song." And now he had more time than ever. Again, failure was his release.

Whitman visited the Astor Library. He asked a Mr. Dwight about the "highest numeral term known" for his romance of immense numbers, and visited Henry Abbot's Egyptian Museum on Broadway. The enthusiasm he had brought to politics, and then to art, and then to Italian opera, he now brought to the study of language. He began to collect words, definitions. His notes contain lists of pithy consonantal words like "cruller, skull, lusty, wicket"; rare words he probably had to look up in a dictionary ("gusset, cincture, tendon, craunch, mandible, pilaster"); a list of definitions for the word *lusty* ("bulky, hardy, strong, stout, powerful, rough, muscular, vigorous, robust, vital, physical"). On another page, he listed medical words: "*Clyster,* the liquid or wash for the injection into the lower intestines. *Clyster-pipe,* the syringe. *Enema,* an injection . . . into the rectum as a medicine or to impart nourishment. *Rectum,* the terminal or excretory part of the lower intestines. . . . *Anus,* the ass-hole. *Scrotum*—the bag of the testicles." During these experimental years, the very rules of language seemed to be ripe for reform:

Drawing language into line by rigid grammatical rules, is the theory of the martinet applied to the processes of the spirit, and to the luxuriant growth of all that makes art.—It is for small school masters, not for great souls.—Not only the Dictionary of the English Language, but the Grammar of it, has yet to be written.

Whitman would go on making lists and adding definitions, hoping to assemble them eventually in his own version of the new dictionary. American English was the crown of all languages, he now felt, and he would soon say so in several remarkable essays. But the time had not come yet for proclamations. Now Whitman read (or read about) the great German philologists, the linguists and historians. He became conscious of language as a medium with its own life, full of resistances, slippery, pliable. As an old man, he would look back over his life's work and call it a "language experiment." In 1853 and 1854 the experiment had begun.

From his house-building years, Whitman kept the workingman's "uniform," now a flaunted, if still unnoticed, answer to the well-dressed literary crowd who would be seriously puzzled by him when, a year or two later, he emerged publicly from his modest Brooklyn neighborhood.

3

On 15 July 1853, the largest industrial exhibition ever held in America opened next to the Croton holding reservoir, far uptown at 42nd Street. The exhibition's glass and cast-iron shed outdid the original Crystal Palace which, two years earlier, had housed the London World's Fair. New York's Crystal Palace was an enormous Greek cross measuring 365 feet 5 inches along each arm, with at its center a 123-foot dome, the highest ever built in America. Alongside this, stood a second conventional structure for the exhibit of moving machinery. The entire exhibition covered four acres, on what is now Bryant Park. On the north side of 42nd Street near Sixth Avenue stood Latting's ice cream parlor, topped by a 280-foot observatory tower. The downtown panorama of the city as seen from the platform on top of the tower, framed by the two rivers and the wide bay, has been preserved in numerous etchings. Latting's tower was New York's first skyscraper, until a fire destroyed it several years later.

For months, the Crystal Palace had been front page news, as 15,000 panes of translucent enameled glass were fitted onto the cast-iron armature. New Yorkers, with their love of immense numbers, were impressed by the catalogue of statistics published by the *New York Times*: 1,800 tons of iron; 750,000 board feet of wood; 55,000 square feet of glass; 173,000 feet of exhibition space in the main structure alone. Clusters of gas lights and drinking fountains of New York's famous Croton water were installed. The exhibits arrived from all over Europe and America: every kind of manufactured product and raw material; quantities of art work; "philosophical machinery," including the daguerreotype; examples of the latest technology and industry; decorative items such as perfumes, clothes, hair dyes, including, in the American exhibit, Mr. Bell of New York's collection of stuffed birds.

President Franklin Pierce and the great English geologist, Charles Lyell, attended the inaugural ceremonies, as New Yorkers crowded uptown to celebrate the opening of this cornucopia of the present age. Among them came Walt Whitman who would return often over the next year, wandering inside the broad arms of the glass and cast-iron cross, like the poet in Samuel Warren's epic, *The Lily and the Bee.* This was Whitman's element: the crowds and the soft gas lights; the eclectic mingling of commerce, art, and science. The promoters claimed that the Crystal Palace inaugurated a new age. Soon war would be replaced by the heroic advances of science and technology. The nations would meet not on battlegrounds but in industrial exhibits. The Crystal Palace stood for the wealth, progress, and democracy of this new age.

The high spirits of the occasion may have been dampened during an afternoon rainstorm by several leaks in the unfinished dome. But it was an exciting day for New Yorkers. For almost a year, the crowds would come, despite the exhibition's inconvenient location far uptown. For a mile around, there would be Crystal Stables, Crystal Cake Shops, Crystal groggeries and ice cream saloons. A dilapidated hotel on Sixth Avenue was renamed the Crystal Hall of Pleasures, and an old woman called her racks of rotting oranges and bananas, the Crystal Fruit Stall. On the streets surrounding the official exhibition arose a popular fair, with colorful health cures, a lung-testing machine, a bearded lady. "I went for a long time (nearly a year)—days and nights, especially the latter," Whitman wrote. He spent hours in the largest art gallery ever assembled in America, including a colossal grouping, "Christ and his Apostles," by the admired Danish sculptor, Bertel Thorvaldsen, and Baron Carlo Marochetti's oafish equestrian statue of George Washington. There were "many fine bronzes," Whitman remembered, along with "pieces of plate from English silversmiths, and curios from everywhere abroad—with woods from all the lands of the earth—all sorts of fabrics and products and handwork from the workers of all nations."

During this climactic year, Whitman worked at his notebooks and experimented with the idea of a "colossal," "perfect" character, who would be himself. He spent days and evenings at the Crystal Palace, enjoying the bands, the art, and the gas lights; enjoying, above all, the festive concentration of modernity displayed as a living "catalogue," a "list-poem" of man's works in all their randomness. As the Crystal Palace announced a new age of productive labor, an age of the common man and the consumer living lives of epic ordinariness, so Whitman, too, would announce this age in another way. Already he was shaping his thought, not systematically but under the pressure of an elusive conception that cast up bits and fragments related by a common tone, a common, as yet unformulated idea. In his notebook, he proposed writing, "A poem in which all things and qualities and processes express themselves—the nebula—the fixed stars—the earth—the grass, waters, vegetable, sauroid, and all processes—man—animals." The poem would be "Song of Myself." Like the Crystal Palace, and like the "poem" sung by the journeyman violinist of *The Countess of Rudolstadt,* it would be a compendium of all knowledge, all experience, housed in a form as outsized, in its way, as the glass and cast-iron cross next to the reservoir: Whitman's capacious "self." The heroism of this "self" would consist in an ability to "digest" all the variousness of man and of life itself; to display it for all to see, in a new sort of poem: not a "linear" account of the violent heroism of warfare, but a profuse, soaring display; not a story, but a feast spread out to be viewed.

These analogies between "Song of Myself" and New York's Crystal Palace are only slightly fanciful. Each expressed in its way the nineteenth century's pleasure in miscellaneous display; each declared for a new age characterized by the triumph of daily living. Let the Crystal Palace stand for these years of 1853 and 1854 when, still an obscure Brooklyn house builder and journalist, Whitman was making the works and making himself, while he spent hours at the exhibition which reflected back to him his own emerging vision of "the immediate age." It is fitting that he recorded a visit to the Crystal Palace on the reverse side of some trial lines for "Song of Myself":

20 March, '54

Bill Guess—aged 22. A thoughtless, strong, generous animal nature, fond of direct pleasures, eating, drinking, women, fun, etc. Taken sick with the small-pox, had the bad disorder and was furious with the delirium tremors. Was with me in the Crystal Palace, a large, broad fellow, weighed over 200. Was a thoughtless good fellow.

Peter_____, large, strong-boned young fellow, driver. Should weigh 180. Free and candid to me the very first time he saw me. Man of strong self-will, powerful coarse feelings and appetites. Had a quarrel, borrowed $300, left his father somewhere in the interior of the State, fell in with a couple of gamblers, hadn't been home or written there in seven years. I liked his refreshing *wickedness,* as it would be called by the orthodox. He seemed to feel a perfect independence, dashed with a little resentment, toward the world in general. I never met a man that seemed to me, as far as I could tell in forty minutes, more open, coarse, self-willed, strong and free from the sickly desire to be on society's lines and points.

George Fitch—Yankee boy, driver. Fine nature, amiable, sensitive feelings, a natural gentleman, of quite a reflective turn. Left his home because his father was perpetually "down on him." When he told me of his mother his eyes watered. Good looking, tall, curly haired, black eyed fellow—age about 23 or 24—slender, face with a smile, trousers tucked in his boots, cap with the front-piece turned behind.

Whitman was not only "out of the game"; sometimes he was in it, too. He was happy to have company on his strolls about the gaily lit exhibit which, by now, had lost some of its novelty for New Yorkers and would soon require P. T. Barnum's tub-thumping to attract visitors. Bill Guess, Peter _____and George Fitch are not just names on Whitman's interminable lists. They are vividly remembered young men with, taken together, a large dose of those traits Whitman would soon dramatize in himself: physically big, thoughtless, good-natured, refreshingly wicked, yet naturally reflective and gentle, too. This reads like a composite portrait of Whitman's "rough"; the very portrait that would soon be immortalized in Gabriel Harrison's photograph, taken a few months later. Here were Whitman's models, even down to the problematical father and the beloved mother. As he walked with his young men, Whitman was observing and shaping his own "self." We must never underestimate his powers of self-observation. Remember the phrenologist's motto: "Self-made or never made." As Whitman "boiled" with poetry, he remade his newly pliable self in the image of men like these: unorthodox, good-natured, physical. Just the sort of men who—in Whitman's rhapsody of rage, "The Eighteenth Presidency"—could become president, or even a great poet, in a true democracy.

By now, Whitman had severed his connection to the Democratic party, and to all parties. For several years, the nation's political life had been dominated by a series of laborious compromises, as Democrats and Whigs tried to play down the sectional conflict that was threatening to tear the country apart. The attempts failed. Webster's Omnibus Bill, and now Stephen O. Douglas's repeal of the Missouri Compromise, reassured no one. Disaster was in the making, and the politicians were helpless to prevent it, or even to formulate the prospect of it. Whitman was not alone in his disaffection. Within two years, the newly formed Republican party would attempt to rally unhappy voters. But Whitman's rage at the "limber-tongued lawyers, very fluent but empty feeble old men, professional politicians, dandies, dyspeptics," whom he saw running the government, was too profound to be satisfied by any arrangement of the parties. What America needed was not new politics but new men, he would write in his "Eighteenth Presidency," or at the very least, in the words of his 1855 preface, "one fullsized man, unconquerable and simple."

The poem "Pictures," crude and mechanical though it was, had sketched the making of such a man, who would justify Emerson's breathtaking reversal: all the collective entities that shaped men and took charge of their lives—the governments, the institutions—were only the lengthened shadow cast by this man. He was a center, from him radiated the circumference; he was "complete"; others, incomplete. Above all, he was the natural product of democracy. If America's "experiment," with freedom succeeded, it would be his work. He would also be the evidence and only unanswerable proof of democracy's triumph:

> I carry the plenum of proof and everything else in my face,
> With the hush of my lips I confound the topmost skeptic.

Whitman wasn't floundering now. In his notebooks he worked out ambitious patterns of prose and verse, preliminaries for the great poem that was coming. Yet his years of public life kept his "language experiment" from becoming a retreat. To be sure, like his future supporters, Emerson and Thoreau, there was in him a brittle core that would not come down into the marketplace; an arrogance, a coldness even, which showed in his flashes of righteous rage and in the sudden shifts of feeling that made him seem impregnable, even a little frightening, to his friends. Yet he did not withdraw now to any shack in the woods to write his poems. His upstairs room was not a solitary platform for the sort of "spiritual astronomy" that characterized Emerson. In one of his notebooks he wrote: "Lofty sirs! you are very select . . . and will have reserved seats in the ninetieth heaven . . . and recognize only the best dressed and most polite angels. . . . As for me I am a born democrat. I take my place by night among the sudorous or sweaty classes, among men in their shirt sleeves—the sunburnt, the unshaven, the huge paws."

In October, Whitman wrote a "memorial" to the Brooklyn City Council, arguing against its decision to shut down the city's railcars on Sundays, so as to preserve the orderliness of the Sabbath. This sort of thing had been a favorite target of his in the *Eagle,* years before. Government had no business meddling in the morals of individuals: "Alas, gentlemen, the civilized world has been overwhelmed with prohibitions for many hundreds of years." In the case at hand, "the stoppage of the Railcars causes much vexation and weariness to many families," on the very day when they are free to enjoy themselves. Let them enjoy themselves; government cannot be "the overseer and dry nurse" of a man's private behavior. In a democracy, less is more; even disorder is better than the arrogant arbitrary imposition of order. As Whitman warms to his subject, we hear echoes of the new vocabulary he was formulating in his notebooks:

We do not want prohibitions. What is always wanted is a few strong-handed, big-brained practical honest men. . . . The citizen must have room. He must learn to be so muscular and self-possessed; to rely more on the restriction of himself than any restrictions of statute books, or city ordinances, or police. This is the feeling that will make live men and superior women. This will make a great athletic spirited city. . . .

There is indeed nowhere any better scope for practically exhibiting the full-sized American idea, than in a great, free, proud, American City. Most of our cities are huge aggregates of people, riches, and enterprise. The avenues, edifices and furniture are splendid; but what is that to splendor of character? To encourage the growth of trade and property is commendable; but our politics might also encourage the forming of men of superior demeanor, and less shuffling and blowing.

Here were Whitman's politics and his poetics too. Democracy was not a structure of laws or a jostling of the parties, but a community of "well-developed men . . . possessed with the eternal American ideas of liberty, friendliness, amplitude and courage." On a piece of paper, he jotted down his sweet, anarchist's fantasy: "In a few years the legislatures national state and municipal will subside into rare sessions." Shelley had rhapsodized about the poet as legislator. For Whitman this was no rhapsody but an urgent call to duty. Under the inept politics of the 1850s, his excitable imagination saw the possibility of an exalted function for some "well-developed man," who could speak to all. *"Rule in all addresses—and poems and other writings etc.—*Do not undertake to say anything however plain to you unless you are positive it will be perfectly plain to those who hear or read. —Make it plain." We hear Whitman's plain-speaking man in this very "memorial," as we will hear him in the celebratory prose of the 1855 preface, in the unpublished "Eighteenth Presidency," in the notes on language that were published after his death under the title *American Primer.* We hear him in Whitman's lecture projects of the next few years. In marginal notes on platform manner, voice, and intonation, he imagined an orator whose words and physical presence would enlarge the diminished lives of his hearers:

Animation of limbs, hands, arms, neck, shoulders, waist, open breast, etc.—the fullest type of live oratory—at times an expanding chest, at other times reaching forward, bending figure, raised to its fullest height, bending way over, low down, etc.

The strong, yet flexible face. By persevering exercise, muscular, mental, copious, practice of face, all the muscles attain a perfect readiness of expression, terror, rage, love, surprise, sarcasm.

Sweeping movements, electric and broad style of the hands, arms, and all the upper joints. These are to be developed just as much as the voice by practice.

In the America Whitman hoped for, there was no limit to the influence such a man could wield. He would be a national bard, a poet-legislator, a priest: "From the opening of the Oration and on through, the great thing is to be inspired as one divinely possessed, blind to all subordinate affairs and given up entirely to the surgings and utterances of the mighty tempestuous demon."

Whitman called his enlarging demon "nature," although, with a paradox that goes to the heart of his conception, he described him in a series of staged poses and calculated vocal effects. Whitman's demon-nature was as deliberate as a dandy. Yet Whitman saw him ranging across the country, succeeding where institutions blundered and failed:

True vista before—The strong thought-impression or conviction that the straight, broad, open, well-marked vista before, or course of public teacher, "wander-speaker",—by powerful words, orations, uttered with copiousness and decision, with all the aid of art, also the natural flowing vocal luxuriance of oratory. That the mightiest rule over America could be thus—as for instance, on occasion, at Washington to be, launching from public room, at the opening of the session of Congress—perhaps launching at the President, leading persons, Congressmen, or Judges of the Supreme Court. That to dart hither or thither, as some great emergency might demand—the greatest champion America ever could know, yet holding no office or emolument whatever . . . and always to hold the ear of the people.

216

Whitman's very syntax creaks with the bulky voice he is imagining. His "wander-speaker" is nature's politician, the president of hearts.

A dozen years later, Whitman called his idea of the American experiment "personalism," emphasizing his belief that democracy stands or falls with its ability to give rise to complete individuals. In doing so, Whitman spoke with the voice of his century which had placed the individual at the heart of social theory. Rousseau, Schiller, Blake, Kierkegaard, Carlyle, Emerson: such a dissonant chorus, yet all making the same potentially revolutionary judgment. Society succeeds in its great-souled individuals, fails wherever it constricts and mechanizes. "Man was born free, yet every where he is in chains," Rousseau had written in the opening line of *The Social Contract,* and a century of writer-philosophers glossed him: Schiller, with his vision of men "fragmented" by modern labor; Carlyle, with his grim view of the machine age:

Not the external and physical alone is now managed by machinery, but the internal and spiritual also. . . . Men are grown mechanical in head and in heart, as well as in hand. Not for internal perfection, but for external combinations and arrangements, for institutions, constitutions—for Mechanism of one sort or another, do they hope and struggle.

If "energy is eternal delight," as in Blake's proverb of hell, then society, by stealing a man's work, has stolen his delight, his very substance. "Alienation," for Marx, becomes a crime against greatness of soul.

Whitman's *Democratic Vistas* would be in this tradition: a sweeping, turbulent, dark outcry. Yet, despite its idiosyncratic style, *Democratic Vistas,* published in 1871, would be a book much like other books, a call for argument and response. In 1854, Whitman was moved by a richer braiding of personal and political hopes. The "personalism" is there—we hear it in his new emphasis on large self-reliant individuals; but it is less a doctrine than a program for Whitman's "wander-speaker" and poet. In the idiom he is preparing, democracy will resemble an immense theater: the "singer" will perform his aria, and the people—those freely spinning atoms of shapeless America—will be brought to a focus, merged in the sort of ecstasy Whitman knew evening after evening at the opera house. To be an audience is to be multiplied, and yet singular; separate, yet enlarged with the massed energies of so many others. Whitman would call this paradoxical feeling "en-masse individuality."

In his day, Americans loved to be part of an audience. They adored their great orators—Daniel Webster, Edward Everett, Wendell Phillips. They made a lecturer, Ralph Waldo Emerson, into a cultural hero. They built opera houses in western boom towns, congregated in evangelical tent meetings, and developed a passion for the street theater of mass political rallies. In a country that was perpetually on the move, repudiating its past and building its future in a din of sawdust and hammers, the social bond stretched thin. Americans recognized themselves all too well in Tocqueville's description:

Among democratic peoples, new families are always rising out of obscurity, others are always falling back, and those that remain are changing; time's pattern is broken at every moment, and the remains of past generations are obliterated. We forget easily those who have preceded us, and have no idea of those who will follow. Only those who are closest appear interesting. Each class moves closer to the others and mixes with them, its members become indifferent and like strangers to each other. Aristocracy had made of all its citizens a long chain climbing from the peasantry to the king; democracy breaks the chain, setting each link apart from the others. . . .

Thus not only does democracy make each man forget his ancestors, it hides his descendants from him, and divides him from his contemporaries; it continually turns him back into himself, and threatens, at last, to enclose him entirely in the solitude of his own heart.

As an audience, however, Americans were brought together; here, in the theater or meeting hall, was society made solid and palpable. That Whitman should have hit upon the poet-orator as a figure for his enlarged selfhood shows how attuned he was to the theatricality of his character—but also to the cultural needs of his reader. His "argument with others" and his flamboyantly staged personage went hand in hand. Writing large-voiced poems; sauntering visibly up Broadway, pink-skinned, bearded, and "limber"; sitting magisterially silent at Pfaff's, or projecting himself in imagination across the country as a voice bursting its confines, transforming inchoate America into a community of hearts: all these constituted for Whitman an act at once personal and political.

4

In nearly all of Whitman's writing in the mid-1850s, there is a feeling of malleability, of unlimited possibility. He will become radically new; he will reinvent literature; he will transform America; he will create a new dictionary, new syntactical forms; he will master all of world literature, all of history and science. His appetite was immense, unreal; more like the fantasies of an adolescent dreamer than the reflections of a thirty-five-year-old man who, for more than a dozen years, had been schooled in the bruising business of actual politics, who had suffered through the recalcitrant cycles of the economy and the demands of a large poor family, with a dying father, a pathologically violent older brother, and a retarded younger brother. "The Eighteenth Presidency," written during these years, is subtitled "Voice of Walt Whitman to Each Young Man in the Nation, North, South, East, and West." Although the text was never published, Whitman set it up in type, as if he expected his closing exhortation to be heard:

To editors of the independent press, and to rich persons. Circulate and reprint this Voice of mine for the workingmen's sake. I hereby permit and invite any rich person, anywhere, to stereotype it, or re-produce it in any form, to deluge the cities of The States with it, North, South, East and West. It is those millions of mechanics you want; the writers, thinkers, learned and benevolent persons, merchants, are already secured about to a man. But the great masses of the mechanics, and a large portion of the farmers, are unsettled, hardly know whom to vote for, or whom to believe. I am not afraid to say that among them I seek to initiate my name, Walt Whitman, and that I shall in future have much to say to them.

By the time Whitman wrote these lines, he had already begun to have his say in the magnificent poems of the 1855 and 1856 editions of *Leaves of Grass.* He had been praised by the "Master,"

Ralph Waldo Emerson, and had received visits from Emerson, Thoreau, Bronson Alcott. On the other hand, his book had not exactly become a household item. He had been vilified by some critics, praised perceptively by others, and virtually deified in several anonymous local reviews which, it turns out, he wrote himself. He had established the beginnings of a controversial literary fame. Not, to be sure, the respectful sort of fame of his colleague and acquaintance, William Cullen Bryant, or the pleasing reputation of a romantic songster, like Longfellow. From the first, Whitman's poetry disturbed in ways that his critics were quick to see. He was not simply criticized; he was reviled as a disgusting barbarian; or—as in the case of Emerson, Thoreau, Fanny Fern, and an odd chorus of literary outsiders, many of them women—he was loved, even looked on with awe. Yet his book constituted a small occurrence in the literary world. All in all, *Leaves of Grass,* in 1855 and 1856, was close to being a non-event. Were it not for the enthusiastic letter that Emerson wrote him in 1855, Whitman might have become just another New York eccentric like McDonald Clarke, the mad street poet of the 1830s whom he had written about years before, in the *Aurora.* Whitman's "success" could hardly serve as a platform for his stratospheric ambitions. Calling his poems a "New Bible" in 1857 was part of a dizzying display of unrealism; a fantasy of power linked maybe to a feeling of release, as well as to a headlong flight from guilt, caused by his father's illness and death days after his book was published in 1855.

What is noteworthy, finally, are not these irruptions of manic fantasy that seized hold of Whitman during his uniquely productive years, but his ability to give a communicable form to his fantasy. In his case, the infantile visionary was also a crafty poet, and he rarely mistook the excitement of the vision for the reality of the poems. Manic vision and an intuitive confidence in the language tool he had been elaborating since the early 1850s went hand in hand. We see this in the poems, which speak with the voice of an adventurous, eloquent, sexually alive man; someone who, if he chose, could dominate the public arena, as Whitman's "wander-speaker"—as Whitman himself—believed he could. We know that Whitman's life and his poems came together in the 1850s.

This coming together was an effect of style. The poems say it was so; and the man, taking his cue from the poems, created himself as living proof of the poems' truth. Shall we call this acting a pose? Yet suppose the actor cannot set aside his part. Suppose the part is all he can allow himself to be. When does the mask melt into the flesh, and the lie become the face? It is probably the mark of a man's genius that he can present the twists of his personal history in a way that touches others. He can write poems, for example, and make his pose the centerpoint of a dialogue:

> I am he attesting sympathy;
> Shall I make my list of things in the house and skip the house that supports them?

The "house" containing Whitman's "lists" is the poem; the poem, in turn, is his channel of sympathy. By means of the poem he is not solitary, like his Louisiana live oak, "uttering leaves of joyous green," without any friend or comrade near. Whitman knew—he tells us in this lovely poem—he could not do that. For the poem is his sanity, and he is its supporting truth:

The soul has that measureless pride which consists in never acknowledging any lesson but its own. But it has sympathy as measureless as its pride and the one balances the other and neither can stretch too far while it stretches in company with the other. The inmost secrets of art sleep with the twain. The greatest poet has lain close with both and they are vital in his style and thoughts.

Let us remember, too, the unique atmosphere of the 1850s, surely some of the strangest years in American history. Civil war was in the offing. The middle years of the decade were gripped by a prolonged economic crisis, paralleled by one of the country's periodic outbursts of religious mania. Locally, New York City was having a civil war of its own between native Protestant "Know-Nothings" and immigrant Irish and German Catholics. When the papal nuncio, Cardinal Bedini, visited the city, he was attacked by hostile "nativist" mobs and had to flee on a tugboat. On several Sundays during the summer of 1854, a sailor calling himself the Angel Gabriel came over to Brooklyn with a bodyguard of Know-

Nothings* in white pre-Ku Klux Klan hats, to preach in a vacant lot on "Purgatory for Popery and the Pope." Brooklyn Catholics attacked them with stones, bricks, and guns in a series of bloody street fights.

In May 1854, an escaped slave named Anthony Burns was arrested by United States marshals in Boston. Suddenly the reviled Fugitive Slave Law was no mere legality: the Federal Government itself was dragging a free man into slavery. Within days, Boston's public halls were packed; Wendell Phillips and the historian Theodore Parker shouted their outrage. There were riots and the marines had to be called; a protestor was killed. Whitman set aside his still formless notes for a long poem, to write a sarcastic "ballad" which he included in his book a year later:

> Clear the way there Jonathan!
> Way for the President's marshal! Way for the government cannon!
> Way for the federal foot and dragoons . . . and the phantoms afterward. . . .
>
> Why this is a show! It has called the dead out of the earth,
> The old graveyards of the hills have hurried to see;
> Uncountable phantoms gather by flank and rear of it,
> Cocked hats of mothy mould and crutches made of mist,
> Arms in slings and old men leaning on young men's shoulders.
>
> What troubles you, Yankee phantoms? What is all this chattering of bare gums?
> Does the ague convulse your limbs? Do you mistake your crutches for firelocks, and level them?
>
> If you blind your eyes with tears you will not see the President's marshal,
> If you groan such groans you might balk the government cannon.

Like "Resurgemus," written in 1850, this is a political melodrama, belligerent, ironic. The poem draws on Whitman's old favorite themes—the ghosts, the graveyard imagery—but with a cocky sureness of touch that surpasses the political poems of 1850.

---

*The "Know-Nothings" were members of a minor political party, the American party, and were hostile to the flood of immigrants—in particular, the Germans and Irish—who were changing American life at the time. The predecessors of the Know-Nothings were small Native American groups, active in the 1840s, especially against the Irish and against Catholics in general. Their narrow nationalism eventually repelled Whitman; but in the early 1840s, as editor of the *Aurora,* he had been violently anti-Irish and anti-Catholic himself.

He speaks to the decade's political despair. We hear the same shrilly disappointed tone as in Emerson's journals of the time: a grim sense that America's "experiment," which a decade before appeared to crown all of history, was failing.

But the 1850s were not simply a time of national self-doubt. This was America's heyday of "progress" and territorial expansion. "Size is only development," time is an "unflagging pregnancy," Whitman would write in "Song of Myself," expressing what appeared to be an unshakable American belief. For the crisis of the 1850s was played against an equally bold scenario of hope, symbolized for New Yorkers by the Crystal Palace: here was "progress" made visible; here for all to see were the inventions that were changing the world—the railroads, the ocean steamers, the telegraph, the Atlantic cable, the elevators, central heating. American optimism drew strength from these miracles of technology. Despite the fires that periodically destroyed their wooden cities, and the economic busts that drove hard-working men into poverty, despite slavery, a flawed political system, and an ever-increasing tide of public anger, Americans still managed to see themselves as the "Adam" of the national myth their writers had created for them. In 1855, Whitman's "poet" would express this undeflatable hope:

He drags the dead out of their coffins and stands them again on their feet. . . . He says to the past, Rise and walk before me that I may realize you. He learns the lesson . . . he places himself where the future becomes present. The greatest poet does not only dazzle his rays over character and scenes and passions . . . he finally ascends and finishes all. . . . He exhibits the pinnacles that no man can tell what they are for or what is beyond . . . he glows a moment on the extremest verge. He is most wonderful in his last half-hidden smile or frown.

It is characteristic of Whitman that he should phrase his historical optimism in terms of personal possibility. The colossus bestriding past and future, is himself. Politics, poetry, geography merge to create this malleable giant, the fleshed and brawling child of Emerson's "central man."

The very grammar of Whitman's preface communicates a sense of unlimited expansion. Its sentences unfold in large syntactical loops, distending and almost vanishing amidst chaplets of nouns; these are sentences like prairies or open stretches of river, or like the pliable unpredictable changes of a living being:

Henceforth let no man of us lie, for we have seen that openness wins the inner and outer world and that there is no single exception, and that never since our earth gathered itself in a mass have deceit or subterfuge or prevarication attracted its smallest particle or the faintest tinge of a shade—and that through the enveloping wealth and rank of a state or the whole republic of states a sneak or sly person shall be discovered and despised . . . and that the soul has never once been fooled and never can be fooled . . . and thrift without the loving nod of the soul is only a fetid puff . . . and there never grew up in any of the continents of the globe nor upon any satellite or star, nor upon the asteroids, nor in any part of ethereal space, nor in the midst of density, nor under the fluid wet of the sea, nor in that condition which precedes the birth of babes, nor at any time during the changes of life, nor in that condition that follows what we term death, nor in any stretch of abeyance or action afterward of vitality, nor in any process of formation or reformation anywhere, a being whose instinct hated the truth.

In his notebooks, Whitman played with neologisms, tried out quirky changes of usage, protested the conventions of naming, and proposed new ones. If *Leaves of Grass* was a "language experiment," as he told Horace Traubel, then here was the laboratory; a litter of half-shaped propositions for reforming the American idiom:

All through a *common* gender ending in *ist* as—
    lovist) both
    hatist) masc
       &
      fem
 —   hater m
     hatress f &c.
a good innovation
    employer —employee
    offender —offendee
       thing offended
    server —servee
    lover —lovee
       thing loved
    hater —hatee
       thing hated

about the controversy respecting words ending in *ick*—the k left out by modern writers—If anything is left out it were better the c—thus musik, stik, lok, brik, apoplektik

The *Girls l'Amour* love-girls

Names of cities, islands, rivers, new settlements &c. These should/must assimilate in sentiment and in sound, to something organic in the place, or identical with it—It is far better to call a new inhabited island by the native word, than by its first discoverer, or to call it New anything—Aboriginal names always tell finely; sometimes it is necessary to slightly Anglicize them—All classic names are objectionable. How much better Ohio, Oregon, Missouri, Milwaukee &c. Iowa (?) than New York, Ithica, &c.

Today we know that languages are not so easily "reformed." Yet Whitman was not simply playing out his extravagant temperament here. A bouyant, almost dreamlike belief in the improvability of man was part of the national mood. Poe attacked it, with his obsessed vision of buried, shrinking enclosures. Melville turned it into a desperate joke, in his "cannibal" epic, *Moby Dick,* in *Pierre,* and in *The Confidence Man.* Whitman himself had little patience with the popular reform movements of the 1850s, which agitated loudly for everything from free love to vegetarianism. He found them narrow-minded, intolerant; no place for a "representative man," whose ambition was to embrace multitudes. Despite his love of comrades, he was not interested in the utopian communities that were springing up around the country: Brook Farm, in Massachusetts; Albert Brisbane's Fourierist phalanstery, in New Jersey; Etienne Cabet's Icarians in Illinois, whom Whitman had seen disembarking in New Orleans. From this time on, Whitman kept his politics closer to his body; he dreamed not of perfect communities but of perfect lovers. His democracy was modeled on an embrace.

Yet Whitman had accepted Orson Fowler's evangelical belief in the ability of individuals to reshape their lives by means of good eating, proper dress, sexual honesty, exercise, etcetera. "Progress" was not simply a matter of new machines and new politics. "What can be a more admirable aim for the most exalted human ambition," Whitman wrote, "than the wish and resolve to be *perfect*? Though the carrying out of this resolve requires some mental purification, the most of it, I think, is of a physical nature."

Whitman's unsettling commitment to the most extravagant propositions was rooted in the idiom of his day. If a single Fourierist phalanstery could transform the world within a calculated number of years; if "reform" could be seen as a broadside attack on all the benighted customs that kept man from becoming "perfect," then we must conclude that Whitman had company in his extravagance. The confidence that enabled him to remake the idiom of poetry was grafted onto a widespread belief that human affairs were malleable; that change was at hand; that a secular millennium could be obtained by finite calculable actions decided on by sensible, somewhat visionary men. As Whitman wrote in the soaring conclusion to his "Eighteenth Presidency":

Never was there more eagerness to know. Never was the representative man more energetic, more like a god, than today. He urges on the myriads before him, he crowds them aside, his daring step approaches the arctic and antarctic poles, he colonizes the shores of the Pacific, the Asiatic Indias, the birthplace of languages and of races, the Archipelagoes, Australia; he explores Africa, he unearths Assyria and Egypt, he re-states history, he enlarges morality, he speculates anew upon the soul, upon original premises; nothing is left quiet, nothing but he will settle by demonstrations for himself. What whispers are these running through the eastern Continents, and cross the Atlantic and Pacific? What historic denouments are these we are approaching? On all sides tyrants tremble, crowns are unsteady, the human race restive, on the watch for some better era, some divine war. No man knows what will happen next, but all know that some such things are to happen as mask the greatest moral convulsions of the earth. Who shall play the hand for America in these tremendous games?

CHAPTER 7

"Song of Myself"

1

SOMETIME DURING 1854, Whitman began to write out the poems of his first book, and his notebooks give us an idea of how he went about this. Many of the poems, as we have seen, developed from prose notes Whitman had made during the preceding years, some of them worked experimentally into a cascade of more or less rhythmic verse. Then, as if the vision of the poems and their long rhythmic line had suddenly become clear to him, Whitman recast all this material into the form we know, with its Biblical parallelisms, its anchoring nouns, and floating, indefinite verbs.

The turning point was almost certainly "Song of Myself": most of the preliminary prose and the rough spills of verse point to it. The existence of "Pictures," his crude earlier attempt at a similar work, makes it likely that this stylistically various poem absorbed Whitman's efforts for some time, perhaps several years. He forged his language instrument and his inclusive, miscellaneous form in order to write it. And, as we will see, he made the poem into one of those modern circular epics that tell the story of their own creation: Wordsworth's *Prelude,* Rimbaud's *Season in Hell,* Joyce's *Ulysses,* Proust's *Remembrance of Things Past.* "Song of Myself" enacts Whitman's birth as a poet. It is the record of an artist's struggle to become himself. Fittingly, it is also the workshop in which the change was accomplished. Here again, the life and the work intertwine, in the very making of Whitman's most ambitious poem.

It is fascinating to see his newly acquired verbal power casting about for an appropriate idiom. Whole lines from the prose would survive into his poems, yet it is not clear that Whitman had poems in mind when he wrote these lines. Many of the notations read like matured versions of the sort of prose he had written years before in "The Sundown Papers" and in his early stories and allegories:

I think the soul will never stop, or attain to any growth beyond which it shall not go.—When I walked at night by the seashore and looked up at the countless stars, I asked of my soul whether it would be filled and satisfied when it should become god enfolding all these, and open to the life and delight and knowledge of everything in them or of them; and the answer was plain to me at the breaking water on the sands at my feet: and the answer was, No, when I reach there, I shall want to go further still.—

I will not be a great philosopher, and found any school, and build it with iron pillars, and gather the young men around me, and make them my disciples, that new superior churches and politics shall come.—But I will take each man and woman of you to the window and open the shutters and the sash, and my left arm shall hook you round the waist, and my right shall point you to the endless and beginningless road along whose sides are crowded the rich cities of all living philosophy, and oval gates that pass you into the fields of clover and landscapes clumped with sassafras, and orchards of good apples, and every breath through your mouth shall be of a new perfumed and elastic air, which is love.—Not I—not God—can travel this road for you.—It is not far, it is within the stretch of your thumb; perhaps you shall find you are on it already and did not know.—Perhaps you shall find it every where over the ocean and over the land, when you once have the vision to behold it.—

Whitman would quarry phrases from these paragraphs and use them in "Song of Myself." The "open road"—we see it here for the first time—will underlie several poems in the book. Eventually it will become Whitman's best known theme:

I tramp a perpetual journey,
My signs are a rain-proof coat and good shoes and a staff cut from the
  woods;
No friend of mine takes his ease in my chair,
I have no chair, nor church nor philosophy;
I lead no man to a dinner-table or library or exchange,
But each man and each woman of you I lead upon a knoll,
My left hand hooks you round the waist,
My right hand points to landscapes of continents, and a
  plain public road. . . .

It is not far. . . . it is within reach,
Perhaps you have been on it since you were born, and did not know,
Perhaps it is everywhere on water and on land.

Whitman's "manuscript doings and undoings" have remade his essaylike prose into poetry. The allegory has been pared down; it has become the cautionary voice of his monologuing self. The prose has not so much been used as it has been plundered for its images, its sketch of a setting.

Whitman's loosely reeled-out line could accommodate a startling variety of tones; its range of subject matter was vast. He picked through his poetic notebooks and his old editorials, the scrapbook of newspaper items he had begun to keep half a dozen years before. He bracketed passages in books on geology and astronomy. These were his sources, and he worked them into the new line, inventing, pastiching, paraphrasing.

There is another, less appreciated side to Whitman's remarkable breakthrough at this time. As he wrote and rewrote the material accumulating on his desk, he began to shape it into a vast poem, and the shaping was unprecedented. Unlike virtually every other long poem of the century, this one did not tell a story or unfold an argument. The material in it included sensational erotic passages, fantasias of geology and astronomy, a series of impressionistic travelogues, a sketch of a sea battle, another of a wartime massacre, remarkable tableaux of a horse, a butcher, blacksmiths at work, a crisp-haired Negro worker, a fleeing slave, a sad lonely woman, vivid dawns and sunsets; the prayerful invocation of natural "miracles" reverberating with echoes from *Sartor Resartus*. All of this contributes to the changeable portrait of a man, named on line 499 as "Walt Whitman," who, we are told, is creating this uninterrupted flow as a form for himself, a celebration of himself.

Whitman was remarkably adroit. Without any narrative or clear subordination of themes, he arranged his armfuls of poetry into a single text. It is fascinating to see how he grouped together lines taken from all over his notebooks, and juggled passages, until they complemented each other and completed each other. The fragments and portraits and "catalogues," the sexual deliriums, and the reflections on poetry contribute to a whole effect, as the sounds of the instruments contribute to an orchestra. Among modern poems, perhaps T. S. Eliot's *The Waste Land* comes closest to "Song of Myself," in its deliberately various styles, its indirect unity consisting in repeated images and themes, its undercutting of narrative.

For half a century, *The Waste Land* has haunted readers, because its intricate balancing of themes seems to call out for interpretation: surely the poem "means" something; yet it slides out of reach, hovers amid a plurality of meanings, until, giving up, the reader understands that the poem is simply itself—a musical whole, spoken by a disembodied voice, in turn playful, mournful, satirical, mystical. "Song of Myself" has puzzled its readers in many of the same ways. Eschewing narrative, Whitman, too, balanced themes and images; he created a voice in turn playful, mournful, satirical, mystical. The idea of a musical structure was promoted by Whitman, who claimed that his method was that of the Italian opera: an interplay of arias and recitatives. The triumph of the poem lies, finally, in its architecture. In this sense, "Song of Myself" dominates the handful of finely constructed poems Whitman wrote: "Crossing Brooklyn Ferry," "Out of the Cradle Endlessly Rocking," "When Lilacs Last in the Dooryard Bloomed." In 1854, he built his most ambitious poem on the model of music rather than narrative; or like a display of items in a department store, overwhelming the viewer with its profusion; or, yet again, like an overabundant meal which stuns the guest, while giving him the pleasure of feasting without constraint. There will be more to say about this long poem which I believe is Whitman's masterpiece and one of the great long poems in our language. We will see Whitman's lanky balancing of themes flow together to suggest an elusive story: an adventure of personal change, told by allusion and by echo.

By the winter of 1854–55, he had completed a dozen poems and assembled them into a book. Did he submit the manuscript to a New York publisher that winter? If he did, he was unsuccessful. On the other hand, he may have chosen, from the first, to create his own book, to give it the shape of its unusual content, supervise its printing, and send it personally into the world. Some friends of Whitman's, James and Thomas Rome, owned a printing shop on the corner of Cranberry and Fulton streets, where they did mostly legal work. The Romes agreed to print Whitman's book, and he spent most of the spring of 1855 in their shop, revising, correcting proof. He himself set about ten pages of type, and had a special chair where he came every morning to read the *Tribune* and then work for a few hours.

He decided on a large quarto format to accommodate his unusually long lines. The Rome brothers printed 795 copies and then, surprisingly, distributed the type. If the country was going to "absorb" Whitman as "affectionately as he absorbed it," as he had written ·in his preface, people were going to have a hard time finding copies of his book. The whole affair was a little haphazard. When the sheets came off the press, the inking looked spotty, the typography was less than perfect. Whitman was a proud printer. He worked on his books personally whenever he could. It was a tribute to the trade he had practiced as a boy and then abandoned when he became a journalist, then a poet. The imperfections in his book cannot have pleased him. But Whitman was also a practical man. He was paying for this, and the money was limited. The Rome Brothers sent 200 copies of the book to a Brooklyn binder, Charles Jenkins who, for thirty-two cents a copy, produced the full effect Whitman sought: embossed green cover, gilded lettering; on the inside, Samuel Hollyer's stipple engraving of the photograph taken a year before by Gabriel Harrison. The remaining 595 copies were sent elsewhere for cheaper binding.

On 15 May, Whitman registered the copyright for his book in the Southern District County Court House, in Brooklyn. As a last touch, he dashed off an introductory essay and had it set in small type with forbidding double columns: not exactly an easy welcome into a book that seemed designed to trouble, more than to please, the reader. In fact, the inside and the outside of Whitman's book reflect two sides of his enterprise. The cover, a rich, dark green cloth with elaborate title letters woven with gilded shoots and tendrils invites the reader to a sentimental pleasure echoing the popular mode of feminine literature. Yet the inner design of the book disconcerts. No author is mentioned on the title page. The page facing it shows the engraved portrait of a man who does not look like a writer at all. Instead of the conventional authorly bust, in waistcoat and tie—a visual complement to the established writer's formal three names—the reader sees the three-quarters portrait of a workingman standing casually with his hand on his hip, his hat on, and his shirt open at the throat.

The introductory prose is untitled. Its small print and long sentences seem almost to bar entry to the book. The first six poems simply repeat the book's title: "Leaves of Grass." The rest of the poems are separated by a double bar, without any title at all. And the poems! The irregular lines of the first poem spill uninterrupted, with neither numbered parts nor significant stanza breaks, across fifty-six large pages. Beckoning with its outside, the book on its inside disturbs, even repels. With his first turn of the page, the reader stands warned. Don't expect the gracious hospitality of literature. This book is rough-spoken, clumsy; it won't make easy reading, won't charm you. Its starkly hewn poems are not simply poems; its author is not merely an author.

With this home-made book, Whitman declared himself uncompromisingly. Over the years, he would republish *Leaves of Grass* six times, adding poems, revising them, grouping them in new arrangements. Revision started only a year later and ended in 1892 with the "death-bed edition" which effectively froze Whitman's reputation for more than half a century. Everyone of these editions was the work of Whitman's hands. He sat with the printers, designed the cover, chose the type face. When, in 1891, he was too sick to worry his book through the press, he had his friend Horace Traubel do it for him. Yet the first edition stands apart, as a bristling anti-literary statement. It is Whitman's most radical venture, unshadowed by the conservative impulse that would coax him back toward "literature" as the years passed. Later would come the struggle for acceptance; the partly bungled attempts to reassure his readers by adopting the accepted themes of "religion," and other higher matters, safely far from the body. As for the sexual "rough," the sayer of home-made poems, he would be fenced in and dimmed. His poems would be recast as poems, with titles and numbered parts reminding the reader that he is proceeding safely toward an end: this delerium of irrupted bits and veering dithyrambs is art after all; it is order playing at disorder; the work of a modern Pindar, a superior Ossian, an incomparably masterful Martin Farquhar Tupper.

The 1855 *Leaves of Grass* shows no such caution. Whitman throws his chunky language at the reader. He cajols and thunders; he chants, celebrates, chuckles, and caresses. He spills from his capacious American soul every dreg of un-Englishness, every street sound thumbing its nose at traditional subject matter and tone. Here is Samson pulling the house of literature down around his ears, yet singing in the ruins.

Whitman arranged to sell his book at Swayne's on Fulton Street (who quickly withdrew because of the book's unsavory reputation) and may also have left some copies at Dion Thomas's on Nassau Street. He sent complimentary copies to a handful of influential people, including Ralph Waldo Emerson. But his main distributor was the phrenological clearinghouse, health bazaar, and catch-all reform publisher, Fowler and Wells, whose spacious quarters were now located at 308 Broadway, across from New York Hospital, near the present City Hall. There, amid copies of the *American Phrenological Journal, The Water-Cure Journal,* and *Life Illustrated* (to which he would soon be a regular contributor); amid such literary publications as Margaret Fuller's *Papers on Literature and Art* and several hundred other titles—mostly in the "how to" realm of health care, household management, botany, shorthand, and chemistry—Whitman deposited the bulk of his small edition. It was a peculiar choice, but also a practical one. Fowler and Wells could provide generous publicity through their various magazines (Whitman would anonymously review his own book in *The American Phrenological Journal,* in 1856). They would forward copies to

their Boston office and, most important, to their English distributor, in London—a key to Whitman's success in England, a dozen
years later. Fowler and Wells provided a curiously appropriate atmosphere for Whitman's anti-literary ambition. Taken at its word,
Leaves of Grass may have been the most ambitious "how to" man-
ual in the Fowler and Wells repertoire. Here was not any mere
poem or literary distraction but a recipe for self-making on a vast
scale:

This is what you shall do: Love the earth and sun and the animals, despise
riches, give alms to everyone that asks, stand up for the stupid and crazy,
devote your income and labor to others, hate tyrants, argue not concerning God, have patience and indulgence toward the people, take off your
hat to nothing known or unknown or to any man or number of men, go
freely with powerful uneducated persons and with the young and with
the mothers of families, read these leaves in the open air every season of
every year of your life, re-examine all you have been told at school or
church or in any book, dismiss whatever insults your own soul, and your
very flesh shall be a great poem and have the richest fluency not only in
its words but in the silent lines of its lips and face and between the lashes
of your eyes and in every motion and joint of your body.

• • •

Stop this day and night with me and you shall possess the origin of all
  poems,
You shall possess the good of the earth and sun . . . there are millions
  of suns left,
You shall no longer take things at second or third hand . . . nor look
  through the eyes of the dead . . . nor feed on the spectres in books,
You shall not look through my eyes either, nor take things from me,
You shall listen to all sides and filter them from yourself.

The Fowler and Wells program of self-change—their vision of
man as a malleable animal with his fate in his hands—could be said
to reach a climax in this irregular text, which offered to launch its
reader on the open road of his appetites, as a living poem—God's,
and Walt Whitman's, other book—unhoused, journeying beyond
the stage-mummery of social roles to a completeness of being personified by Whitman's epithet "kosmos."

The 1892 "death-bed edition" of *Leaves of Grass*—438 closely
packed pages—would be Whitman's legacy of a lifetime. A windy,

often abstract book, introduced by a sheaf of beginning poems, concluded by a sheaf of goodby poems, whose reworkings and reorderings produced little more than an eccentric series of parts with a hazy chronology. This was the face Whitman offered to posterity, accompanied by all his photographs: large, wispy-haired, grizzled, benign; a lover of butterflies and of humanity; not a man almost, but a spirit pressing outward from his large body. His excitable friend Maurice Bucke cited him as the example of an evolutionary trend toward "cosmic consciousness": an advance messenger from a future higher race. How odd that Whitman, the argumentative freethinker and despiser of spirit rappings, should have been lifted to posterity on a wave of adoration that echoed, however distantly, theosophy, Madame Blavatsky, and the end-of-century's dabbling in sentimental cults. His own book, however, had diffused its rebellious core in a sea of piety. Even Bucke had to admit he preferred the poems of Whitman's first unbridled outpouring.

For all his printer's skills, he never learned to organize his own books. In the "death-bed edition" of *Leaves of Grass,* he was still groping for wholeness; and in *Specimen Days,* he frankly abandoned all hope of a form. None of the various editions of *Leaves of Grass* are unified masterpieces on the order of, say, Wordsworth and Coleridge's *Lyrical Ballads,* Blake's *Songs of Innocence and Experience,* or Baudelaire's *Fleurs du Mal.* The twelve poems in his first edition are uneven. Several are simply spillovers from the great long poem that became "Song of Myself," but lack that poem's stunning development. The political poems—"Europe: The 72d and 73d Years of These States" and " A Boston Ballad"—seem tossed in to fill the book out. The concluding poem—"Great Are the Myths"—is so weak that it was eventually dropped from future editions. Long poems come first, and short poems last: that seems to be the extent of Whitman's organizing impulse. And he would never substantially improve on it. As a printer, he made his books with care. As the architect of a grand design, he never got beyond hopeful slogans about a "New Bible" that would be constructed like a "cathedral" or, alternately, like a growing organism. Whitman's lifelong enterprise existed on this margin between order and

disorder, but never was the effect so direct as in the "do it yourself" volume that, on 6 July 1855, received a cramped notice in the
New York *Tribune*:

WALT WHITMAN'S POEMS "LEAVES OF
GRASS" 1 vol. small quarto, $2 for sale by
SWAYNE. No. 210 Fulton st., Brooklyn,
and by FOWLER & WELLS No. 308 Broadway, N. Y.

So Whitman's book, with its curious title, was announced to the
American public that, four years before, had refused to read *Moby
Dick* and, only a year before, had found nothing worth remarking
in *Walden*. Now a middle-aged Brooklyn journalist and journeyman printer had fashioned another book that no one could read:
loud, bizarrely sexual, often so obscure the phrasing resembled
some sort of practical joke. Did he really expect his workingman
friends to read this? Did he expect anyone to read it? At first, not
many people did. There is no evidence that Cornelius Matthews or
Evert Duyckinck—Whitman's tutors in literary nationalism—noticed any unusual occurrence that summer of 1855. Melville and
Whitman, neighboring giants, passed each other without a nod.
Although Whitman had admired the young author of *Typee*, he
seems never to have heard of *Moby Dick, Pierre,* or *The Confidence
Man*. Melville is known to have grumbled at Whitman's later
slightly shabby fame; but in the 1850s, he apparently didn't notice
the only other literary genius in New York City.

Yet Whitman knew what he had accomplished. In a way, that is
what astonishes most, for nothing like this glossy green volume
had ever been produced in America. Only William Blake, in England, had been so stubbornly new. Yet Whitman would always
have a disconcerting ability to see himself as if he were another
person. When he sat down to write his preface, with a dozen
completed poems under his belt—in particular a long, anomalous
masterpiece, the tale of a metamorphosis such as Ovid never
dreamed—he launched into one of those third-person self-portraits
that would become his trademark:

America does not repel the past or what it has produced under its forms
or amid other politics or the idea of castes or the old religions . . . accepts

the lesson with calmness . . . is not so impatient as has been supposed that the slough still sticks to opinions and manners and literature while the life which served its requirements has passed into the new life of the new forms . . . perceives that the corpse is slowly borne from the eating and sleeping rooms of the house . . . perceives that it waits a little while in the door . . . that it was fittest for its days . . . that its action has descended to the stalwart and well-shaped heir who approaches . . . and that he shall be fittest for his days.

In one provokingly physical, multiclaused sentence, the "well-shaped heir" steps confidently into the dead father's place. The private saga begun in the blood-curdling stories of Whitman's youth—the sons destroying themselves in order to punish the fathers—has reached its culmination. Now it is the father who is carried, dead, from the house. Already, the son has taken his place. Sturdy, uncannily sure of himself, he announces himself to the world: this book will be his house, his very body; it will also be his father's coffin. As we know, a week after *Leaves of Grass* was published, Whitman, Sr., died. The son's self-willed rise had paralleled his father's decline, as if the empty place left by the father provided room for the son to change his life.

The preface is Whitman's most forceful prose work. Along with "The Eighteenth Presidency" and the essay on language called *An American Primer,* it forms the corpus of Whitman's early prose. Exuberant and richly imaged, expanding into layered clauses and repetitions that all but burst a sentence from its grammatical linkages, the preface is not so much an essay as an exploratory voice, beside itself with fullness of thought. In later years, Whitman would write a great deal of prose: *Democratic Vistas,* the lovely *Specimen Days.* During his last decade, there would be many reminiscing essays and summings-up of his life's work. The style would be deliberately garrulous, quirky, and personal, the voice of a musing old man. But the prose of the 1850s is another thing entirely. The influence of Emerson is likely here. Whitman's declarative tone, his episodic paragraphs never fully focused into an argument, his brilliant concreteness, all reflect Emerson's revolutionary style. But Whitman has taken his "Master" onto new terrain. Emerson had started with rough passages from his journal, which he polished and sharpened until they became a tight flashing prose that seemed to burst from the page. Whitman's preface, on the other hand, wanders loosely, repeats itself, never gives one example when it can give ten. There is a feeling of leisurely expansion, the kind of stretching and overreaching of syntax that characterizes ordinary speech. Whitman's preface is a living journal. It is a voice thinking aloud, alternately groping for clarity, asserting, celebrating.

Like Emerson, Whitman was not really a philosopher. The ideas in his preface are few and simple: all of history culminates on the American continent; because time has ripened to fullness here, Americans can also be considered "the greatest poems," marrying nature and culture as never before. America's unique achievement is not its material wealth but the expanded personality of its citizens, or even of one citizen: "fullsized . . . unconquerable and simple." This citizen thrives on liberty, candor, prudence, nature, love. He is the "greatest poet," because, more than anyone else, he can "translate" the silent poems of the actual world into language. His poems flow from his uninhibited relationship to the world; they are works of love, not of literature: "The known universe has one complete lover and that is the greatest poet." Emerson had asked: "Why should not we . . . enjoy an original relation to the universe?" We do, we must, says Whitman's preface. Not only says it, speaks with the voice of that relationship:

His spirit responds to his country's spirit . . . he incarnates its geography and natural life and rivers and lakes. Mississippi with annual freshets and changing chutes, Missouri and Columbia and Ohio and Saint Lawrence with the falls and beautiful masculine Hudson, do not embouchure where they spend themselves more than they embouchure into him . . . On him rise solid growths that offset the growths of pine and cedar and hemlock and liveoak and locust and chestnut and cypress and hickory and limetree and cottonwood and tuliptree and cactus and wildvine and tamarind and persimmon . . . and tangles as tangled as any canebrake or swamp . . . and forests coated with transparent ice and icicles hanging from the boughs and crackling in the wind. . . .

High up out of reach he stands turning a concentrated light . . . he turns the pivot with his finger . . . he baffles the swiftest runners as he stands and easily overtakes and envelops them. The time straying toward infidelity and confections and persiflage he withholds by his steady faith . . . he spreads out his dishes . . . he offers the sweet firmfibred meat that grows men and women. His brain is the ultimate brain. He is no arguer . . . he is judgement. He judges not as the judge judges but as the sun falling around a helpless thing. As he sees the farthest he has the most faith. His thoughts are the hymns and praise of things. In the talk on the soul and eternity and God off of his equal plane he is silent. He sees eternity less like a play with a prologue and denouement . . . he sees eternity in men and women . . . he does not see men or women as dreams or dots.

The voice is astonishingly physical—by turns expansive, aphoristic, lovingly indiscriminate, tender, declarative, sometimes a little preachy. Whitman's introductory prose is not, truly speaking, a preface—Whitman nowhere refers to it as such—but the bold opening voice of the book itself. It is a monologue spoken by the "greatest lover"; a self-portrait in the third person, providing the basis for a dramatic unveiling when, in the opening lines of the opening poem, he becomes "undisguised and naked": "I celebrate myself and sing myself."

Whitman's announcing voice reminds us how close he still was in 1855 to prose. Much of his book was first written down as prose. His most influential models were not poems at all but Carlyle's gnarled prose, Emerson's essays, the King James Bible, Ruskin, maybe even Thoreau. There was far more great prose than poetry in Whitman's "foreground." His achievement was to incorporate the advantages of prose—its flexibility, its ability to mold itself freely to an actual speaking voice—into a new line that was subtly accented, yet never far from the extended rhythms of prose. The anonymous reviews Whitman wrote of his book during the months following its publication were virtually prose extensions of his poems, blurring further the almost unnoticeable line between his writing and the grandiose personage he had created for himself.

Whitman's prose and poetry would quickly move further apart. His ear would be so haunted by his rhythmic line that prose became a chore and a trial. In 1856, he dropped his extraordinary preface from the new edition and replaced it with a strident "tribute" to his "Master," Ralph Waldo Emerson. This postface, in the form of a "letter," was a thin exterior addendum to the poems, not a preparatory voice. By 1860, it too was dropped. Whitman never wrote the "lectures" he planned in 1856 and 1857, and the reason may be found in this note he wrote to himself: "The trouble in

Lecture style is often the endeavor (from the habit of forming the rhythmic style of *Leaves of Grass*) involuntarily to preserve a sort of rhythm in the Lecture sentences." As he moved away from prose, his poems became more recognizable as poems. "Crossing Brooklyn Ferry" and "Out of the Cradle Endlessly Rocking" are choral and lyrical; they recapitulate, offer echoes of image and theme with visible artistry, unlike the anti-poem which, like a Dickens novel, expands shaggily across half of the 1855 edition. In 1855, prose was Whitman's ground level. Like his workingman's background, his easy knowledge of the trades, it guaranteed a specific weight and concreteness to the language he created. Prose underlay what Emerson called the "buffalo strength" of these poems, their ability to digest quantities of unpoetic material, to assert, bluster, and mourn with the rank authority of the streets.

In the preface, Whitman is riding the crest of his achievement. The dozen poems are finished, maybe already set up in type. Whitman knows what they represent. That, finally, is the pleasure of this prose. It is not a program or a manifesto (in years to come, Whitman would write his share of those) but a shout of triumph. In the house out on Portland Street, Whitman lived amid his uncomprehending family. The weight of illness and approaching death lay upon the house. His older brother Jesse was already showing the violent temperament that would cause him to be committed to the King's County Lunatic Asylum in 1864. Youngest brother Eddie, Whitman's roommate and lifelong care, was growing to a man, helpless and strange in his simple-mindedness. Sister Hannah was writing her miserable self-centered letters from Vermont. Every morning Whitman went down to the Rome brothers' printing shop, and that must have been a satisfying time in his day: the part of poetry writing that resembled a regular job, although, to be sure, it didn't earn him any money. Whitman was now the man of the family, a role he had sought with the deepest urges of his character, ever since he rejoined the household ten years before. Yet nothing—not the troubled family prospect or his remarkable literary isolation—could dim the feeling of triumph, and the lucid understanding of what he had accomplished, that broke in upon him during that culminating spring:

Let the age and wars of other nations be chanted and their eras and characters be illustrated and that finish the verse. Not so the great psalm of the republic. Here the theme is creative and has vista. Here comes one among the wellbeloved stonecutters and plans with decision and science and sees the solid and beautiful forms of the future where there are now no solid forms.

• • •

A heroic person walks at his ease through and out of that custom or precedent or authority that suits him not. Of the traits of the brotherhood of writers savans musicians inventors and artists nothing is finer than silent defiance advancing from new free forms. In the need of poems philosophy politics mechanism science behavior, the craft of art, an appropriate native grand-opera, shipcraft, or any craft, he is greatest forever and forever who contributes the greatest original practical example. The cleanest expression is that which finds no sphere worthy of itself and makes one.

Whitman had made a new "sphere," a new free "form," and he knew it.

Eventually the dozen poems of the 1855 edition would acquire titles and separate identities. Now they are shuffled together, almost inadvertently. Some poems begin on new pages; some simply fill out a page and run onto the next. None, as I have said, are separately titled. This seems clumsy and ill thought out. Yet Whitman was probably acting on a hunch that the poems belong to a single conception. To his first readers, they seemed not like poems at all, but arbitrary lengths of language, defying the impulse to form. And this appearance is partly right. The poems themselves play abundantly on all the suggestions of openness, as in Whitman's figure of the "open road," which appears and reappears throughout the book:

I am he that walks with the tender and growing night.

My ties and ballast leave me. . . . I travel. . . . I sail. . . . my elbows rest
   in the sea-gaps,
I skirt the sierras . . . . my palms cover continents,
I am afoot with my vision.

Storming enjoying planning loving cautioning,
Backing and filling, appearing and disappearing,
I tread day and night such roads.

241

Cycles ferried my cradle, rowing and rowing like cheerful boatmen

Pleasantly and well-suited I walk,
Whither I walk I cannot define, but I know it is good.

I wander all night in my vision,
Stepping with light feet . . . swiftly and noiselessly stepping and
stopping.

Sauntering the pavement or riding the country byroads here then are
faces.

The Lord advances and yet advances:
Always the shadow in front . . . always the reached hand bringing up
the laggards.

There was a child went forth every day.

The poems wander, saunter, and tramp. They visit busy workshops and list the tools, stroll along city streets, set off across country, or stride into the cosmos. They journey through time and death: from human life, into the grass, and back again. Metempsychosis, too, becomes a journey, which turns endings into beginnings, dissolves the endings of poems:

I bequeath myself to the dirt to grow from the grass I love,
If you want me again look for me under your bootsoles.

A year later, Whitman would write "Song of the Open Road," but the road is already the connective thread of his vision, turning the world into a panorama for the traveling mind. The road becomes a figure of change, growth, and learning. Traveling is Whitman's principal activity in the 1855 *Leaves of Grass,* measuring the distance his conceptual powers had come in the last year or so since he wrote "Pictures," with its idea of the mind as a gallery of photographs in the fixed house of the self. Now Whitman's open road takes him out of doors:

Houses and rooms are full of perfumes . . . . the shelves are crowded
with perfumes,
I breathe the fragrance myself, and know it and like it,
The distillation would intoxicate me also, but I shall not let it.

The atmosphere is not a perfume . . . . it has no taste of the distillation
. . . . it is odorless,

It is for my mouth forever . . . . I am in love with it,
I will go to the bank by the wood and become undisguised and naked.

• • •

I swear I will never mention love or death inside a house,
And I swear I never will translate myself at all, only to him or her who
    privately stays with me in the open air.

These figures of the open road and the open air gather Whitman's
1855 poems into a single loosely defined text. In his book, he
unhouses himself, shucks off his clothing, opens his eyes and all his
senses. He becomes the moving center of a colossal plenitude.
Street scenes and country scenes, the random vividness of countless
events and places, scenes from the historical past, the old gods, the
backward panorama of geological times and the dizzying expansions of space, the stars, and nebulae, the "apple shaped earth": all
swing in orbit around Whitman's perceiving self, who becomes
their principle of order, their pivot and reason for being. There is
no transcendentalist "over-soul" hovering behind the forms of
Whitman's world; there is only the hungering self, "taking in"
everything he sees, "digesting" it. No wonder he calls himself a
"kosmos." Hegel might have recognized, in the Whitman of these
poems, the subjective Romantic spirit personified. The visible
world finds its haven and meaning in the inwardness of this giant:
the world is food for his thought, pasture for his appetites. Without him, it is a random heap of riches, like the overstocked display
of a cosmic department store or the chaos of cargoes heaped along
the Manhattan waterfront. Whitman calls his poet a "hub of the
wheeled universe"; he is a moving hub; his universe, expanded to
infinity, is a wheel with its center everywhere, its circumference
nowhere.

    In 1855, the road was still America's symbol of opportunity. In
the American idiom, progress and personal betterment were not
merely hopeful ideas. Actual roads led to their fulfillment: roads
heading west from New England's rocky fields to the "Valley of
Democracy" in Ohio, to California and gold; from country to city,
and city to country. The Whitman family's decades-long swing, in
Walt's youth, between their West Hills, Long Island, farm, and
Brooklyn was a small reflection of the mobility that Americans

considered a national privilege. The Yankee peddler, Johnny Appleseed, the Conestoga wagon, Horace Greeley's "Go west, young man," were on the road and defined the road. "Manifest Destiny" was a politics of the road. Thomas Hart Benton's obsession with a transcontinental railroad was road thinking raised to a higher power. When Thoreau chose to walk a mere mile out of town, and then write about his "journey," using images of wilderness and vast travel, he was inverting America's passion with fine irony.

As for the "open air," what did America stand for in the eyes of the world, and in its own eyes, but a gargantuan out-of-doors, symbolized by the waterfalls at Niagara, the half-legendary Rocky Mountains soon to be painted and photographed by Albert Bierstadt, the gloomy forests rendered by Thomas Cole and Frederick Church.

America's obsession with the out-of-doors drove Poe to imagine his heroes locked up in coffins, vaults, and thickly draped rooms, as if to escape the din of the national temperament. But Whitman did something more difficult. Having heard the din (he had made his share of it over the years, as a "screetch-eagle" journalist,) he took the vulgar symbols and filled them with his own meanings. He made them into literature, without betraying their raucous origins. Not only did Whitman unhouse himself in his poems, he unhoused the poems. Here is another measure of the complexity he was capable of in managing his symbols. His "perfumes" and "shuttered houses" stand for the distilled language and closed forms his poems forsake, as they expand openly on their "road." In Whitman's view, his poems *are* a kind of out-of-doors; they are language at one with nature, not set against it by the "chains" of rhyme and formal rhythm. They are leaves of grass, not the leaves of books: "The rhyme and uniformity of perfect poems show the free growth of metrical laws and bud from them as unerringly and loosely as lilacs or roses on a bush, and take shapes as compact as the shapes of chestnuts and oranges and melons and pears, and shed the perfume impalpable to form."

Whitman was a masterful poet of personal change. In a handful of important poems, he evokes the elusive shifts in temperament and sensation, the slides of perception. Whitman's self speaks with many voices and many moods. He is unpredictable and changing. In "There Was a Child Went Forth," he experiences the objects of the world "with wonder or pity or love or dread." These shifting feelings remake him; he becomes what he sees on his day-long, and then life-long, journey.

I touch here on Whitman's most intuitive subject matter. The "melting in" effect of the Luminist painters he had admired becomes a subtly shifting grasp of the moods and impulses by means of which the psyche searches for new strengths, discards old ones. Change, for Whitman, was the raw material of inwardness, as in "The Sleepers" (a dark twin of "Song of Myself") and one of the great poems of the 1855 edition. Like Whitman himself, the voice of "The Sleepers" is restless at night. While others are in bed, he wanders the city peering into windows, seeing even through walls and closed eyes into the interior night of people's minds: "Bending with open eyes over the shut eyes of sleepers;/ Wandering and confused . . . lost to myself . . . ill-assorted . . . contradictory." As he goes, the night and his dark feelings merge in a phantasmagoria of "corpses," "gashed bodies," and "the insane." But the darkness is also a healer, a resolver of tensions:

> I stand with drooping eyes by the worstsuffering and restless,
> I pass my hands soothingly to and fro a few inches from them;
> The restless sink in their beds . . . . they fitfully sleep.

Stanza by stanza, the darkness changes: it is a nightmare, a spiritual medicine, a resolver of conflict. As he glides across the nightscape of the city, Whitman's wanderer becomes a kind of Proteus. He is a dervish intoxicated by his dance, a clairvoyant seer:

> I am the everlaughing . . . it is new moon and twilight,
> I see the hiding of douceurs . . . . I see nimble ghosts whichever way I
>   look,
> Cache and cache again deep in the ground and sea, and where it is
>   neither ground or sea.

Well do they do their jobs, those journeymen divine,
Only from me they hide nothing and would not if they could;
I reckon I am their boss, and they make me a pet besides,
And surround me, and lead me and run ahead when I walk,
And lift their cunning covers and signify me with stretched arms, and
  resume the way;
Onward we move, a gay gang of blackguards with mirthshouting mu-
  sic and wildflapping pennants of joy.

His whirling dance awakens him sexually. The dancer becomes a
woman waiting for her "truant lover" and also the lover; the two
meet in darkness, like Cupid and Psyche, or like "self" and "soul"
in a famous passage of "Song of Myself":

O hotcheeked and blushing! O foolish hectic!
O for pity's sake, no one must see me now! . . . . my clothes were
  stolen while I was abed,
Now I am thrust forth, where shall I run?

Pier that I saw dimly last night when I looked from the windows,
Pier from the main, let me catch myself with you and stay . . . . I will
  not chafe you;
I feel ashamed to go naked about the world . . .

The cloth laps a first sweet eating and drinking,
Laps life-swelling yolks . . . laps ears of rose-corn, milky and just
  ripened:
The white teeth stay, and the boss-tooth advances in darkness,
And liquor is spilled on lips and bosoms by touching glasses, and the
  best liquor afterward.

The "pier" rubbing its length in the moonlight is so close to saying what it means that Whitman's language dissolves into an erotic
gibberish, as if only by that means could he keep his masturbatory
secret. Eventually he would remove this whole passage from the
poem.

With each succeeding stanza, Whitman weaves the associations
of the night: the guilty erotic climax; visions of death and mourn-
ing; and then the life-destroying, life-giving sea—that other
night—where a "courageous giant . . . in the prime of his middle
age" is dashed against the rocks:

Steady and long he struggles;

He is baffled and banged and bruised . . . he holds out while his
    strength holds out,
The slapping eddies are spotted with his blood . . . they bear him away
    . . . they roll him and swing him and turn him:
His beautiful body is borne in the circling eddies . . . it is continually
    bruised on rocks,
Swiftly and out of sight is borne the brave corpse.

The middle-aged swimmer is surely Whitman himself—another
of his third-person portraits—who had lived most of his life near
the ocean and loved to swim. But now Whitman's "road" begins a
delicate climb toward dawn. He thinks of his mother, of a mysteri-
ously appealing Indian girl, of the vast dark bulk of a whale, sleepy
but powerful: "Warily sportsman! though I lie so sleepy and slug-
gish, my tap is death."

The nineteenth century loved the theme of release in darkness.
The Heraclitean dictum—"The way down and the way up are the
same"—could be its motto. Baudelaire, Rimbaud, Poe, Swinburne:
all drew on the torment of the old Gothic romances, to create a
vision of downward release, as if Dante's *Inferno* would have had
no *Paradiso.* This great literature of descent had only occasional
echoes in nineteenth- century America. Its American masterpiece is
probably *Moby Dick,* where America's "open road" and "open air,"
are wrenched into tragedy: the reader last glimpses Ahab rushing
into the ocean depths, while Ishmael floats to survival on a coffin.

In "The Sleepers," too, the way down becomes a way up, as
night climbs into dawn, and the release of nightmare purges the
dreamer. The dawn approaches, and the night with its guilty lover,
its killing ocean, becomes a mother exhaling peace and reconciliation. The pain of separation has been healed by sleep which is to
Whitman's night wanderer what soil is to grass: a nourishing
ground anchoring him to a life beyond himself.

"The Sleepers" is one of Whitman's finest poems, and I don't
mean to exhaust its possibilities in these few pages. I want simply
to emphasize Whitman's variable voice when he was writing at the
height of his power. In such poems, his "road" becomes an inward
thread, a path in his own mind. When his poet speaks from a
platform of acquired knowledge, he can be repetitive and dull, as in
the pious poems which flay us with their static lists and slogans.

The 1860 *Leaves of Grass* is thick with them. They are part of Whitman's program: they fill out his "New Bible" with Old Testament prophecy and orations in the large manner. But when he speaks to find out who he is and what he knows; when his poems present a mind altered by its own actions, a mind changing before our eyes because it is speaking not only to us but to itself, then Whitman is at his best. We have seen that the voice of *Leaves of Grass* reflects two vastly popular hortatory modes: the penny newspaper and the revivalist sermon. The programmatic Whitman tended to write versified editorials; his book was a pulpit. But Whitman could let a private voice into his poems. Then the editorialst-preacher's discourse became tangled with private meanings. It veered unpredictably along an inspired thread of associations. Whitman's "open road" is a metaphor for this thread of surprises. His great poems are not secular sermons but records of self-making, open-ended, delighting in the "indirections" by which the mind tricks itself into knowledge.

3

The greatest of these poems is "Song of Myself," which may also be the most problematic and difficult of Whitman's works. The task of organizing an extremely long poem without any overarching narrative is formidable. Some of Whitman's finest middle-length poems are framed by a single setting: the night ("The Sleepers"), or the East River just before sunset ("Crossing Brooklyn Ferry"), or a beach on Long Island ("Out of the Cradle Endlessly Rocking"). But "Song of Myself" takes the universe and all of time as its setting. Within the poem, there are occasional smaller unities: a sun rising unobtrusively through several stanzas, two staggeringly busy journeys taking up almost half the poem, an ecstatic awakening of the senses through half a dozen stanzas. Nonetheless, the poem flows from surprise to surprise; nothing seems too peculiar to find a place in it. The catalogues are bristling and random, and their randomness is important. For they are extended symbols of a mind that excludes nothing. A random list is, by definition, merely a sample of an unspoken list containing everything; and "Song of Myself," similarly, contains everything.

The great epic poems have been masterpieces of inclusion. To the classical Greeks, *The Iliad* was a kind of Bible, not only because of its solemn heroic code, but because the poem moved in expanding circles of knowledge. While telling about Troy and Helen, Hector and Achilles, it scrupulously caught up quantities of knowledge about rituals and the gods, techniques of warfare, a medically exact description of serious wounds, weapons making, and, in the extended similes, countless tableaux of ordinary living. In this sense, "Song of Myself," too, is an epic. It, too, is a masterpiece of inclusion, although it deliberately inverts the familiar epic ambition: it does not tell a story; its hero has not accomplished any grand actions; or, rather, his grand action is the poem itself. The hero of "Song of Myself" is an ordinary man (Hollyer's engraving makes sure the reader knows this) who has led a remarkably commonplace life, as Whitman insists when he invokes the

> People I meet . . . the effect upon me of my early life . . . of the ward
>   and city I live in . . . of the nation,
> The latest news . . . discoveries, inventions, societies . . . authors old
>   and new,
> My dinner, dress, associates, looks, business, compliments, dues,
> The real or fancied indifference of some man or woman I love,
> The sickness of one of my folks—or of myself . . . or ill-doing . . . or
>   loss or lack of money . . . or depressions or exaltations.

Whitman's "singer" glories in his anonymity. We don't know his name or how he earns his living. His actions of any sort are few, but everything—the "everything" that is the poem—happens to him. The "singer" bestrides the poem and is the poem, reciting, celebrating, ironizing. Whitman's unified setting for "Song of Myself" is not a place but a voice various and broad enough to say "everything." The poem is an extravagant monologue; or, rather—to use Whitman's model for the genius of pure voice—it is an opera; an opera, moreover, in which all the voices are one. Whitman's "singer" resembles no one more than that extraordinary celebrator of his own irruptive nature: Diderot's character of Rameau's Nephew, who also bursts the confines of his social self, in a hilarious, moving, endlessly surprising performance that deliberately evokes an operatic aria.

The critic, Richard Chase, called "Song of Myself" a comic masterpiece, reminding us of Whitman's elusively various tone, which is as capable of comedy as it is of erotic ecstasy, of sardonic political satire as of cosmic voyaging. Remember the lines he added to the final version of "Song of Myself":

> I harbor for good or bad, I permit to speak at every hazard,
> Nature without check with original energy.

Whitman is trying to help the reader here, by seeding his poem with parenthetical comments, like stage directions inserted between the lines of a play or, more exactly, like the unspoken plea of a novelist whose näively truthful tone tells his reader: what you are reading here really happened, I didn't make it up; this is not literature, but fact.

As our first great anti-literary genre, the novel took its readers by ruse, developing a remarkable bag of tricks by which it claimed to tell only the truth. The novelist openly renounced his claim to be an artist: he was an amanuensis, a mere scribe of history; facts spoke through him. Yet it was all art, and the reader knew it. One neither believed or disbelieved the novelist's false modesty. One suspended disbelief, agreeing to be beguiled by a new kind of artistry which consisted in "lying like the truth," as was said of Daniel Defoe, the first modern novelist.

"Nature without check with original energy." Whitman, too, is saying, there is no art here, and no poem; there is only "nature," only spontaneous utterance. Don't look here for second thoughts or cunning echoes, for foreshadowings and formal development. Here is a voice speaking before it thinks, "for good or bad." Now everything is explained: the overabundant images, the vagaries of subject matter, the sudden shifts and leaps, the sense of a voice reeling out of control. There is a kind of brinkmanship, as the poem veers from surprise to surprise. It is the brinkmanship of life itself, which takes place at the very edge of an unwritten future. To be sure, it is all art no less than a novel is art. Whitman's bag of tricks is deep. His claim, too, is the novelist's: this is merely truth, not literature.

"Song of Myself" is not only a voice, then; it is a voice that can not stop "singing," delighted with its own fullness, plunging into its unuttered future. The poem's present tense is so reckless and hurried ("I speak at every hazard . . . without check") that it seems to have no past, no memory: that is to say, the poem is not about anything, any more than life is about something. It is simply happening; it is about itself. How much like Whitman, to have written a provokingly unliterary poem (a frank outpouring, pure "nature") which yet plays humorously, even erotically, with the theme of its own creation. Here again we see an effect of Whitman's "twoness," his ability to watch himself act, to know and orchestrate his presence. An important example of this ability occurs in a celebrated passage near the beginning of the poem:

> I believe in you my soul . . . . the other I am must not abase itself to you.
> And you must not be abased to the other.
>
> Loafe with me on the grass . . . . loose the stop from your throat,
> Not words, not music or rhyme I want . . . . not custom or lecture, not even the best,
> Only the lull I like, the hum of your valved voice.
>
> I mind how we lay in June, such a transparent summer morning;
> You settled your head athwart my hips and gently turned over upon me,
> And parted my shirt from my bosom-bone, and plunged your tongue to my barestript heart,
> And reached till you felt my beard, and reached till you held my feet.
>
> Swiftly arose and spread around me the peace and joy and knowledge that pass all the art and argument of the earth;
> And I know that the hand of God is the elderhand of my own,
> And I know that the spirit of God is the eldest brother of my own,
> And that all the men ever born are also my brothers . . . . and the women my sisters and lovers,
> And that a kelson of the creation is love;
> And limitless are leaves stiff or drooping in the fields,
> And brown ants in the little wells beneath them,
> And mossy scabs of the wormfence, and heaped stones, and elder and mullen and pokeweed.

251

Does this remarkable love song record an actual experience, as critics have often wondered? It is, for example, one of the rare stanzas in "Song of Myself" to be written in the past tense. Whitman's version of the peace that passeth all understanding is of the body and from the body. It expands like a gathering sexual storm and "droops" like the subsidence of feeling after the sexual climax.

Of course, we will never know whether Whitman experienced such a moment and became a poet because of it. We have seen how piecemeal and incremental his literary advances were over half a dozen years: the result of persistent work and of the half-formed conviction of a goal that became clear only by jolts and leaps. On the other hand, there are the notebook experiments, Whitman's attempts to describe his overwhelming physical passion for color, the hypnotic power of the human voice, an "oceanic" orgasm without a partner. His marriage of self and soul in "Song of Myself" draws these experiments into a triumphant lyric: the song of an illuminated moment when Whitman's "twoness" dissolves in an act of love.

In the line of the poem following this excerpt, a child (born of this marriage?) asks him a question—"What is the grass?"—to which the entire poem will be an answer: it is a "hieroglyphic"; it is a bed of love; it is what the earth utters, to remind man that death is not final; it is a symbol of the countless varieties of experience that Whitman catalogues on his world-circling journeys:

> This is the grass that grows wherever the land and the water is,
> This is the common air that bathes the globe.

All flesh is grass, laments Isaiah in a passage Whitman surely knew; after a season, it dies. But the grass grows again; and leaves of grass—those "hieroglyphics" of the self, that book not a book, of poems that are not poems—they, too, will grow again, if the reader will stoop to gather them up.

Whitman's scene of love making on the grass is curiously elusive. Self and soul loaf tenderly, and yet they hardly seem to touch each other. Instead of touching, they listen: everything is in the voice, a summery *bel canto* without words, rhyme, or "custom"; only a "valved voice"—in effect, a new kind of poetry. At last, the "tongue" brings self and soul together in an act of phantasmic oral sex; an orgasm accomplished by voice alone, surpassing "all the art and argument of the earth." Whitman's love making is also an act of poetry, so intimate and vivid that whoever listens becomes a loving partner and accomplice ("Stop this day and night with me and you shall possess the origin of all poems"). Whitman, here, is describing his own poetry, this very poem. Self and soul embrace, as Whitman dreamed of embracing his reader. The next poem in his book will begin:

> Come closer to me,
> Push close to me and take the best I possess,
> Yield closer and closer and give me the best you possess.
>
> This is unfinished business with me. . . . how is it with you?
> I was chilled with the cold types and cylinder and wet paper between
> us.
>
> I pass so poorly with paper and types. . . . I must pass with the contact
> of bodies and souls.

The voice "sings" about itself, insists on its loving appeal. In 1860, it would say:

> Camerado, this is no book,
> Who touches this touches a man,
> (Is it night? are we here together alone?)
> It is I you hold and who holds you,
> I spring from the pages into your arms—

It is a book only by disguise or by ruse. This unpredictable poem denies that it is a poem, yet it is about the efficacy of poetry: as erotic tool, as voice, as extension of the body:

> My voice goes after what my eyes cannot reach,
> With a twirl of my tongue I encompass worlds and volumes of worlds.

I have pointed out the curious resemblance between "Song of Myself" and the classical nineteenth-century novel. Both claim not to be "literature"; both want to be read naïvely, as windows on the truth, mere daguerreotypes; as history, not fantasy. On the whole, readers have probably done better with both than have critics. It is, after all, an austere wish to resist the novel's story-telling rapture in order to unearth its bag of tricks. "Song of Myself," too, I suspect, has been easier to read than understand. Analysis slides off the poem; yet the reader follows the shifting images and tone, the rising and falling cadence, the casual leap from theme to theme, as one follows the rhythms of a voice speaking its mind. The voice never lets one down. There is a flow, an exploratory reaching for the next thought and image, which is Whitman's profoundest verisimilitude. A mind must move like that; it must veer and surprise and amble forward, just like that. It must sidestep, change moods unpredictably, avoid statements in favor of suggestion, abstractions in favor of urgently physical images.

Critics have tried, with dubious success, to identify the five or seven or nine major divisions of the poem. They have enumerated the poem's central ideas, its statements, its developments. In short, they have tried to read it as other great poems have been read. Yet these critics have seemed, if not more wrong, somehow less useful than when reading, say, Keats's great odes, or Wordsworth's "Tintern Abbey," or Milton's "Lycidas." There is a danger in defying the author's instructions, and Whitman is unequivocal: this is no poem, he says; this is a reckless present tense; this is a voice becoming naked to you ("I will go to the bank by the wood and become undisguised and naked") and catching its own meanings as they fly; a voice discovering itself to you and to itself.

"Song of Myself" is an engine of self-making: that I believe is the clue we must follow to unravel its story. Whitman's "singer" is made and remade by his poem. He is a creature of language, grounded in his voice—as Whitman suggests through his conflation of themes. The poem is a body ("who touches this touches a man") but also a flirtatious commentary on itself as a poem. It is the flesh that is grass, but it is also a meditation on the capabilities of language. Flesh is grass, and grass is song: here Whitman's celebration of bodily feelings becomes doubled with artistic self-awareness, shaped by the poem's feeling for itself as a poem. Remember the double meanings that shimmer in Whitman's scene of love making on the grass, which is at once erotic song, and commentary on the new poetry Whitman invents in this very poem. No matter how fast the fit whirls him, the watcher still watches. The watcher is the dancing master and orchestrator of Whitman's themes. When watcher and dancer come together on the grass in an act of poetry performed by the "tongue," their partnership is sealed. Dancer and watcher, self and soul combine to answer the child's question: "What is the grass?" The answer will be multitudinous and long—it will be the poem itself; and the answerer will be caught up in the whirlwind of his answer. He will take in his own words, digest them, and become a new man:

> I find I incorporate gneiss and coal and long-threaded moss and fruits
>   and grains and esculent roots,
> And am stucco'd with quadrupeds and birds all over.

This is the literal scenario of the poem: the process by which Whitman's singer becomes a man of his words. I have described Whitman's fantasy of incorporation, in which "digestion" becomes the underlying figure for all learning and perception. Learning to be a man, we take in what we see; we enrich our substance with the perceived substance of what our senses, those carnal hunters, bring to us as prey.

Aroused by his voice, Whitman's singer rises from his bed of grass and journeys forth. What follows in the poem is not so much catalogue, as impressionistic journey and gargantuan menu. It is the "open road" of Whitman's "tenacious, acquisitive" senses, taking it all "for me . . . for me . . . for me." I called "Song of Myself" an epic, a masterpiece of inclusion. Here is the epic work itself. It is a labor of "merging"—Whitman's characteristic figure—of becoming naked, in order to strip from others their illusory separateness: "Undrape . . . I see through the broadcloth and gingham whether or no." Whitman's "open road" is also a tireless peristalsis: the world enters the maw of the awakened self, who comments with varied refrains:

> This is the grass.

> I fly the flight of the fluid and swallowing soul.

> All this I swallow and it tastes good.

Whitman's singer is not ecstatic solitary; he is not solipsist or idealist. The world exists for him as food, and he devours it with his song. Whitman's idea plays elusively throughout the text: the singer travels within his poem, which is a road going nowhere and everywhere; yet the poem is also a body feeding itself indiscriminately with all its senses. Before we insist, however, on Whitman's infantile magic-thinking or on his naïve and primitive belief in the efficacy of language, we must remember the third strand in his play of meanings: the poem is, after all, a poem; the body and its digestive actions are figures of speech, they are maneuvers of the voice dramatizing its desires. The poem is a symbolic action, threaded with refrainlike commentaries on voice, body, and appetite as figures for the poetic act and the cognitive life of the mind. These are some of the double and triple takes of meaning that constitute Whitman's "indirections" in "Song of Myself."

Whitman's catalogues extend across half the poem, in a broad associative flow. They are the very workings of self-change. The digestive and devouring action of the poem passes through them. The open road is also an open mind, an open body, and an open mouth. The singer emerges from the journey, fleshed with his increased substance.

> Who goes there! hankering, gross, mystical, nude?
> How is it I extract strength from the beef I eat?

We know now what he's been eating—the very world—and we will learn shortly who he is. Meanwhile, as I have said, we hear the boastful American voice that Whitman extracted from the booster journalism of his day, from the tall stories and the folklore—that American glamor of exaggeration that had made Mike Finn and Daniel Boone into frontier giants, and the Founding Fathers into saints. Whitman's fleshed and awakened self speaks American on the large scale:

> One world is aware, and by far the largest to me, and that is myself,
> And whether I come to my own today or in ten thousand or ten million years,
> I can cheerfully take it now, or with equal cheerfulness I can wait.
>
> My foothold is tenoned and mortised on granite,
> I laugh at what you call dissolution,
> And I know the amplitude of time.

Here is the voice that suggested "something a little more than human" to Thoreau. It has enlarged itself in the poem, and the poem has made it. The shy solitary self, observing a spear of grass in the first lines of the poem, has "extracted strength" from his "beef," and now he will shout his name:

> Walt Whitman, an American, one of the roughs, a kosmos,
> Disorderly fleshy and sensual . . . eating drinking and breeding,
> No sentimentalist . . . no stander above men and women or
>   apart from them . . . no more modest than immodest.
>
> Unscrew the locks from the doors!
> Unscrew the doors themselves from their jambs!

The anonymity is broken; the singer reveals himself as an American, "one of the roughs." He has eaten and drunk; he has lain naked on the grass and traveled along an open road of appetizing sensations. He has also made this poem, and now his name bursts from his lips. Like Odysseus crowing his name to the blinded Cyclops, Whitman's singer has made a name for himself. On line 499 of the first poem in his first book, the name "Walt Whitman" enters literature. For more than a decade he had been signing his short stories "Walter Whitman," and his editorials, "WW" or "Paumanok," when they were signed at all. His byline in James J. Brenton's 1849 anthology, *Voices from the Press*, had been "Walter Whitman." The receipts from his contracting work as late as 1854, are usually signed "Walter Whitman, Jr." To his family and friends, on the other hand, he had been "Walt" all along, "probably because his father was Walter," George Whitman remembered. "It was a way we had of separating them."

Now he would be "Walt" to everyone, as Emerson, growing up, had decided to be "Waldo" instead of the hated "Ralph," and Thoreau had decided to be "Henry David" instead of the "David Henry" he had been born with. While these are not new names, they are not quite the old ones either. There has been a shuffling of identities; a choice subtly but definitely made to be *this* man. Whitman chose to make his life and his work speak with one voice and to name that voice "Walt Whitman." He refused to separate his private and public identities, refused to climb the ladder of accepted

ambitions. He had not switched, for example, from the profession
of journalism to the profession of literature. Unlike "Walter
Whitman, Jr," "Walt Whitman" did not claim to be a professional
anything. He was simply himself: an irresistibly public man created
by his poems, who lived in his words and was nourished by them:

> I do not press my finger across my mouth,
> I keep as delicate around the bowels as around the head and heart,
> Copulation is no more rank to me than death is.
>
> I believe in the flesh and the appetites,
> Seeing hearing and feeling are miracles, and each part and tag of me is
> a miracle.
>
> Divine am I inside and out, and I make holy whatever I touch or am
> touched from;
> The scent of these arm-pits is aroma finer than prayer,
> This head is more than churches or bibles or creeds.
>
> If I worship any particular thing it shall be some of the spread of my
> body;
> Translucent mould of me it shall be you,
> Shaded ledges and rests, firm masculine coulter, it shall be you,
> Whatever goes to the tilth of me it shall be you,
> You my rich blood, your milky stream pale strippings of my life;
> Breast that presses against other breasts it shall be you,
> My brain it shall be your occult convolutions,
> Root of washed sweet-flag, timorous pond-snipe, nest of guarded du-
> plicate eggs, it shall be you,
> Mixed tussled hay of head and beard and brawn it shall be you,
> Trickling sap of maple, fibre of manly wheat, it shall be you;
> Sun so generous it shall be you,
> Vapors lighting and shading my face it shall be you,
> Winds whose soft-tickling genitals rub against me it shall be you,
> Broad muscular fields, branches of liveoak, loving lounger in my wind-
> ing paths, it shall be you,
> Hands I have taken, face I have kissed, mortal I have ever touched, it
> shall be you.
>
> I dote on myself . . . there is that lot of me, and all so luscious,
> Each moment and whatever happens thrills me with joy.

These lines, climaxing a portion of the poem, contain all of Whitman's humor and sensuality and outrageousness. He sings out
about "worship" and "prayer"—the language of churchgoing—

but also about "armpits," "copulation," a charmingly timorous penis, the wind's "soft-tickling genitals." Whitman's church is his body. Aroused from head to toe, he describes himself as a well-fed and bearded erection, so deliciously happy that the trees, the fields, and the wind have become his lovers.

But the song is not over. For there is a problematical side to Whitman's unbridled expansion. As he peels away the boundaries of house, clothes, even place; as social and moral distinctions fall away, he comes to the very edge of language. He has been a voice, his body has been the poem. Now body and poem blur together:

> My voice goes after what my eyes cannot reach.
> With the twirl of my tongue I encompass worlds and volumes of
>   worlds.
>
> Speech is the twin of my vision . . . it is unequal to measure itself.
> It provokes me forever,
> It says sarcastically, Walt, you understand enough . . . why don't you
>   let it out then?
>
> Come now I will not be tantalized . . . you conceive too much of
>   articulation.
>
> . . . .
>
> My final merit I refuse you. . . . I refuse putting from me the best I am.
>
> Encompass worlds but never try to encompass me,
> I crowd your noisiest talk by looking toward you.
>
> Writing and talk do not prove me,
> I carry the plenum of proof and every thing else in my face,
> With the hush of my lips I confound the topmost skeptic.

There is an overreaching here. This is not the mystic's helpless admiration for an unsayable truth or Rousseau's romantic *je ne sais quoi*. Walt Whitman teeters beyond himself. What does he need the poem for? He is already the poem, and he is perfect. Whitman's question is the ancient unanswerable one of the theologians. Why did God, who is perfect and beyond need, create anything at all? As the heroes of epic discovered, to be "a little more than human" is to stand at the edge of a strangely dissolving solitude. Is Walt Whitman in the poem, or is he out of it? His silence is spoken: "the hush of [his] lips" is, after all, a phrase. Yes, he is in

the poem, caught in it, carried by it. And now it becomes headlong, more than he had bargained for.

His unfettered senses have been so aroused that the experience of
a sunrise almost destroys him. A wild crescendo of sounds over-
whelms him:

> I am exposed . . . cut by bitter and poisoned hail,
> Steeped amid honeyed morphine . . . my windpipe squeezed in fakes of
> death.

"Touch" floods him with fire, betrays and almost annihilates him:

> On all sides prurient provokers stiffening my limbs,
> Straining the udder of my heart for its withheld drip.
> Behaving licentious toward me, taking no denial,
> Depriving me of my best as for a purpose,
> Unbuttoning my clothes and holding me by the bare waist,
> Deluding my confusion with the calm of the sunlight and pasture
> fields,
> Immodestly sliding the fellow-senses away,
> They bribed to swap off with touch, and go and graze at the edges of
> me.
> . . . .
>
> I am given up by traitors;
> I talk wildly . . . . I have lost my wits . . . . I and nobody else am the
> greatest traitor,
> . . . .
>
> You villain touch! what are you doing? . . . . my breath is tight in its
> throat;
> Unclench your floodgates! you are too much for me.

The unshielded life is dangerous; physical ecstasy can be a kind of
death. The poem will circle this danger several times. Several
times, Whitman will push to the edge of his paradox: to be a self,
with a name, and yet to be everything and everyone. And each
time he will spiral into a wider orbit, discovering that "Walt
Whitman's" journey is unendable, that his appetite can never be
satiated, and the world never completely internalized. Having tried
to end his poem in a swaggering celebration, he accepts at last that
the poem can have no end.

Here begins the poem's second catalogue, grappling up into its mesh of language all religions, the geological past, the violence of history, walking with Jesus in Judea. Whitman's road opens ever wider:

Rise after rise bow the phantoms behind me,
Afar down I see the huge first Nothing, the vapor from the nostrils of
    death,
I know I was even there . . . . I wait unseen and always,
And slept while God carried me through the lethargic mist,
And took my time . . . . and took no hurt from the foetid carbon.

and

This day before dawn I ascended a hill and looked at the crowded
    heaven,
And I said to my spirit, When we become the enfolders of those orbs
    and the pleasure and knowledge of every thing in them, shall we be
    filled and satisfied then?
And my spirit said No, we level that lift to pass and continue beyond.

The sun that has begun rising on line 552—introduced casually, in the previous line, by an association with "morning glory"—continues to rise, clouded by panics and momentary fears, busy with "lovers," filled with an ever more solid acceptance of the unendable journey that is the poem. Finally, it is sunset. Whitman's singer sees himself as a wild hawk, sounding his non-language—his "barbaric yawp"—over the roofs of the world, while the daylight dims, and the almost setting sun casts enormous shadows. The poem ends with dusk. But the grass will continue to grow, the singer will be waiting for you; the cycles of death and resurrection, like the cycle of day and night, will continue. The poem's end will not be a true ending, merely an articulation of endlessness:

I depart as air. . . . I shake my white locks at the runaway sun,
I effuse my flesh in eddies and drift it in lacy jags.

I bequeath myself to the dirt to grow from the grass I love,
If you want me again look for me under your bootsoles.

You will hardly know who I am or what I mean,
But I shall be good health to you nevertheless,
And filter and fibre your blood.

Failing to fetch me at first keep encouraged,
Missing me one place search another,
I stop somewhere waiting for you.

4

I described "Song of Myself" as an engine of self-making. "Walt Whitman," we remember, is not merely a character in a poem—a "persona," "the singer," or even simply "Self," as he has been called by various critics. What is being made here is a man, and a man's name. Every inflection of tone, every particularity of style, theme, and form—the entire work of the poem—has been intended to erase the boundary between art and life, between "Walt Whitman" and the actual man who lived out along Myrtle Avenue, in Brooklyn, and had just delivered several hundred copies of his book to the Fowler and Wells establishment on Broadway.

This collaboration between the life and the work had long since changed the status of art in the nineteenth century. With Rousseau and then Byron, the writer had become flamboyant, intensely mannered. His work was offered as the broadcast form of his personality, and his personality gave a weight of personal truth to his work. Rousseau had publicly renounced the stylish Parisian life led by many *philosophes,* and gone to live in the country. This "reform," as he loudly called it, was meant to bring his personal habits into line with his philosophy of nature. Byron wrote daring Gothic poems and launched them with his publicly scandalous behavior. William Blake walked naked in his garden; Wordsworth retired to a country valley; Gerard de Nerval appeared in the Luxembourg Gardens with a lobster on a leash; Baudelaire dressed in black and cultivated his miseries; Rimbaud subverted conventional poetic forms and conventional morality. These were not simply personal eccentricities but a form of public privacy. The artist's behavior was purposeful, a part of his art; his work flowed into his gestures; his clothes were a form of rhetoric, to be deciphered along with his book. From Rousseau's self-righteous bravado, to the bohemian

262

bars of nineteenth-century Paris filled with artists and writers acting out the radicalism of their art, to Thoreau's literary retreat into the woods, there was a clear connection.

Whitman, too, would have his bohemian period. In the late 1850s and early 1860s, he would be a regular customer at Pfaff's, on Broadway just north of Houston Street. This basement restaurant, with its long tables, its tankards of good beer, and its racks of newspapers, was the headquarters of New York's bohemia. Every evening a ragtag crowd of artists, actors, and literary people could be found there. Whitman, sitting quietly in his florid working-man's outfit and his beard, glowing pink and plump, like a Rabelaisian wiseman, was a feature of the place. Usually he was silent, a listener not a talker. But his notorious book spoke for him, and he was surrounded by free-lovers, radicals, and vegetarians who supposed he had joined them in the life of reform and freedom. At the time, he let the misunderstanding go, and probably liked it. It went along with his overall air of provocation. It gave him allies, a platform. One of his Pfaff friends, the magazine editor and literary bohemian, Henry Clapp, became Whitman's champion for a while. In 1859, Clapp published "A Word Out of the Sea" (later renamed "Out of the Cradle Endlessly Rocking") in the *Saturday Press,* an influential magazine he edited until the money ran out, several years later. He nursed controversies concerning Whitman, published reviews of his work, and kept Whitman in the public eye as a radical new voice. Clapp's influence helped to make Whitman known and also located him on the margin of literary respectability.

In his bohemian years, Whitman loved to eat and drink well. Late in the evening, he would go over to the rough Bowery beer-houses with a group of friends, or sit talking at Pfaff's with off-duty doctors from nearby New York Hospital. He was something of a local celebrity: a literary rebel and an eccentric with his peculiar way of dressing, his strangely aged appearance, in the company of a drinking crowd almost half his age. Yet there was a sadness, too. This marginal bohemia was not what he had in mind when he had launched his "Voice" to the working men and women of America only a few years before. In the poems, he was "coarse and strong . . . suffused as with the common people . . . . —O they are truly me!" he wrote in an 1859 notebook, continuing:

> But that shadow, my likeness, that goes to and fro seeking a livelihood, chattering, chaffering,
> I often find myself standing and looking at it where it flits—
> That likeness of me, but never substantially me.

Again the watcher was watching, and what he saw seemed disturbingly unreal. Although Whitman's "voice" still reached confidently for its lovers, the bearded listener at Pfaff's felt separate, lonely. He was celebrated, yes, but Pfaff's and its friendly crowd—the slightly shady "actresses," the acidly witty journalists and down-at-the-heels drinkers—were not America. At times, its underground vaults, for all their clinking and gaiety, felt like a tomb:

> —The vault at Pfaff's where the drinkers and laughers meet to eat and drink and carouse
> While on the walk immediately overhead pass the myriad feet of Broadway
> As the dead in their graves are underfoot hidden
> And the living pass over them, recking not of them,
> Laugh on laughers!
> Drink on drinkers!
> Bandy and jest!
> Toss the theme from one to another!
> Beam up—Brighten up, bright eyes of beautiful young men!
> Eat what you, having ordered, are pleased to see placed before you— after the work of the day, now, with appetite eat,
> Drink wine—drink beer—raise your voice,
> Behold! your friend, as he arrives—Welcome him, where, from the upper step, he looks down upon you with a cheerful look
> Overhead rolls Broadway—the myriad rushing Broadway
> The lamps are lit—the shops blaze—the fabrics vividly are seen through the plate glass windows
> The strong lights from above pour down upon them and are shed outside,
> The thick crowds, well-dressed—the continual crowds as if they would never end
> The curious appearance of the faces—the glimpse just caught of the eyes and expressions, as they flit along,
> (You phantoms! oft I pause, yearning, to arrest some one of you!

Oft I doubt your reality—whether you are real—I suspect all is but a
   pageant.)
The lights beam in the first vault—but the other is entirely dark.

In 1855, the aim had been different. The man behind the book
had been not a literary bohemian holding court in a restaurant, but
an anonymous Brooklyn workingman who lived in his poems and
was created by them. America's dream of liberation had seemed to
be concentrated in him: liberation from the "feudal" past, from
English manners and English literature; liberation from social roles
and the artificial distinctions conferred by the tailor. Liberation,
too, from sexual prudishness, the fear of death, and death itself. His
cultural ancestors had been Gargantua and Pantagruel, and Rousseau's "natural man," and Wordsworth's country poet. His road
was William Blake's "road of excess." The mystical German shoe-
maker Jacob Boehme had come before; and those self-reliant
Christian heretics who were ruled by the "inner light" and by the
anarchic purity of impulse: those antinomians who, as Quakers,
had become so improbably respectable in Whitman's America. All
of these, and more, had contributed to Walt Whitman's larger-
than-life voice.

The man, too, had seemed larger than life. Thoreau had seen it
and, overcoming his discomfort at Whitman's staginess, was fascinated. During several visits with Whitman in the fall of 1856,
Bronson Alcott had been amused by Whitman's oversized manner;
yet he, too, felt himself in the presence of a phenomenon:

Broad-shouldered, rouge-fleshed, Bacchus-browed, bearded like a satyr,
and rank, he wears his man-Bloomer in defiance of everybody, having
these as every thing else after his own fashion, and for example to all men
hereafter. Red flannel undershirt, open-breasted, exposing his brawny
neck; striped calico jacket over this, the collar Byroneal, with coarse cloth
overalls buttoned to it; cowhide boots; a heavy roundabout, with huge
outside pockets and buttons to match; and a slouched hat, for house and
street alike. Eyes gray, unimaginative, cautious yet melting. When talking will recline upon the couch at length, pillowing his head upon his
bended arm, and informing you naively how lazy he is, and slow. Listens
well; asks you to repeat what he has failed to catch at once, yet hesitates in
speaking often, or gives over as if fearing to come short of the sharp, full,
concrete meaning of his thought. Inquisitive, very; over-curious even;

inviting criticism on himself, on his poems—pronouncing it "pomes". In fine, an egotist, incapable of omitting, or suffering any one long to omit, noting Walt Whitman in discourse. Swaggy in his walk, burying both his hands in his outside pockets. He has never been sick, he says, not taken medicine, nor sinned; and so is quite innocent of repentence and man's fall.

Alcott and Thoreau were the first in a long line of friends who saw Whitman as he wanted to be seen: free of social niceties, toweringly physical, yet observant and gentle, healthy, innocent; a man acting and dressing as he pleased, who was in all things, exactly speaking, the man of his poems. As a young Boston clergyman Moncure Conway had put it the year before, in a letter to Emerson: "His eye can kindle strangely; and his words are ruddy with health. He is clearly his Book."

We must try to imagine Whitman's state of mind during the summer and fall of 1855. He had just written a provokingly original book, and he knew it. The book was a gauntlet thrown down to the powers of acceptable literature, and the reactions he had gotten must not have surprised him.

[a] gathering of muck . . . entirely destitute of wit.

The volume . . . fortifies the doctrines of the Metampsychosists, for it is impossible to imagine how any man's fancy could have conceived such a mass of stupid filth, unless he were possessed of the soul of a sentimental donkey that had died of disappointed love.

Who is this arrogant young man who proclaims himself Poet of Time, and who roots like a pig among the rotten garbage of licentious thoughts?

Reactions like this excited Whitman, and he included a few scathing reviews among the notices of his book he bound into a second batch of the 1855 *Leaves of Grass*. In a few of the books, he pasted the copy of a letter from Emerson he had received a few weeks after the book was published. Emerson's letter had "set him up," George Whitman remembered, and he carried it around in his pocket all summer. In October, Whitman got his friend Henry Dana to publish it in the *Tribune,* and, a year later, embossed one of Emerson's sentences on the spine of his second edition: "I greet you at the beginning of a great career."

When Emerson first opened *Leaves of Grass,* he must have seen what the reviewers also saw: that this rowdy New York book expressed "the bolder results of a certain transcendental kind of thinking," in the words of the unfriendly critic Rufus Griswold; that its author, appallingly crude and ill-mannered, but also witty and adventurous, had been sparked by Emerson's ideas, was, in some way, his—Emerson's—responsibility. In 1855, Emerson was no longer the stubborn rebel of twenty, or even fifteen, years before, but was well on his way toward being canonized as America's best-known and most high-minded man of letters. For the most part, he had retreated from the stylistic daring of his first essays. But he recognized in Whitman an answer to his earlier call for a self-reliant American poet who could shrug aside the fetters of tradition and conventional meter in favor of a "meter-making argument." Emerson "rubbed his eyes" and wrote America's most famous literary letter:

> Concord 21 July
> Masstts 1855

> Dear Sir,
> I am not blind to the worth of the wonderful gift of *Leaves of Grass.* I find it the most extraordinary piece of wit and wisdom that America has yet contributed. I am very happy in reading it, as great power makes us happy. It meets the demand I am always making of what seemed the sterile and stingy Nature, as if too much handiwork or too much lymph in the temperament were making our western wits fat and mean.
> I give you joy of your free and brave thought. I have great joy in it. I find incomparable things said incomparably well, as they must be. I find the courage of treatment, which so delights us, and which large perception only can inspire.
> I greet you at the beginning of a great career, which yet must have had a long foreground somewhere, for such a start. I rubbed my eyes a little, to see if this sunbeam were no illusion; but the solid sense of the book is a sober certainty. It has the best merits, namely of fortifying and encouraging.
> I did not know until I last night saw the book advertized in a newspaper, that I could trust the name as real and available for a post-office. I wish to see my benefactor, and have felt much like striking my tasks, and visiting New York to pay you my respects.
> R. W. Emerson.

For years Emerson would be a loyal supporter of Whitman.

Once, he came out, unannounced, to the Whitman family's house in Brooklyn; another time, he invited Whitman to dine with him at his New York hotel, and Whitman took him on a visit (he would never quite forgive) to the rowdy Mercer Street firehouse. Emerson also sent numerous visitors to Whitman, including Conway, Thoreau, and Alcott, and instigated several excellent reviews of *Leaves of Grass*. Despite the shocked dislike of numerous friends, and despite his irritation at Whitman's tasteless use of his letter, Emerson continued to stand by Whitman. On 6 May 1856, he wrote his friend Carlyle a letter that would have thrilled Whitman had he known about it:

One book, last summer, came out in New York, a nondescript monster which yet had terrible eyes and buffalo strength, and was indisputably American—which I thought to send you; but the book throve so badly with the few to whom I showed it, and wanted good morals so much, that I never did. Yet I believe now again, I shall. It is called *Leaves of Grass*—was written and printed by a journeyman printer in Brooklyn, New York, named Walter Whitman; and after you have looked into it, if you think, as you may, that it is only an auctioneers inventory of a warehouse, you can light your pipe with it.

There was always an element of misunderstanding in the friendship between the two men. Emerson clearly felt a responsibility to coax Whitman toward greater self-control as a writer. He saw Whitman as a shaggy genius who had to outgrow his shagginess. Many years later, when asked why he had left Whitman out of his anthology of American poetry, Emerson replied that Whitman had not yet gotten out of the firehouse and into the drawing room. That 1856 visit still rankled.

Yet in 1855, Emerson plucked Whitman from obscurity to an improbable fame. It was fame in a teacup, to be sure, but it was real, and it served as a platform for the gradual establishment of Whitman's reputation in later years. From the first, *Leaves of Grass* made its way. Although the book never sold readily, as Whitman claimed a year later, neither was it a total failure, as he liked to remember when he had become old and celebrated. Fowler and Wells got the book into people's hands. A copy may have found its way to a law office in Springfield, Illinois, where Lincoln is said to have read it. Another was discovered by a young Philadelphia Quaker, who remembered her initial impression of its power. A later friend of Whitman's, John Swinton, told of picking up a copy in a bookstore on Fulton Street. In Boston, the writer John Trowbridge and, in Providence, William O'Connor, laid their hands on copies. Somehow, the edition was disposed of; and a year later, Fowler and Wells agreed to publish an expanded edition of the book.

This was a high moment of Whitman's life. With an "iron will"—his phrase in the story "The Shadow and Light of a Young Man's Soul"—he had remade himself and made his book, and the two labors had been one. His daring long poem, taking up half the book, recorded the change, or, rather, offered itself as the very instrument of change: an ordeal by language. And he had succeeded. There was Emerson's letter to help him believe it. There was the young clergyman, Moncure Conway, the first of many pilgrims. And Thoreau, Alcott, Longfellow's younger brother, Sam, coming over on the ferry to his frugal neighborhood, to meet him and hear what he had to say. And there was the shocked anger of his enemies, generating a higher class of vituperation than the rivals of his newspaper days. At this moment of victory, it must have seemed to him that anything could happen, and was happening. When he wrote an answer to Emerson and included it in the 1856 *Leaves of Grass,* he thought of Longfellow's fame and Tupper's vast popularity: why couldn't he do what they had done? In this floodtide of the machine age, was there any limit to the power of the printed word?

Of authors and editors I do not know how many there are in The States, but there are thousands, each one building his or her step to the stairs by which giants shall mount. Of the twenty-four modern two-double, three-double, and four-double cylinder presses now in the world, printing by steam, twenty-one of them are in These States. The twelve thousand large and small shops for dispensing books and newspapers—the same number of public libraries, any one of which has all the reading wanted to equip a man or woman for American reading—the three thousand different newspapers, the nutriment of the imperfect ones coming in just as usefully as any—the story papers, various, full of strong-flavored romances, widely circulated—the one-cent and two-cent journals—the political ones, no matter what side—the weeklies in the country—the sporting and pictorial papers—the monthly magazines, with plentiful imported feed—the sentimental novels, numberless copies of them—the low-priced flaring tales, adventures, biographies—all are prophetic; all waft rapidly on. I see that they swell wide, for reasons. I am not troubled at the movement of them, but greatly pleased. I see plying shuttles, the active ephemeral myriads of books also, faithfully weaving the garments of a generation of men, and a generation of women, they do not perceive or know. What a progress popular reading and writing has made in fifty years! What a progress fifty years hence!

Whitman is writing about his origins here. This tide of popular reading—newspapers, popular novels, and tracts—had been his compost. He came from it, and now he hailed in it the possibility of an audience. Fantasy and truth blur in Whitman's exuberance. The thousand copies of his first edition sold "readily," he claimed; and now he was planning "several thousand copies" of his new book. "The way is clear to me. A few years, and the average annual call for my Poems is ten or twenty thousand copies, more, quite likely." But first he must go out to "meet people and The States face to face, to confront them with an American rude tongue. . . . In poems or in speeches I say the word or two that has got to be said. . . . Every day I go among the people of Manhattan Island, Brooklyn, and other cities, and among the young men, to discover the spirit of them, and to refresh myself."

Like "The Eighteenth Presidency," written about the same time, Whitman's "letter" boils with uncontrolled ambition. It is a fantasy of power, a program for a wild man. That, too, was American enough. If exaggeration and outrageousness were, at every level, America's native dance—then Whitman could say what he wanted, he could bring taste and restraint down about his ears. It was an old theme with him: "Always America will be agitated and turbulent. This day it is taking shape, not to be less so, but to be more so, stormily, capriciously, on native principles, with such vast proportions of parts! As for me, I love screaming, wrestling, boiling-hot days."

What Emerson made of this tribute we can only imagine. The whole "letter" reels with hype: it is "screaming," "boiling-hot."

Whitman's "lazy" nature contained an opposing streak of verbal delirium. His kindliness had a wild underside, and rarely has it spoken so uninhibitedly as in this unpleasant letter, which Whitman wisely suppressed in later editions of *Leaves of Grass.* Yet the letter tells us about the heights Whitman inhabited at the time. Not only had he erased, for his reader, the boundary between art and life, he had erased it for himself. Whitman's ordeal by language, we have seen, was not only a theme for a poem, but a lived program, an internalized form of the great American hope. Whitman lived between his book and his body. Perfection of the life *was* perfection of the work. The poems said it, and now the man said it, too, and he said it about himself.

5

In the fall of 1855, Whitman wrote the first of several unsigned reviews of his book. Admirers of Whitman have often been unsettled by his lifelong maneuvering for publicity. Over the decades, there would be numerous inserts in newspapers relating the doings, the state of health, and the general welfare of "Walt Whitman." Whitman wrote most of these inserts, and editors, grateful for a little filler, printed them. These third-person glimpses are Whitman's trademark, as we have seen. They signify that exterior glance—the man watching himself live—that Whitman made repeatedly. His notion of becoming "perfect" was, curiously, not far from Baudelaire's in the autobiographical story *La Fanfarlo,* whose hero, Samuel Cramer, lives in front of a mirror, not to admire himself with facile narcissism but to discipline his face, his dress, his gestures, until he becomes the work of his hands: a living poem, a dandy.

Whitman's anonymous reviews rank with his famous butterfly photograph as examples of his reckless, and slightly dishonest, staginess. He kept up the fiction for years and even included the anonymous reviews in a curious anthology of critical articles, panegyrics, attacks, and parodies of his work, which he collected and published in 1860, to accompany his great third edition of *Leaves of Grass*; he called the anthology *Leaves of Grass Imprints*. Questions of propriety aside, these early self-reviews tell us how Whitman wanted to be read in 1855; more important, how he wanted to be seen and heard. Like *Leaves of Grass* itself, they are segments of the legend he had set about creating for himself. Here is Whitman's autobiography on the grand scale. Here is the perfection he willed for himself and presented to the public, not as a concealing lie, but as a vision that seemed to him to be anchored in his very flesh:

Self-reliant, with haughty eyes, assuming to himself all the attributes of his country, steps Walt Whitman into literature, talking like a man unaware that there was ever hitherto such a production as a book, or such a being as a writer. Every move of him has the free play of the muscle of one who never knew what it was to feel that he stood in the presence of a superior. Every word that falls from his mouth shows silent disdain and defiance of the old theories and forms. Every phrase announces new laws; not once do his lips unclose except in conformity with them.

• • •

He makes audacious and native use of his own body and soul. He must recreate poetry with the elements always at hand. He must imbue it with himself as he is, disorderly, fleshy, and sensual, a lover of things, yet a lover of men and women above the whole of the other objects of the universe.

• • •

Doubtless in the scheme this man has built for himself, the writing of poems is but a proportionate part of the whole.

A year later, in the Brooklyn *Daily Times*—a newspaper he would soon be editing—he amplified this fabulous portrait of a man whose poems are casual outgrowths of his gigantic and various nature:

First be yourself what you would show in your poems—such seems to be this man's example and inferred rebuke to the schools of poets. He makes no allusions to books or writers; their spirits do not seem to have touched him; he has not a word to say for or against them, or their theories or ways. He never offers others; what he continually offers is the man whom our Brooklynites know so well. Of pure American breed, large and lusty—age thirty-six years (1855)—never once using medicine—never dressed in black, always dressed freely and clean in strong clothes—neck open, shirt-collar flat and broad, countenance tawny transparent red, beard well-mottled with white, hair like hay after it has been mowed in the field and lies tossed and streaked—his physiology corroborating a rugged phrenology—a person singularly beloved and looked toward, especially by young men and the illiterate—one who has firm attachments there, and associates there—one who does not associate with literary people—a man never called upon to make speeches at public dinners—never on platforms amid the crowds of clergymen, or professors, or aldermen, or congressmen—rather down in the bay with pilots in their pilot-boat— or off on a cruise with fishers in a fishing-smack—or riding on a Broadway omnibus, side by side with the driver—or with a band of loungers over the open grounds of the country—fond of New York and Brooklyn—fond of the life of the great ferries—one whom, if you should meet, you need not expect to meet an extraordinary person—one in whom you will see the singularity which consists in no singularity—whose contact is no dazzle or fascination, nor requires any deference, but has the easy fascination of what is homely and accustomed—as of something you knew before, and was waiting for.

The tone of these articles is as remarkable as their content. There is a confidence, a largeness of reach. One hardly notices the outrageousness of Whitman's self-description; it is at home with itself and happy in its power.

What did Whitman think readers would make of these so-called reviews? What *did* they make of them? We can assume that at least some readers of the Brooklyn *Daily Times* knew Whitman or knew of him. He was a local citizen; only a few years before, in political and journalistic circles, he had been a small celebrity.

It is a measure of Whitman's remarkable achievement—the fusing of his poetry and his personality—that Alcott, Thoreau, and Conway described Whitman in terms that are not so far from these extravagant puffs. To his New England visitors, he seemed, and perhaps was, "a little more than human." All his life, he would be seen this way. His friend John Burroughs would be awed by his cold blue eyes which resembled apertures of empty sky. Maurice Bucke would describe someone—probably himself—who experienced a euphoric glow for months after meeting Whitman. After the Civil War, soldiers described the magnetic effect of his presence in the hospital wards. By the sheer power of his personality, he seemed to haul the sick bodies to safety, like the healer in "Song of Myself":

To any one dying . . . thither I speed and twist the knob of the door,
Turn the bedclothes toward the foot of the bed,
Let the physician and the priest go home.

I seize the descending man. . . . I raise him with resistless will.

O despairer, here is my neck,
By God! you shall not go down! Hang your whole weight upon me.

I dilate you with tremendous breath. . . . I buoy you up;
Every room of the house do I fill with an armed force . . . lovers of
    me, bafflers of graves:
Sleep! I and they keep guard all night;
Not doubt, not decease shall dare to lay finger upon you,
I have embraced you, and henceforth possess you to myself,
And when you rise in the morning you will find what I tell you is so.

For years the Whitman family had been obsessed with health, and
we can see why, with their pitiable declining fortunes, their sick-
nesses, their unraveling heredity. The undersong to Whitman's
"iron-willed" remolding of self was his sister Hannah's repellent
letters: here was another song of self, shrill, self-pitying, and hypochondriac. The family's flawed heredity affected Whitman, too. At
forty, he looked like an old man. Even before going to Washington, he had begun to suffer from dizzy spells and periodic weaknesses, which he attributed to sunstroke. By his mid-forties, his
health had permanently failed; and a few years later, he was partly
paralyzed by a stroke. But in 1855 and 1856, he sang out about his
"magnetism" and his radiant bodily health and offered to pull his
readers—and all of America—up to his gigantic level.

It is an astonishing combination of poetic genius, street theater,
and fraud. And something else, too: a feeling of power, a genuine
physical aura which was the outreaching form of Whitman's celebrated egotism: "What good is it to argue about egotism," he
wrote in one of his anonymous reviews, "There can be no two
thoughts about Walt Whitman's egotism. That is avowedly what
he steps out of the crowd and turns and faces them for."

"What a man wishes for in his youth, he obtains abundantly in
his old age," Goethe wrote in his *Autobiography* which had served
as one of Whitman's models. Whitman wished powerfully that he
could be a new man. He wished he could transcend the limits of

the ordinary, while yet remaining a representative, ordinary man. He wished to be the focus of a vast flow of personalities, lovers, bodies, skills, voices, and he called this flow "democracy." So many intertwining wishes. And there were the private wishes, too. He wished to be his mother's champion, a father to his brothers and sisters; to wrench himself free of his family's aura of failure and ill health. These wishes were a lens concentrating his will. And now it seemed he had gotten what he wished for.

CHAPTER 8

"Whoever You Are Holding Me Now in Hand"

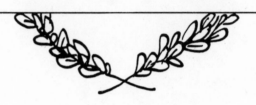

1

IN 1854, Whitman began a creative surge that did not end with his first book or even with his second a year later. For more than three years, he wrote poems at a headlong pace. His 1856 edition contained twenty new long poems. Less than a year after that, he had finished seventy-eight more poems, writing them out on squares of unused pink endpaper left over from the 1855 *Leaves of Grass*. Whitman would never throw himself into his writing this way again. During these years, in addition to the poems, he wrote his remarkable essay on American vernacular (posthumously called "An American Primer"); he wrote the "Eighteenth Presidency," in which he called for a new American politics based on the "voice of Walt Whitman." He compiled volumes of notes on world culture, for his role as one of the "Wander Teachers," or "Mediums":

> Strong and sweet shall their tongues be—poems and materials of po-
> ems shall come from their lives—they shall be makers and finders,
> Of them, and of their works, shall emerge divine conveyers, to convey
> gospels,

Characters, events, retrospections, shall be conveyed in gospels—
  Trees, animals, waters, shall be conveyed,
Death, the future, the invisible faith, shall be conveyed.

This outpouring of poems was the text of Whitman's wild oration. They are poems of the voice, and they are about voices: the voices of "Mediums," "savans," "oratists," and "poets to come." They are about the power of "vocalism": "When you hear it, the merciless light shall pour, and the storms rage around." Whitman's model is theater, as we have seen, but a theater that is out of doors, created by the larger-than-life voice of the "young giant" who is democracy personified, but who is also Walt Whitman of Ryerson Street in Brooklyn—a man of whom anything, apparently, could be expected.

Whitman's designs were in flux. Even before publishing the 1856 *Leaves of Grass,* he was at work on the prologue to a further, more ambitious book:

In the Year 80 of The States,
My tongue, every atom of my blood, formed from this soil, this air,
Born here of parents born here,
From parents the same, and their parents' parents the same,
I, now thirty-six years old, in perfect health, begin,
Hoping to cease not till death.

By the time this long poem—called by then "Protoleaf"—became the prologue to Whitman's next volume, in 1860, and to every edition after that, Whitman's grand design had undergone many changes. In a note dated June 1857, he wrote: "The Great Construction of the New Bible. Not to be diverted from the principle object—the main life work—the three hundred and sixty-five.—It ought to be ready in 1859." With more than one hundred poems already written, Whitman saw himself creating a veritable scripture of democratic life. To complete it, he would need two more years of total commitment, three hundred sixty-five days a year. Or did he mean that he was preparing to write another two hundred and sixty-five poems, to fill out a complete cycle of the sun, which rises and sets through many of these poems? Whitman's ambition was measureless, and his peculiar talent, we have seen, was to devise a measureless voice to fulfill it.

Carlyle's *Sartor Resartus* had also been a "New Bible" of sorts, as had Tupper's *Proverbial Philosophy* and Blake's *Prophetic Books*; Hugo's *Voix de Satan* would be another, and Nietzsche's *Zarathustra* yet another. The nineteenth century specialized in "New Bibles" and in virtuoso geniuses to write them. Whitman's wild aim is less unique, finally, than his creative appetite which, in 1856 and 1857, absorbed endless data from his newspaper skimming and his hours at the library and spilled them in rhythmic heapings into his catalogue like poems.

Around the time Whitman was thinking about a "New Bible," he wrote his friend Sarah Tyndale of another, very different plan:

Fowler & Wells are bad persons for me. They retard my book very much. It is worse than ever. I wish now to bring out a third edition—I have now *a hundred* poems ready (the last edition had thirty-two)—and shall endeavor to make an arrangement with some publisher here to take the plates from F. & W. and make the additions needed, and so bring out the third edition. F. & W. are very willing to give up the plates—they want the thing off their hands. In the forthcoming Vol. I shall have, as I said, a hundred poems, and no other matter but poems—(no letters to or from Emerson—no notices, or anything of that sort.) I know well enough, that *that* must be the *true* Leaves of Grass—I think it (the new Vol.) has an aspect of completeness, and makes its case clearer. The old poems are all retained. The difference is in the new character given to the mass, by the additions.

There is no mention here of any grand conception. The book Whitman was thinking about is more modest: to the plates of the 1856 edition, he would add about 78 new poems, probably the ones he had copied out on pink paper. On the back of a rejected poem, he made a list of numbered titles beginning with 33 and running to 103. Whitman's book was going to be a "mass" of numbered poems. It would really be two books bound together. "Protoleaf," on which he had been working for two years, would simply be merged in the "mass," a sign that Whitman had given up on the grand work he had been hoping for, and was willing to settle for a mere book. Yet this book, too, he felt, would have an "aspect of completeness" and be the "true *Leaves of Grass*." While writing almost two thirds of his life's work in less than three years, Whitman had no time to plan. The poems were a long flurry, on a level of wildness with his "open letter" to Emerson. The idea of a "New Bible"—a vast cyclical poem, a "Great Construction"—that would nonetheless be full of native "grossness. . . . savageness and freedom," pleased Whitman; he even wrote a long prologue for it. But the randomly shuffled poems that he copied out on pink paper were a more practical, maybe even a truer sort of book. As in his first home-made volume, only two years before, the impression of a formless accumulation, overrich and overabundant—an outdoor market or traveling trunk of a book—had, in Whitman's esthetic, a truth of its own.

Whitman's collaboration with Fowler and Wells had never been secure. Although they agreed to publish his second book, they preferred to keep their name off the title page. Whitman had never been their idea of a poet anyway. His raucous evangelism was too concrete and direct, too tinged with the possibility of scandal. His celebration of sex was a bit warm, even for the enthusiastic Fowlers and especially for their cooler son-in-law, Samuel Wells. What were these crusading businessmen to make of Whitman's biblical rage at the contortions of Victorian euphemism, or of the dripping, drenching, and effusing of sexual juices; of the men caressing female bodies in bed; of the lonely eroticism that erupts and subsides throughout these poems? Besides, Whitman's books did not sell. The 1856 edition went almost unnoticed, and apparently he was too caught up in his writing to campaign for it as he had for the first book a year before. By June 1857, Whitman was ready to look for another publisher or perhaps to do the new book himself.

Nothing came of the plan Whitman wrote about to Sarah Tyndale, although she sent him fifty dollars toward buying the plates of his book back from Fowler & Wells. Things had come crashing down around Whitman's ears that spring. His free-lance writing was not supporting him; and during the winter, he borrowed two hundred dollars from the biographer James Parton. Parton's wife, Sara, under the penname Fanny Fern, was an immensely popular writer of the time and became one of Whitman's fervent early supporters. But the fervor went sour. It is a familiar story: women, stirred by Whitman's attack on the hypocrisy of Victorian morals, were often drawn to his easy physicality, only to find him impregnable and elusive, a ghost in a floridly sexual body. Ellen O'Con-

279

nor and Anne Gilchrist were two of the women who fluttered around Whitman in later years. But Sara Parton was not the fluttering type. When his two-hundred dollar note to her husband came due that spring, and Whitman had not paid, she sent her lawyer to seize some of Whitman's personal belongings, including a painting by his friend Jesse Talbot. The whole thing was humiliating, and it came back to haunt Whitman a quarter of a century later, when the critic T. W. Higginson, exasperated by Whitman's raucous saintliness, dredged up this unpleasant affair as proof that the Good Gray Poet was, in reality, a very bad gray poet, who didn't even pay his debts.

In May, with the Parton affair still rankling, Whitman took a job as the editor of the independent local newspaper, The Brooklyn *Daily Times*. For the first time in nine years, he was working for a living. Those late mornings writing poems in the room under the eaves; the walks along Fulton Street to the ferry; the unhinged routine, arriving anywhere, leaving anywhere at his whim: that was gone for now. In his "letter" to Emerson, the year before, Whitman had boasted of his book's vast sales, of a writer's life supported by his pen. In the "Eighteenth Presidency," he had exhorted "Rich Persons" to step forward and print his political jeremiad. Whitman seems at times to have had a fairy-tale relationship to money. One of his pink-paper poems, entitled "To Rich Givers," pursues the same curious fantasy:

> What you give me, I cheerfully accept,
> A little sustenance, a hut and garden, a little money—these as I rendezvous with my poems,
> A traveller's lodging and breakfast as I journey through The States—
> Why should I be ashamed to own such gifts? Why to advertise for them?
> For I myself am not one who bestows nothing upon man and woman,
> For I know that what I bestow upon any man or woman is no less than the entrance to all the gifts of the universe.

Not only was America going to "absorb" her poet; but, in a dreamlike circulation of gifts, she was going to support him while he ranged over the twin roads of his poem and his country. This was Whitman's hope during those adventurous years when he poured out poems and welcomed his first pilgrims. So much for the Loco-foco pride of an American poor man. In Whitman's vision, death, air, grass, laughter, and money circulated freely. The hat that, in a moment of wounded pride, he had twisted into a rope and battered an usher over the head with at posh Grace Church, was now, in his fantasy, available for a handout.

The year 1857 brought Whitman down hard. Only a year before, he had declared that "the work of my life is making poems": "a hundred, and then several hundred—perhaps a thousand." Now the money had run out; and the poems, too, dried up. He was back to his old frantic life of filling newspaper pages with miscellaneous items from the surface of his mind, the surface of the age. Two years later, Whitman assembled the poetry of 1856 and 1857 into a manuscript which he asked his friends, the Rome brothers, to set up in type. The Romes's proof pages have since disappeared; Whitman probably used them as part of the manuscript he brought up to Boston, in March 1860, to be printed by a new publishing firm, Thayer and Eldridge, as the third edition of *Leaves of Grass*. But the Romes held onto the manuscript, and it passed through the hands of collectors, becoming the basis for a remarkable piece of literary detective work by the scholar Fredson Bowers. Whitman copied out the poems for the Rome brothers on several kinds of paper: the coarse pink endpaper, scissored into page-sized squares from larger sheets; the backs of blue tax forms printed by the City of Williamsburg; various other kinds of white and blue paper. Bowers cross-checked a handful of hints (the draft of an article scrawled on the back of one poem; the fact that the Williamsburg tax forms became obsolete in 1855 and could be used as scrap only after that date, probably no earlier than 1857; a list of titles written on the back of a poem, corresponding, most likely, to the hundred poems Whitman had in mind in his letter to Sarah Tyndale) and concluded that all the poems on pink paper were copied out consecutively by the middle of 1857 and represented Whitman's extraordinary activity of the previous year. The blue tax form poems probably are revisions and, in a few cases, new poems. The rest of the paper, which came into use in 1859 and reflected renewed activity, contained some of Whitman's greatest poetry and a startlingly new tone—in fact, a new subject matter.

Whitman's creative surge ended in the spring of 1857, probably because he was too busy earning a living to devote himself to poetry, although he continued to read and make notes and to develop theories about the powers of "vocalism" and oratory. But he may simply have outrun himself. Having written so much in a short time, he may have exhausted his material. Whitman's pink-paper poems and the poems of the 1856 edition are, for the most part, swarming, celebratory. Their technique is the catalogue; they portray the world entering "with electric swiftness safely and duly without confusion or jostling or jam [into] the space of a peachpit." That is to say, they pursue Whitman's epic of perception, the creation of a new world by a new mind, which he had defined in his 1855 preface as the work of the "greatest poet." The tone is set by the bouyant assemblages of a poem like "Our Old Feuillage," which plays on Whitman's characteristic pun of these years: leaves ("feuillage") that are sheaves of perceptions; poems that grow and are harvested as the greenery of a formidably natural continent:

America always!
Always me joined with you, whoever you are!
Always our own feuillage!
Always Florida's green peninsula! Always the priceless delta of Louisiana! Always the cotton-fields of Alabama and Texas!
Always California's golden hills and hollows—and the silver mountains of New Mexico! Always soft-breath'd Cuba!
Always the vast slope drained by the Southern Sea—inseparable with the slopes drained by the Eastern and Western Seas,
The area the 83rd year of These States—the three and a half millions of square miles,
The seven millions of distinct families, and the same number of dwellings—Always these and more, branching forth into numberless branches;
Always the free range and diversity! Always the continent of Democracy!
Always the prairies, pastures, forests, vast cities, travellers, Kanada, the snows;
Always these compact lands—lands tied at the hips with the belt stringing the huge oval lakes;
Always the West, with strong native persons—the increasing density there—the habitans, friendly, threatening, ironical, scorning invaders;

All sights, South, North, East—all deeds, promiscuously done at all
  times,
All characters, movements, growths—a few noticed, myriads
  unnoticed,
Through Mannahatta's streets I walking, these things gathering.

Whitman's voice here is declarative, confident. It is an epic
voice, inclusive in the mode of the random list. All of "Our Old
Feuillage" could be a passage in "Song of Myself," except for the
booster tone ("America always!") which is far more muted in the
poems of 1854 and 1855.

In poem after poem written out on pink paper, Whitman takes
off. He circles the world as far as Hindustan, "the house of mater-
nity," and returns, "joyous, after long travel, growth and sleep." In
another poem, he prowls the American air in the company of his
"lover," and his poem-body opens wide, as in the superb catalogues of "Song of Myself":

We become plants, leaves, foliage, roots, bark,
We are bedded in the ground—we are rocks,
We are oaks—we grow in the openings side by side. . . .
We are also the coarse smut of beasts, vegetables, minerals;
We are what the flowing wet of the Tennessee is—we are two peaks
  of the Blue Mountains, rising up in Virginia,
We are two predatory hawks—we soar above and look down,
We are two resplendent suns—we it is who balance ourselves orbic and
  stellar—we are as two comets;
We prowl fanged and four-footed in the woods—we spring on prey;
We are two clouds, forenoons and afternoons, driving overhead.

Elsewhere he confronts time and death with a physical exuberance
that he will edit out of the published version of one of his future
"Calamus" poems:

Throwing far over the head of death, I, full of affection,
Full of life, compact, visible, thirty eight years old the eighty first year
  of The States,
To one a century hence, or any number of centuries hence,
To you, yet unborn, these, seeking you.

Whitman would group most of these poems in the "Chants Democratic" and "Leaves of Grass" sections of the 1860 edition. They

are the "spine" of that edition and of his work as a whole. It is largely through these poems that we have learned to see Whitman, or a certain Whitman: the result of the labor of self-making that had puzzled and enchanted Thoreau; that his future publishers, Thayer and Eldridge, would worship; that the naturalist John Burroughs and the fiery polemicist William O'Connor would admire, even adore. This is the Whitman who was "a little more than human," devoting himself in poem after poem to outrageous, almost humorous self-celebration:

Illustrious the yet shining light! Illustrious the soft reflection of the
  moon in the eastern sky
Illustrious world whatever I see or hear or touch. . .

To speak! To walk! To seize something by the hand!
To be conscious of my body, so perfect, so large!
To be this incredible God I am!
To move among these other Gods—these men and women!

Wonderful how I celebrate you and myself!
How my thoughts play subtly at the spectacles around!
How clouds pass silently overhead!
How the earth darts on and on! And how the sun, moon, stars, dart on
  and on!

How the water sports and sings! (Surely it is alive!)
How the trees stand out there with strong trunks—with branches and
  leaves! (Surely there is something more in each of the trees—some
  living soul!)

As I sailed down the Mississippi,
As I wandered over the prairies,
As I have lived—As I have looked through my windows, my eyes,
As I went forth in the morning—as I beheld the light breaking in the
  east,
As I bathed on the beach on the Eastern Sea, and again on the beach on
  the Western Sea,

As I roamed the streets of inland Chicago—Whatever streets I have
  roamed,
Wherever I have been, I have been charged with a charge of contentment and triumph.—

As we read many of these pink-paper poems, we cannot help but feel a straining for effect, the sense of a concerted effort to keep to the high plateau. For all their richness of detail, the poems are univocal. For all their physicality and formlessness, they often seem programmatic, not an advance toward new themes, but a repetition of old ones. "Our Old Feuillage" makes the catalogue into a separate form. "Poem of Joys" isolates the tone of celebration which gives substance to "Song of Myself," and makes it into a subject of its own. "Song of the Open Road" organizes the elusive, often oblique theme of the 1855 poems into a single assertion. These are good poems, but they represent tidyings, consolidations. In them, Whitman is massing his themes, organizing his territory as the American bard. He is also flattening his poems, by limiting their range of feeling. Reading them, we forget the terrors, the darknesses, the exquisite tenderness that contribute to the "story" of "Song of Myself." We forget the agonies and resurrections of "The Sleepers," the creeping lines of mourners in "To Think of Time." The 1855 *Leaves of Grass* was an impulsive book, not a programmatic one. But the pink-paper poems belong already to the "New Bible." Already Whitman is editing himself. The speaker of these poems is the towering personage of his anonymous self-reviews, and the accomplishment of the poems, as we have seen, is to make Whitman's personage believable. But he cannot manage it indefinitely. A sign of Whitman's straining to graft a program onto his gift is the poem he worked on for almost five years as his program opener, the gateway to his Bible: "Protoleaf" or, as he would eventually call it, "Starting from Paumanok." He began working on the poem in 1855; and two years later, it was still weak, full of nationalistic posturing, as almost all his introductory poems would be. "Starting from Paumanok" is a replay of "Song of Myself," without the hermetic inward-turning and the incremental self-building, which create the drama of Whitman's first poem. The leaning and loafing observer has become a rugged traveler, starting from his Long Island childhood and ranging west across time and space:

> How curious! How real!
> Underfoot, the divine soil—Overhead the sun.

Whitman turned this phrase over and over in his notebook, as if to parlay it into the rhythm of his high-ranging self. He rarely labored so over a poem. "Protoleaf" kept escaping him and descending into purple prose, a kind of inflated editorializing:

> Here lands female and male,
> Here the heirship and heiresship of the world—Here the flame of materials,
> Here Spirituality, the translatress, the openly avowed,
> The ever-tending, the finale of visible forms......
> I will make a song for These States, that no one State may under any circumstances be subjected to another State,
> And I will make a song that there shall be comity by day and by night between all The States, and between any two of them,
> And I will make a song of the organic bargains of These States—And a shrill song of curses on him who would dissever the Union;
> And I will make a song for the ears of the President, full of weapons with menacing points.

By 1857, Whitman had closed the circle. He had tidied and consolidated; he had written one hundred poems that were "a little more than human," perhaps too much more. In one of the pink-paper poems, he had written: "What am I after all but a child pleased with my own name? repeating it over and over." When Whitman took his job with the Brooklyn *Daily Times,* it was time to stop the repetitions that had become strident and pat. His conservative side had reined him in in the midst of his great labor. Instead of enlarging his range, he had simply gotten louder, and now he stopped.

Yet the poems of these years are not as monolithic as I have implied. A handful of poems, probably written late in this period, are new and promising. Love poems, they are quiet, reflective. Where previously he had been a player before an audience, in these poems he finds himself face to face with a person. The intransitive ecstasies of "Song of Myself" are muted and suddenly socialized, as if, despite the lid of silence that his psyche imposed, Whitman had momentarily lit the lamp and seen his lover I called these love poems; "almost" love poems would be better, for they are still muffled and fragmentary, compared with the poems that Whitman would write in 1859. Here, the love reaches across separations. It is a modulation of his excited celebration of lovers passing on a street, in "Song of Myself." His lover is still a stranger but has become singular now:

> Passing stranger! you do not know how longingly I look upon you,
> You must be he I was seeking, or she I was seeking, (It comes to me, as of a dream,)
> I have somewhere surely lived a life of joy with you.

and

> Of him that I love day and night, I dreamed I heard he was dead,
> And I dreamed I went where they had buried the man I love but he was not in that place,
> And I dreamed I wandered searching among burial places, to find him,
> And I found that every place was a burial place,
> The houses full of life were equally full of death, (This house is now,).

Whitman was already making his long lists of young men, and these fragmentary poems hint at a new dimension in his feelings. His "lover" is a man, but he is forbidden; he is a "stranger," or he is dead. It is the old theme of love and loss of which the troubadors had sung: love spiritualized by distance, preserved by impossibility. We see it stirring in these poems, combined with another of Whitman's themes: the confession of some fault that, if fully known, would overthrow his manly personage:

> May-be one is now reading this who knows some wrong-doing of my past life,
> Or may-be a stranger is reading this who has secretly loved me,
> Or may-be one who meets all my grand assumptions and egotisms with derision,
> Or may-be one who is puzzled at me.
>
> As if I were not puzzled at myself!
> Or as if I do not secretly love strangers! (O tenderly, a long time, and never avow it;)
> Or as if I did not see, perfectly well, interior in myself, the stuff of wrong-doing,
> Or as if it could cease from transpiring from me until it must cease.

The love poems would develop powerfully in 1859; they would represent a new maturity for Whitman, perhaps a larger, more flexible self-acceptance. Yet there, too, the theme of manly love, the lighting of Psyche's lamp, would be fraught with tensions.

Love and longings for death went together for Whitman. Love and the hidden "fault"—the "secret" he hinted at to Horace Traubel almost forty years later?—were compulsive partners in his mind, and these two slight notes, amid the exuberance of the pink-paper poems, hint at another reason for his silence in 1857. As he circled the flame of the forbidden, he found himself speaking plainly, maybe too plainly, until finally he recoiled and fell silent. If the blue tax-form poems represent, in part, writing done over the next year or two, then we hear in one of them an echo of Whitman's inner turmoil, the struggle to speak, and yet not to speak, which accompanied his feelings of sexual guilt. I give the poem in its manuscript form, which is more pointed than the published version:

> I go no farther till I confess myself in the open air, in the hearing of this time and future times,
> Also till I make a leaf of fair warning.
>
> I am he who has been sly, thievish, mean, a prevaricater, greedy,
> And I am he who remains so yet.
>
> What foul thought but I think it?
> What in darkness in bed at night, alone or with a companion, but that too is mine?
> You prostitutes flaunting over the trottoirs, or obscene in your rooms?
> Who am I that I should call you more obscene than myself? . . .
>
> Beneath this impassive face the hot fires of hell continually burn—within me the lurid smutch and the smoke;
> Not a crime can be named but I have it in me waiting to break forth,
> Lusts and wickedness are acceptable to me,
> I walk with delinquents with passionate love.

As always, Whitman theatricalizes. The hot fires and smutch within are Byronic; they are American Gothic. This is still the gigantism of Whitman's pink-paper poems. With the crumbling of his "impassive face," a colossal débris falls to the earth. Whitman's "Confession and Warning"—the title of this poem—is made at the top of his lungs. When he speaks out again, in a year or so, his voice will be softer, more puzzled. Not a "little more than human," but simply human, often wrenchingly so.

2

Meanwhile, Whitman took up his new job at the Brooklyn *Daily Times*. He visited his friends the Prices and argued genially with their Swedenborgian neighbor. His notebooks are full of names, addresses; he was socially busy . One of them reads: "Miss Ellen Grey, Bowery Theater, cor. Hicks and Amity, before May 1, tall high house free stone." The mysterious Ellen Grey, perhaps an actress, left no other trace in Whitman's life, unless the photograph of a long-haired, dark young woman, pasted in another of Whitman's notebooks, is of her. He thought about visiting his sister Hannah, already embroiled in her sad marriage to the landscape painter Charles Hyde, and took note of the train schedule to Rutland, Vermont (the train arrived in Rutland toward nine at night). Traveling was on Whitman's mind. He recorded a visit to the Fourierist Albert Brisbane in Irvington, New Jersey. He thought of visiting a friend named William Place at a public house on the Delaware River frequented by raftmen.

Whitman was full of writing projects that came to nothing. He had the idea for a "Book of Letters": to a prostitute, to a felon, to someone about to die. Example, to a prostitute: "I salute you, my love, with a kiss on your lips that you do not forget me." Another project is for a "Poem of Wise Books," and another for "a poem (or passage in a poem) giving an account of my way of making a poem." His healing fantasy of a happy old age was still alive: "Poem expressing the sentiment of old age. . . . o my old manhood! my children and grandchildren! My white hair and beard! My largeness, calmness and majesty from many years."

His lists of young men are interspersed with lists of books. Whitman was still gathering facts for the compendious poems he had stopped writing, or for the lectures he hoped to give, or maybe simply to "exercise" the organs of his brain, to cultivate himself. He reminded himself to ask a Mr. Arkhurst about insects, for a poem of insects. He listed Eduard Winkelmann's *History of Ancient Art,* and Schlegel's *History of Literature,* R. W. Piper's, *Trees of America* and Joseph Gostick's *Spirit of German Poetry.* He noted a conversation with a friend of the Prices, Mrs. Elizah Farnham, a former matron of Sing Sing Prison, about the new territory of California, and the note gives vent to his Westward-looking dream of an America to match the gigantism of his "New Bible":

Everything [in California] seems to be generated and grow on a *larger scale*—fruits, vegetables for cooking, trees, etc.—Humanity is also freer and grander. —The children seem cast on a fuller pattern, grow better, breathe more air, make more blood, are sounder every way a superior type. The passions are also stronger, the soul more clarified and apparent, life seems more intense and determined—there is more individuality and character."

As usual, we do not see Whitman much with friends or in the society of writers. We glimpse him in the streets with his young men or watching a baseball match or two boys wrestling in an empty lot. Through his *Daily Times* editorials, we see him going to public lectures, visiting churches and evangelical tent meetings, observing the prostitutes on Broadway, near Houston Street. It was an uneventful life, as his brother George would say, but full of the city, centered as always on his family and now, for a few years, on his job. He wrote in an 1857 notebook: "All poems or any other expression of literature that do not tally with their writer's actual life and knowledge, are lies." How Whitman accomplished this tally in his own mind, we cannot know. Perhaps we see here the impulse to open his poems, even dangerously, to the complete man, which in a few years would give the poems a new tone. Meanwhile, the bard of the "New Bible" and the small-time journalist had to get along as best they could.

A year or so later, Whitman annotated a new edition of Plato: "by love [Plato] evidently means the passion inspired in one man by another man, more particularly a beautiful youth. The talk seems to hinge on the question whether such a youth should bestow his 'favors' more profitably on a declared 'lover' or on one not especially so." Whitman found the subject "astonishing to modern ideas," although it may not have been so astonishing to him, with his lists of "beautiful youths." In another annotation, he may have been thinking of his own "love poem" on the grass, in "Song of Myself": "he makes an ingenious comparison—the gross and the spiritual in a human being in love—. . . They 'lie down together' 'kiss and fondle each other etc. etc.'" In all of Plato, here is what stirred Whitman: he himself would soon be writing about the "gross" and the "spiritual" lying down together and fondling each other; "self" and "soul," poet and stranger, the drama of a "human being in love."

For two years, Whitman worked hard and wrote little poetry. Every morning, he came to the *Daily Times* office wearing the bluff outfit of a New York "rough": a jacket of heavy dark blue cloth open at the top to show a woolen undershirt, and a red handkerchief tied around his neck; pants tucked into his high boots; a battered broad-brimmed hat. He made friends with a young German poet, Frederick Huene, who worked in the composing room of the newspaper. Huene described Whitman walking around the office for long periods without saying a word; one thinks of his father's moody silences.

In his editorials, Whitman made a point of holding himself aloof from practical politics. He wrote of his usual strolls about town, of a visit to a porcelain factory, of a campaign for a new Brooklyn waterworks (he later called it his proudest accomplishment at the *Times*). As usual, his book notices are hurried and cursory. He is an ardent booster of Brooklyn's future: "this great city's wharves will one day be crowded with shipping and its streets vocal with the clash of machinery." Two years earlier, he had written to Washington requesting the latest government census reports and other vital national statistics; now he meditated on the signs of progress signaled by "the fat volumes of Patent Office Reports," and exhorted his readers to "bless your star that fate has cast your lot in the year of our Lord 1857":

Think of the numberless contrivances and inventions for our comfort and luxury which the last half-dozen years have brought forth—of our baths and ice houses and ice-coolers—of our fly-traps and mosquito nets—of house bells and marble mantels and sliding-tables—of potent ink-stands and baby-jumpers—of serving machines and street sweeping machines.

He wrote about physical fitness and exercise, especially swimming, as he had in the *Eagle* nine years before. For all his "healthy-

291

mindedness," however, he was more repelled than ever by the shrill optimism of the "reform" movements that swarmed in the 1850s: the "free-lovers, ultra-nationalists, trance-media, female atheists, vegetarians, phrenologists," who inveighed against

ignorance and rum and debauchery. . . . One imagines the millennium would be at hand if a Bible were in every household. . . . Another finds his universal panacea for the ills that flesh is heir to in turning humans into amphibious animals, in deluging the inside and outside with the liquid element, and in foreswearing beefsteak for bran bread and turnips.

The problem of evil has "puzzled all developed thoughtful minds through all the ages," yet these reformers, with their "farthing rush-light . . . seek to illumine the illimitable caverns of the infinite. With [their] favorite (pint) measure [they] would ladle out the ocean. It is pitiful."

This is not the Whitman who worked to make himself "perfect" and broadcast his perfection in assertive poems. His "two-ness" is still intact. In the *Daily Times,* we recognize his familiar opinions on prostitution, on physical health, on the "union" as a political, almost a metaphysical, hope. We hear his lingering fascination with the South ("we like the refreshing openness of the southern character"), his delight in the city's new buildings, its ferries and shipping, its milling streets. All of this is Whitman as we know him in the poems, but it is a curiously colorless Whitman. Reduced to his opinions, as he is in these editorials, his enthusiasms become interchangeable with the enthusiasms of the age. It is another proof, were one needed, that "Walt Whitman" is a creation of style. He is the language that expands in ruffled flows across one hundred remarkably original poems. In the stripped-down form of his editorials, he is thinner, almost anonymous. At times, it stretches our credulity—and our willingness to accept Whitman's famous "contradictions"—to recognize him here at all. In "Song of Myself," three years before, he had written:

> The negro holds firmly the reins of his four horses . . . the block swags
>   underneath on its tied-over chain,
> The negro that drives the huge dray of the stoneyard . . . steady and tall
>   he stands poised on one leg on the stringpiece,

His blue shirt exposes his ample neck and breast and loosens over his
hipband,
His glance is calm and commanding . . . he tosses the slouch of his hat
away from his forehead,
The sun falls on his crispy hair and moustache . . . falls on the black of
his polish'd and perfect limbs.

and

Hell and despair are upon me . . . crack and again crack the marksmen,
I clutch the rails of the fence . . . my gore dribs thinned with the ooze
of my skin,
I fall on the weeds and stones,
The riders spur their unwilling horses and haul close,
They taunt my dizzy ears . . . they beat me violently over the head
with their whip-stocks.

But in the *Daily Times,* we hear another voice, virtually another
man, reminding his reader that slavery has its "redeeming points,"
although, with a century or so, "it is likely to become extinct."
Meanwhile, he approves of Oregon's new constitution prohibiting
"colored persons, either slave or free, from entering the State."
That, he feels, is the only way to protect "White Labor" from the
"interference and competition of Black Labor." For "who believes
that the Whites and Blacks can ever amalgamate in America? Or
who wishes it to happen? Nature has set an impassable seal against
it." Whitman never ceases to surprise. He may have thought of
himself as the "greatest lover" and called his poems a house of
"sympathy," but in the Brooklyn *Daily Times,* despite his silences
and his rough costume, he was still the unreconstructed and unimaginative Walter Whitman.

That summer, he wrote to a friend:

O you should see me, how I look after sea-sailing. I am swarthy and red
as a Moor—I go around without any coat or vest—looking so strong,
ugly and nonchalant, with my white beard—People stare, I notice, more
wonderingly than ever. . . . I have thought for some time past, of beginning the use of myself as a public Speaker, teacher, or lecturer. (This, after
I get out the next issue of my "Leaves")—Whether it will come to anything remains to be seen. . . . My immediate acquaintances, even those
attached strongly to me, secretly entertain the idea that I am a great fool
not to *"make something"* out of my talents and out of the general good will
with which I am regarded. Can it be that some such notion is lately
infusing itself into me also?

Privately, "Walt Whitman" is still intact. "I am so non-polite," he wrote to another friend, "so habitually wanting in my responses and ceremonies. That is *me*—much that is bad, harsh, an undutiful person, a thriftless debtor, is me." Evidently the Parton affair still rankled, but here he turns it to account as part of his personage: outrageous, unpredictable.

Apparently his busy days at the *Daily Times* had not prevented him from planning for the future: a new issue of "Leaves"; a plan to "use" himself as a public speaker. A year later, lecturing was still on his mind, and he drew up a circular:

WALT WHITMAN'S LECTURES

I desire to go by degrees through all These States, especially West and South, and through Kanada: Lecturing, (my own way,) henceforth my employment, my means of earning my living—subject to the work elsewhere alluded to that takes precedence.—

Of this, or through the list present and to come, any [lecture] will be recited before any society or association of friends, or at the defrayment of some special person.—

AMERICA
A Programme, &c

Some plan I seek to have the vocal delivery of my Lectures free, but at present a low price of admission, One Dime—Or my fee for reciting, here, $10, (when any distance expenses in addition.)
Each lecture will be printed, with its recitation, needing to be carefully perused afterward to be understood. I personally sell the printed copies.

Whitman was ready to talk about anything. "Geography, Language, Politics, a person (as Elias Hicks, Voltaire, Emerson)." He planned to carry on his lifelong invective against the clergy:

As we look around on Nature, the facts of life, how real they are—how unconscious then all these passing chrysalis Religions, with all the churches and the insane statements of the ministers—appear but as empty shells. They know it not—so melancholy. The bodies are dead—the spirits have flown to other spheres—yet they keep on the same celebrating over the coffins.

He filled his notebooks with an encyclopedia of homespun comments about Chaucer, Cromwell, Milton, Rousseau and prepared himself to deliver "live modern orations, appropriate to America, appropriate to the world." "Washington made free the body of America. . . . Now comes one who will make free the American soul."

Outwardly, Whitman may have been a second-rank newspaper editor, his poetry may temporarily have dried up, but in private his personage still simmered. The real subject of these "Lessons" was himself, "divinely possessed, blind to all subordinate affairs and given up entirely to the surgings and utterances of the mighty tempestuous demon." He saw himself "wrestling" with his audience in an "agonistic arena." It was a kind of opera, transposed from New York's baroque theaters to the nation itself. Instead of Sontag or the great Marietta Alboni, there would be "Walt Whitman . . . aboriginal fashion."

By June 1859, Whitman had lost his job at the Brooklyn *Daily Times*. A tradition has it that he ran afoul of "certain orthodox deacons" and was fired by the paper's owner, George C. Bennett. If so, it would certainly have been in character. In one of his last editorials, he suggested, provocatively, that the police ought to "tolerate" well-run houses of prostitution. In another editorial two days later, he claimed to understand how unmarried young women could be tempted to escape from the sexless castle of propriety, for "one glimpse of real life and nature—one taste of substantial joys and sorrows that shall wake all the pulses of womanhood; even though the experience be brief and dearly bought." These articles may have been the last straw, for within days Whitman was unemployed, a sadly familiar experience for the thirty-nine-year-old poet and journalist. Four days later, he wrote in his notebook: "It is now time to *stir* first for *Money* enough *to live and provide for M—.** To *stir*—first write stories and get out this slough."

The "slough" would last more or less until December 1862 when, on a moment's notice, he packed his bags and left for the Virginia battlefield where his brother George had been reported wounded. In a letter to Emerson, written from Washington a few weeks later, he referred to his "New York stagnation" and his

---

*The identity of "M" remains a mystery. "M" could refer to mother, but why the enigmatic abbreviation? Or "M" could refer to a lover, but there is no confirming reference in any notebook or from any other source.

"horrible sloughs." Yet the "slough" had been accompanied by a remarkable new surge of poetry; and it had contributed in its way to Whitman's new voice. A book, perhaps his finest single volume, had been published by a legitimate Boston publisher. He had become a public figure, albeit in a small way.

Some time during the spring or the summer of 1859, Whitman copied a dozen poems into a notebook of white wove paper, under the heading "Live Oak with Moss." The poems bear Roman numerals I to XII and can be read as an impassioned story, announced in the opening lines of the sequence:

Not the heat flames up and consumes,
Not the sea-waves hurry in and out,
Not the air, delicious and dry, the air of ripe summer, bears lightly along white down-balls of myriads of seeds, wafted, sailing gracefully, to drop where they may,
Not these—O none of these, more than the flames of me, consuming, burning for his love whom I love—O none, more than I, hurrying in and out; Does the tide hurry, seeking something, and never give up?—O I, the same, to seek my life-long lover.

The dozen numbered poems are love poems, and they are not furtive or deceptively hearty and athletic, like the few pink-paper poems on the same subject written several years before. In "Live-Oak with Moss," Whitman burns openly for his lover. He hurries "in and out" with a frankly sexual motion, or he "flames up" and ejects his myriads of white "seeds." Whitman had sexualized nature in "Song of Myself," but the eroticism had been solitary; it had been a "religion" of lone ecstasy. Here there is another person; they are two. Nature is present as a source of images to express the inner world of the lover's feelings. The voice of the poem, too, is new. The flush of delight is mingled with a suggestion of vulnerability. As a lover, Whitman is not self-contained. He can no longer simply "effuse [his] flesh in eddies, and drift it in lacey jags," like a polymorphously perverse child. He must concentrate on his elusive partner; accept the estrangement of his very self, which now exists far from him, in the guise of a beloved but uncontrollable face, moved by an obscure will. In lines he later suppressed, Whitman wonders at his former solitary grandeur:

> Was it I who walked the earth disclaiming all except what I had in
> myself?
> Was it I boasting how complete I was in myself?

As a "young giant," he had boasted of his oneness with nature,
inhaling it silently, exhaling it as "song." But now he perceives a
sadness. In poem II of the sequence, the "live oak" "glistening out
joyous leaves," as he himself had uttered joyous "leaves," makes
him aware of a difference between them. The oak stands alone,
without any "companion" near; its leaves are addressed to no one.
Like the omnipresent "grass" in "Song of Myself," they grow and
flourish, a lone celebration of the life force. But Whitman knew
he could not endure such aloneness. His own "leaves" reach out,
calling for lovers; that is their reason for being. His love longings
have opened a gulf between himself and nature's rude impassive-
ness. In this poem, he is not out-of-doors but in his room, trying to
remember the friends and lovers who would make his life full, if
only they were near. He cannot produce "leaves" of his own now
but plucks them from the live oak tree, and places them in his
room where he can see them.

The "live oak" is Whitman's former self—"rude, unbending,
lusty"—writing alone in his attic room, self-sufficient by default, a
"giant" because he could not simply be a man. Behind it is the boy
whose family moved from house to house, unsettling his life and
making it impossible to have friends. Just the year before, Whitman had written an editorial in the Brooklyn *Daily Times* about the
fracturing of lives by constant moving: children uprooted from
school, "all sorts of forebodings and anticipations," families "perhaps maimed for life by moving." The lonely pattern of Whitman's childhood had never been effaced. It had been overlaid by
his hearty workingman's posture and, before that, by his public life
as journalist and militant party worker. But Whitman's private life
had always seemed curiously vacant. His "open road" never completely transcended the "forebodings" and the hurt of solitary
movement.

But now, from among the young men Whitman passed on the
street or met at the Mercer Street Fireman's Club, or on the Fulton
Ferry, or wherever he compiled his long, touching lists ("the fre-

quent and swift flash of eyes offering me love"), a single lover
emerged; or—we cannot wholly exclude the possibility—an absorbing fantasy lover, made up of Whitman's longings, as, in the
late Middle Ages, a troubadour of Provence idealized his beloved.
Thus, Whitman:

> When I heard at the close of the day how I had been praised in the
>   Capitol, still it was not a happy night for me that followed;
> Nor when I caroused—Nor when my favorite plans were accom-
>   plished—was I really happy,
> But that day I rose at dawn from the bed of perfect health, electric,
>   inhaling sweet breath,
> When I saw the full moon in the west grow pale and disappear in the
>   morning light,
> When I wandered alone over the beach, and undressing, bathed, laugh-
>   ing with the waters, and saw the sun rise,
>
> And when I thought how my friend, my lover, was coming, then O I
>   was happy;
> Each breath tasted sweeter—and all that day my food nourished me
>   more—And the beautiful day passed well,
> And the next came with equal joy—And with the next, at evening,
>   came my friend.
>
> And that night, while all was still, I heard the waters roll slowly con-
>   tinually up the shores
>
> I heard the hissing rustle of the liquid and sands, as directed to me,
>   whispering, to congratulate me,—For the friend I love lay sleeping
>   by my side,
> In the stillness his face was in-clined towards me, while the moon's
>   clear beams shone,
> And his arm lay lightly over my breast—And that night I was happy.

This may be the loveliest of the poems Whitman later included in
the "Calamus" grouping of his 1860 edition. The radical shape-
lessness of the 1855 poems is absent here. "Song of Myself" was a
poem without an end; the poet's journey was beginningless and
endless. In this poem, he has found an end: he has exchanged the
cosmos for a lover's embrace; the "open road," for a room in hearing of the ocean, invaded by moonlight, but sheltered, apart from
the tides and waters and lands he had celebrated in the one hundred poems of his "New Bible."

We have met this private man before: he is the quiet, almost shy observer of the spear of grass, at the beginning of "Song of Myself." It is he who, a few lines later, goes to "a bank by the wood," to become naked and enjoy the open air. His encounter on the grass is, for all its intensity, solitary, a meeting of self and soul. Here, in the love poems of "Live Oak with Moss," he is center stage. There is a solemn peacefulness in his manner, a contentment. The houseless, but also homeless rover has found a home in his beloved's arms. The poem is a lover's fairy tale. It stands in the high tradition of love, which renounces the world for the private fulfillment of a beloved's presence. The theme of renunciation runs through these poems. Whitman renounces his nation-making stance, his gigantism; he renounces his desire for "knowledge" and orations in the grand manner. "Song of Myself" had also contained a moment of curious spoken quietude:

My final merit I refuse you—I refuse putting from me the best I am.
Encompass worlds, but never try to encompass me,
I crowd your sleekest talk by simply looking toward you.

Writing and talk do not prove me,
I carry the plenum of proof, and everything else, in my face,
With the hush of my lips I confound the topmost skeptic.

In these twelve poems, Whitman celebrates the privacy that had little place in the work of two years previous. The public man retires to a room now or to a quiet wood, or he walks the streets noticing, not the pageant of the city,

But the two men I saw to-day on the pier, parting the parting of dear friends.
The one to remain hung on the other's neck and passionately kissed him—while the one to depart tightly prest the one to remain in his arms.

This is Whitman's reversal: the world for a lover; exuberant display for the withdrawn silence of a passion that may not even have been expressed:

As I walk by your side or sit near, to remain in the same room with you,

Little you know the subtle electric fire that for your sake is playing
within me.

Several poems in the sequence are outcries of jealousy and abandonment; several are wistful attempts to transmute the pain of love
to a safer sentiment of universal friendship. These are the poems
that give us the sense of an actual lover and a coy, changeable
beloved living out some personal drama, as we feel the gritty particularity of the man Shakespeare, in the cycle of his sonnets. Only
an actual Psyche and his fleeing Cupid could produce such convulsions of shame and wounded pride:

Hours continuing long, sore and heavy-hearted,
Hours of the dusk, when I withdraw to a lonesome and unfrequented
spot, seating myself, leaning my face in my hands;
Hours sleepless, deep in the night, when I go forth, speeding swiftly
the country roads, or through the city streets, or pacing miles and
miles, stifling plaintive cries;
Hours discouraged, distracted—for the one I cannot content myself
without, soon I saw him content himself without me;
Hours when I am forgotten, (O weeks and months are passing, but I
believe I am never to forget!)
Sullen and suffering hours! (I am ashamed—but it is useless—I am
what I am;)
Hours of my torment—I wonder if other men ever have the like, out
of the like feelings?
Is there even one other like me—distracted—his friend, his lover, lost
to him?
Is he too as I am now? Does he still rise in the morning, dejected,
thinking who is lost to him? and at night, awaking, think who is
lost?
Does he too harbor his friendship silent and endless? harbor his anguish and passion?
Does some stray reminder, or the casual mention of a name, bring the
fit back upon him, taciturn and deprest?
Does he see himself reflected in me? In these hours, does he see the
face of his hours reflected?

The dozen poems of "Live Oak with Moss" break Whitman's
relative silence of two years. In earlier poems, he had withdrawn
from a core of subject matter that, to Horace Traubel, he would
call his "secret." His sympathy with the downtrodden and the

excluded had been general, a form of radical Christian charity, insisting that the last shall be the first: the defeated, the prostitutes, the sick. In "Song of Myself," Whitman offered to be their savior, lifting them by the main force of his "magnetism" from the bed of sickness or from opprobrium. The "greatest lover's" feast—his poem—had been open to all and required the presence of all. It was Psyche circling her flame, leaving her love in darkness, but casting side glances, offering suggestive, almost revealing hints. But here is the "secret" fully spoken: Whitman loves a man; he takes him to his bed, redefines himself as the poet of this love. He renounces his promiscuous love affair with the "present age" and becomes absorbed in a private love. He is relieved to say at last what he is. Yet even in his frankness, there are depths that frighten him: "toward him there is something fierce and terrible in me, I dare not tell it in words—not even in these songs." There is "indirection" within "indirection." Whitman would never truly say all; he was after all, not a moralist or a saint, but a poet. His life was an opera, with climaxes and hints of further dénouements.

It may be that Whitman fell in love in 1858 or 1859, as he would again half a dozen years later with the Washington streetcar conductor, Peter Doyle. We can only speculate, for the twelve poems of his notebook are no more anecdotal than is "Song of Myself." Whitman's beloved is not a recognizable man but a focus of longing or delight. In the poems, exhilarating fantasy mingles with collapses into humiliation. These, on the other hand, have a ring of truth; here, Whitman lets us more deeply into his defensive personage than anywhere in his poetry. If appetite was the tutelary spirit of his flurry of poems through 1857, loss and the labyrinth of feelings associated with merely being human alter the shape of his poetry now.

"Live Oak with Moss" did not survive as an independent group. Whitman pulled apart the notebook and dispersed the poems into the larger series he was preparing for the Rome brothers. He was not through, though, with the subject matter of these poems. His poems of 1859 are filled with illicit confession. His love is perilous, he warns. It is marginal and disruptive, flourishing only in hidden places. His beloved must watch out, "lest any person, for miles around, approach unawares." Even then, "the way is suspicious—the result slow, uncertain, may-be destructive." In many of these new poems, the drama of sexual love becomes the more innocuous love of comrades. It takes on overtones of robustness and American frankness. There is a veering toward abstraction, which culminates in Whitman's use of the term "adhesiveness," strangely bloodless and philosophical, compared to his fulsome expressions of passion. Yet he enjoys flirting with the homosexual feelings of these poems. Sexual guilt exhilarates him now. His coyness is a little feminine: he is the flustered prey, warding off the pursuer, but not entirely escaping him, not denying him. In one of the new poems, he seems to be thinking of his lists of young men:

> soon a silent troop gathers around me,
> Some walk by my side, and some behind, and some embrace my arms or neck,
> They, the spirits of friends, dead or alive—thicker they come, a great crowd, and I in the middle,
> Collecting, dispensing, singing in spring, there I wander with them.

There is a fairy-tale quality here, as in many of the poems that follow upon "Live Oak with Moss." Whitman portrays himself as a benign tempter surrounded by his troop of lovers; or as a god of natural abundance, distributing tokens of his sexual magnetism. And the "tokens" take Whitman back to his irrepressible theme: poetry. The renunciation expressed in "Live Oak with Moss" was a passing moment. Again, Whitman's poems circle upon themselves, celebrating the self-conscious act, the making of poems, as the highest gift he can offer:

> Here! lilac, with a branch of pine,
> Here, out of my pocket, some moss which I pulled off a live-oak in Florida, as it hung trailing down,
> Here, some pinks and laurel leaves, and a handful of sage,
> And here what I now draw from the water, wading in the pond-side,
> (O here I last saw him that tenderly loves me—and returns again, never to separate from me,
> And this, O this shall henceforth be the token of comrades—this calamus-root shall,
> Interchange it, youths, with each other! Let none render it back!)
> And twigs of maple, and a bunch of wild orange, and chestnut,
> And stems of currants, and plum-blows, and the aromatic cedar;

These I, compassed around by a thick cloud of spirits,
Wandering, point to, or touch as I pass, or throw them loosely from
  me,
Indicating to each one what he shall have—giving something to each,
But what I drew from the water by the pond-side, that I reserve,
I will give of it—but only to them that love, as I myself am capable of
  loving.

There is a slippage of theme—a kind of spiraling—in these poems. Whitman distributes the tokens of his love happily and freely. Love has made him as abundant as nature herself. But the celebration modulates. Under it all there is a more secret love, destined for a special lover. Its token, disclosed in a parenthesis, is a calamus root and is meant, apparently, for someone capable of loving beyond comradeship, like Whitman himself. Comradeship and manly good feeling have an underside ("I am what I am") which Whitman intrudes into the poem, to tantalize and intrigue. Having told all, he hints that there is more to tell, and the more is secretive, secluded, sexual. The calamus root becomes the emblem of this further dimension of feeling, and it raises interesting questions.

The calamus stalk, growing in marshland all over the northeast, is a stiff phallic plant, just the sort of veiled symbol that Whitman loved. But the calamus root is something else again. Cleaned and prepared, it is a medicinal plant. Perhaps, Whitman, with his wide reading in the health literature of his day, knew that and made the calamus root a combined symbol of sexual secrecy and health (was it the health of at last telling the secret that had been "stifling" him?). In "Song of Myself," he had referred to "washed sweet flag," another name for calamus; and again the medicinal reference is intriguing. Sweet flag, or calamus, was a digestive; in early spring, the crisp stalks could be eaten in a salad. The root, washed and dried, was known to local New York Indians—and, indeed, around the world wherever the calamus grows—as an aphrodisiac and possibly a hallucinogen. How much of this did Whitman know? His circling of the calamus theme is so elusive that we cannot pin him down. Calamus, he tells us, stands for the secret core of his emotions. It is also the poetry—a different species of leaves now—rising from its hidden source, more shaded by complex feelings than ever before, but franker, almost nakedly expressive:

Here the frailest leaves of me and yet my strongest lasting,
Here I shade and hide my thoughts, I myself do not expose them,
And yet they expose me more than all my other poems.

But what exactly do these esoteric leaves expose? Whitman's
guilty erotic longings? Or some even more secret exaltation due to
the ingestion of an initiatory drug? Or somehow both? The following note makes curious reading: "Sweet flag. Sweet fern. Illuminated face. Clarified. Unpolluted. Flower corn. Aromatic Calamus. Sweet gum, bulb and melons with bulbs grateful to the
hand." This is surely one of Whitman's more suggestive word
lists. Calamus and illumination are linked. The melons nestle erotically in hands, but it is an innocent eroticism, as if calamus not
only stood for the sexual stirrings of "adhesiveness," but transfig-
ured them, made them "unpolluted" and healthy, perhaps because
of the root's health-giving properties, combined with its ability to
stimulate feelings of expansive ecstasy—the root feelings, we remember, of Whitman's enterprise as a poet, three years before. In
his striving to become "perfect," he could be rhapsodic about the
sensation of physical health, when "the whole body is elevated to a
state by others unknown—inwardly and outwardly illuminated,
purified, made solid, strong, yet bouyant. . . . A man realizes the
venerable myth—he is a god walking on earth."

Whitman's nest of meanings will not be unraveled. Calamus
reveals all and yet conceals all: it stands for Whitman's "secret" of
manly love and yet sprays that secret abroad as a sweet aroma, the
scent of its tall, rushlike leaves, poetry. These are puzzling poems,
overflowing their ostensible theme of manly love, defying analysis,
and yet, circling their subject matter, they are oddly clear in tone.
The most extraordinary of them, "Scented Herbage of My Breast,"
moves with an almost drugged rhythm, from the dark, erotic
"body leaves," which express inner feelings but also longings for
death, to the celebration of comrades, to a uniquely downward sort
of transcendence proposing what one might call an under-soul, a
unified bass note which plays "patiently," "behind the mask of
materials," and is what life is for—death:

Scented herbage of my breast,
Leaves from you I yield, I write, to be perused best afterwards,

Tomb-leaves, body-leaves, growing up above me, above death,
Perennial roots, tall leaves—O the winter shall not freeze you, delicate
    leaves,
Every year shall you bloom again—Out from where you retired, you
    shall emerge again;
O I do not know whether many, passing by, will discover you, or
    inhale your faint odor—but I believe a few will;
O slender leaves! O blossoms of my blood! I permit you to tell, in your
    own way, of the heart that is under you,
O burning and throbbing—surely all will one day be accomplished;
O I do not know what you mean, there underneath yourselves—you
    are not happiness,
You are often more bitter than I can bear—you burn and sting me,
Yet you are very beautiful to me, you faint-tinged roots—you make me
    think of Death.

Remember Arthur Stedman's unfriendly gibe about Whitman as
Osiris, with his chest hairs sprouting under his open shirt. This is
the poem Stedman was referring to, and Whitman must have clued
him into the Osiris reference. Osiris was one of the Mediterra-
nean's dying gods: a pagan foreshadowing of Christ. Osiris died,
and his decay fed the "leaves" of the new season. Poetry and death
commingle here, along with the strange assonance of the erotic
theme, the call for comrades. There is no reasoning this poem. It is
a welded unity of voice. Why death and fertility, the self-conscious
punning of "leaves" and the "secret" of adhesive love, should
weave among each other here only Whitman's compulsively elusive mind could tell us.

4

Although Whitman dissolved the "Live Oak With Moss" series,
the idea of a group of poems continued to intrigue him; and some
time after the summer of 1859, he turned to it again. On the back
of a fair copy of "I Saw in Louisiana a Live Oak Growing," he
wrote himself a reminder: "A cluster of poems, pommets expressing the thoughts, pictures, aspirations etc. . . . Fit to be perused
during the days of the approach of Death." Given the braiding of

themes in several of the poems devoted to manly love, Whitman could be referring here to the "Live Oak" series, which he eventually renamed "Calamus." Somewhat later, he thought of a matching "cluster": "a string of Poems (short etc.) embodying the amative love of woman—the same as Live-Oak Leaves do the passion of friendship for men."

Gradually the cluster idea took hold until, by the spring of 1860, Whitman had recast his book in its entirety and made it largely the *Leaves of Grass* we have become familiar with: an assemblage of parts, clusters, numbered series, introduced by a poem clumsily named "Proto-Leaf," and ended by a sentimental farewell entitled "So Long." Gone was the roughshod book of 1855: the overlapping, interleaving lengths of poem; the "Bible" of open-endedness, of unfinished and unfinishable impulse. Now Whitman planned a book divided into sections named "Calamus," "Enfans d'Adam," "Leaves of Grass," "Chants Democratic." There were smaller groupings, too: "Messenger Leaves," "Says," "Thoughts." As usual, Whitman was not adept at this sort of architecture. Many poems did not fit, and he let them stand separately. The effect was, again, eccentric: a bristling table of contents, with too much typography, too many subdivisions. The organization lapsed into semidisorder. Whitman's "New Bible" was half new and half old. It was radically different from the book he had been planning in 1857: appreciably longer, organized as I have indicated. The tone, too, was different. The brash poems of his long surge are dispersed among the various sections. "Calamus" and "Enfans d'Adam" focus Whitman's erotic venturesomeness as never before.

Whitman's "slough," too became part of his "New Bible." The sagging spirits that had periodically dogged him, and made him doubt everything—himself, the reality of nature, even other people (this had been the nightside of his solitary exaltation)—now became a new subject matter.

These were shaky years. The feelings bared by the "Calamus" poems were probably part of it. Whitman did not know who he was any more. If not America's "giant," then who? Maybe the lone boy without friends; the job-hopping and house-hopping young man; the failure who, like his father, had a stubborn, angry streak that often brought his professional activities to nought. Whitman had fought off his father—borne him, dead, from the house. He had tried to edit out of his poems, and out of his personality as well, the angers, the paralyzing glooms. To his brothers and sisters, and to America entire, he wanted to be the father whose lack obsessed him: not an angry, helpless father, but a benign magnetic one, potent, serene; "the good grey poet." But now the failure was there, and this time Whitman did not turn away. In an odd way, father and failure went together for Whitman, giving rise now to a remarkable poem, which he published in the new *Atlantic Monthly,* in April 1860—one of his few legitimate publications of these years—under the title "Bardic Symbols," later "As I Ebbed with the Ocean of Life."

The poem opens with the poet walking on a Long Island beach. The tide is out, and the wet sand near the water is strewn with "lines" of débris:

> chaff, straw, splinters of wood, weeds, and the sea gluten,
> Scum, scales from shining rocks, leaves of salt lettuce, left by the tide.

Here, indeed, are "symbols," or, should we say "tokens"? But, unlike the tokens he had plucked for his lovers in "These I Singing in Spring," they stand here for deflated hope, failed poems, abandonment. They have been stranded by the ocean, that "fierce old mother":

> a little washed up drift,
> A few sands and dead leaves to gather.

As always, Whitman's drama of experience is expressed in metaphors of poetry. He wrote about writing because living to him was writing; and writing—poetry—was the root activity of life, as it was for Shelley, Wordsworth, and Blake. Not only is *Leaves of Grass* a "language experiment," its subject, irrepressibly and often surprisingly, is language. In his low spirits, he sees a resemblance between himself and the stranded "lines" at his feet. He, too, is shrunken; his glorious miscellanies have become heapings of débris abandoned by the surges of the inspiriting mother-ocean. The old "twoness," which had haunted Whitman—the watcher peeled from his actions and chilling them with self-doubt; the "twoness" which had been dissolved by the erotic marriage of self and soul in "Song of Myself"—reappears now, in a figure of savage self-mockery:

> O baffled, balked,
> Bent to the very earth, here preceding what follows,
> Oppressed with myself that I have dared to open my mouth,
> Aware now, that, amid all the blab whose echoes recoil upon me, I
>   have not once had the least idea who or what I am,
> But that before all my insolent poems the real Me still stands un-
>   touched, untold, altogether unreached,
> Withdrawn far, mocking me with mock-congratulatory signs and
>   bows,
> With peals of distant ironical laughter at every word I have written or
>   shall write,
> Striking me with insults till I fall helpless upon the sand.

There is a kind of crazed honesty, a fierce self-acceptance, in this poem. One thinks of Yeats's dirge for the collapse of his creative powers, in "The Circus Animal's Desertion." The scene of the poem is the scene of Whitman's strength: the Long Island beaches of his childhood and early manhood. The sound is the rolling surf he would one day identify with the rolling rhythm of his long lines. But now, ironically, he has no access to that strength. The creative tide has ebbed, stranding at his feet these pitiful tokens of failed language. And now Whitman makes one of those leaps of association that are so improbable, yet so filled with the voice's own authority, that one hears the unconscious at work: a slip of impulse—an inspiration—that suddenly says everything:

> You friable shore, with trails of debris!
> You fish-shaped island! I take what is underfoot;
> What is yours is mine, my father.
>
> I too Paumanok
> I too have bubbled up, floated the measureless float, and been washed
>   on your shores;
> I too am but a trail of drift and debris,
> I too leave little wrecks upon you, you fish-shaped island.
>
> I throw myself upon your breast, my father,
> I cling to you so that you cannot unloose me,
> I hold you so firm, till you answer me something.

Kiss me, my father,
Touch me with your lips, as I touch those I love,
Breathe to me, while I hold you close, the secret of the wondrous
    murmuring I envy,
For I fear I shall become crazed, if I cannot emulate it, and utter myself
    as well as it.

Whitman calls upon his father, kisses and implores him. From the scene of his vanished strength, he reaches out, in a brotherhood of failure, to the father he had buried. Buried, in fact, four years earlier; buried, symbolically, when he came home as a young man, to become the central influence in his family; buried, more problematically, in the almost unbroken silence of his poems which, with rare exceptions, never mention any father. Yet here now is his father, come back from the dead, as psychopomp, or spirit guide, a companion of dark moods. The father Whitman had fled in his "gigantism" and his lusty assertions catches up with him. This is the scene that is missing from the Gothic melodrama of his early stories. There the son punished the father, by mutilating himself before his eyes. Here, his hurt has enabled him to see his father as if for the first time, and draw from him a kind of negative strength: the ability to endure and thrive in failure. The poem ends with this note of negative triumph. The "young giant," who had cockily refused to take his hat off, even to God, now accepts his shrunken feelings. He embraces what the religious philosopher Rudolf Otto has called the sentiment of "creatureliness": the crushing conviction of one's own smallness and insignificance before the immensity of God:

Me and mine!
We, loose winrows, little corpses,
Froth, snowy white, and bubbles,
(See from my dead lips the ooze exuding at last!
See—the prismatic colors, glistening and rolling!)
Tufts of straw, sands, fragments,
Buoyed hither from many moods, one contradicting another,
From the storm, the long calm, the darkness, the swell,
Musing, pondering, a breath, a briny tear, a dab of liquid or soil,
Up just as much out of fathomless workings fermented and thrown,
A limp blossom or two, torn, just as much over waves floating, drifted
    at random,

Just as much for us that sobbing dirge of Nature,
Just as much, whence we come, that blare of the cloud-trumpets;
We, capricious, brought hither, we know not whence, spread out be-
fore You, up there, walking or sitting,
Whoever you are—we too lie in drifts at your feet.

Whitman's work evolved powerfully in 1859 and 1860. If, as he later claimed, his aim in *Leaves of Grass* had been to put on record the complete life and personality of an American in the second half of the nineteenth century, he made a stride here toward completeness. His loosely rhythmic line shows itself capable of expressing every variation of feeling, every shade of exuberance and self-doubt. It can be "indirect," almost indecipherable, or movingly straightforward; candid in the grand manner of Chateaubriand and Rousseau, or coy, almost furtive. These were his "contradictions": the illogical juggling of thoughts, feelings, needs, and convictions, along with their opposites, which make up a self.

5

In 1859, Whitman was reborn as a poet, and that may be the story he tells in his most famous poem of these years, "A Word Out of the Sea," later renamed "A Child's Reminiscence," and, finally, "Out of the Cradle Endlessly Rocking." Whitman first published the poem in Henry Clapp's *Saturday Press,* as the magazine's "Christmas offering" for 1859. An editorial preface (written by Whitman) shows how aware he had become of the demands his poems made upon the unaccustomed reader:

Like the "Leaves of Grass," the purport of this wild and plaintive song, well-enveloped and eluding definition, is positive and unquestionable, like the effect of music.
The piece will bear reading many times—and perhaps indeed only comes forth as from recesses, by many repetitions.

It is, indeed, an elusive poem, a braiding of voices, evocations of place and feeling. The musical effect is prominent in the prayerlike introductory stanza—which he first called "Preverse"—and in the conclusion, calling hypnotically for the tidal resolution of "death death death death death." Like the modernist poems that have influenced contemporary taste—"The Wasteland," "The Cantos," many poems by William Carlos Williams and Wallace Stevens—it is best read in repetition, as Whitman instructs: not read, but re-read, as a balancing of images, voices, and themes. The music of the poem is visibly operatic: the bird singing of tragic passion; the boy, downstage, singing separately and yet participating in a duet of companion feeling.

There is a new kind of exuberance in "Out of the Cradle Endlessly Rocking": not the exuberance of gigantic feelings, but an artist's exuberance; a sense of verbal powers; the confidence that his combinations are daring, but right and new. The prelude is a dazzling text: twenty-three lines layered into a single multiclaused sentence. Its rocking syntax, which becomes the rocking of the waves and the rocking of death, is the cradle of the poem's title. The bird's aria, broadly operatic, alternates with the boy's chant of self-discovery. As always, the subject of the poem is "song," poetry. The poet remembers a night in his boyhood: a moonlit beach, with twining shadows and the rustling of the surf; the moon, heavy and yellow; a bird singing all night. It is one of those vivid early memories that often mark a turning point in a person's life. Hearing the bird sing of lost love and death, the boy's own song starts up, for he, "of all men," understands the bird and, understanding, finds his inner self launched in a song of loss and despair. Like the bird, he, too, longs for the whispered resolution which he hears at first confused and then suddenly clear: "death," the word out of the sea, answering all loss with its ambiguous fulfillment.

Reduced to its story, the poem even sounds like an opera, as Whitman surely intended. It is linked to other poems he was writing at the time. The setting is the same Long Island beach as in "As I Ebbed with the Ocean of Life," and, most likely, as in the lovely "Calamus" poem, "When I Heard at the Close of the Day." The themes of many of these poems, too, are similar: love, its solemn pleasure, its loss; the shrunken feelings that result from lovelessness; the need to reassemble one's powers and make a song, even out of loss and loneliness.

Because "Out of the Cradle Endlessly Rocking" is about the birth of the poetic faculties, it is often supposed that the poem is, to some extent, autobiographical. Did Whitman, as a boy, spend late spring evenings on the beach one year, spying on a lone mockingbird? Did he imagine a story about the bird, as children will—a story that told more about his own feelings of abandonment than about the bird? Did this memory lie dormant until, years later, Whitman burst his cocoon of mediocrity and became a poet? He never said so, and we will never know. The songs that burst from the boy's throat that spring night certainly do not resemble Whitman's chants of 1855 and 1856, with their raucous self-confidence and their "healthy-mindedness":

Bird! (then said the boy's Soul,)
Is it indeed toward your mate you sing? or is it mostly to me?
For I that was a child, my tongue's use sleeping,
Now that I have heard you,
Now in a moment I know what I am for—I awake,
And already a thousand singers—a thousand songs, clearer, louder,
    more sorrowful than yours,
A thousand warbling echoes have started to life within me,
Never to die.

But they do resemble the dozen poems of "Live Oak with Moss" and the many other poems that Whitman assembled in the "Calamus" section of his book. They resemble "As I Ebbed with the Ocean of Life." Perhaps "Out of the Cradle Endlessly Rocking" tells a different story than has usually been supposed: not Whitman's birth, but his rebirth, as a poet in 1859 when, shaken by new feelings and a new moral daring, he remembered and accepted the solitary boy he had once been. His "slough" had forced open sources of experience that his earlier poetry had largely avoided, except for glancing side references which are often moving but are not sustained. The voice of those earlier poems was designed to absorb such lapses and transform them. But they re-emerged; and in 1859, Whitman gathered them into a remade voice. He learned again how to sing. In "Out of the Cradle Endlessly Rocking," he tells the story of that awakening.

CHAPTER 9

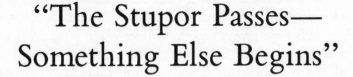

"The Stupor Passes—
Something Else Begins"

1

Aᴼᴛᴇ FTER losing his job at the Brooklyn *Daily Times* in the spring of 1859, Whitman again had time on his hands. He wrote in the mornings or went over to the Rome brothers' printing shop. In the late afternoon, he took the Fulton Street Ferry to Manhattan and rode the Broadway stage up to Pfaff's. For the next three years he "loafed" and rode the New York stages. A Boston paper reported that he earned his living as a driver. But Pfaff's was his haunt. Whitman sat a little apart from the mordant crowd of journalists and writers who had made the basement restaurant their headquarters. Sharp talk had never been his style. "My own greatest pleasure at Pfaff's," he recalled, "was to look on—to see, talk little, absorb. I never was a great discusser anyway." When William Dean Howells visited Pfaff's in August 1860, and was introduced to Whitman, he remembered how the poet

leaned back in his chair, and reached out his great hand to me, as if he were going to give it to me for good and all. He had a fine head, with a cloud of Jovian hair upon it, and a branching beard and mustache, and gentle eyes that looked most kindly into mine, and seemed to wish the liking which I instantly gave him, though we hardly passed a word, and our acquaintance was summed up in that glance and the grasp of his mighty fist upon my hand.

Even in the caustic atmosphere of Pfaff's, with its coterie of wits and beauties, Whitman dominated: by his bulk and his silences; by a feeling of benign power which, in later years, often stirred visitors: it seemed to shine from him in Washington, when he went through the hospital wards; it was part of his aura as an old man on Mickle Street. At Pfaff's, Whitman shored up his shaky ambitions; he dominated his glooms and his intractable money problems. It was a small stage, but on it he was free to play his part, and he played it so casually, the part sunk its roots so deeply into his nature, that it was a part no longer but the man himself.

A cult was already forming around this half-respectable young/ old man. In the spring of 1860, a woman named Juliette Beach wrote in Clapp's *Saturday Press:* "Walt Whitman on earth is immortal as well as beyond it, God bless him," adding that *Leaves of Grass* was sure to be "the standard book of poems in the future of America." "Walt Whitman is a genius," "*defacto* our poet laureate," announced another critic. This would always be Whitman's paradox. Not Emerson or Clapp or, later, William O'Connor could break down the literary world's hostility to Whitman. His name would always be synonymous with scandal and rowdy self-indulgence. But he and his poems cast a spell. In the eyes of many readers, they stood for honesty and spiritual daring, sexual frankness, freedom from social taboos. To these readers, Whitman was hardly a poet at all: he was a prophet, a liberator. Thus, Juliette Beach's "God bless him." And thus, an extraordinary letter Whitman received in February 1860—a letter that changed his life, by offering him a wider stage than Pfaff's cocoon of wits, or Henry Clapp's magazine.

A month before, Whitman had announced in the *Saturday Press* that a new *Leaves of Grass* was in the works. It would be

the fuller grown work of which the former two issues were the inchoates. . . . indeed, "Leaves of Grass" has not yet been really published at all. Walt Whitman, for his own purposes, slowly trying his hand at the edifice, the structure he has undertaken, has lazily loafed on, letting each part have time to set—evidently building not so much with reference to any part itself, considered alone, but more with reference to the ensemble.

Then, in mid-February came this letter from Boston:

Walt Whitman,

Dr. Sir. We want to be the publishers of Walt Whitman's Poems— Leaves of Grass.—When the book was first issued we were clerks in the establishment we now own. We read the book with profit and pleasure. It is a true poem and writ by a *true* man.

When a man dares to speak his thought in this day of refinement—so called—it is difficult to find his mates to act amen to it. Now *we* want to be known as the publishers to Walt. Whitman's books, and put our name as such under his, on title pages.—If you will allow it we can and will put your books into good form, and style attractive to the eye; we can and will sell a large number of copies; we have great facilities by and through numberless Agents in selling. We can dispose of more books than most publishing houses (we do not "puff" here but speak *truth*).

We are young men. We "celebrate" ourselves by acts. Try us. You can do us good. We can do you good—pecuniarily.

Now Sir, if you wish to make acquaintance with us, and accept us as your publishers, we will offer to either buy the stereotype plates of Leaves of Grass, or pay you for the use of them, in addition to regular copyright.

Are you writing other poems? Are they ready for the press? Will you let us read them? Will you write us? Please give us your residence.

Yours Fraternally
Thayer & Eldridge

For years, Whitman had scavenged for every crumb of publicity he could get. He had written reviews of his own book, planted items in newspapers, written anonymous editorial copy about himself for Clapp's magazine. At most, he had managed to create a few ripples of notoriety. His book, as he admitted a month before, had not really been published at all. For all his genial presence and his eccentric dress, he was stymied, broke; he was in a slough, with no apparent way out. But now, from Boston, the very heartland of America's literary respectability, came an offer to publish his book, from a legitimate publisher whom he would not have to pay, but who would pay him.

William Thayer and Charles Eldridge were ambitious young

men, of the very sort Whitman had been calling to in his poems, and now they had heard him. They had just published James Redpath's polemical biography of *John Brown* and had made a financial success of it. They were paying a fiery young writer, William O'Connor, a monthly salary to write an abolitionist novel, *Harrington*. And now they wanted to publish Walt Whitman, the free spirit and literary revolutionary. They wanted to allow him to design his own book, to put into it whatever he pleased, and to pay him as well. Within a month, Whitman was in Boston. With him were the Rome brothers' proof sheets—to serve as manuscript copy for the new book—along with a handful of major poems written just that winter, and a further spurt of poems that may have come during the weeks before he left for Boston. Suddenly Whitman's New York "stagnation" was replaced by an almost bewildering prospect of success.

Thayer and Eldridge were not dalliers. They took Whitman to the best stereotype foundry in Boston and left word to follow his instructions. Within two weeks, 120 pages were set up in type. At first the printers were befuddled by Whitman's eccentric design and the mix of type faces that he chose. The printers thought he was "crazy," he wrote his brother Jeff, "and there were all sorts of supercilious squints . . . but since it has been through the press, they have simmered down. Yesterday the foreman . . . pronounced it, in plain terms, the freshest and handsomest piece of typography that had ever passed through his mill." As the book took form, Whitman felt that a "great weight" had been taken from him, a "great obstacle that has been in my way for the last three years. . . . It is quite curious, all this should spring up so suddenly, ain't it."

Whitman was happy in Boston. Every morning he corrected proof at the foundry. He strutted like a New York peacock along Washington Street. Emerson had gotten him a temporary membership to the Boston Atheneum, and he went now and then to leaf through magazines in the prosperous atmosphere of the library's reading room. John Trowbridge, a writer and journalist who had read *Leaves of Grass* five years before, heard that he was in town, and went to see him at the foundry one morning. Trowbridge found a "grey-bearded, plainly dressed man, reading proof-sheets in a little dingy office, with a lank unwholesome-looking lad at his elbow, listlessly watching him." The lad was another candidate for Whitman's lists of young men. He explained to Trowbridge that he wanted to strengthen the boy, by imparting some of his "magnetism" to him. Trowbridge found Whitman in a subdued mood, and the two men talked quietly. Looking over the spread-out proof pages of his book, Whitman remarked, "I am astonished to find myself capable of feeling so much." It is a telling remark. However much Whitman managed to be his book, as Moncure Conway had put it, there would always be a startled bystander in his mind—the isolated boy, or the mocking and bowing watcher of "Out of the Cradle"—who found himself hard to believe.

Trowbridge invited Whitman to dinner the following Sunday, and Whitman came in a livelier mood. He told Trowbridge that the main influences on his poetry had been the Bible, the Italian opera, and Emerson. Emerson had helped him to "find himself," he said. And Emerson still stood behind his difficult New York friend. He introduced Whitman to whoever would consent to meet him. James Russell Lowell, Longfellow, and Oliver Wendell Holmes refused, even though Lowell had just published Whitman's "Bardic Symbols" in the *Atlantic Monthly*. James Redpath and the abolitionist Charles Sanborn were not so aloof. They welcomed Whitman, and the men became lifelong friends. During Whitman's stay in Boston, Sanborn was brought to trial for aiding some of John Brown's followers; and Sanborn remembered Whitman sitting in the courtroom in his workingman's outfit—to make sure justice was done, Whitman later said, and help rescue Sanborn if necessary. Sanborn, Redpath, and Whitman's other new Boston friends would be of great help to him three years later, when he started making his hospital rounds in Washington. They collected small sums of money for Whitman to distribute to the wounded soldiers or to use to buy gifts of food, candy, or writing paper.

During his visit to Boston, Whitman also met the man who, for a dozen years, would be his tireless champion. William O'Connor, who was writing *Harrington* for Thayer & Eldridge, had, like Trowbridge, read *Leaves of Grass* in 1855 and been impressed. Within three years of their meeting, he would virtually merge his life with Whitman's. O'Connor, twelve years Whitman's junior, was a volatile polemicist and fiction writer. By the time he was nineteen, he had been artist, daguerreotypist, and poet. As a young man, he had published poems and stories, and, shortly before meeting Whitman, had been fired as editor of the *Saturday Evening Post,* in Philadelphia. By temperament and by conviction, O'Connor was a radical. Along with his wife, Ellen, he supported women's rights and abolition. But "support" is hardly the word for O'Connor's stormy convictions. Hawthorne, in *Our Old Home,* called him "a young man of genius and enthusiasm," who, to his repertoire of "causes," had added the controversy over Bacon's putative authorship of Shakespeare's plays. (Virtually alone in America, O'Connor would fight the Bacon fight all his life.) But in 1863, another cause possessed him. He fought the battles, roused the troops, wrote defenses and counterdefenses, raged at the scoundrels who ruled public opinion. He developed a curiously dependent fame, as the honorable champion of a doubtful cause—the doubtful cause being Walt Whitman. O'Connor lost himself in Whitman, and Whitman, to a surprising degree, lost himself equally in O'Conner. To Horace Traubel, he admitted with his usual telescoping of time, that without his mother and O'Connor, *Leaves of Grass* could hardly have been conceived at all.

In the spring of 1860, O'Connor wrote to his friend Sara Helen Whitman, Poe's muse and almost lover (his "Helen"): "The great Walt is very grand and it is health and happiness to be near him; he is so large and strong—so pure, proud and tender, with such an ineffable bon-hommie and wholesome sweetness of presence; all the young men and women are in love with him." There is a whole future in this letter. To those who met him, and especially to O'Connor, Whitman was very much his book, and the book and the man seemed grander for the identification. With his self-scrutinizing eye, Whitman was aware of his "magnetism" and was not shy of amplifying it with his vivid dress, his beard, and his broad, even-tempered manner.

The tone of worship is even stronger in a letter from William Thayer a few months after Whitman had returned to New York:

We too wish you could be with us in Boston, for we have *so* much to say: and our "fanatic" wants to get under the refreshing shelter of Walt's spirit; he does not ask Walt to talk, but only for the privilege of looking into those eyes of calm, and through them to enter into that soul, so deep in its emotions, so majestic in all its thought-movements, and yet so simple and childlike. Yes, Walt Whitman, though men of the world and arch-critics do not *understand* thee, yet there be some among men and women who *love* thee.

This was heady, and probably disorienting, it came so close to fulfilling Whitman's deepest wishes. His isolation had burst; not only did he have an audience now, he had acolytes. Not sad accounting sheets of the names of passing faces, but the very comrades he had imagined in "These I singing in spring. . . ." There he had offered his comrades flowers, herbs, tokens of song. And now they had come: O'Connor, Trowbridge, Thayer, Eldridge. They had received those tokens in the form of his new book, with its ornate orange cover: a globe floating on clouds; along the spine, a finger with a butterfly perched on it.

Boston marked a turning point for Whitman, although its full consequences would not become apparent for several years. In Boston, he began to see the kind of awe his personage and his book could inspire in just the sort of educated men who had always been beyond him. The interest of Emerson, Alcott, and Thoreau was confirmed and expanded. Five years after the carpenter's son from Brooklyn had become a figure of scandal, and the object of the puzzled admiration of America's greatest man of letters, Whitman was becoming a beloved sage. The vituperation of the critics would continue: he was an easy target. But the cult that flowered in the last decades of his life was already stirring. Leading it were his publishers, who felt they had a great success on their hands. Within two months of publication, they had sold a thousand copies, and were planning a second printing. They saw the book selling steadily over the long haul, not exploding as had *Uncle Tom's Cabin* in 1852. Meanwhile, they put their resources behind it. They printed a separate sixty-four-page advertising pamphlet, containing reviews and articles about Whitman, including his own anonymous puffs. They wrote announcements and planned advertisements that were so inflated that Whitman took the copy home with him one night and burned it.

In Boston, too, he began to defend his book in a new way. Before, his poems had been written in spurts of enthusiasm that left no time to plan or worry about consequences. But now his long mornings of composition in the attic room he shared with poor inarticulate Eddie had produced this book. Only months, or perhaps weeks before, the shape of it had become clear. At its heart were "Song of Myself," now simply called "Walt Whitman," and the poem clusters called "Enfans d'Adam" and "Calamus": self-creation, sex, and homosexual love were the book's foundations. And anchored to these motifs, the ample celebration of American nature, of democracy, and the pervasive exploration of the poetic act itself took form.

Upon Whitman's arrival in Boston, Emerson had come to see him almost immediately, and the two men went out walking on the Common. For two hours, under the leafless March elms, Emerson tried to persuade Whitman to leave certain poems out of his book: not many, perhaps only a handful of passages. The problem was the "Enfans d'Adam" cluster. The public was not ready for the sexual frankness of poems like "Spontaneous Me" or "I Sing the Body Electric." It was not prepared for a poet who celebrated prostitutes and masturbation. The question was not moral, argued Emerson, but practical: "he wanted the book to sell," Whitman remembered, "thought I had given it no chance to be popularly seen, apprehended: thought that if I cut out the bits here and there that offended the censors I might have a book that would go through editions—perhaps many editions." Emerson was "keen," "magnetic," advancing his arguments like a general marshaling his troops. Whitman listened and was convinced; but, as so often when challenged in his beliefs or simply in his behavior, he found himself stiffening. It was a kind of revelation. Listening to Emerson, Whitman discovered that his book was inviolable. That all of it stood, or all of it fell. To cut out, or even to mute the sex was to cut the book off from its "root." That day, walking under the elms with his benefactor, the man who more than any other had helped to make his book a fact of literary life, Whitman discovered that, for him, as for his gathering devotees, *Leaves of Grass* was a cause to be stubbornly defended, preserved not only as a book but as a token of wholeness, of liberation.

On balance, Whitman probably was right. Sex was indeed the root. We have no trouble with that idea today. In his intuitive way, Whitman knew himself; and more than any writer of his day, he was willing to pursue the consequences of that knowledge. The sexual frankness; the remarkable carnal ecstasies that burst from the page in numerous poems; his style of suspended, cumulative clauses, breaking apart the syntax of the sentence, breaking apart time and meaning and the logic of explanation—all this surely held together. Emerson talked about acceptability and the "public"; Whitman, the stubborn son of a stubborn father, built a fence around his book. Whitman's final defense was: "I feel more settled than ever to adhere to my own theory, and exemplify it."

Whitman paid a price for defending his book; for Emerson, too, was right. The sexual passages would never be acceptable to the nineteenth-century reading public; Whitman would never make it into the drawing room. When, twenty-years later, he revisited Boston to supervise another complete edition of his work, Emerson had faded into a benign senility. Whitman went out to see him and stayed to dinner. It was, for Whitman, a reconciliation, for the two men had long been estranged. Afterward, Whitman spoke of Emerson only with reverence, even awe. The trip ended badly, however, for yet again the sex came to haunt Whitman's campaign for respectability. His publisher, James R. Osgood, threatened by Boston's attorney general, backed out of the contract, and the book was withdrawn from publication.

There was another price, too. Over the years, Whitman stiffened into a militant of his own book. He became a guerrilla at the edge of culture, with his sharp-shooting defender, William O'Connor, and later his coterie of Philadelphia friends who regarded him as a neglected prophet. As Whitman stiffened, his book, too, stiffened. It became a sacred text, a relic; indeed, a "Bible" that could not suffer compromise. In the end, Whitman's idea of himself as a beleaguered prophet restricted him. The more untouchable his book became, the harder it became for him to write poems for it. Perhaps that is why the finest writing of Whitman's last decades is his prose. There he had nothing to live up to as, thirty years before, he had had simply the excitement of the pen and the paper.

The Boston bubble did not last. By July, Thayer & Eldridge was planning a third printing of *Leaves of Grass,* to be accompanied by a cheaper ($1.00) edition. While the publishers noticed "considerable opposition among the trade to the book," they were convinced that strong advertising would create "an overwhelming demand among the mass public" and sweep away the "cowardice" and "prejudice" of the booksellers. A few months later, their zeal began to waver. Apparently moral fervor alone did not suffice to make a profit, for their books were not succeeding. In December, they wrote Whitman warning him not to cash a check they had just sent him. Three days later, they declared bankruptcy. The plates for Whitman's book fell into the hands of a rival publisher, Horace Wentworth, who threatened to pirate the book unless Whitman bought the plates from him. Whitman refused, and Wentworth eventually did run off new printings from which Whitman never got a cent. It is ironic that this pirated edition was far more widely read than the original Thayer & Eldridge edition had been.

After a year of making new friends and publishing his book in a convincing new form, after coming to the verge of a genuine national fame, Whitman was back where he started. He was more broke than ever. His friend Henry Clapp was awash in drink and desperate for money. Again, Whitman was at Pfaff's, listening, not talking: a king of bohemia who spent his evenings with a group of hard-drinking, nonliterary friends, rather than with the wits and arguers of Clapp's circle. He had the same supporters as before: Clapp and his friends, the bohemian writers and actresses, Ada Clare and Adah Isaacs Menken. As always, there were the women, sensing in Whitman an ally in their battle against the desexualizing myths of Victorian respectability: one Connecticut woman wrote Whitman inviting him to conceive a child with her on a mountain top. But, on the whole, his book had not been well received. Even Clapp, apparently by mistake (he was usually a little drunk), published in his magazine a wild attack on it by an upstate correspondent, who concluded by advising Whitman to commit suicide. Hostile notices poured in from all over the country. The *Westminster Review,* Whitman's favorite among the British literary magazines, attacked him. Whitman had become famous, but it was an eccentric, unsatisfying fame, as the author of a vile book; someone to parody and mock; someone whose morals were unspeakable. He had sought this battle; he had chosen to speak out, where his generation did not speak at all. He had chosen to violate the polite norms of his age, but he may not have understood the savagery with which those norms would be defended. He may not have bargained for the depth of the repudiation he now faced.

He lapsed into his New York life again; but he was older now. The lack of money hurt. Pfaff's must have seemed a smaller stage than ever. He went on collecting names. He threw himself in more than ever with the stage drivers and ferryboatmen he'd been friendly with for almost ten years. Occasionally he visited New York Hospital, when some of his stage-driver friends ended up there with broken bones or a bad fever. The hospital stirred him strangely, and he kept going back. One of the young surgeons remembered him coming through the wards and then stopping to talk afterward in the hospital office. Whitman was not faint-hearted in the operating room; he asked pertinent medical questions; and eventually he wrote a series of articles about the hospital for the *Leader,* under the penname Velsor Brush.

For a decade, health had been everything to Whitman: it had been his religion, his muse. "Walt Whitman" was the man poetry had made healthy. But now the New York Hospital spoke a darker poetry to him: "What a volume of meaning, what a tragic poem there is in every one of those sick wards! Yes, in every individual cot with its little card-rack nailed at the head." He watched a young student die slowly of a broken spine. Another man fell off a train in Jersey City, and Whitman thought how strong and good-looking he had been only a few weeks before. The man lay unconscious in his bed; soon his friends would carry him to the "dead house." In Whitman's poetry, death had been a dark "merging." But in the hospital, death happened to individuals: it was painfully specific. Whitman would "absorb" this lesson and make it his in the long nightmare of the Civil War.

Before going bankrupt, Thayer and Eldridge had announced another book by Whitman, "Banner at Daybreak"; and five years later, a handful of these poems found their way into *Drum-Taps,* where they were its weakest part. These were not creative years.

Whitman limped along on the few dollars he earned as Velsor Brush. He lived on loans which he paid back as best he could. In the fall of 1860, Abraham Lincoln defeated Stephen O. Douglas for the presidency, and Whitman was present when Lincoln visited New York toward the end of February 1861. Whitman remembered the hostile crowd jamming the street in front of the Astor House; the premonition of violence. Lincoln, wearing a black suit with a black stovepipe hat on his head, stepped down from his carriage, stretched, and walked slowly up the steps to the hotel.

War was in everyone's mind, and two months later it came. On 12 April, Whitman had gone to hear an opera at the Academy of Music, on Fourteenth Street. He was walking down Broadway after the performance when he heard the newsboys shouting. He bought a paper and crossed over to the Metropolitan Hotel to read it under the steady light of the gas lamps. Fort Sumter had been attacked. It was war. A crowd stood silently in the pool of light in front of the hotel and then gradually dispersed. A few days later, Whitman wrote in his notebook: "I have this day, this hour, resolved to inaugurate for myself a pure, perfect, sweet, clean-blooded robust body, by ignoring all drinks but water and pure milk, and all fat meats, late suppers—a great body, a purged, cleansed, spiritualized, invigorated body." Thus, Whitman experienced public crises in his flesh. It is as if he wanted to cure himself of the war and, at the same time, to make himself equal to it.

That spring and summer, Whitman's life did not change much. His brother George enlisted for a hundred days with New York's Thirteenth Regiment and may have been among the optimists who marched to war with a length of rope tied to their musket barrels, for the prisoner each was going to lead home in a noose. Later in the year, George re-enlisted and served out the whole war. Whitman wrote a rousing topical poem, with the refrain: "Beat! beat! drums!—Blow! bugles! blow!" and published it in the *Leader* and in *Harper's Weekly*. His notebook filled obsessively with the names of young men: stage drivers, soldiers, several of whom he brought home to "sleep with" him. He went often to the hospital, which now had a wing reserved for wounded soldiers. They were so young, he remarked: mostly farm boys who had never been to a city before. On a Sunday night, he sat in the dimly lit ward with seven convalescent boys from Maine. The comradeship and warmth made them seem like "old friends."

That fall, the young naturalist John Burroughs came to New York to meet Whitman. Henry Clapp told Burroughs that Whitman had been eking out his living as a copyist and free-lance journalist. In the evenings he was mostly at Pfaff's with the crowd of drinkers he would soon be writing to from Washington: Hugo Fritch, Nat Bloom, Charlie Saunders, and others. Whitman was in a slough, but he had not lost the ability to enjoy himself. He would always be resilient, pulling himself erect by force of will. It was this bouyancy that imparted a glow to his declining years in Camden, when pain and physical weakness could not diminish the florid old man of Thomas Eakins's portrait. Now, it kept Whitman afloat while he was trapped in "stagnation," made worse by the shocking defeats the northern armies had been suffering for most of the year.

2

Such was Whitman's situation in December 1862 when, on a Tuesday morning, he opened the newspaper to discover that his brother George had been wounded at the battle of Fredericksburg. That afternoon he was on the train to Washington, determined to find George at all costs. It was a miserable journey. He was pickpocketed while changing trains in Philadelphia, and arrived in Washington without a cent. Once there, he went from hospital to hospital looking for his brother. It seemed hopeless to find anyone in the confusion of makeshift hospitals that surrounded the city. During his treks across the half-finished capital, Whitman ran across his former publisher, Charles Eldridge, and his Boston friend William O'Connor. Eldridge worked in the army paymaster's office, and O'Connor was a clerk for the Light House Board of the Treasury Department. When George could not be found in any of the Washington hospitals, Eldridge obtained a military pass for Whitman to go down by boat to Aquia Creek and then by train to the Virginia battlefield where the New York Fifty-first was camped. A day later, on 19 December, Whitman disembarked at Falmouth, opposite Fredericksburg, in southern Virginia. It took him half a day to find his brother in the sprawling camp. A metal sliver had pierced George's cheek, but the wound was already healing.

Until George was captured late in 1864, to spend four hellish months in a southern military prison, he would lead a charmed life during the war. He fought in a dozen arduous battles. He endured the freezing winters and the parched, dusty summers, was promoted several times in the field. Year in year out, his companions died of cholera and typhoid as much as of southern bullets. But George, the one solidly healthy Whitman, slipped between all the dangers.

The bond between the brothers would never be as intense as during these years of the war. In letter after letter, Whitman traced George's movements and tried to reassure his mother. In 1865, he wrote an article for the Brooklyn *Daily Union* about George's remarkable war record. The Whitman family hung on George's safety. He was their emissary to the war. The war was the one thing he and Walt would ever share. When George was captured, Whitman haunted the war office, to obtain George's exchange, and he finally succeeded.

For ten days, in December 1862, Walt shared his brother's tent at Falmouth. During the blustery gray days after the battle of Fredericksburg, he picked his way from group to group of encamped soldiers. He ate and talked with the men and filled his notebook with a vivid accumulation of names, descriptions, battle reports. The troops huddled in flimsy shelter-tents or in "shebangs" of freshly cut branches that barely cut the wind. The young soldiers, fresh from their farms and workshops, had been hardened by a year of campaigning. Death had become a casual, almost jocular companion. On the night after he arrived at Falmouth, Whitman described a walk among the campfires:

My walk out around the camp, the fires burning,—groups around—the merry song—the sitting forms—the playing light on the faces—they would tell stories—one would tell a story of a dead man sitting on the top rail of a fence—he had been shot there at sundown, mortally wounded, clung with desperate nerves and was found sitting there, dead, staring with fixed eyes in the morning.

Whitman's notebook reflects his state of mind. He has been pulled out of his "slough"—out of himself—by the grim scenes of the late battle and by the soldiers: young men like his New York stage drivers and ferryboatmen, made lean and curiously hearty by the experiences of the war. He walks along the Rappahannock River and sees Fredericksburg, "splintered, bursted, crumbled, the houses—some with their chimneys thrown down—the hospitals—the man with his mouth blown out." On a bright, freezing day, he admires a regimental inspection, the men "sifted by death, dismemberment, etc. from eleven hundred men (including recruits) to about two hundred." He sits around fireplaces improvised in holes in the ground, and is stirred by the "brightly beautiful" scene of wagon trains, encampments, locomotives, and stacked rifles, spread out over miles of battlefield. Everywhere there are graves; bodies on stretchers, covered with brown and gray blankets:

Death is nothing here. As you step out in the morning from your tent to wash your face you see before you on a stretcher a shapeless extended object, and over it is thrown a dark grey blanket—it is the corpse of some wounded or sick soldier of the reg't who died in the hospital tent during the night—perhaps there is a row of three or four of these corpses lying covered over. No one makes an ado. There is a detail of men made to bury them; all useless ceremony is omitted. (The stern realities of the marches and many battles of a long campaign make the old etiquets a cumber and a nuisance.)

There is a terse, terrible clarity in these notes that is already stirring toward poetry. But a poetry that is new for Whitman, quieter, more pictorial, as if the powerful scenes of the war could almost speak for themselves. The poet needed only open his eyes and report the casual truths that lay about him, dense with unspoken, unspeakable meanings. The row of bodies in front of the hospital tent would become the subject of one of Whitman's finest poems:

A sight in camp in the daybreak gray and dim,
As from my tent I emerge so early sleepless,
As slow I walk in the cool fresh air the path near by the hospital tent,
Three forms I see on stretchers lying, brought out there untended lying,
Over each the blanket spread, ample brownish woolen blanket,

Gray and heavy blanket, folding, covering all.

Curious I halt and silent stand,
Then with light fingers I from the face of the nearest the first just lift
   the blanket;
Who are you elderly man so gaunt and grim, with well-gray'd hair,
   and flesh all sunken about the eyes?
Who are you my dear comrade?
Then to the second I step—and who are you my child and darling?
Who are you sweet boy with cheeks yet blooming?

Then to the third—a face nor child nor old, very calm, as of beautiful
   yellow-white ivory;
Young man I think I know you—I think this face is the face of the
   Christ himself,
Dead and divine and brother of all, and here again he lies.

These were days that changed Whitman's life. The previous summer, he had been oppressed by the war and by his own aimlessness.
New York had weighed on him. He had written a handful of
blustering war poems and sentimental fables. But his feelings were
best captured in a fragmentary poem he culled from his notebooks:

Year that trembled and reel'd beneath me!
Your summer wind was warm enough, yet the air I breathed froze me,
A thick gloom fell through the sunshine and darken'd me,
Must I change my triumphant songs? said I to myself,
Must I indeed learn to chant the cold dirges of the baffled?
And sullen hymns of defeat?

Now, only a few months later, in freezing Virginia, among men
collecting themselves after the battle for further battle, among new
sights and new feelings, Whitman was renewed. Already, a remarkable handful of poems is germing that will form the core of
"Drum-Taps." They are short, casual poems; the poet is hardly
present in them. F. O. Mathiessen compared them to certain
Dutch and Flemish genre paintings: understated and precise; realistic in the way that Stephen Crane would be realistic in *The Red
Badge of Courage.* The poems register a stripping down, a setting
aside of personality, which Whitman had praised in his great early
poems, where nakedness and the open road had been figures for
self-renewal—had praised, but not practiced, for his naked self had
caroused, more like a gigantic opera singer than a simplified seer.

3

The men told him about their forced marches; they described the eerie scenes of wounded and dead; and Whitman, caught by the passion of these young men, saw with their eyes, felt with their bodies. When he wrote, his voice—which had been floridly his own—became transparent, almost humble:

> A march in the ranks hard-prest, and the road unknown,
> A route through a heavy wood with muffled steps in the darkness,
> Our army foil'd with loss severe, and the sullen remnant retreating,
> Till after midnight glimmer upon us the lights of a dim-lighted build-
> ing,
> We come to an open space in the woods, and halt by the dim-lighted
> building,
> 'Tis a large old church at the crossing roads, now an impromptu
> hospital,
> Entering but for a minute I see a sight beyond all the pictures and
> poems ever made,
> Shadows of deepest, deepest black, just lit by moving candles and
> lamps,
> And by one great pitchy torch stationary with wild red flame and
> clouds of smoke,
> By these, crowds, groups of forms vaguely I see on the floor, some in
> the pews laid down,
> At my feet more distinctly a soldier, a mere lad, in danger of bleeding
> to death, (he is shot in the abdomen,)
> I stanch the blood temporarily, (the youngster's face is white as a
> lily,). . . .

Whitman heard this story from a Maine soldier who had been at the battle of White Oaks Church in Virginia. By the time he wrote the poem, he had seen plenty of war hospitals. Already at Falmouth, he visited hospital tents where men lay on the ground or on mattresses of pine boughs. One of the first things he noticed in camp, he wrote his mother, "was a heap of feet, arms, legs, etc., under a tree in front of a hospital, the Lacey House," where the worst cases were brought. Whitman would see plenty of amputated limbs during the next three years. Doctors sawed arms and legs off from morning till night. Stories were told of soldiers who saved their limbs by taking a pistol with them to the operating room, and leveling it at the surgeon.

At the Lacey House, Whitman wrote letters for the wounded soldiers. He gave a Confederate captain a newspaper, and he talked to whoever seemed lonely or needy. Men died while he watched. ("Death is nothing here.") It was an upheaval, an overthrowing of all his feelings. For a decade he had written poem-sermons on the health and youth of the flesh. The poems had reverberated with a kind of invulnerability. Yes, there had been a dark side, culminating in the "death death death death death" of "Out of the Cradle," but it had been romantic and songlike. Death had been a nervous tune, edging around his song of health. But here were actual men dying; here were bodies ripped open by shrapnel, drained by disease. "Now that I have lived for 8 or 9 days amid such scenes as the camps furnish," he wrote his mother, ". . . really nothing we call trouble seems worth talking about."

On 29 December, 1862 Whitman returned to Washington. The ten days at Falmouth had washed New York out of his life, and he was determined to stay as close to the war as possible. That meant staying in Washington which, as virtually a Union enclave in the Confederacy, was filled with constant troop movements in case of surprise raids by General Lee's mobile army. On the day Whitman arrived back in Washington, he wrote to Emerson asking for help in procuring a government job; and the letter gives us a notion of Whitman's mood:

Dear Friend,

Breaking up a few weeks since, and for good, my New York stagnation—wandering since through camp and battle scenes—I fetch up here in harsh and superb plight—wretchedly poor, excellent well, (my only torment, family matters)—realizing at last that it is necessary for me to fall for the time in the wise old way, to push my fortune, to be brazen, and get employment, and have an income—determined to do it, (at any rate until I get out of horrible sloughs).

Whitman was penniless and had only a few friends in Washington; he had no idea how he was going to make a living. But he had decided to stay. He was not always "cautious"; sometimes, in the upsurge of new feelings, he leaped first and considered later. So he had gone to New Orleans, fourteen years before. And now he was in Washington, determined, somehow, to settle there.

Within days, Eldridge had gotten Whitman a part-time job as a copyist for an army paymaster, Major Hapgood. Whitman found himself a "werry little bedroom," in a roominghouse on L Street where the O'Connors also lived. A few days later, sitting in Major Hapgood's office on the top floor of a tall house on Fifteenth and F streets, with a view of the Potomac and Georgetown to the south, and the houses of Washington spreading around, Whitman wrote his sister-in-law Martha about his first few days in Washington. Everyday, crowds of "poor sick pale tattered soldiers" climbed the stairs to the paymaster's office, only to find they were in the wrong place or had the wrong papers, and were forced to leave, disappointed and tired. It was awful. The day before, he had gone out to the Campbell Hospital to visit two Brooklyn boys from George's regiment:

Yesterday I went out to the Campbell Hospital to see a couple of Brooklyn boys, of the 51st. They knew I was in Washington, and sent me a note, to come to see them. O my dear sister, how your heart would ache to go through the rows of wounded young men, as I did—and stop to speak a comforting word to them. There was about 100 in one long room, just a long shed neatly whitewashed inside. One young man was very much prostrated, and groaning with pain. I stopt and tried to comfort him. He was very sick. I found he had not had any medical attention since he was brought there—among so many he had been overlooked. So I sent for the doctor, and he made an examination of him—the doctor behaved very well—seemed to be anxious to do right—said that the young man would recover—he had been brought pretty low with diarrhea, and now had bronchitis, but not so serious as to be dangerous. I talked to him some time—he seemed to have entirely give up, and lost heart—he had not a cent of money—not a friend or acquaintance—I wrote a letter from him to his sister—his name was John A. Holmes, Campbello, Plymouth county, Mass. I gave him a little change I had—he said he would buy a drink of milk, when the woman came through with milk. Trifling as this was, he was overcome and began to cry. Then there were many, many others. I mention the one, as a specimen. My Brooklyn boys were John Losery, shot at Fredericksburgh, and lost his left forearm, and Amos H. Vliet—Jeff knows the latter—he has his feet frozen, and is doing well. The 100 are in a ward (6)—and there are, I should think, eight or ten or twelve such wards in the Campbell Hospital—indeed a real village. Then there are some 38 more Hospitals here in Washington, some of them much larger.

The next day, and the next, Whitman went back to the Campbell Hospital. He stopped at the bedsides of the wounded soldiers; he talked with the doctors and brought whatever he could afford—some writing paper, fruit juices, a little tobacco—to cheer up the young men, many of whom had been brought up by boat and then ridden in brutally jolting army wagons, half dead from their wounds or from diarrhea. The scenes in the hospitals overwhelmed Whitman. So many suffering young men, so much loneliness and need. Within days, he knew that he was not on the fringes of the war any longer, but at its heart. His job hunting was forgotten. In mid-January 1863, Emerson wrote him letters of recommendation for Salmon P. Chase, the Secretary of the Treasury, and William Seward, the Secretary of State; but Whitman did not use them for more than a year. His whole being was absorbed by these young men who haunted his days and his nights: the farmers' sons and the young factory workers, most of them away from home for the first time in their lives. Now they lay in the whitewashed buildings that had been thrown up on empty land around the city to house the Union wounded.

For years, Whitman had made a habit of talking with strangers; and his life, as I have said, had been a form of street theater. Now the theater had come indoors into the long hospital sheds. He still talked with strangers; he gave of himself, as a man throws a buoy to someone who is drowning. Suddenly the "health" and "magnetism" Whitman had celebrated in his poems, or radiated playfully on his walks along Broadway, were no longer sources of egotistical pride: they were a medicine; they helped men live.

Whitman's Washington existence organized itself almost immediately. For several hours each day, he worked in Major Hapgood's office and then went to one of the dozens of hospitals that surrounded Washington. We see him looking out over the city and the Potomac from Major Hapgood's high window—the panoramas of snow or rain; the clear days and the dusty parched days, all curiously peaceful and still, even in the midst of the war; and we see him, for hours and days at a time, going from bedside to bedside in the hospitals. Sometimes he sat down to write a letter for a wounded boy, or give a small gift, or help dress a wound. Sometimes he simply stopped and talked for a while. It quickly appeared that he was a born nurse. As a poet, he had the ability to lose himself in what he saw, to see it from its own point of view, so to speak. Now, as a hospital nurse, he seemed to feel the boys' needs as if they were his own.

For the first time in fourteen years, Whitman was on his own. He supported himself meagerly by writing "letters" to New York newspapers and by copying for Major Hapgood. His room on L Street was little more than a place to sleep: four bare walls, a bed, and a coal stove; almost a monk's cell, or an urban Walden, as Justin Kaplan has called it. It was a precarious existence, but Whitman was not thinking about his comforts. "It doesn't seem to me it makes so much difference about worldly successes," he wrote to his brother Jeff in April, "(beyond just enough to eat and drink, and shelter, in the moderatest limits) any more, since the last four months of my life especially, and that merely to *live*, and have one fair meal a day, is *enough*."

In January, he had asked Jeff to help him raise money for his hospital visits, and Jeff's colleagues at the Brooklyn Water Works had contributed a few dollars each. They and other friends would continue to send Whitman money for most of the war. Whitman spent the money on small items—peaches, raspberry syrup, tobacco, a little brandy—which he distributed on his visits. When a soldier was destitute, Whitman gave him some money. His notebooks are filled now with the names of soldiers, their regiments, their wounds and illnesses, what they want him to bring on his next visit: some preserves maybe, or peppermints, a Bible or a newspaper. Sometimes there is more:

Ward K bed 47, Oscar F. Wilber co G 54th N.Y. talked with him July 22nd '63 afternoon—asked me to read a chapter in the New Testament— I complied asking him what, "make your own choice" said he. I opened at the close of one of the books of the evangelists in the first part testament describing the latter hours and crucifiction of Christ—he asked me to read the following chapter how he rose again. It pleased him very much, the tears were in his eyes—asked me if I "enjoyed religion," I said "probably not my dear in the way you mean"—he said it was his main reliance, he smiled sweetly said he did not fear death—I said "Why Oscar don't you think you will get well" He said I may but it is not probable—he then told me his condition—his wound was very bad, it discharged much—he had also for quite a long time diarroeha altogether prostrating him—he behaved very manly calm and sweet, spoke slow and low, had large fine eyes very eloquent."

For months, and then years, Whitman's life centered on the hospitals. Although he apparently received an authorizing letter from a church organization called the Christian Commission, he had no use for official visitors who were often cold and distant and looked as though they were simply doing a job. The soldiers shrank from them, Whitman observed. Whitman was not doing a job. There was an exaltation in his work, a flush of love and horror with which he often had to struggle to keep his bearings.

In February 1863, the Government Patent Office was transformed into a hospital, and Whitman noted the irony of the setting. "Rows of sick, badly wounded and dying soldiers," were jammed between "high and ponderous glass cases, crowded with models in miniature of every kind of utensil, machine or invention it ever entered the mind of man to conceive." The Patent Office had been America's temple of "progress." But here was the undersong of progress: these hurt bodies and suppurating wounds and cries of pain. Two years later, Whitman again walked through the halls of the Patent Office, just before Lincoln's second inaugural ball was to be held there, and reflected on the contrast: "To-night, beautiful women, perfumes, the violin's sweetness, the polka and the waltz; then the amputations, the blue face, the groans, the glassy eye of the dying, the clotted rag, the odor of wounds and blood, and many a mother's son amid strangers, passing away untended there."

Whitman eventually recorded his hospital visits in *Memoranda during the War*, which became a section of *Specimen Days*. He scattered further notations in *November Boughs* (1888). It all came from the smudged, penciled notes he took day after day, as he walked between the rows of beds, stopping here and there with his little gifts and his inspiriting presence. He gave expert care, sensed what the soldiers needed: here were the "delicate hands guiding the cart." Over and over again, in letters and in his notes, Whitman described his days in the hospitals. It was an unvarying routine, and yet not a routine, because the unshielded presence of the dying was all around him:

Thursday, Jan. 21.—Devoted the main part of the day to Armory—Square hospital; went pretty thoroughly through wards F, G, H, and I; some fifty cases in each ward. In ward F supplied the men throughout with writing paper and stamp'd envelope each; distributed in small portions, to proper subjects, a large jar of first-rate preserv'd berries, which had been donated to me by a lady—her own cooking. Found several cases I thought good subject for small sums of money, which I furnish'd. (The wounded men often come up broke, and it helps their spirits to have even the small sum I give them.) My paper and envelopes all gone; but distributed a good lot of amusing reading matter; also, as I thought judicious, tobacco, oranges, apples, etc. Interesting cases in ward I; Charles Miller, bed 19, company D, 53d Pennsylvania, is only sixteen years of age, very bright, courageous boy, left leg amputated below the knee; next bed to him, another young lad very sick; gave each appropriate gifts. In the bed above, also, amputation of the left leg; gave him a little jar of raspberries; bed 1, this ward, gave a small sum; also to a soldier on crutches, sitting on his bed near. . . . (I am more and more surprised at the very great proportion of youngsters from fifteen to twenty-one in the army. I afterwards found a still greater proportion among the southerners.)

Evening, same day, went to see D. F. R., before alluded to; found him remarkably changed for the better; up and dress'd—quite a triumph; he afterwards got well, and went back to his regiment. Distributed in the wards a quantity of note-paper, and forty or fifty stamp'd envelopes, of which I had recruited my stock, and the men were much in need.

The hospital wards were Whitman's setting now. He was no longer the nimble-footed poet of Manahatta, as in his early poem, "Pictures," or the rough, splendid workingman waving to passers-by from the top of a Broadway stage. He was a mother-man distributing his care among hundreds and thousands of helpless young men who filled the hospital sheds and the tent cities, which multiplied as the war's toll grew:

During those three years in hospital, camp or field, I made over six hundred visits or tours, and went, as I estimate, counting all, among from eighty thousand to a hundred thousand of the wounded and sick, as sustainer of spirit and body in some degree, in time of need. These visits varied from an hour or two, to all day or night; for with clear or critical cases I generally watch'd all night. Sometimes I took up my quarters in the hospital, and slept or watch'd there several nights in succession.

Almost from the first, Whitman thought about collecting his notes into a book. He would give America a view of her own suffering soul; he would make the invisible visible: the hospitals, those forgotten places where the débris of war had been cast up—a débris of living young men suffering from the grotesque wounds of war. A boy with a pierced bladder dribbles urine through his wound. Another boy gives off a smell of rot from a gangrenous leg. Another, dying of a stomach wound, looks untouched and peaceful, sleeping the sleep of youth that degenerates day by day into a fever-ridden anguish and then death. After only a few weeks in Washington, Whitman wrote to Emerson:

I desire and intend to write a little book out of this phase of America, her masculine young manhood, its conduct under most trying of and highest of all exigency, which she, as by lifting a corner in a curtain, has vouchsafed me to see America, already brought to Hospital in her fair youth—brought and deposited here in this great, whited sepulchre of Washington itself—(this union Capital without the first bit of cohesion—this collect of proofs how low and swift a good stock can deteriorate—) Capital to which these deputies most strange arrive from every quarter, concentrating here, well-drest, rotten, meagre, nimble and impotent, full of gab, full always of their thrice-accursed party—arrive and skip into the seats of mightiest legislation, and take the seats of judges and high executive seats—while by quaint Providence come also sailed and wagoned hither this other freight of helpless worn and wounded youth, genuine of the soil, of darlings and true heirs to me the first unquestioned and convincing western crop, prophetic of the future, proofs undeniable to all men's ken of perfect beauty, tenderness and pluck that never race yet rivalled. . . .

As I took temporary memoranda of names, items, etc. of one thing and another, commissioned to get or do for the men—what they wished and what their cases required from outside, etc.—these memoranda grow bulky, and suggest something to me—so I now make fuller notes, or a sort of journal, (not a mere dry journal though, I hope)—This thing I will record—it belongs to the time, and to all the States—(and perhaps it belongs to me).

The distance between the hospitals and the brightly lit magnificence of the Capitol building, with its domed chambers, frescoes, and gold leaf, enraged Whitman. And the rabble of office seekers, the swarming politicians, the never-ending rhetoric of Congress. It was a circus enclosed in a ring of terrible truth; an incarnation of the trivial neighboring with the awful simplicity of the war's direst result. By October 1863, Whitman's book was all but written. It is a miscellany of observations; a pell-mell heaping of journal entries, battle scenes told to Whitman by wounded soldiers, hospital visitings, reports of living and dying, longer accounts of special cases. The book is Whitman's notebook amplified; it is Teufelsdröckh's bag of scraps, recounting the biography not of the poet but of the hospitals and, in Whitman's view, of the war itself: America's soul-making ordeal. Whitman wrote to his Boston friend James Redpath, who earlier that year had published Louisa May Alcott's *Hospital Sketches:*

> My idea is a book of the time, worthy the time—something considerably beyond mere hospital sketches—a book for sale perhaps in a larger American market—the premises or skeleton memoranda of incidents, persons, places, sights, the past year (mostly jotted down either on the spot or in the spirit of seeing or hearing what is narrated). . . .
>
> I have much to say of hospitals, the immense national hospitals—in them too most radical changes of premises are demanded—(the air, the spirit of a thing is every thing, the details follow & adjust themselves). I have many hospital incidents, [that] will take with the general reader—I ventilate my general democracy with details very largely & with reference to the future—bringing in persons, the President, Seward, Congress, the Capitol, Washington City, many of the actors of the drama—have something to say of the great trunk America, the West etc etc—do not hesitate to diffuse myself—the book is very rapid—is a book that can be read by the five or ten minutes at (being full of small parts, pieces, paragraphs with their dates, incidents etc)—I should think two or three thousand sale ought to be certainly depended on here in hospitals in Washington, among departments etc.

It was to be an inexpensive book, selling for one dollar at most, and ready for the holiday season. But Redpath had his doubts, and Whitman's book did not see the day until, as usual, he published it himself a dozen years later. Whitman's belief in the order of disorder; the random heaping of notes reflecting a deeper order of actual experience, was not more acceptable to literary minds of his day than was his sexual frankness. For the time being, Whitman's trunk would hold onto its miscellaneous treasure.

Neither *Memoranda during the War* nor *Specimen Days* hints at the troubled intensity of Whitman's fascination with the hospitals. This world of dying young men stirred emotions he had never fully allowed himself to feel before. It was as if his fugitive lists of names—a glance, the invitation of a passing face—had materialized and become inescapable. He went back every day, living the role of healer and life giver he had imagined in "Song of Myself" seven years before:

> To any one dying . . . thither I speed and twist the knob of the door,
> Turn the bedclothes toward the foot of the bed,
> Let the physician and the priest go home.
> I seize the descending man. . . . I raise him with resistless will.

In the hospitals, Whitman saw himself lifting the wounded from their beds by the force of his sympathy and loving care. Every day, he peered and watched, like his night wanderer in "The Sleepers"; and as he went through the wards, the beds became a miniature of the country at large, a geography of America's young men, with whom he exchanged vows of love, more potent, in his eyes, than any medicine:

O what a sweet unwonted love (those good American boys, of good stock, decent, clean, well raised boys, so near to me)—what an attachment grows up between us, started from hospital cots, where pale young faces lie & wounded or sick bodies. My brave young American soldiers—now for so many months I have gone around among them, where they lie. I have long discarded all stiff conventions (they & I are too near to each other, there is no time to lose, & death & anguish dissipate ceremony here between my lads & me)—I pet them, some of them it does so much good, they are so faint & lonesome—at parting at night sometimes I kiss them right & left—The doctors tell me I supply the patients with a medicine which all their drugs & bottles & powders are helpless to yield.

In his letters to his mother and friends, Whitman seems awed by the bond that grew up between him and the boys he visited. It is a sweet, brooding feeling, thriving on desperation, on the need of frightened young men for reassurance and tender care. In the crude hospital sheds, surrounded by dying and hopeless strangers, the soldiers must have grasped at this large, friendly man, with his easy manner, who entered their lives as if he had known them for a long time. Whitman had rehearsed this role, too, in his poems. In "Calamus," he had distributed tokens of love and sympathy to young men: the sprigs of lilac, moss, pinks, and laurel leaves had stood for his best self, his poems. Now the tokens changed: they were candies, tobacco, slices of cake, and peaches cut up in some cream; they were sheets of letter paper, stamps, and a few coins of money. The young men took them—small comfort in a dire place—knowing that they stood for more—for the intense, at times puzzling feelings of this bearded man who came to visit them in high boots, thick jacket, and hat. He still smelled of soap, for he had scrupulously bathed before coming out to whatever cluster of buildings he chose for his visit each day.

Amid the "butcher sights" of the hospitals Whitman felt himself flooded with love for the young soldiers. He kissed and fondled them as if they were his sons: "I never before had my feelings so thoroughly and (so far) permanently absorbed, to the very roots, as by these huge swarms of dear, wounded, sick, dying boys." It was not unusual for him to spend half the night going from bed to bed spooning out jam or stewed fruit from a pot.

Yet after all this succoring of the stomach (which is of course most welcome & indispensible) I should say that I believe my profoundest help to these sick and dying men is probably the soothing invigoration I steadily bear in mind, to infuse in them through affection, cheering love, & the like, between them and me. It has saved more than one life. There is a strange influence here. I have formed attachments in hospital, that I shall keep to my dying day, & they will the same, without doubt.

It is clear that the hospitals were vital places for Whitman. During four years, he rarely missed a day, with his knapsack full of gifts and his florid fatherliness. Even when the war was over, and the country labored to forget its four years' ordeal, Whitman went on visiting the chronic cases that lingered in a few outlying hospitals. He thrived as a bringer of comfort. For once, his "doubts" about "appearances," the undertone of meaninglessness that had dogged the larger-than-life voice of his poems, were laid to rest. For the hospitals were a field of action beyond all doubting. In his poems, he had invited his readers to an adventure of self-change, full of danger and erotic delight. But it had been a lonely activity, with uncertain results. The suspicion of failure was never far. In the hospitals, Whitman set aside his metaphors, in order to live them. His poet had been a bringer of health; his poet's world had been an "open road," and the poet had opened his mind to embrace whatever came his way. Now the hospitals were his open road. As he went up and down the wards, it seemed to him that all of America was at his feet, represented by this gathering of the sick and the dying, these young men from all over the country, whom Whitman had once imagined as citizens in his republic of comrades or as his companions in the aromatic springtime of "Calamus" love:

While I was with wounded and sick in thousands of cases from the New England States, and from New York, New Jersey, and Pennsylvania, and from Michigan, Wisconsin, Ohio, Indiana, Illinois, and all the Western States, I was with more or less from all the States, North and South, without exception. I was with many from the border States, especially from Maryland and Virginia, and found, during those lurid years 1862–63, far more Union southerners, especially Tennesseans, than is supposed. I was with many rebel officers and men among our wounded, and gave them always what I had, and tried to cheer them the same as any. I was among the army teamsters considerably, and, indeed, always found myself drawn to them. Among the black soldiers, wounded or sick, and in the contraband camps, I also took my way whenever in their neighborhood, and did what I could for them.

In the wards, Whitman tried to save the boys' lives, and sometimes he succeeded. Often he had to watch them die, and there were days when he felt overwhelmed by the destructive rage of the war. But he knew that the hospitals gave him something, too. In the hospitals, the coy play of Cupid and Psyche—the "indirections" that gave his poems their suggestive weaving of themes—was replaced by frank and open acts of love. Here his homosexual ardor was not suspicious or shameful: it was a medicine; it buoyed up the sick and the dying. There was no need to veil it in euphemisms or to project it in grand notions of comradeship and democracy. There was no need even to make poetry out of it. Whitman could simply hug, and kiss, and hold hands. He could let his emotions flow "without check, with original energy."

The hospitals were a release for Whitman. They were a way around the self-censoring and the Victorian self-accusations that erupted even amid his strongest "Calamus" poems. We see the terrible extremes of the hospitals in all of his letters. In one, he describes "wounds full of crawling corruption," and the "dreadful" sadness of the suffering men—this was his heavy refrain in the letters—while also exulting in the new-found release of his deepest desires:

In the hospitals among these American young men, I could not describe to you what mutual attachments & how passing deep & tender these boys—some have died, but the love for them lives as long as I draw breath—those soldiers know how to love too when once they have the right person & the right love offered them. It is wonderful.

It was wonderful. And also terrible. And Whitman swung between the extremes, in a tension that sometimes exhausted him. By 1864, his health had begun to suffer, and a slow slide into sickness began. He had bouts of prolonged weakness and dizziness. On hot sunny days, he walked around Washington with an umbrella, for fear of sunstroke. Late in the year, he had to return to Brooklyn to rest and regain his strength. In the light of his weakening health, the humorous descriptions he gives of himself in the letters—he is always fat, red-faced, and hearty—become ominous. The red face was probably a sign of vascular problems and hypertension, fed by his exhausting involvement in the hospitals. The stroke that disabled Whitman in 1873 was apparently already brewing in his system.

Sometimes, in the emotionally heated atmosphere of the hospitals, Whitman became reckless and poignant. There are sad beautiful letters in which he takes chances, expresses his homosexual longings with troubled directness. In the spring of 1863, he fell in love with a young soldier, Thomas Sawyer, who had been a patient at the Armory Square Hospital. When Sawyer got better and went back to his regiment, Whitman bought some underwear and a shirt for him, but Sawyer forgot to stop by Whitman's room to pick them up. Whitman wrote Sawyer letters that must have puzzled him, they are so tense with emotion:

I was sorry you did not come up to my room to get the shirt & other things you promised to accept from me and take when you went away. I got them all ready, a good strong blue shirt, a pair of drawers & socks, and it would have been a satisfaction to me if you had accepted them. I should have often thought now Tom may be wearing around his body something from me. . . .

My dearest comrade, I cannot, though I attempt it, put in a letter the feelings of my heart—I suppose my letters sound strange & unusual to you as it is, but as I am only expressing the truth in them, I do not trouble myself on that account.

In another letter, he embroidered a fantasy for the future: he and Sawyer, and maybe another hospital friend, Lew Brown, whose leg was amputated later in the year, would live together after the war and share everything and never be lonely again.

One more time after the war was over, Whitman laid himself bare in his long, troubled love for the streetcar conductor, Peter Doyle. But it was in the hospitals that Whitman opened his emotions for the first time. To John Trowbridge he had confessed that he was surprised, in reading his poems, at his ability to feel so much. The poems lived an open life, apart from the furtive inwardness of the poet, who strove to become his book and yet, in this matter of full, spontaneous feelings, had not succeeded. But now he had truly become his poems. His fantasy of comradeship was now expressed not in a book but in a letter to a young friend.

The hospitals aroused Whitman in every way. It was there that his extravagant idea of the 1850s was unexpectedly realized. He had wanted to write poems that poured from his enlarged life. He had dreamed of a kind of omnipresence: the "voice of Walt Whitman" would penetrate every corner of America; the "travelling soul" of his poems would enter everywhere, see everything, establishing a web of relationships, like his "patient spider," spinning out "filament, filament" into the surrounding emptiness. The dream was wild; and by the end of the decade, it had palpably failed. But now the dream had become unexpectedly true. Whitman's experience in the hospitals had been written out first in his book; his book had been a program, and now, against all hope, he was building it in his acts and feelings.

This man-myth of the 1860 *Leaves of Grass* had made of the hospitals a "found poem" to live within. Yet how terrible that found poem was! Here was the tragedy for Whitman: his dream of love was inextricably tangled up with death, as it had been in his poems. The refrain of "Out of the Cradle"—"death death death death death"—had become ugly and concrete. The boy in the poem singing of lost love was now a man finding love all around him in the hospital wards, but the refrain had become deafening.

The hospitals were the culmination of Whitman's years of experiment. He had produced a book, and now he had produced a self; and it was all perched on a precarious edge. In many respects, his book appeared to be a failure, its greatness barely glimpsed by a handful of friends. Even Emerson had become remote and cool. Whitman's self, bathed in the erotic, fed on suffering; it lived off the helplessness of a dying generation. No wonder then that these "contradictions" tore him apart and finally helped to make him sick. By the war's end, he had retreated from the vitality of his ten-year experiment. For the war was not only an ending, but a beginning: it was the beginning of his old age; the beginning of his public legend, and his stiffened, defensive stance as the "good grey poet," a subtly pious bard who stood for wholesome religious feelings and progress. This was the Whitman whom William Rossetti helped to make famous in England, making possible the grudging acceptance of Whitman in America in his last decades. It was the Whitman we have all come to know, with his grizzled beard and his frozen optimism.

5

The Washington hospitals were the beginning of a long, often touching end for Whitman. There he lost his health while still in the prime of life. There, too, he made new friends who came to his aid, as his New York and Boston friends never had. William and

Ellen O'Connor fed Whitman and gave him a home away from home. They, Burroughs, Eldridge, and a handful of friends met almost every week, to drink and talk. Sometimes they made dinner or a Sunday breakfast. Whitman was the central figure of the group. They were all devoted to him. And Ellen O'Connor may secretly have been in love with him, little as Whitman would have suspected it. The group was a focus for agitated talk about the war, about slavery, about "Walt Whitman," who promised a new freedom and appeared, to William O'Connor at least, as a secular Christ. Whitman made the punch and led the games of Twenty Questions. Often he argued loudly, and once a policeman knocked to see whether any violence was being done. Whitman's angry streak had long been buried; but the strain of the hospitals, and also maybe the confidence of his adoring circle of friends, brought it up again.

O'Connor and Burroughs were formidable allies. Both were passionate, intelligent men. O'Connor never gained any independent fame. When in 1865, Whitman was ingloriously fired from a clerk's job in the Interior Department for being an obscene poet, O'Connor got him another job almost immediately in the Attorney General's Office, where he worked until his stroke in 1873. In 1866, in his defense of Whitman, O'Connor wrote a powerful treatise on freedom of speech, which many of his contemporaries compared to Milton's *Areopagitica,* and which launched Whitman belligerently as the "Good Grey Poet," the title of O'Connor's book. At the time, O'Connor's polemic earned him a certain renown as the brilliant defender of an unworthy cause. Henry Raymond, a founder of the *New York Times* and no friend of Whitman's, offered O'Connor a job as cultural columnist, but O'Connor hesitated to leave the security of his Treasury Department job. That was the man: angry, incisive, fiercely moral; yet inwardly vacillating and timid. He remained in Whitman's orbit, even as Burroughs was diplomatically edging away, to begin his own career. Before he went on to become America's leading naturalist, Burroughs's first published work was a surprisingly insightful book on Whitman: *Notes on Walt Whitman as Poet and Person* (1867), parts of which were probably written, or at least strongly suggested, by Whitman himself.

Thus, in the mid-1860s, flanked by his two remarkable defenders, Whitman seems to have accepted the public image of himself. He began to see himself in a new way: not as a verbal adventurer, with the courage of the unknown, but as a prophet and a man of wisdom. The turning that had begun in Boston, in 1860, was accentuated. His weakening health may have been part of it. A feeling that nothing could ever match the intense fulfillment of the hospitals may have also contributed. But Whitman pulled back from his creative edge. He wrote a dozen great short poems out of his war experience, and these formed the substance of his Civil War volume, *Drum-Taps*, published in 1865. As we have seen, the poems showed a breakthrough into a new style, but the breakthrough was aborted. Whitman never developed his new mode. Even as he tried to concentrate on his poems for a last effort, he sensed the decline that had begun, and wrote about it to Charles Eldridge as early as November 1863: "I feel to devote myself more to the work of my life, which is making poems. I must bring out *Drum-Taps*. I must be continually bringing out poems—now is the hey day. I shall range along the high plateau of my life & capacity for a few years now & then swiftly descend."

Whitman was aroused to a final greatness, in 1865, by Lincoln's assassination, to which he responded with the magnificent ode, "When Lilacs Last in the Dooryard Bloomed." After that, there was not silence but sporadic effort, sparse and diminished. During the Civil War, Whitman's "language experiment" had ended in a violent commingling of life and art.

6

But his great work was done. The middle decade of the nineteenth century had seen the publication of his rowdy, ramshackle book. Eccentric, supercharged with words and energy, *Leaves of Grass* was launched on a collision course with its age. Whitman's work assaulted the institution of literature and language itself and, in so doing, laid the groundwork for the anti-cultural ambition of much modernist writing. He is the ancestor not only of Henry Miller and

Allen Ginsberg but of Kafka, Beckett, André Breton, Borges—of all who have made of their writing an attack on the act of writing and on culture itself.

Yet *Leaves of Grass* spoke for its age, too—and truly erupted out of it. If art is a measure of a culture's deepest understanding, of its felt reality, then Whitman's contribution cannot be underestimated. Even today, few of us are able fully to accept the immense numbers that have come to measure our world: light-years, expanding and contracting universes, billions of years of earthly evolution. In the literature of our century, the richest figures have been ones of enclosure: Proust's cork-lined bedroom, or Gregor Samsa's bedroom; Becket's garbage cans; a small Irish city, imposed on the shoreless oceans of the original Ulysses. A few decades earlier in a *Season In Hell*, Rimbaud managed to see all of Europe as a sort of haunted house. Our civilization has taken a dizzying inward dive, expressed by a new and complex esthetic. Does this tendency represent a collective shrinking from the "silence of infinite spaces"? Have we turned inward in order not to lose ourselves in the blankness of the cosmos? Whitman knew no such problem. He unhoused himself with glee, turning geology, astronomy, and all the turbulence of his age into a stage set for the immense self.

NOTES

Abbreviations

Allen   Gay Wilson Allen, *The Solitary Singer* (New York, 1955).

Bowers   Fredson Bowers, ed., *Whitman's Manuscripts: "Leaves of Grass" (1860)*, (Chicago, 1955).

Bucke   Richard Maurice Bucke, *Walt Whitman* (Philadelphia, 1883).

Corr.   Edwin Haviland Miller, ed., *The Correspondence*, 6 vols., 1961–1977, New York University Press edition of *The Collected Writings of Walt Whitman*.

CPW   *The Complete Prose Works* (New York, 1902).

DBN   William White, ed., *Daybooks and Notebooks*, 3 vols., 1978, New York University Press edition of *The Collected Writings of Walt Whitman*.

Eagle   Thomas L. Brasher, *Whitman as Editor of the Brooklyn "Daily Eagle"* (Detroit, 1970).

EPF   Thomas L. Brasher, ed., *The Early Poems and the Fiction*, 1963, New York University Press edition of *The Collected Writings of Walt Whitman*.

Faner   Robert D. Faner, *Walt Whitman and Opera* (University Park, Pa., 1951).

Furness   Clifton Joseph Furness, ed., *Walt Whitman's Workshop* (Cambridge, Mass., 1928).

GF   Cleveland Rodgers and John Black, eds., *The Gathering of the Forces*, 2 vols. (New York, 1920).

Glicksberg   Charles I. Glicksberg, ed., *Walt Whitman and the Civil War* (Philadelphia, 1933).

In Re   Horace Traubel, Richard Maurice Bucke, and Thomas Harned, eds., *In Re Walt Whitman* (Philadelphia, 1893).

ISL   Emory Holloway and Vernolian Schwarz, *I Sit and Look Out* (New York, 1932).

Kaplan   Justin Kaplan, *Walt Whitman: A Life* (New York, 1980).

LC   Manuscript Division, Library of Congress, Washington, D.C.

LG   *Leaves of Grass*, The Library of America (New York, 1982).

LG, 1855, facsimile Eakins Press (New York, 1966).

LG, 1860   *Leaves of Grass*, Boston, 1860; facsimile edition, with an introduction by Roy Harvey Pierce (Ithaca, N.Y., 1961).

LG, Norton   *Leaves of Grass*, Norton Critical Edition (New York, 1982).

Miller   Perry Miller, *The Raven and the Whale* (New York, 1956).

NYD   Emory Holloway and Ralph Adimari, *New York Dissected* (New York, 1936).

Notes

Perry   Bliss Perry, *Walt Whitman*, AMS Press, New York, 1969; reprinted
               from the 1906 edition.
Rubin   Joseph Jay Rubin, *The Historic Whitman* (University Park, Pa., 1973).
Shepherd   Esther Shepherd, *Walt Whitman's Pose* (New York, 1938).
Stovall   Floyd Stovall, *The Foreground of "Leaves of Grass"* (Charlottesville,
               Va., 1974).
UPP   Emory Holloway, ed., *The Uncollected Poetry and Prose of Walt Whit-
               man,* 2 vols. (Garden City, New York, 1921).
WWC   Horace Traubel, *With Walt Whitman In Camden,* 5 vols., (1906–
               1964): vol. I, Boston, 1906; II, 1908; III, 1914; IV, Philadelphia,
               1953; V, Carbondale, Ill., 1964.

Introduction: "The Long Foreground"

Page
4   Whitman's anonymous review of *Leaves of Grass, LG,* 1855, facsimile, addendum.
5   Emerson quotation from *LG,* p. 1326.
7   "The direct trial," *LG,* p. 23.
       "The newspaper," *WWC,* IV, p. 2.
8   Emerson quotation from Gay Wilson Allen, *Waldo Emerson* (New York 1982),
           p. 582.
       "No one will," *LG,* Norton, p. 574.
9   Randall Jarrell, *Poetry and the Age* (New York, 1953), pp. 101–21.
10   "Make no quotations," *CPW,* VI, pp. 4, 34.
11   Whitman's remark about not reading a poem, *LG,* p. 611.
       "Push close," *LG,* p. 89.
12   "The place of the orator," Furness, p. 37.
       "Love the earth," *LG,* p. 11.
13   F. O. Matthiessen, *The American Renaissance* (New York, 1941).
14   "Have you reckoned," quoted in *LG,* p. 28.
       Daniel Boorstin, *The Americans: The National Experience* (New York 1965).
15   "I create," *Corr.,* I, p. 50.
       "A hundred years hence," *LG,* p. 308.
16   George Whitman's remark from *In Re,* p. 34.
       Thoreau's remark, in Allen, p. 204.
       The "fraud" criticism was made by Shepherd.
19   Letter to the New York friend, *Corr.,* I, p. 142.
20   Letter to his mother, *Corr.,* I, pp. 114, 118.

Chapter 1. "The *Bhagavad Gita* and the New York *Tribune*"

Page
25   This description of Whitman from *In Re,* p. 34.
27   Herman Melville quoted in Edwin H. Miller, *Melville* (New York, 1975), p. 114.

Notes

Page

28   Charles Dickens, *American Notes* (London, 1842), pp. 135–36.
     Horace Greeley, 19th Century Crusader, Glyndon G. Van Deusen (Philadelphia, 1953), p. 52.

29   "Principles. . . . in," *GF*, I, p. 108.
     "Experiment" and "test," *GF*, I, pp. 11–12.
     "O dark were," *GF*, I, p. 28.

30   "By mere politicians," *GF*, I, p. 60.
     "We would hunt immorality," *GF*, I, p. 64.
     Whitman's comment on the workingman, *Eagle*, p. 130.
     "Why, all that is good," *GF*, I, pp. 5–6.

32   "Uncorrupted core," *GF*, I, p. 38.

33   "Here and there," *LG*, pp. 75–76.

34   "Wild Frank's Return, *EFP*; quotations on p. 64.

35   "Bervance," *EFP*.

36   George's remark from *In Re*, p. 34.
     Frances Wright, *A Few Days in Athens* (New York, 1822).

37   Comments on Whitman's youth from Perry, p. 19.
     "From the moment," *CPW*, VI, p. 148.

38   George's remark from *In Re*, pp. 34ff.

39   Material on Walter, Sr., from Allen, p. 2.
     Vignette of Walter, Sr., from *LG*, p. 139.

40   Alexis de Tocqueville, *De la Democratie en Amerique*, vol. II (Paris, 1835), p. 82 (my translation).

41   "Great heyday" from Ann Douglas, *The Feminization of American Culture* (New York, 1977).
     "The mild virtues," *GF*, II, pp. 268–69.
     "If goodness," *GF*, II, pp. 88–89.

43   Long Island *Democrat* quotation in *UPP*, I, p. 37.
     "Where is," *GF*, II, p. 246.

44   "At this hour," *GF*, II, pp. 246–47.

45   "Some of the wisest," Stovall, p. 141.
     Charles Knight, ed., *Half-Hours with the Best Authors* (New York 1849).

46   Astor Place Opera House description from Douglas T. Miller, *Jacksonian Democracy* (New York, 1967), pp. 169–70.

47   "We see the rows," *NYD*, pp. 18–21.
     "It is a full house," *NYD*, pp. 18–21.
     "The stale, second hand," *Eagle*, p. 205.

48   "An exquisitely played flute," *Eagle*, p. 207.
     "Her voice," *GF*, II, pp. 352–53.
     "O what is it," *LG*, 1860, p. 240.
     "I want that tenor," *UPP*, II, p. 85.
     God as "a vast pure tenor," Faner, pp. 42–43.

49   "A new world," *NYD*, p. 22.
     "We consider," *GF*, II, p. 321.

50   "Though we never," *GF*, II, pp. 322–23.
     Whitman on being an actor, *GF*, II, p. 333.
     On Edwin Forrest's "robustous" performance, *LG*, p. 1188.

51   "I can, from my good seat," *LG*, p. 1191.
     Constantin François Chasselboeuf, Comte de Volney, *Les Ruines, ou Meditation sur les Revolutions (Paris, 1791)*.
     "Seems to me," *LG*, p. 1288.
     Whitman on an "amateur-theater," *LG*, p. 1293.

Notes

Chapter 2. "I Saw in Louisiana"

Notes

Page

76   "Both H. and M'C," *UPP*, II, p. 78.

Henry Lees quoted in Rubin, p. 206.

79   Newspaper quoted In Allen Nevins, *The Ordeal of the Union*, vol. I (New York, 1947), p. 192.

Banner of Freedom quote from LC.

Quotation from the *Evening Post*, Allen, p. 102.

80   The Buffalo convention, Nevins, *Ordeal*, p. 207.

81   The *Advertiser*'s prediction, Rubin, p. 206.

"Hardly anyone," Rubin, p. 211.

82   An acquaintance on Whitman, Shepherd, p. 53.

"Good farm," Rubin, p. 220.

83   "After the present date," Rubin, p. 222.

84   "I cannot understand," *UPP*, II, p. 66.

"The Shadow and Light of a Young Man's Soul," *UPP*, I, pp. 229–34.

85   Louisa Whitman on Walter's "strangeness," *UPP*, I, p. 230.

Archie Dean's Long Island neighbors, *UPP*, I, p. 232.

"By his long walks," *UPP*, I, p. 232.

86   "The change was not," *UPP*, I, pp. 233–34.

"I am not glad," *UPP*, II, pp. 88–89.

88–89   Table and phrenological analysis from Madeleine B. Stern, *Heads and Headlines: The Phrenological Fowlers* (Norman, Oklahoma, 1971), p. 105.

90   The skulls at Fowler & Wells, Stern, *Heads and Headlines*, p. 31.

"Breasting the waves," Stern, *Heads and Headlines*, p. 100.

"One of the choice places," *LG*, p. 1291.

92   "O adhesiveness!," *LG*, p. 274.

"All beauty comes" and "His brain," *LG*, p. 9.

93   "Extreme caution," *LG*, p. 20.

"Everything yet," *UPP*, II, p. 76.

94   "The effusion," *UPP*, II, P. 65.

"Writing and talk," *LG*, p. 53.

The meeting of body and soul, in "Song of Myself," *LG*, pp. 30–31.

95   Orson Fowler on his own mental organs, Stern, *Heads and Headlines*, p. 32.

The nineteenth-century admirer is quoted in Stern, *Heads and Headlines*, p. 32.

96   Orson Fowler on phrenology, in John O. Davies, *Phrenology, Fad and Science* (New Haven, 1955), p. 42.

"Phrenological gypsies," Davies, *Phrenology*, p. 45.

98   "In that condition," *LG*, p. 1272.

99   "Of pure American breed," *LG*, facsimile, addendum.

100   The *Advertiser*'s swansong for Whitman, from Rubin, pp. 223–24.

101   "Letters from A Travelling Batchelor," in Rubin, pp. 311–54.

102   "Here, and all along," *LG*, p. 698.

103   "All of a sudden," Rubin, p. 313.

Whitman on the blue fishermen, from Rubin, p. 314.

104   Whitman on a Long Islander, from Rubin, p. 312.

105   Whitman on a farmer's wife, Rubin, p. 321.

105–106   Whitman on a sail to Montauk, Rubin, 346.

106   Whitman on the Croton Reservoir, Rubin, p. 337.

107   "Others will enter," *LG*, p. 308.

"It avails not," *LG*, p. 308.

108   Whitman on a ramble about town, Rubin, p. 347.

Chapter 3. "A Blessing on the Young Artist Race"

Page
112   "Walt Whitman's early years" passage from Bucke, pp. 19–20.
113   George Whitman on Walt's habit of talking to strangers, *In Re*, p. 34.
114–115 Stories and sketches of the early 1850s, LC.
117   "Tomb Blossoms," *Voices From the Press*, ed. James J. Brenton, New York, 1850.
        William Seward quoted in Allan Nevins, *The Ordeal of the Union*, vol. I (New York, 1947), p. 300.
        "I tell you Americans," Rubin, p. 249.
118   Whitman at political meetings, Rubin, p. 247.
        Old Testament text, Zechariah, 13:6.
        "If thou art balked," *EPF*, pp. 36–37.
119   "Of olden time," *EPF*, pp. 47–48.
120   "God, 'twas delicious!" *EPF*, p. 38.
121   Whitman on Henry Ward Beecher, *UPP*, p. 234.
        Personal slogans from Whitman's notebook, *CPW*, vol. VI, p. 7.
        "Backward I see," *LG*, p. 30.
        Whitman on Jenny Lind, in Rollo G. Silver, "Whitman in 1850: Three Uncollected Articles," *American Literature*, January 1948, pp. 314–15.
122   "Music, in the legitimate," Silver, "Whitman in 1850."
        Whitman on art's highest aim, Silver, "Whitman in 1850."
        Whitman on the librettos of Italian opera, *UPP*, I, p. 259.
        Whitman on his first visit to a theater, Silver, "Whitman in 1850," p. 312.
123   Whitman on a painting of Walter Libbey, *UPP*, I, pp. 237–38.
124   Whitman on daguerreotypes, Silver, "Whitman in 1850," p. 310.
        Whitman on Libbey and the Dusseldorf school of painters, from Rubin, p. 264.
124–125 Whitman on the painting called "The Death of Bayard," from Silver, "Whitman in 1850," pp. 305–6.
125   Whitman on realism in painting, from Silver, "Whitman in 1850," p. 306.
        "Smile O voluptuous coolbreathed earth!," *LG*, p. 47.
126   "To behold the daybreak!" *LG*, p. 52.
127   Whitman calling for a counterdemocracy of the arts, from *UPP*, I, p. 237.
        Whitman on Brown's sculpture studio, from *WWC*, II, p. 502.
128–129 Emerson's question from *Selected Writing of Emerson*, ed. Brooks Atkinson (New York, 1940), p. 3.
129   "Who would not mourn," *UPP*, I, pp. 242–43.
        "In the temple of the Greeks," *UPP*, I, pp. 244–45.
        William James's words from *The Varieties of Religious Experience*, Mentor ed., (New York, 1958) pp. 80–83.
130   Whitman on his "singular eyes," *NYD*, p. 130.
        "The singer" who "bends an arm," *LG*, p. 30.
        Abby Price's remark from Bucke, p. 30.
130–131 "Scented herbage," *LG*, p. 268.
131   Emerson on the poet as the "complete man," from *Selected Writings of Emerson*, p. 320.
        Whitman on the "perfect man," from, *UPP*, I, p. 245.
        Whitman on "orthodox specimens," *UPP*, I, p. 245.
131–132 Whitman counseling the artist, *UPP*, I, p. 246.
133–134 Whitman on vocabulary of the trades, LC.
134   Whitman on workingmen's voices, LC.

Page

George Whitman's recollection, *In Re,* p. 34.

Henry Thoreau on Whitman as a democrat, quoted in Allen, p. 204.

134–135 "The anvil and tongs," *LG,* p. 95.

136 "Barbaric yawp," *LG,* p. 87.

D. H. Lawrence's comparison, from *Studies in Classic American Literature,* (New York, 1951).

137 "Urge and urge and urge," *LG,* p. 28.

"The Eighteenth Presidency," *LG,* pp. 1307–25.

Whitman writing to John Parker Hale, *Corr.,* I, p. 39.

139 Whitman on a burly workingman, *NYD,* p. 130.

Whitman on lower Broadway, *NYD,* p. 132.

141 Thoreau's complaint quoted in Allen, p. 205.

141–142 A contemporary article on the New York "rough," quoted in Clarence Gohdes, "Whitman as One of the Roughs," *Walt Whitman Review,* March 1962, p. 18.

Chapter 4. "A Copious Book Man"

Page

143 Whitman's "uneventful" life, *In Re,* pp. 33–40.

Marianne Moore on the ostrich in her *Collected Poems,* p. 102.

144 Gay Wilson Allen, *The Solitary Singer* (New York, 1955); and Floyd Stovall, *The Foreground of "Leaves of Grass"* (Charlottesville, Va., 1974).

Allen, pp. 125ff.

144–145 Thomas Carlyle, *Sartor Resartus,* Everyman's Library (London, 1908); originally published in 1833–34); the quotation about George Fox is on p. 157.

145 Carlyle on the "toil-worn Craftsman" and the artist, from *Sartor Resartus,* pp. 171–72.

Whitman on reading George Sand's *Consuelo,* from *WWC,* III, pp. 422–23.

George Sand, *Consuelo* (Paris, 1842).

Whitman on a "new school" of oratory, Shepherd, p. 191.

Passage from Sand's *Consuelo,* quoted in Shepherd, p. 191.

145–146 George Sand, *The Countess of Rudolstadt* (Paris, 1843); the quotation on the journeyman laborer is from Shepherd; the description of the journeyman violinist is quoted in Shepherd, p. 293.

147 Sand, *Countess,* on the unknown, quoted in Shepherd, p. 178.

Whitman's paraphrase of Sand, *UPP,* II, p. 65.

"Every existence," *LG,* p. 130.

Sentences from Sand, *Countess,* quoted in Shepherd.

148 Jules Michelet, *The People* (New York, 1846), quoted in Gay Wilson Allen, *The New Walt Whitman Handbook* (New York, 1975), pp. 268–69.

Philip Bailey, *Festus* (originally published in 1839), quoted in Rubin, p. 277.

149 Alexander Smith, *A Life Drama* (New York, 1853), quoted in Rubin.

Martin Farquhar Tupper, *Proverbial Philosophy* (New York, 1838).

Whitman on "the proof of a poet," *LG,* p. 26.

150 Perry on journals of Emerson and Thoreau, Perry, p. 89.

William Blake, preface to his *Prophetic Books* (originally published 1793–1804), quoted in Perry, p. 89.

151 Perry on Whitman and the Bible, p. 96.

Page

Samuel Warren, *The Lily and the Bee, A Lyrical Soliloquy* (originally published 1851, 1853), quoted in Perry, pp. 93–95.

153   Whitman's "Thoughts on Reading," Stovall, p. 268.

154   Margaret Fuller's taunt, quoted in Shepherd, p. 56.

Margaret Fuller, *Papers on Literature and Art* (originally published in 1846), quoted in Shepherd, p. 57.

Sidney Lanier, quoted in Shepherd, p. 268.

155   Cornelius Matthews's poem, quoted in Shepherd, p. 59.

157   Whitman on Broadway's "many lessons," *NYD*, p. 30.

157–159 Whitman on Dr. Abbot's Egyptian Museum, *NYD*, p. 28.

159   The acquaintance's description of Whitman from Shepherd, p. 266.

Whitman on human time and Egypt, *NYD*, p. 32.

160   "This Compost," *LG*, p. 495.

161   "I am an acme," *LG*, pp. 79–80.

Joseph Beaver, *Walt Whitman and Science* (New York, 1972).

Chapter 5. "A Strange Miscellany"

Page

164   Bronson Alcott quoted in Milton Hindus, ed., *Walt Whitman: The Critical Heritage* (New York, 1971), p. 65.

166   Whitman on his "diary-jottings," *LG*, p. 689.

Herman Melville, in *Moby Dick*, Signet ed. (New York, 1961), p. 149.

167   Sören Kierkegaard on his notebooks, *The Journals of Kierkegaard*, ed. Alexander Dru (New York, 1958), p. 58.

"I harbor for good or bad," *LG*, p. 188.

168   "Incongruous," *LG*, p. 689.

169   Thomas Carlyle, *Sartor Resartus*, Everyman's Library (London, 1908); originally published 1833–34), p. 58.

170   Articles torn out of magazines, LC.

Whitman on a scrapbook of clippings, *WWC*, II, p. 54.

D. H. Lawrence on America's having been born old, *Studies in Classical American Literature*, (New York, 1951).

171   "Make no quotations," *CPW*, VI, pp. 4, 6, 7, and 34.

Whitman's report of a remark of Emerson's, *WWC*, III, pp. 401–2.

172   Whitman on the stage drivers, *LG*, p. 703.

"Rapid the trot," *LG*, pp. 101–2.

173   Whitman to Ellen O'Connor, from Ellen Calder, "Personal Recollections of Walt Whitman," *Atlantic*, June 1907.

Keats on "negative capability," from John Keats, *Selected Letters*, Anchor Books (New York, 1956), p. 103.

Whitman's catalogues, *LG*, pp. 703–4.

173–174 "Every hour of the day," *CPW*, VI, p. 144.

174   Whitman as a "fluid and swallowing soul," *LG*, p. 63.

"All this I swallow," *LG*, p. 64.

"The soul or spirit," *UPP*, II, pp. 64–65.

175   Ralph Waldo Emerson, "Nature," *The Selected Writings of Ralph Waldo Emerson*, ed. Brooks Atkinson (New York, 1950), pp. 28–29.

Page

      Whitman's description of a touch, *LG*, p. 55.

      "What is marvellous?" *LG*, p. 10.

176   "I will not be the cart," *UPP*, II, p. 64.

177   Passages from the notebooks on Whitman's publicness, *UPP*, II, p. 65.

178   "I am not glad to-night," *UPP*, II, pp. 88–89.

      "O, Nature!," *UPP*, II, pp. 88–89.

      "Depression," LC.

179   George Whitman on his brother, *In Re*, pp. 33–37.

180   "Of Insanity," *CPW*, vol. VI, pp. 63–64.

      Whitman on his walk along "old Clover Hill," *UPP*, I, pp. 255–56.

      "Dazzling and tremendous," *LG*, p. 52.

181   "I want that tenor," *UPP*, II, p. 85.

182   "I have seen corpses," *UPP*, II, p. 84.

      "The proof of a poet," *LG*, p. 26.

183   "Have you practiced," *LG*, p. 28.

      "Hasting, urging, resistless," *CPW*, VI, p. 8.

184   Whitman on poems that purported not to be poems, *LG*, p. 611, and *CPW*, VI, p. 8.

      "My final merit," *LG*, p. 53.

185   Joseph Frank, *The Widening Gyre* (Bloomington, Ind., 1968), pp. 3–14.

186   "Bridalnight," LC.

187   "*Faith*" and "Joy Joy!" LC.

188   Whitman on his "secret," WWC, IV, p. 2.

188–189 Excerpts from 1850s notebooks on young men, LC.

189   Whitman's list-poems, Berg Collection, New York Public Library.

190   The remark about Whitman's seeming "to hate women" is from Allen, p. 33.

      Whitman's former student's recollection from Allen, pp. 35–36.

      Whitman on "making a pet of the boy," from Calder, "Personal Recollections,"

191   Abby Price's letter about Whitman, from Bucke, p. 29.

192   Whitman on affection, to Traubel, *WWC*, I, p. 125.

      "A mighty pain" (doggerel Whitman recited), Calder, "Personal Recollections."

192–193 "Sit a while," *LG*, 1860, p. 98.

193   " . . . I record of two simple men," *LG*, 1860, pp. 372–73.

      Journal confession, *UPP*, II, pp. 95–96.

194   "Depress the adhesive nature," *UPP*, II, p. 96.

195   "Poem incarnating," *UPP*, II, p. 79.

195–196 "This man was of wonderful," *LG*, pp. 119–20.

196   Note appended to Whitman's confession, *UPP*, II, p. 94.

      "Outline sketch," *UPP*, II, p. 96.

Chapter 6. "Self-Made or Never Made"

Page

202   "Speech is the twin," *LG*, p. 53.

      "I am a dance," *LG*, p. 108.

203   Whitman writing to Sarah Tyndale, *Corr.*, I, p. 44.

      "Backward I see," *LG*, p. 30.

      "The rich coverlet," *LG*, p. 260.

Notes

Page

204 "In a little house," *LG*, Norton, p. 642.

Whitman's self-portrait *LG*, Norton, p. 644.

204–206 "Pictures," *LG*, Norton, pp. 642–49.

207 Prose introduction to Whitman's new book of poems, *LG*, p. 5.

208 Whitman's collections of words, LC.

208–209 "Drawing language," LC.

209 Whitman on the Crystal Palace exhibition, Allen, p. 120.

211 "A poem in which," *DBN*, III, p. 776.

212 Visit to the Crystal palace, 20 March 1854, *CPW*, VI, pp. 133–34.

213 Whitman's rage at the "limber-tongued lawyers," Furness, p. 92.

"One fullsized man," *LG*, p. 6.

214 "I carry the plenum," *LG*, p. 53.

"Lofty sirs!" LC.

214–215 "Memorial" to the Brooklyn City Council, *UPP*, I, p. 262.

215 Whitman's anarchist's fantasy, LC.

Whitman on some "well-developed man," LC.

216 Whitman on an orator, Furness, p. 38.

"From the opening," Furness, p. 37.

"*True vista before,*" *CPW*, VI, pp. 7–8.

217 Jean-Jacques Rousseau, *The Social Contract* (1762).

Thomas Carlyle, quoted by Paul Zweig, *The Heresy of Self-Love* (Princeton, 1981), p. 247.

218 Alexis de Tocqueville, quoted in Zweig, *Heresy*, p. 19.

219 Passage from "The Eighteenth Presidency," *LG*, p. 1323.

221 "I am he attesting," *LG*, p. 46.

"The soul has," *LG*, p. 13.

222 "Clear the way there," *LG*, pp. 135–36.

223 "He drags the dead," *LG*, p. 13.

224 "Henceforth let no man," *LG*, pp. 19–20.

224–225 Word lists from Whitman's notebooks, *DBN*, III, p. 705.

225 "What can be," LC.

226 "Never was there," *LG*, pp. 1424–25.

Chapter 7. "Song of Myself"

Page

228 "I think the soul," *UPP*, II, pp. 66–67.

229 "I tramp a perpetual journey," *LG*, p. 82.

231 For production of Whitman's first edition see Rubin, pp. 307–9.

234 "This is what you shall do," *LG*, p. 11.

"Stop this day and night," *LG*, p. 28.

236–237 "America does not repel," *LG*, p. 5.

237 On Whitman's preface to *Leaves of Grass*, see Ivan Marki, *The Trial of the Poet* (New York, 1976).

238 Quotations from the preface to *Leaves of Grass*, *LG*, pp. 6, 11.

Emerson on "the known universe," *The Selected Writings of Ralph Waldo Emerson*, ed. Brooks Atkinson (New York, 1950), p. 3.

Notes

Page
238–239   "His spirit" and "High up," *LG*, pp. 7–9.
239–240   Whitman's note on "lectures," Furness, p. 35.
241   "Let the age and wars," *LG*, p. 8.
        "A heroic person walks," *LG*, p. 14.
        "I am he," *LG*, p. 47.
        "My ties and ballasts," *LG*, p. 59.
        "Storming enjoying planning," *LG*, p. 63.
242   "Cycles ferried my cradle," *LG*, p. 80.
        Pleasantly and well-suited," *LG*, p. 106.
        "I wander all night," *LG*, p. 107.
        "Sauntering the pavement," *LG*, p. 125.
        "The Lord advances," *LG*, p. 127.
        "There was a child," *LG*, p. 138.
        "I bequeath myself," *LG*, p. 88.
        "Houses and rooms," *LG*, p. 27.
243   "I swear I will never," *LG*, p. 84.
244   "The rhyme and uniformity," *LG*, p. 11.
245   "There Was a Child Went Forth," *LG*, pp. 138–39.
245–248   "The Sleepers," *LG*, pp. 107–17.
245   "I stand with drooping eyes," *LG*, p. 108.
        "I am the everlaughing," *LG*, p. 108.
246   "O hotcheeked and blushing!," *LG*, pp. 109–11.
246–247   "Steady and long," *LG*, p. 111.
247   "Warily sportsman!," *LG*, p. 113.
248–262   "Song of Myself," *LG*, pp. 27–88.
249   "People I meet," *LG*, p. 28.
250   "I harbor for good or bad," *LG*, p. 188.
        "I speak at every hazard," *LG*, p. 188.
251   "I believe in you my soul," *LG*, p. 30.
252   "What is the grass?" and "This is the grass," *LG*, p. 43.
253   "Stop this day," *LG*, p. 28.
        "Come closer to me," *LG*, p. 89.
        "Camerado, this is no book," *LG*, p. 611.
        "My voice goes after," *LG*, p. 52.
254   "I will go to the bank," *LG*, p. 27.
255   "I find I incorporate," *LG*, p. 57.
        "Undrape . . . I see," *LG*, p. 33.
        Lines of Whitman's varied refrain, *LG*, pp. 43, 63, 64.
256   "Who goes there!," *LG*, p. 45.
        "One world is aware," *LG*, p. 46.
257   "Walt Whitman, an American," *LG*, p. 50.
        George Whitman's recollection, *In Re*, p. 35.
258   "I do not press," *LG*, p. 51.
259   "My voice goes after," *LG*, pp. 52–53.
260   "I am exposed," *LG*, p. 54.
        "On all sides," *LG*, p. 55.
261   "Rise after rise bow," *LG*, pp. 79–80.
        "This day before dawn," *LG*, p. 82.
261–262   "I depart as air," *LG*, p. 88.
264   "Coarse and strong" and "But that shadow, my likeness," *UPP*, II, p. 91.

Notes

Page

264–265 "The vault at Pfaff's," *LG*, Norton, pp. 660–61.

265–266 Bronson Alcott quote from Milton Hindus, ed., *Walt Whitman: The Critical Heritage* (New York, 1971) pp. 64–65.

266 Moncure Conway quote from Hindus, *Walt Whitman*, p. 30.

Various criticisms of the time to *Leaves of Grass* from Hindus, *Walt Whitman*, pp. 32–33, 69, respectively.

267 Rufus Griswold criticism from Hindus, *Walt Whitman*.

Emerson's letter to Whitman on *Leaves of Grass*, *LG*, p. 1326.

268 Emerson's letter to Carlyle, quoted from Gay Wilson Allen, *Waldo Emerson*, (New York, 1982), p. 583.

269–270 "Of authors and editors," *LG*, p. 1329.

270 Whitman on future sales of his book, *LG*, p. 1327.

"Meet the people and The States," *LG*, pp. 1327–28.

"Always America," *LG*, pp. 1335–36.

272 Whitman's self-reviews, *LG*, 1855, facsimile, addendum.

272–273 Whitman's self-portrait in the Brooklyn *Daily Times*, *LG*, 1855, facsimile, addendum.

274 "To any one dying," *LG*, p. 73.

Whitman on his own egotism, Hindus, *Walt Whitman*, p. 46.

Chapter 8. "Whoever You Are Holding Me Now in Hand"

Page

276–277 "Strong and sweet," *LG*, 1860, pp. 189–90.

277 "In the Year 80," *LG*, 1860, p. 8.

"The Great Construction," Bowers, p. *xxxv*.

278 Whitman's letter to Sarah Tyndale, *Corr.*, I, p. 44.

279 Sarah Tyndale's $50, Kaplan, p. 224.

280 The "bad grey poet," Kaplan, p. 224.

"What you give me," *LG*, 1860, p. 399.

281 "The work of my life," *LG*, p. 1327.

Fredson Bowers, ed., *Whitman's Manuscripts: "Leaves of Grass" (1860)* (Chicago, 1955).

282–283 "America always!," *LG*, 1860, pp. 159ff.

283 Whitman on circling the world, *LG*, 1860, p. 312.

"We become plants," *LG*, 1860, pp. 309–10.

"Throwing far over," Bowers, p. 122.

284 "Illustrious the yet shining light!," Bowers, pp. 142–44.

285 "Starting from Paumonok," *LG*, pp. 176–188.

"How curious!," LC.

286 "Here lands female and male," *LG*, 1860, pp. 9–10.

"What am I after all," *LG*, 1860, p. 241.

287 "Passing stranger!," *LG*, 1860, p. 366.

"Of him that I love," *LG*, 1860, p. 362.

"May-be one is now reading this," *LG*, 1860, pp. 361-62.

Notes

Page

288   "I go no farther," Bowers, pp. 170–72.

289   "Miss Ellen Grey," LC.

         Whitman's various writing projects, LC.

290   Whitman's note on conversation with Mrs. Elizah Farnham, LC.

         Note in an 1857 notebook, LC.

290–291 Whitman's notes on Plato and "an ingenious comparison," LC.

291   Description of Whitman, ISL, p. 12.

         Whitman on Brooklyn, ISL, p. 147.

         Whitman on signs of progress, ISL, p. 133.

292   Whitman on reform movements of the 1850s, ISL, p. 44.

292–293 "The negro holds firmly," LG, p. 37.

293   "Hell and despair," LG, p. 65.

         Whitman on Oregon's new constitution, ISL, p. 90.

         "O you should see me," Corr., I, pp. 44–45.

294   Whitman's circular for lectures, Allen, p. 219.

295   Whitman's lifelong invective against the clergy, Furness, p. 42.

         Notebook comments, Furness, pp. 35, 37.

         Whitman on unmarried young women escaping from propriety, ISL, p. 122.

         "It is now time to stir," ISL, p. 15.

         Whitman's letter to Emerson, Corr., I, p. 61.

296   "Live-Oak with Moss, Bowers, pp. 92ff.

         "Not the heat flames up," Bowers, p. 92.

         "Effuse [his] flesh," LG, p. 88.

297   "Was it I who walked," Bowers, p. 68.

         Whitman's editorial in the Brooklyn Daily Times, ISL, p. 125.

297–298 "The frequent and swift," LG, p. 279.

298   "When I heard," Bowers, pp. 86–88.

299   "My final merit," LG, p. 53.

         "But the two men I saw," Bowers, p. 116.

299–300 "As I walk by your side," LG, p. 286.

300   "Hours continuing long," LG, 1860, pp. 355–56.

301   Toward him there is something," Bowers, p. 114.

302   "Soon a silent troop," LG, 1860, p. 347.

302–303 "Here! lilac," LG, 1860, p. 348.

303   I owe my knowledge of the calamus root's properties to an unpublished paper by Steven McClure.

304   "Here the frailest leaves," LG, p. 283.

         "Sweet flag. Sweet fern," LC.

         Whitman on the sensation of physical health, LG, p. 1272.

304–305 "Scented herbage of my breast," LG, p. 268.

305   Whitman's note on a copy of "I Saw in Louisiana a Live Oak Growing, Berg Collection, New York Public Library.

306   Whitman on a matching "cluster" of poems, Allen, p. 250.

307   Quotations from "Bardic Symbols," LG, pp. 394–96.

         "O baffled, balked," LG, p. 395.

         "You friable shore," LG, pp. 395–96.

309   Rudolph Otto, The Idea of the Holy, Oxford, 1923.

309–310 "Me and mine!," LG, p. 396.

310–312 "Out of the Cradle Endlessly Rocking," LG, pp. 388–94.

310   "Like the 'Leaves of Grass,'" Berg Collection, New York Public Library.

312   "Bird! (then said the boy's Soul,)," LG, 1860, pp. 275–76.

Chapter 9. "The Stupor Passes—Something Else Begins"

Page
313   Whitman on visiting Pfaff's, quoted in Kaplan, pp. 245–46.
313–314 William Dean Howells, quoted in Allen, pp. 230–31.
314   Juliette Beach, *Saturday Press,* Kaplan, pp. 242–43.
        Critic on Whitman as "our poet laureate," Kaplan, pp. 242–43.
314–315 Whitman's announcement of a new *Leaves of Grass,* quoted in Allen, p. 232.
315   Letter from Thayer & Eldridge, in Allen, pp. 236–37.
316   Whitman's letter to his brother Jeff, *Corr.,* I, p. 52.
        Whitman on the book's taking form, *Corr.,* I, p. 51.
        John Trowbridge, quoted in Allen, p. 241.
317   Whitman's remark to Trowbridge, Allen, p. 241.
        Whitman on Emerson's influence, Allen, p. 242.
318   Hawthorne on William O'Connor, *Our Old Home,* from Florence B. Freedman,
          "New Light on an Old Quarrel: Walt Whitman and William O'Connor,"
          Walt Whitman Reviews, June 1965.
        O'Connor's letter to Sara Helen Whitman, from Freedman, "New Light."
318–319 Letter from William Thayer to Whitman, *Corr.,* I, pp. 48–49.
320   Whitman on Emerson, *WWC,* I, p. 439.
321   Whitman's Visit to Emerson, *LG,* p. 915.
322   Thayer & Eldridge on the third edition of *Leaves of Grass, Corr.,* I, p. 48.
323   Whitman on the New York Hospital, Glicksberg, p. 29.
324   "I have this day, this hour," LC.
        "Beat! beat! drums!," *LG,* p. 419.
326   Whitman describing a walk among the campfires, Glicksberg, p. 69.
327   Whitman on Fredericksburg, Glicksberg, p. 70.
        "Death is nothing here," Glicksberg, pp. 73–74.
327–328 "A sight in camp," *LG,* p. 441.
328   "Year that trembled," *LG,* p. 442.
329   "A march in the ranks hard-prest," *LG,* pp. 439–40.
        Whitman to his mother on one of the first things he noticed in camp, *Corr.,* I,
          p. 59.
330   Whitman's letter to his mother after "8 or 9 days," *Corr.,* I, p. 59.
        Whitman's letter to Emerson from Washington, D.C., *Corr.,* I, p. 61.
331–332 Whitman on his visit to the Campbell Hospital, *Corr.,* I, pp. 62–63.
333   Justin Kaplan on Whitman's room on L Street, in Kaplan, p. 289.
        Whitman's letter to his brother Jeff, *Corr.,* I, pp. 63–64.
333–334 "Ward K bed 47," LC.
334   Whitman on hospital in Government Patent Office, *LG,* p. 717.
        Whitman on Patent Office as site of the Inaugural Ball, *LG,* p. 761.
335   "Thursday, Jan. 21," *LG,* p. 714.
335–336 "During those three years," *LG,* p. 775.
336   "I desire and intend to write," *Corr.,* I, pp. 69–70.
337   "My idea is a book of the time," *Corr.,* I, pp. 171–72.
338   "To any one dying," *LG,* p. 73.
        "O what a sweet unwonted love," *Corr.,* I, p. 122.
339   "I never before had," *Corr.,* I, p. 77.

Notes

Page

        "Yet after all this succoring," *Corr.,* I, p. 102.

340   "While I was with wounded and sick," *LG,* p. 776.

341   "In the hospitals," *Corr.,* I, p. 163.

342   Passages from Whitman's letters to Thomas Sawyer, *Corr.,* I, pp. 93, 107.

345   Whitman's letter to Charles Eldridge, *Corr.,* I, p. 185.

INDEX

Index

Index

Index

Index

Index

Index